Mormons, Scripture, and
the Ancient World

FARMS Publications

Teachings of the Book of Mormon

The Geography of Book of Mormon Events: A Source Book

The Book of Mormon Text Reformatted according to Parallelistic Patterns

Eldin Ricks's Thorough Concordance of the LDS Standard Works

A Guide to Publications on the Book of Mormon: A Selected Annotated Bibliography

Book of Mormon Authorship Revisited: The Evidences for Ancient Origins

Ancient Scrolls from the Dead Sea: Photographs and Commentary on a Unique Collection of Scrolls

LDS Perspectives on the Dead Sea Scrolls

Images of Ancient America: Visualizing Book of Mormon Life

Isaiah in the Book of Mormon

King Benjamin's Speech: "That Ye May Learn Wisdom"

Periodicals

Insights: An Ancient Window

FARMS Review of Books

Journal of Book of Mormon Studies

FARMS Reprint Series

Book of Mormon Authorship: New Light on Ancient Origins

The Doctrine and Covenants by Themes

Copublished with Deseret Book Company

An Ancient American Setting for the Book of Mormon

Warfare in the Book of Mormon

By Study and Also by Faith: Essays in Honor of Hugh W. Nibley

The Sermon at the Temple and the Sermon on the Mount

Rediscovering the Book of Mormon

Reexploring the Book of Mormon

Of All Things! Classic Quotations from Hugh Nibley

The Allegory of the Olive Tree

Temples of the Ancient World

Expressions of Faith: Testimonies from LDS Scholars

Feasting on the Word: The Literary Testimony of the Book of Mormon

The Collected Works of Hugh Nibley

Old Testament and Related Studies

Enoch the Prophet

The World and the Prophets

Mormonism and Early Christianity

Lehi in the Desert; The World of the Jaredites; There Were Jaredites

An Approach to the Book of Mormon

Since Cumorah

The Prophetic Book of Mormon

Approaching Zion

The Ancient State

Tinkling Cymbals and Sounding Brass

Temple and Cosmos

Brother Brigham Challenges the Saints

Published through Research Press

Pre-Columbian Contact with the Americas across the Oceans: An Annotated Bibliography

New World Figurine Project, vol. 1

A Comprehensive Annotated Book of Mormon Bibliography

Mormons, Scripture, and the Ancient World
Studies in Honor of John L. Sorenson

Edited by Davis Bitton

Foundation for Ancient Research and Mormon Studies
Provo, Utah

Foundation for Ancient Research and Mormon Studies
at Brigham Young University
P.O. Box 7113
University Station
Provo, Utah 84602

Library of Congress Cataloging-in-Publication Data

Mormons, Scripture, and the ancient world : studies in honor of John L.
  Sorenson / edited by Davis Bitton.
        p.   cm.
    Includes bibliographical references and index.
    ISBN 0-934893-31-4 (hardcover)
    1. Church of Jesus Christ of Latter-Day Saints—History. 2. Book of
Mormon—Evidences, authority, etc. 3. Book of Mormon—Antiquities.
4. Mormon Church—History. I. Sorenson, John L. II. Bitton, Davis, 1930–
BX8611.M674 1998
298.3'09—dc21
                                                    98-9753
                                                    CIP

Printed in the United States of America
06 05 04 03 02 01 00 99 98   6 5 4 3 2 1

CONTENTS

Acknowledgments vii

Introduction
Davis Bitton ix

MORMON HISTORY AND CULTURE

1   Baptized, Consecrated, and Sealed: The Covenantal
Foundations of Mormon Religious Identity
Steven L. Olsen 3

2   Mormon Funeral Sermons in the Nineteenth
Century
Davis Bitton 27

3   Parley P. Pratt and the Pacific Mission: Mormon
Publishing in "That Very Questionable Part of the
Civilized World"
David J. Whittaker 51

4   The Rise and Decline of the LDS Indian Student
Placement Program, 1947–1996
James B. Allen 85

5   Mormon Intruders in Tonga: The Passport Act
of 1922
R. Lanier Britsch 121

ELUCIDATING THE BOOK OF MORMON

6   Nephite Kingship Reconsidered
Noel B. Reynolds 151

7   Nephi and His Asherah: A Note on 1 Nephi
    11:8–23
    Daniel C. Peterson 191

8   A Singular Reading: The Māori and the Book
    of Mormon
    Louis Midgley 245

9   Pattern and Purpose of the Isaiah Commentaries
    in the Book of Mormon
    Garold N. Davis 277

    THE ANCIENT WORLD

10 Resist-Dyeing as a Possible Ancient Transoceanic
    Transfer
    Stephen C. Jett 307

11 Pre-Columbian American Sunflower and Maize
    Images in Indian Temples: Evidence of Contact
    between Civilizations in India and America
    Carl L. Johannessen 351

12 Doubled, Sealed, Witnessed Documents: From
    the Ancient World to the Book of Mormon
    John W. Welch 391

13 Festivals as Context for Exchange in the
    Great Basin–Columbia Plateau Region of
    Western North America
    Joel C. Janetski 445

    A Bibliography of the Published and
    Unpublished Works of John Leon Sorenson
    compiled by David J. Whittaker 479

    Index 503

ACKNOWLEDGMENTS

To the officers and staff of FARMS who initiated this project and entrusted me with it I wish to express thanks, especially to M. Gerald Bradford and Melvin J. Thorne. David J. Whittaker, of Brigham Young University's Harold B. Lee Library, in addition to preparing the bibliography included in this work, arranged for the transcription and processing of the John L. Sorenson oral histories, which should be of value to future researchers as they study twentieth-century Latter-day Saint scholars and their faith.

A work like this does not see the light of day without much behind-the-scenes labor. Thanks to Daniel B. McKinlay and Reed D. Andrew for carefully checking sources and verifying quotations and to Wendy C. Thompson and Emily L. Johnson for proofreading. The major responsibility of editing each of the separate contributions and preparing the entire manuscript for publication has been that of Donald L. Brugger, to whom I express special thanks.

The drawings and map have been prepared by illustrator Michael P. Lyon. The typesetting and design are the work of Mary Mahan.

Truly this volume has been a team project. I know that all who have participated join me in the wish that it will stimulate, add to our knowledge, and demonstrate respect and admiration for John L. Sorenson.

Davis Bitton

INTRODUCTION
Davis Bitton

How did John L. Sorenson become the person he is? Tall, thin, and gray-haired, he is a courtly gentleman, a model of kindness and consideration. As bishop of a student ward at Brigham Young University, he patiently guided young married couples, recalling in the process his own years as a virtual "professional student." Friends testify of his unfailing helpfulness. Many colleagues, especially his junior ones, have benefited from his unasked dispatch to them of clippings or articles that he thought might aid their projects or spur a new line of effort from them.

Yet one is always aware of his mind, and some who do not know the whole man encounter only this. An extraordinary mind it is, formed and disciplined by an uncommonly dynamic and fecund combination of native intelligence and varied experience. Its formation has included lengthy formal education and the vigorous exercise of academic skills, as well as stimulating interaction with other good minds. Yet, as we shall see, John Sorenson's intellectual development has not been limited to the classroom or academic study.

Drawing from an extensive oral history and from a personal friendship of more than thirty years, I will summarize a dozen periods of notable growth in John's life. What we discover is the result of a layering process by which a succession of rich experiences combined to produce a man of remarkable ability. At a certain early stage, John was perhaps not strikingly different from any number of other young males, but before long no one else had exactly his combination of background and expertise. As his life has continued and deepened, personal and work experiences have forged the unique, extraordinary person we honor in this volume.

Childhood and Youth

Born in 1924 to poor parents in the small northern Utah community of Smithfield, John L. Sorenson would seem to have been a poor prospect for advancing very far in life. The youngest of six children, he remembers his parents as always being elderly and in poor health. Even before the Great Depression of the 1930s, they could do little more than keep food on the table and clothing on their children. The family depended heavily on the classic pioneer resources of a large garden, fruit trees, a cow, a pig, and chickens. Survival rather than bright expectations characterized the family's hopes.

Yet John's memories are positive. For one thing, his family was close-knit: the parents were always there for their children, and older siblings away from home provided a reinforcing network while John was growing up. The accomplishments of the preceding five children against heavy odds had garnered them some sense of pride in family. To be a Sorenson was to hold some promise and also to feel some responsibility to society. In addition, the community offered security and calm. Residents could walk in safety anywhere they needed to go, and few felt the need to lock their doors. "Smithfield was a three-ward town," John recalls, noting that such a designation not only communicated the size of a community but also implied the dominance of Mormonism in the fabric of community life.

Much of life in Smithfield revolved around the ward. One beloved bishop presided over the ward during most of John's childhood and youth, a time when John enjoyed attending the children's Primary class and, later, Sunday School. Ordained a deacon at age twelve, he faithfully fulfilled his priesthood responsibilities. As president of his deacons and teachers quorums and as secretary in the priests quorum, he proved reliable. With rare exceptions he attended all his meetings in a day when regular church attendance among Latter-day Saints was far from the norm. John found the church to be a source of security. "For me church did take," he remarks, "and I took to it."

In school John was consistently an excellent student, an accomplishment he attributes to the pattern established by his older siblings and to excellent teachers. "Smithfield was a town where the schools and education were held in particularly high esteem," he remembers. His report cards throughout his primary and secondary schooling would show essentially nothing but A grades.

In contrast to his academic success, John remembers feeling socially rather marginal. Sensitive to the poverty of his family, he avoided involvement with children from wealthier homes. He liked neighborhood sports, especially hoop-on-the-barn basketball, but never excelled in them. Having skipped the second grade, John was always a year younger than his classmates, a fact that probably exacerbated his sense of distance from many of them.

Yet the teachers certainly knew of young John Sorenson. Because the classwork was relatively easy for him, he spent a good deal of time helping those who struggled to learn. Many

students must have come to know him as a valued friend or
pleasant and capable acquaintance, for he was elected student
body president of his junior high school. In high school his
social life expanded: he was business manager of the yearbook,
and he participated in debate and wrote for the school paper.
He was also active in seminary, where he had "outstanding
teachers." "I hope I avoided snobbery," he says, revealing a continuing concern with something he considers to be a reprehensible social sin.

Even though church, school, and home chores filled his
days, John always made time to read. The local library, which
was constructed with the help of funds from Andrew Carnegie,
provided treasured books and magazines such as *Boy's Life* and
National Geographic. When the *Deseret News* published a series
of profiles entitled "Know Your World," John clipped and filed
them. This early interest in the wider world helped establish a
basis for his later interest in cultures and geography.

Utah State Agricultural College

At age seventeen, having graduated from North Cache
High School, John entered Utah State Agricultural College
(now Utah State University) in Logan. A brother and two sisters of his had already graduated from there. With the campus
located only seven miles from Smithfield, John could pursue a
higher education while living at home. "It was a foregone conclusion that I would attend college," he says. "There was simply
no other prospect."

His older brothers, Curtis and Randall, had become electri-
cal engineers, and John followed their example. Taking courses
heavy in mathematics and physics, he also prospered in general
education courses such as anatomy, writing, drafting, and metal

shop. Because the school was a land-grant college, all male students participated in ROTC.

During his first quarter at Logan came the attack on Pearl Harbor and America's entry into World War II. Some form of military service was inevitable for him, for despite his sickly childhood, he was now in generally good health. (Until middle age, though, his six-foot frame almost never carried more than 135 pounds.) Because John and his friends in the sciences would complete a year of classes before they became eligible for the draft, they set about to turn their education to their advantage in the military. John and his hometown buddy Grant Athay (who eventually became a rather famous astrophysicist) signed up to be trained as meteorologists in the Army Air Corps. They became reservists awaiting call-up, and this enabled them to complete a total of five quarters in college before they were drafted.

Military Life

Like many other young Americans in the military, John Sorenson found himself a minor actor in something much larger than himself. As a rural youth, he had little experience of a broadening nature beyond what he had learned through school, books, and the radio. He had never traveled more than 150 miles from his home.

At first his military service meant simply more college education. His six months of pre-meteorology training was in Albuquerque at the University of New Mexico, in what could be termed a semimilitary setting. The students in his group—most of them from Oklahoma, Arkansas, Texas, and California—were housed in college dorms and ate at the campus cafeteria, but they wore privates' uniforms and went through daily physical

training and close-order drill to give them a soft version of the
basic military training that most servicemen endured. Taught
by regular University of New Mexico faculty, they studied English, geography, and courses featuring the primary menu of
mathematics and physics. Because all the students had been
chosen for their outstanding college records, competition was
fierce, and the usual A grades they expected occasionally came
out as disappointing Bs and Cs. Part of the incentive to succeed
was the rumor that dropouts would be sent to tail-gunner school!

After their training in Albuquerque, the class members became aviation cadets (a rank between enlisted man and officer)
and were sent to the California Institute of Technology (Caltech)
in Pasadena for formal training in meteorology. Regular faculty
taught the courses, and Air Corps officers served as laboratory
assistants. The classes carried regular Caltech graduate-level
credit. Facilities were again a far cry from those in the regular
military, for these cadets lived in a large hotel with maid service.
Once more only a minor military component was incorporated
into the heavy academic grind. This course work added a more
intensive dimension to John's previous studies at Utah State
Agricultural College and the University of New Mexico.

Probably more educational, however, were the occasional
weekends John spent exploring the southern California ambi-
ence. Hitchhiking on Los Angeles's recently opened first freeway, visiting the Hollywood Canteen and the Rose Bowl, shop-
ping in the glittering Wilshire district—all this was a formative
experience for a rural Utahn. During John's time in California,
a coterie of four Latter-day Saints in the group gave him comfort and support.

When John completed his military training in mid-1944,
he was commissioned a second lieutenant. He fulfilled one
short assignment at a base in Nevada, his only one as a regular

forecaster. "I didn't think anyone could really forecast the weather," he notes. "I certainly couldn't do it with any confidence." Because of his electronics experience, John was soon sent to Air Corps weather headquarters in North Carolina for special training as a communications facilitator. For the next year and a half he instructed and encouraged those in the Air Corps communications field to more speedily transmit weather data from bases on Ascension Island in the South Atlantic and from Natal and Fortaleza, Brazil. These locations were fueling stops for bombers being ferried from Brazil to Africa, the Middle East, and India. "We always said that those of us in the South Atlantic didn't go overseas," John notes wryly; "we just went abroad."

John was discharged as a first lieutenant in the spring of 1946, long after the war in Europe had ended. Thirty-nine months had passed since he left Cache Valley.

Missionary in Polynesia

In the summer of 1946 John enrolled for another quarter at Utah State Agricultural College but found himself at loose ends because the sciences no longer seemed attractive to him. Like many other service people trying to settle down after seeing the world, he was restless.

John told his bishop in early August that he would like to serve a mission. It was not generally assumed in those years that every young man should serve a mission; in fact, in his hometown during the 1930s, John had seen only a handful of young men leave for missions. Many returning veterans, however, were eager to serve missions immediately, and John was part of that wave. His savings from the military made a mission feasible. When he opened the letter from church headquarters,

he found that he had been called to serve in the New Zealand
Mission. His departure date was in question, however, because
of the lack of civilian transportation.

While waiting to leave, John met Kathryn Richards of Magna,
Utah, who was living temporarily with her married sister next
door to the Sorenson family. The two fell in love in short order
and decided to marry immediately rather than wait until after
John's mission. They were wed in the Salt Lake Temple in November 1946. There was never any question that John would
still serve his mission, and although marrying in such circumstances was unusual, it was not unknown in the wake of the
war. After John's departure in early January, Kathryn lived first
with her sister and later with her parents, in whose home
Kathryn and John's first son, Jeffrey, was born in 1947. Kathryn
supported herself by working in Salt Lake City because she did
not want to deplete John's savings. The couple would not be
reunited until mid-1949.

The LDS Church was then still very much a local phenomenon, not the worldwide operation it now clearly is. Conditions
in the crowded mission home on State Street in Salt Lake City
were indicative of that intimacy. Almost half the General Authorities could take time to speak to the departing missionaries
during their three or four days in the mission home. One day
when John and two companions were walking past the LDS
Church Office Building while returning from the temple to the
mission home, someone approached them from behind and
put his arms around their shoulders. "Well, boys," he said, "I
hope you enjoy your mission as much as I enjoyed mine." It was
white-bearded George Albert Smith, president of the church.

After a long ocean voyage on a crowded converted troop-
ship, Elder Sorenson arrived in Auckland, New Zealand, where
he was greeted by his former stake president who also was a member of his home ward in Smithfield: mission president A. Reed

Halverson. President Halverson immediately assigned John to a new field of labor in the Cook Islands, fifteen hundred miles northeast of Auckland. After laboring for some weeks in the New Zealand metropolis while awaiting transport, Elder Sorenson finally boarded a tiny six-passenger ship for the week-long voyage to Rarotonga, the capital island of the isolated Cook group.

For the next two years John would live in this little island paradise. With a formerly volcanic peak in its middle and a ring of coral enclosing its lagoon, the ten-mile-long island was occupied by some fifteen thousand Polynesians and a handful of Europeans. The inhabitants lived in six villages situated around the shore of the island. The rain forest, the abundant flowering trees, and the picturesque beach and lagoon provided an environmental experience for John that could hardly be further from familiar Cache Valley. The people were friendly, smiling, and apparently carefree. The entire scene was, in John's words, "absolutely gorgeous—no place in the world is more beautiful."

Mormonism already had a foothold on the island. In the village of Muri Enua a small branch met in a whitewashed meetinghouse, a thatched-roof structure that contained three tiny rooms for the missionaries adjacent to a little chapel. Elder Sorenson and his companion, Elder Donlon Delamare of Salt Lake City (also a war veteran), were, along with a New Zealand couple, the first American missionaries on the island. The elders' language study depended mainly on the Bible, the only published item in the Rarotongan Maori language; the translation had been done by missionaries of the London Missionary Society who had arrived on the island 125 years earlier. The elders had no grammar or dictionary of significant value. Despite this lack of resources, John was able to give what he terms a "reasonable" talk within two months. Perhaps a spiritual gift, his mastery of the language was also undergirded by a strong desire and incessant study. Before John's two years on Rarotonga were over,

with local help he had translated two tracts and written a Rarotongan grammar for the benefit of subsequent missionaries.

Working as a missionary among a native people to whom
the church was new provided John and his companions an intense experience in adaptation. Far from mission headquarters
(only two planes per month brought mail, and the mission
president visited only once a year), they had to depend on inspiration and the faithful support of loving and admiring but inex-
perienced members. Another challenge was that relations with
the New Zealand government and the country's dominant
church were not always smooth. But the missionaries kept their
focus on the gospel. They emphasized service to the young in
their teaching activities, taught informal English lessons, and
organized Primary groups in several villages. In two years more
than a hundred new members had been baptized.

Although John Sorenson the future anthropologist did not
realize it at the time, this was an incomparable field experience,
for it forced him to recognize and deal with cultural differences.

The University Years

In mid-1949 John returned home from New Zealand via a
forty-four-day voyage on a freighter and was able to see his son
for the first time. John and Kathryn made their first home in
Provo, and with the help of the GI Bill's education subsidy,
John enrolled at Brigham Young University. During his mission
he had read articles by Sidney B. Sperry, Hugh W. Nibley, and
M. Wells Jakeman in the *Improvement Era*. "What those men
were doing with scripture studies, comparing them with external sources, using scholarly methods, seemed very much worth
my doing," he recalls. Consequently, John gave up the idea of
pursuing a degree in science or engineering and instead enrolled in BYU's new archaeology program.

Brigham Young University

It was a special point in time for John, whose interest in applying scholarly methods to Book of Mormon studies was about to be nourished into a lifelong passion. M. Wells Jakeman, a new professor at BYU with a Ph.D. in ancient history, had studied the Mayan language and the civilization of the area of Central America where he was convinced the Book of Mormon events had taken place. He was eager to promote his version of "Book of Mormon archaeology" and had grand hopes of being able to confirm the scriptural accounts once the proper overall geographical location was determined. After starting classes with Jakeman in the rudiments of archaeology and its application to the Book of Mormon, John explored the library, where he discovered dimensions of the discipline—some progressive or even avant-garde—that he did not encounter in the classroom. He quickly established himself as a mature student and within a year became a student teacher.

"I feel that I received an excellent education at BYU," John says. Courses in the humanities and social sciences broadened his understanding in ways that his previous focus on the hard sciences had not permitted. Some of the master teachers he remembers with fondness and respect include Russell Swenson (history), Tommy Martin (bacteriology), Gerritt de Jong (linguistics), Reed Bradford (sociology), Wayne Hales (physics), and Hugh Nibley (ancient history and philology). By working hard and reading voraciously, John graduated in 1951 with a bachelor of science degree in archaeology. With that degree in hand, he could apply for the master of science degree at Caltech that he had already earned. He did so and was awarded his master's degree in 1952.

Because his acquaintance with archaeology was still very limited, John decided to stay at BYU to pursue a master's degree in that field. He and his growing family were still supported by the GI Bill as well as by John's regular student teaching appointments. His master's thesis, finished in 1952, was entitled "Evidences of Culture Contacts between Polynesia and the Americas in Precolumbian Times." The choice of this topic reflects a convergence of John's missionary experience in Polynesia, his familiarity with and critical attitude toward speculation surrounding the Hagoth account in the Book of Mormon, and the excitement of Thor Heyerdahl's 1949 voyage. The thesis was the start of an interest in transoceanic diffusion that Sorenson has pursued ever since. He quotes Thoreau: "Know your own bone; gnaw at it, bury it, unearth it, and gnaw it still" (*The Correspondence of Henry David Thoreau,* ed. Walter Harding and Carl Bode [New York: New York University Press, 1958], 216).

While a student at BYU, John realized the importance of publishing in academic and intellectual life. He began work on articles that in the next few years demonstrated that he was a rising young scholar. Well-read, meticulous, with a mind of his own, and with unusual multidisciplinary breadth, he seemed primed to make his mark. What was not yet clear was how he would do that.

Expedition to Mexico

Working toward a Ph.D. was the next logical move for John, but in 1952 he had no financial resources. To provide him a bare survival income, Professors Sperry and Jakeman cobbled together some teaching tasks for him that fall. Then a break came. Thomas Stuart Ferguson of Orinda, California, an amateur enthusiast in Book of Mormon archaeology, had, with support from leading non-Mormon archaeologists interested in promoting more digging in the remains of ancient cultures in Mexico and Central America, organized the New World Archaeological Foundation. With more faith than money, Ferguson planned an expedition to southern Mexico in order to work from January to May 1953. John and fellow BYU student Gareth Lowe committed themselves to go along, and a pittance from Ferguson's scarce funds helped their wives keep groceries on the table.

John's experience in Mexico was a powerfully formative one. Some of the non-Mormon archaeologists were heavyweights in the field: Dr. Pedro Armillas, a Spaniard well-known for his Marxist-influenced "materialist" position as well as for competent fieldwork; William Sanders, a star Harvard graduate student who has since become one of the deans of Mesoamerican archaeology while on the Pennsylvania State University faculty; and Roman Pina Chan, who was later recognized as one of the top Mexico archaeologists. Gareth Lowe later became director of the New World Archaeological Foundation and a noted authority on Mesoamerican cultures. (In the 1970s John encouraged BYU's awarding Lowe an honorary doctorate.) The actual excavating of sites and the interminable discussions of data, method, and theory that the crew engaged in during their four months in the field near Huimanguillo, Tabasco, provided a marvelous antidote to the idealistic but arid discussions about archaeology in the classroom at BYU.

The area the group studied was chosen according to Ferguson's ideas about the Book of Mormon. The field investigations, for reasons explained by Armillas and Sanders, showed that Ferguson's hopes were ill-grounded. No great "Book of Mormon city" awaited discovery in that area of Tabasco. In a last-ditch effort to find something that would impress donors to fund a second expedition the next year, Ferguson listened to John's reasons for continuing their investigations in the state of Chiapas to the south.

John and Ferguson flew to Chiapas just as the rainy season

was beginning. In ten days of jeep trekking over obscure roads, they located more than seventy-five archaeological sites that John believed he could directly relate to the Book of Mormon. Although the Chiapas reconnaissance did not yield the kind of "quick-proof" artifacts (figurines of horses, for example) that Ferguson sought, John's position—an interest in the overall cultural and geographical context of the area as it may relate to Book of Mormon peoples—has prevailed in the field. The work opened up in Chiapas in 1953 was renewed three years later under the patronage of the LDS Church. Under BYU administrative control for the next forty-one years, the New World Archaeological Foundation has carried out high-quality archaeological research in Chiapas that has earned its team of scientists professional accolades.

In 1953 a position as an archaeology instructor opened up for John in Provo. Over the next two years he taught many classes, published significant professional pieces, and saw his family grow to include five sons.

University of California at Los Angeles

The next year John applied for a National Science Foundation predoctoral fellowship, which was being extended to anthropologists for the first time. Only three fellowships were awarded, and John was delighted to learn he was one of the recipients. With that prestigious prize in hand (full college costs and family subsidy renewable for three years), John evaluated where he wished to pursue a doctorate. He intended to specialize in Mesoamerican archaeology, and eschewing the stodgier though more famous departments, he chose the University of California at Los Angeles, where anthropology was vigorously breaking new ground and where Maya ceramist George Brainerd was a key faculty member.

Although the fellowship stipend represented an increase in compensation over John's previous salary as a BYU instructor, the family faced the problem of finding affordable housing in Los Angeles. A generous personal loan from BYU president Ernest L. Wilkinson (one of scores he made to students without seeking publicity) solved the problem. In his later years at BYU, John disagreed vigorously with some of the president's public pronouncements, but he could never forget the man's private grace.

Older than many of the graduate students he encountered in his department, John found himself generally well prepared even though he lacked some of the curricular requisites. Because he lived far from campus and was not a teaching assistant, John missed out on much of the informal banter between students, but he excelled in his course work. "My education there was really top rate," he is quick to affirm.

Two months into the fall 1955 semester, Professor Brainerd, with whom John had formed a positive relationship, died of a heart attack. This situation could have placed the renewal of John's National Science Foundation fellowship in serious jeopardy because he had been counting on Professor Brainerd's letter of recommendation. Fortunately, however, John had been taking courses in ethnology and social anthropology from Walter Goldschmidt, Ralph Beals, and William Lessa, all first-rate anthropologists. Goldschmidt, who was on the verge of assuming editorship of the *American Anthropologist,* the flagship journal of the discipline, agreed to supervise John's work. John's impressive performance in several classes and the resulting strong letters of recommendation led to a renewal of John's fellowship.

Among John's research projects during his graduate days were those about American (including Mormon) funerals, Japanese-American Buddhist funerals, and Japanese language schools. A paper John wrote on the extension of "emic" analysis from its home in linguistics to ethnography was stimulating

enough to linguistics teacher Harry Hoijer that he urged its publication and nominated John for associate membership in the
international scientific research society Sigma Xi.

Goldschmidt's research had once dealt with the sociocultural accommodation of "Okies" into central California agricultural towns, and he had become one of the exponents of
anthropological study of American culture, a specialization
most anthropologists carefully avoided. John and Goldschmidt
agreed on a dissertation study that would examine the change
of a community from an agricultural base to an industrial one.
As it turned out, the most promising example that seemed
treatable was in Utah. Lowry Nelson, a rural sociologist, had
studied American Fork more than twenty-five years earlier, and
now a study was designed to examine the consequences of the
Geneva Steel plant completed in 1942. Santaquin, a "control"
community, was included to represent the unimpacted agricultural town that American Fork likely would have been had the
steel plant not been constructed. Doing the study meant moving to American Fork in the summer of 1957 to begin a fifteen-
month stay. The dissertation, completed in 1960, was accepted.

Return to BYU

While he was in American Fork, John Sorenson, *pater-
familias,* needed a job to support a wife and eight sons, but the
pickings were slim. At the last minute, S. Lyman Tyler, a friend
and historian who was the director of the library at BYU, came
up with a job for John. For the 1958–59 academic year, John
was appointed social science librarian. His charge was to stock
the new library, still under construction, with expanded, quality
holdings. John also arranged to teach an anthropology class in
the sociology department. By the next year the sociologists had
accepted him as a full-fledged faculty member teaching an-

thropology. Before John's second year as a teacher was over, a major was being offered in anthropology (including work in archaeology) and the name of the department had been changed to include both sociology and anthropology.

Until 1963 John was *the* anthropologist at BYU. During a two-year cycle, with the help of a few faculty members in other fields, he taught all the essential courses. A number of students completed the anthropology major and went on to graduate school or into varied employment. Eventually a second anthropologist came aboard: Merlin Myers, a recent graduate of Cambridge University. Anthropology had taken its place in the intellectual spectrum at BYU.

When John first started teaching anthropology, the salary schedule at BYU was not strong. With Kathryn working hard to manage the household, the family of ten (all eight sons had now been born) was barely able to survive. They bought a large old home in Springville, and before long, Kathryn's remodeling efforts provided an additional room. Meanwhile, John nursed an ulcer at home, promoted the cause of anthropology at work, read papers at professional meetings, and served on a committee for the American Anthropological Association.

Applied Anthropology

John always thought anthropology was too stimulating to be limited to the esoteric reports that seemed to satisfy most ivory-tower academics in the profession. A chance to make the discipline useful came in 1959 when Lyman Tyler asked John to help him support the attorney for the Hopi tribe's land-claim lawsuit. They examined early documents to try to pinpoint when the Navajo settled on Hopi lands.

Another opportunity for John to apply his anthropological skills came when Paul Hyer, Asia historian at BYU and an old friend, drew him into a project on South Vietnam. A U.S. Navy office had contracted through David Pack, a Latter-day Saint employee of the Navy, with BYU professors to construct an in-depth profile of South Vietnam. Hyer insisted that a broad anthropological view would be essential, and John, along with political science and economics faculty members as well as student assistants, worked on the study through the summer of 1961 and part-time through the following academic year. The detailed picture they developed addressed military, social, political, and economic organization in Vietnam; its ethnic and religious groups; and its key public actors. John's anthropological view proved to be key to integrating the myriad data, and he ended up codirecting and cowriting the monographic report. Pleased with the results, the Navy commissioned another study of the same kind on Venezuela, where a guerrilla movement was then operating, for the summer of 1962. Again John essentially wrote the report.

The income from these projects eased the family's financial strain and permitted them to add on to their Springville home. They hoped that in 1964, the start of a sabbatical year for John, they could arrange to get away from their regular grind, but limited funds made that seem unlikely. In the spring, however, a providential telephone call came. People at the Defense Research Corporation in Santa Barbara, California, had come across the Navy studies on Vietnam and Venezuela and were impressed. They were looking for a social scientist to lead them through new contracts with the U.S. government on counterinsurgency. John flew to Santa Barbara for an interview, and soon after his return he was offered a job at two and a half times his BYU salary. "I'll talk to my wife and get back to you," John said, trying to sound cool and detached. Within a few days he started consulting work with the corporation, leaving Kathryn to sell the house in Springville and move the family to California.

The Sorensons settled in an old ranch-style house on three-quarters of an acre on "the Mesa." Using their rooftop telescopes, the boys could see the beautiful Santa Barbara Channel and its whales. The home had been built in the 1920s by a Czarist diplomat who, with much of the embassy's funds and all of its wine, fled Washington at the time of the Russian Revolution. With large citrus, palm, live oak, and avocado trees and a forty-acre azalea nursery next door, the homesite was a veritable paradise for growing boys. In time, as the higher salary made a dent in the family's debts, John's ulcer disappeared.

As always, John and Kathryn were active in their LDS ward. She worked with children in the Primary organization and later became Relief Society president, and John taught gospel doctrine to the adults in Sunday School, as he has done for much of the last forty-five years. The Sorensons enjoyed the climate (including the fog) and walking on the beach, growing their flowers, and many other activities associated with the amenities Santa Barbara afforded. John's mother lived with them for part of the time they were in California.

They also made many dear friends. Meeting on the beach at the University of California, Santa Barbara, with brown-bag lunches, John and one of his friends, a historian, discussed starting a periodical for LDS scholarly interchange. Unknown to them, a group at Stanford was already preparing to launch *Dialogue* a few months down the road. John and Kathryn participated in a new Sunday evening study group that read and discussed a different book each month. Now, more than thirty years later, branches of the group still function in Santa Barbara and in Provo and Salt Lake City.

The Defense Research Corporation (soon renamed General Research Corporation) primarily studied intercontinental ballistic missile strategies by using simulations and gaming. The general intellectual mode of operation was that of a think

tank: proposed programs and strategies were subjected to exhaustive critical questioning in every aspect, from axioms to logic to
outcomes. All this was normally done under the pressure of ur-
gent deadlines. It was a far cry from the leisurely life of academe.

The company's principals, who were scientists or engineers
wanting to make a profit and go public with their stock, sought
to diversify and expand their market. In the 1960s counterinsurgency was a research growth area among their clients, who
were military or quasi-military agencies. Discovering that it
would need a person knowledgeable in social science, the company hired John as the first and nominal head social scientist. His
first responsibility was to direct a study on urban insurgency,
with political scientists, economists, military people, and operations research experts all contributing their expertise.

The biggest challenge for John was to transcend the conceptual frameworks and languages of the company's existing
"scientific" experts. He found that he would need to adapt anthropological and other social science models and terminology
to the ongoing in-house discussion, and although this forced
him to question some of the details of his own discipline, he
appreciated more than ever the power of its overall approach.

It was not simply a competition between disciplines, for the
key questions always came down to nondisciplinary matters.
Rather, the aim was to get at the real questions behind the obvious ones. Military analysts routinely asked questions such as
how guerrillas might attack a village, but the systems critic had
to probe further: Will village defenders risk death if they do not
trust their leaders? Who can be bribed and with what? The process was intense, never ending, and intellectually subversive of
every casual assumption. John realized that most of the academics involved in these discussions asked rather tame, artifi-
cial questions whose answers had little relation to the real
world. He also came to realize that for some problems there are

simply no adequate answers. For example, when this think-tank mode of critical analysis was used in a massive study of urban transportation for the Department of Housing and Urban Development, the panoply of data on vehicle speeds, subway capacities, freeway pollution, and the social costs of failing to fix the current systems made only marginal difference. The overriding fact was that only very expensive, high-tech changes would make marked improvement in traffic flows, and because of the political economy, they were impossible to implement.

John also realized that relatively few clients—private as well as government—do research to find out the real answers. Rather, research is mainly cosmetic, a political ploy used to delay an uncomfortable decision or to justify why an already-determined course will be followed. Huge studies are often shelved if they do not fit the predisposition of those in high places. As John observes, "It was interesting, but highly discouraging, to see the mind-set of the bureaucrats."

John welcomed the high salary he received at the General Research Corporation, but as time went on he began to enjoy less and less the challenge of that kind of work. Under the high stress of dealing with government clients, he began to long for what he recalled (perhaps inaccurately) as the quieter pace of the university. In 1969 company management agreed to John's forming a subsidiary, the Bonneville Research Corporation, which he would operate from Provo and which would handle the social science end of the General Research Corporation's contracts. John planned to utilize BYU faculty members and other LDS experts as consultants.

Moving the family back to Utah was not entirely pleasant. Kathryn wondered why they had left behind what she considered paradise, and John did not really want to be a businessman pressured to locate funds and projects mainly on his own now that the heyday of government support for such contracts was

xxx   Introduction

over. Yet the advantages of the move seemed to outweigh the disadvantages. After the Sorensons relocated to Provo, John had two years of relative success as the large Bonneville team developed new language programs for the Army Language School in Monterey, California. But eventually the General Research Corporation, under its own pressures, withdrew support and the Bonneville Corporation folded.

Final Years at BYU

While working for the General Research Corporation, John had maintained many connections with Brigham Young University. Some faculty members had worked on research projects, including Martin Hickman, dean of the College of Social Sciences, who had served on Bonneville's board of directors. When the company dissolved, Hickman invited John to take an open faculty position at the rank of full professor.

John taught classes in political science and sociology, but not in his old department, which had been renamed the Department of Anthropology and Archaeology. "I have never taught anything but Sorenson," John maintains, "whatever the department label." His primary responsibility was to work with the dean's office in facilitating research proposals made by the college's faculty.

For the next academic year (1972–73), Hickman assigned John to serve on the staff of a university-wide committee attempting to reform the general education curriculum and simultaneously appointed him chair of the university studies department. The general education staff—chiefly John Sorenson, Arthur Henry King, and Marion Bentley, all under the advisement of Dean Terry Warner—strove for two years to arrive at a new curriculum that was both innovative and acceptable to the faculty. However, disciplinary vested interests forced painful political compromises. The result was so far below the visionary hopes of the staff and the reform committee that even now John is not pleased to recall the effort.

Working with the university studies program, on the other hand, was a pleasure for him. The program helped students design a personalized curriculum aimed at meeting a specific graduation need they felt strongly about and could defend. John counseled hundreds of students. Part of his role was to screen out any efforts by individual students looking to complete their programs via an easy set of courses. The unwillingness of some departments to cooperate with the program was a more difficult problem, one caused by the notion that everyone must fit into an already established major or not receive a degree. "I learned a lot I didn't want to learn," John recalls. Eventually the university studies program was restricted and then discontinued.

In 1978 Hickman appointed John chair of the Department of Anthropology and Archaeology. John was to deal with particularly hard questions involving faculty retention and a general stasis in the program, but because he had not been on the inside of the department for fourteen years, he faced a difficult task. He worked prodigiously to resolve these issues for the next eight years.

John's first step was to move his people from obscure basement quarters into the new Kimball Tower, where they could be integrated into the university environment. Eventually he succeeded in having the department name shortened to the anthropology department. Also, a number of changes were made in faculty positions, including hiring the first non-Mormons in the department.

Conceiving the little departmental museum collection more broadly as a semiautonomous entity, John renamed it the Museum of Peoples and Cultures and found it new quarters in the old Allen Hall, where it became the center for BYU's archaeological research. For some years the department's archaeologists had contracted to do a limited amount of archaeology for government agencies and utility companies. Now John sought to promote and regularize that kind of service. The Office of Public Archaeology was established within the museum, a shoestring operation that grew under the leadership of Asa Nielson, a master's graduate of the department. Within a few years a steady flow of projects was under way, resulting in the hiring of additional full-time staff. BYU archaeology students received hands-on experience at archaeological sites in Utah and the surrounding states and then went on to take professional positions in a network of government agencies. A newsletter subtitled "Anthropology at BYU" was produced at and circulated from the museum.

Students in sociocultural and archaeological anthropology learned to attend and give presentations at professional meetings. Africanists Tom and Pam Blakely's lobbying for one such trip saw success when, in 1983, a contingent of two dozen BYU students and faculty traveled to the national meetings of the Society for Applied Anthropology, an organization in which John was a fellow for a quarter century. "Well, I'll be damned," said an older lapsed-Mormon anthropologist from Colorado, surprised that BYU had brought its anthropology program to such a scale. Field schools of archaeology were developed in several venues in the intermountain West, and Professor John Hawkins held a BYU ethnographic field school in southern Mexico.

In the midst of his administrative work, John taught five or six classes per year. Sensitive to his colleagues, he never tried to teach "their" courses, even though he was qualified to do so in many cases. He instead filled in around the edges of the curriculum and developed new specialties of his own, including modern American culture. He particularly enjoyed teaching a course in psychological anthropology, a class he came to consider crucial to the synthesis of the field that anthropologists always claimed to be seeking.

Because he was experienced in the wider world of applied anthropology, John was not one to remain confined within rigid departmental boundaries. He branched out to serve as consultant to the Charles Redd Center for Western Studies, the BYU Language Research Center, the Thrasher Research Fund, the LDS Motion Picture Studio, and a committee studying the LDS missionary program. For more than twenty-five years, he labored consistently to build the anthropology collection within the BYU library system to the point where it is now one of the best collections in the western U.S., and on the subject of Mesoamerica it has few equals anywhere. During his twenty-five years on the faculty, John took only one leave, a semester he spent in St. George in 1985 doing research on the local school system for the BYU College of Education.

In 1985 John suffered a heart attack. Angioplasty treatment limited the organic damage, but the psychic shock proved greater than the physical trauma. He suddenly realized that stress caused by his overambitious agenda was the prime contributor to his condition. Moreover, he realized that nobody really cared about his plans and that most of his concerns at BYU were actually of small moment. Lying in the intensive care unit, he thought about his life. A sympathetic visit from a friend, an apostle in the LDS Church, urged him to believe that he still had a long, productive life ahead. He just needed to correct the course his ship had been sailing. It was a time for major reassessment of what really mattered.

Book of Mormon Scholarship

Retiring from BYU at age sixty-two, John never looked back with longing to either his department or his field. What

he had always wanted to do but had never been professionally
positioned to accomplish was to pursue research on the Book of
Mormon. Now, perhaps, the chance had arrived.

Since 1949, the year he realized the importance of what he
could contribute to Book of Mormon studies, John had accomplished a great deal in that area through spurts of effort. Although heavily involved in other commitments, he had tried
each year to devote at least a few weeks to intensively reading
about Mesoamerican archaeology. He was rarely able to travel
in Mexico and Central America, where he was sure the Nephite
lands lay, but he did master a vast array of primary and secondary materials on ancient life there. In 1969, while working at
the General Research Corporation, he had prepared a landmark paper comparing ancient Near East and Mesoamerican
cultures. First presented a year earlier in a symposium in Santa
Fe, New Mexico, it was published in 1971 in *Man across the
Sea: Problems of Pre-Columbian Contacts,* an important volume
assessing what was known of ancient voyages to the Americas.

John's views on Book of Mormon geography had taken
early form under M. Wells Jakeman's tutelage, but the definitive
solution to the long-argued problem occurred to him during
the 1953 New World Archaeological Foundation season, when,
as he recalls, he studied the scriptures at night as intensively as
he did the ruins during the day. It was clear to him that, as
Jakeman and others had insisted for years, the text itself de-
mands that its setting be restricted to a relatively small territory
that does not include the Hill Cumorah in New York. Rather,
the picture of geography and culture in the Nephite account fits
at point after point into the setting of ancient Mesoamerican
civilization. More specifically, John believed, the "land of
Zarahemla" comprised mainly the drainage area of the Grijalva
River in southern Mexico, while the "land of Nephi" was mostly
in highland Guatemala.

But geography was only one aspect of the correlation that had to be worked out, in John's view, and archaeology provided only partial data. For the correlation between the Book of Mormon lands and Mesoamerica to be convincing, historical traditions, languages, racial types, the whole range of culture, and every other aspect of ancient life had to relate as well. Fortunately, John had always taken the broadest possible approach to studying Mesoamerica, and everything he learned fit with and filled out the picture that had crystallized for him in 1953. Only a few friends and students, however, were aware of the details of his position.

In 1974 David A. Palmer of Naperville, Illinois, a chemical engineer and Book of Mormon buff, urged John to make public his views along with the substantial supporting materials. To overcome John's reluctance to publicize what John considered work in progress, Palmer proposed that students of Book of Mormon geography confer by mail about a written presentation of John's basic views and a contrasting interpretation by V. Garth Norman. Most of the commentators accepted John's views and urged publication of them. Palmer then opened the way for John to give weekly lectures at the LDS Church Office Building in Salt Lake City for several months. One of the listeners was Jay M. Todd, managing editor of the *Ensign,* who not only accepted Sorenson's views but strongly urged that they be published.

But like all new theories, John's proposal encountered opposition. A few people in key church positions felt comfortable with the traditional view that the Nephites had occupied North America and had been exterminated in New York, an impossibility according to the limited geography model and John's reading of the scriptural text. "Don't challenge tradition" was the viewpoint that prevailed. John strove to be patient with the decision not to publish his articles, because he did not want to be seen as a troublemaker, especially a futile troublemaker. He would bide his time.

Finally, circumstances combined to make church authorities realize that the status quo about Book of Mormon geography was actually harmful. For Latter-day Saints to accept ill-informed traditions allowed critics of the Book of Mormon to have a field day. John was asked to produce two articles conveying the gist of his interpretation, and their appearance in the *Ensign* in September and October 1984 constituted a fundamental breakthrough in LDS Church publishing on the Book of Mormon. While the editor's introduction carefully avoided any claim of church approval for these landmark articles, the limited approval that could be inferred from their publication in the *Ensign* opened up new vistas for public discussion of the subject. The chapters that had been blocked from the magazine for so long were quickly published by Deseret Book and the Foundation for Ancient Research and Mormon Studies (FARMS) in mid-1985 as *An Ancient American Setting for the Book of Mormon.*

Coincidentally or not, John's heart attack occurred early in the fall of 1984, just as John was putting all this work to bed and as the new school year was starting. He had also recently finished serving as a bishop.

Meanwhile, John had been heavily engaged in pushing forward the Foundation for Ancient Research and Mormon Studies. John W. Welch founded the organization in 1979 and soon afterward left his southern California law practice to join the faculty of the J. Reuben Clark Law School at BYU. From the first time he heard about FARMS, John Sorenson was an enthusiastic supporter of it. He had been active in Jakeman's Society for Early Historic Archaeology but had given up on it because of the narrowness of the approach and the dominance of personalities in what should have been a more scholarly activity. Since then he had tried to bring Book of Mormon scholars together but was unsuccessful. Now Welch's dynamism, scholarship, and legal and fiscal skills promised a different level of success. FARMS quickly became a cooperative, if not communal, effort. Support and resources mushroomed. Like everyone else at FARMS, John Sorenson helped with the nitty-gritty details. As the organization has tried to bring reliable research on the Book of Mormon and its setting to a wide audience, John has contributed much because of his unique knowledge and perspective. He has written and edited in the FARMS publication program, and for several years he was chairman of the board. Although no longer a member of the board of trustees, John has recently been selected as the editor of the *Journal of Book of Mormon Studies.*

With an unrivaled breadth of experience in fields and skills ranging from dirt archaeology and anthropological theory to systems analysis and the history of science, and having learned to function in an atmosphere of relentless questioning and mutual criticism, John is not easily cowed. He does not, as the saying goes, suffer fools gladly. With either a brief or a lengthy response, he dismisses critics who have not invested neither time nor attention to issues surrounding the Book of Mormon. He tries to give the benefit of doubt when judging the motives of critics, although he cannot grasp the basis of anti–Book of Mormon diatribes, which he finds invariably poorly informed. At the same time, however, he recognizes that his own answers are tentative and that study is an ongoing process that should never cease. He is also eager to supply those willing to learn with facts and viewpoints intended to invite them to seek further truth. One can anticipate that John will continue to contribute significantly to the stream of Book of Mormon scholarship that, thanks partly to FARMS, now depends more on the cooperative efforts of many rather than on the isolated efforts of individuals.

Personal and Family Life

Throughout his years as a scholar, John Sorenson was a husband and a father. Although he and Kathryn pursued different interests according to their different talents, they did many things together and gave each other love and support. While they lived in Santa Barbara, longing for the daughter that they could not conceive, the Sorensons took in Stacy, first as a two-year-old foster child and eventually as an adopted and sealed daughter. As the boys grew up and left home, they showed an independence of spirit sometimes painful to their parents, but the increasing covey of grandchildren lightened John's and Kathryn's lives.

Following John's heart problem and retirement, the couple gave heavy priority to spending time together. Because Kathryn was diabetic, her future health was in question. She and John wanted to enjoy together what they could of their remaining good years. Money was no longer an issue, for their income was comfortable. A measure of the wisdom that comes with age told them both to relax and simplify their lives, and in response they managed to put some of their concerns about their children out of their minds as well.

The flexibility of retirement allowed them to spend a month or so in the winter of 1989 on the lower Colorado River in Arizona. John took his computer and did some writing, but mainly they simply relaxed. The next year they spent a longer time at the beach in Carpinteria, near their beloved Santa Barbara. That respite was so pleasant that they wanted to repeat it. Arriving on New Year's Day 1991, they took a late walk on the beach and then retired. During the night Kathryn passed away of a heart attack, thus being spared the slow, painful decline from diabetes that she had always dreaded.

All the children and many grandchildren gathered for a funeral in Provo that reflected the creativity, humor, service, and unselfish support to John that had characterized Kathryn's life. She was buried in a plot they had jointly chosen in the cemetery in Smithfield, near where their four parents lay and where John's father had planted many of the towering trees sixty years before.

Immediately after the funeral, John traveled alone to Zion Canyon and Springdale, its gateway, one of his favorite spots. For weeks he walked the trails and climbed the ridges and found peace in that gorgeous place. Before long, however, he was back at work on his computer. Peace without work was hard for him to imagine.

In March 1993 John married Helen Christianson, a widow from his ward who had been a close friend of Kathryn and had spoken at her funeral. Their eighteen children (then ranging between forty-seven and fourteen years of age) are the backbone of a joint clan that now numbers more than seventy-five, including three great-grandchildren. The couple's loving relationship is a blessing not only to them but also to hundreds of relatives and friends around them.

John has continued his habit of hard work, and his health is excellent. Nearly every day he walks or buses from his and Helen's home on Canyon Road to his office in BYU's Amanda Knight Building on University Avenue, where he continues the same kind of research and writing that he long prepared to do. He believes life is good to him.

Scholarly Contributions

The incessant flood of scholarship in many languages throughout the world sometimes prompts John to describe himself as an ex-scholar or an ex-anthropologist. The fact is, however, that his determined effort to keep abreast of research in the areas of his interest has paid off. Those who tangle with him will not find him pontificating on his own authority; rather, he calls attention to false assumptions, flaws in reasoning, and articles or books whose premises are weakened by easy generalizations. A well-known Maya scholar has been heard to say that he was reluctant to face Sorenson: "He is too intimidating." This intimidation, if that is the right word for it, comes not from impoliteness or name-calling but from the simple fact of superior preparation—knowing the scholarship combined with having carefully thought about it.

Bibliographical Contributions

A bibliographical contribution sure to have a lasting impact is the two-volume *Pre-Columbian Contact with the Americas across the Oceans: An Annotated Bibliography* (1996), which John prepared in collaboration with Martin H. Raish. The bibliography contains some fifty-one hundred entries. No one considering the possibility of transoceanic contacts can afford to ignore what Betty Meggers of the Smithsonian Institution has described as an "impressive bibliography and monumental effort." Those who deny that any such contacts ever occurred, unwisely presuming to prove a negative, could profitably peruse what anthropologist George F. Carter of Texas A&M University calls an "unbelievably useful" and "magnificent" work.

Epistemological Approach

Unlike almost all people and a surprisingly large number of scholars, John has considered carefully what can and cannot be known and what can and cannot be proved. Because he knows the limitations of scholarship, he possesses a salutary humility. In the scholarly arena everything is subject to change. John is quite comfortable with the tentativeness of human inquiry, realizing that some questions simply stand outside the unaided human mind's capacity to solve. But another result of this awareness of the limits of scholarship is John's impatience with the pretense of some scholarly claims. His paper "'Understanding' the 'Real World'" summarizes his recognition of the tentativeness of human concepts and theories. His natural inclination is to quickly reduce a controversial issue to its rudiments: What are the presuppositions? What evidence should we expect? How thorough have the investigations been? Willing to subject his own work to these same questions, John is not always patient with those who forge ahead and yet are ignorant of their assumptions and the limitations of all human inquiry.

Internal Textual Analysis

In Book of Mormon studies a standard Sorenson rejoinder is to ask how familiar someone is with the text. If the person has not read it carefully, John asks why the opinion should be granted much weight. Even ecclesiastical leaders are not immune from this question. John believes that the authority on what the Book of Mormon claims is the Book of Mormon itself.

Although he is not the only person involved in textual analysis of the Book of Mormon, John has carefully scrutinized a variety of specific questions. His methodical mind manifests itself through his preparation not only of articles on such subjects as the Mulekites and the relationship of warfare to the seasons of the year but also of thorough compilations. What are the Book of Mormon's own geographical references and requirements? One had better consult Sorenson's *The Geography of Book of Mormon Events: A Source Book* (1992). What animals are mentioned in the Book of Mormon and how might they correspond to what we know of pre-Columbian fauna in the Western Hemisphere? One had better consult Sorenson's *Animals in the Book of Mormon: An Annotated Bibliography* (1992). And on and on.

If John has written little on the religious ideas or theology of the Book of Mormon, this does not reflect his lack of interest in this area. Rather, it simply shows that his chosen area of contribution is elsewhere.

External Comparisons

To appreciate John's unique contribution, we must remind ourselves of the two extremes that seemed to dominate Book of Mormon studies when he came on the scene in the late 1940s. On one hand, there were flat denials by all the "big scholars" that anything like the Lehite migrations could have occurred. On the other hand, some Mormons made extravagant claims on their own. Paying little attention to geography or chronology, and ignoring complexity and context, they jumped to the strained conclusion that photographs of ancient ruins confirmed the authenticity of the Book of Mormon. Between these extremes, a small number of Mormon scholars sought to proceed more carefully, and John quickly identified with them.

Rather than look for specific "proofs," however, John raised different questions: What do we know about ancient Mesoamerica? What can be said of the cultural world of the Book of Mormon? Are there compatibilities? Are the apparent incongruities truly irreconcilable, or should they be considered more carefully? No one seems to have been raising these questions when John, as a brilliant graduate student in 1955, delivered a series of lectures titled "The World of the Book of Mormon." Such an approach, buttressed by much additional detail and a willingness, finally, to advance a possible geographical locale for the events of the Book of Mormon, resulted in John's magnum opus, *An Ancient American Setting for the Book of Mormon* (1985).

John is willing to cite specific parallels between the setting of the Book of Mormon and Mesoamerica, but he does so with proper tentativeness. Who other than John Sorenson, we might ask, was in a position in the 1940s or 1950s to write "The Book of Mormon as a Mesoamerican Codex" (1976)? John claims no monopoly on this idea, but although others have made important external comparisons, John's extensive files on parallels and specific comparisons continue to make him a leader in discussions of the Book of Mormon in its external setting.

Mormon Studies

Not well-known to those familiar only with John's Book of Mormon contributions are his analytical and empirical studies of Mormon culture. His important doctoral dissertation comparing American Fork and Santaquin has already been discussed, and fourteen of his essays on Mormon culture and personality have been reprinted in *Taking a Closer Look: Four Decades of Essays on Mormon Culture and Personality* (1997). Although Mormon culture is not the center of his scholarly and teaching interest, John has nevertheless given it significant thought. A kind of capstone of this thought is *Mindful of Every People: Anthropological Perspectives on Mormons* (1997), a work he coedited with University of Maryland anthropologist Mark P. Leone. Although John wrote only one of the chapters, the project, which grew out of sessions he organized in 1980 on the topic "The Anthropology of Mormons," is intended to lay a foundation for future anthropological studies of Mormon culture.

* * *

As professional colleagues, fellow scholars, and friends, we present the following token of our esteem—articles of varying content that all connect with John's interests.

MORMON HISTORY AND CULTURE

BAPTIZED, CONSECRATED, AND SEALED: THE COVENANTAL FOUNDATIONS OF MORMON RELIGIOUS IDENTITY

Steven L. Olsen

One of the "elementary forms of religion" identified by Emile Durkheim is that a society's fundamental concept of God expresses, from a cultural point of view, its highest and most ambitious ideals projected onto eternity.[1] If this is true, we should be able to reflect these spiritual realities back onto empirical cultural phenomena in order to understand the basic and most distinctive sociocultural features of a religion like Mormonism. Before outlining the conceptual benefits of this theoretical perspective, I would like to explain its assumptions and limitations so that its advantages can be more fully appreciated. The following premises define this approach:

1. Religious identity is defined by core theological concepts that are established principally by and through authoritative sources. In Mormonism these sources include, but are not limited to, the canonical standard works—the Bible,

Steven L. Olsen, adjunct assistant professor of anthropology at Brigham Young University, is manager of operations at the Museum of Church History and Art in Salt Lake City, Utah.

the Book of Mormon, the Doctrine and Covenants, and the Pearl of Great Price—and the official writings of Mormon Church leaders.

2. The core concepts that define the religious identity of a people approximate a theological system whose components are structurally interrelated and mutually coherent.

3. These basic concepts and their interdependent and mutually coherent relationships constitute the structure of the religious system.

4. This theological system constitutes a prescriptive model for meaningful religious behavior and social action. However, human behavior is rarely a complete and perfect reflection of theological ideals. Any religious society usually has a degree of dynamic tension between the structural foundations of the theological system and the behavior of those who accept those ideals.

5. Real-world experiences, including those associated with imperfect human behavior, often condition, qualify, or transform the interpretation of theological ideals, but rarely in a deterministic manner. This premise implies that religious identity is contextualized by historical, environmental, social, and other conditions as recognized and interpreted by the believers, particularly by the group's key decision makers or the culture's central institutions. Despite the changeable nature of religious identity, the basic theological concepts that constitute the specific expressions of religious identity tend to persist over time.

This chapter will identify the conceptual foundations of Mormon religious identity and indicate some of the major implications of this perspective for the understanding of Mormon history.

Nine years after his first visit from the angel Moroni, Joseph Smith received one of his most important revelations, section 84 of the Doctrine and Covenants. Ostensibly its subject was priesthood—the authority, by Mormon reckoning, given to righteous men on earth to act in God's stead. In this concise but far-reaching explication of the tradition, doctrine, and power of the priesthood, the twenty-six-year-old Mormon prophet identified those who would eventually be saved in the Father's kingdom by virtue of this divine power. Collectively they would be known as "the church and kingdom, and the elect of God" (D&C 84:34). If these three institutions—the church, the kingdom, and the elect—define the essential social structure of Mormon heaven as suggested by this and other revelations of Joseph Smith (see, for example, D&C 76:50–70; 88:21–5; 132:6–24), then, in light of Durkheim's sociological model, they provide an important basis for interpreting much of the historical and social experience of the Latter-day Saints.

This approach suggests that Mormon religious identity can be understood as being initially constituted and periodically refined in terms of the core sociotheological concepts of the Church of Christ (the Church of Jesus Christ of Latter-day Saints), the kingdom of God (Zion), and the elect people of God (collectively known as the house of Israel). I will demonstrate the analytical value of viewing these concepts, which overlap considerably in ordinary Mormon discourse, as distinctive but complementary concepts in Mormon thought. Although these concepts have been conditioned, transformed, and refined over time by historical tradition and empirical and spiritual experiences, as interpreted by key church leaders, Mormon public discourse and social behavior can be seen as efforts by Latter-day Saints to express and practice in their daily lives the spiritual ideals of Christ's Church, Zion, and the house of Israel. Thus the present analysis describes the historical origins, structural foundations, and social consequences of Mormon identity in terms of three ideal-typic covenanted communities.

Historical Origins of Mormon Identity

The latter-day Church of Christ was organized by Joseph Smith in a remote farmhouse in Fayette Township, New York, on 6 April 1830. By Mormon reckoning, this event effected the restoration to earth of Christ's primitive church, with its divinely appointed officers, priesthoods, and doctrines. At least a few dozen of Smith's followers witnessed this event, but six men constituted the legal participants in the act of organization. Following a formal opening with prayer, events included the congregation's official acceptance, or sustaining, of Joseph Smith and Oliver Cowdery as their leaders; the ordination of Smith and Cowdery to the respective callings of "first elder" and "second elder" (D&C 20:2–3); the administration of the sacrament of the Lord's supper to the congregation; the confirmation of those who had been baptized as members of the church and the ordination of several men to the priesthood; and prophetic and other inspired discourses about members' duties and the future of the Church of Christ.[2]

The Book of Mormon mandated this event as one of the essential preparations for the second coming of Christ and the advent of the millennium at the end of time (see 2 Nephi 9:1–2; 3 Nephi 21:22–9). As the words of the Book of Mormon fell from his lips, Joseph Smith apparently came to understand that his prophetic mission extended beyond his being an agent in restoring ancient scriptures; he was also to be the prophet of Christ's restored church. Supporting this understanding were several revelations that Smith received during this same period. These revelations specifically anticipated the "coming forth of [Christ's] church out of the wilderness—clear as the moon, fair as the sun, and terrible as an army with banners" (D&C 5:14; see 10:53–69; 11:16; 18:4–5). According to Joseph Smith, the Church of Christ began its divinely ordained march out of obscurity on 6 April 1830.

The Book of Mormon also required the establishment of the kingdom of Zion and the gathering of the house of Israel in the latter days (see, for example, 2 Nephi 25–30; 3 Nephi 20–2; Ether 13). Joseph Smith was no less intent on fulfilling these ancient prophecies than he had been on organizing the Church of Christ. At one point Smith declared that the establishment of Zion—a worldwide millennial kingdom of God—was "the most important temporal object in view" of the Latter-day Saints.[3] The revelations he received from 1831 to 1834 reflect this preoccupation with Zion and reveal its gradual unfolding.[4]

In accordance with these divine directives, Smith and a number of his most trusted associates gathered in Jackson County, Missouri, in late July 1831 to dedicate Zion's "center place" (D&C 57:3). Twelve elders, representing the twelve tribes of Israel, ritually laid a log as the foundation of an appropriate habitation in the kingdom. On 2 August the Prophet laid the cornerstones of Zion's main temple, the sacred center of this urban society.[5]

The City of Zion, as defined by Joseph Smith, was to "fill up the world in the latter days" with an innumerable series of mile-square settlements, called squares, having fewer than twenty thousand residents each. Life in Zion was to be characterized by consolidated family residential patterns; concentric spheres of public, residential, and occupational activity, each legitimized and controlled by priesthood authority; and face-to-face patterns of social interaction.[6]

The gathering of the house of Israel—the ethnic identity of the people of God—was formally inaugurated at the dedication of the first Mormon temple, which was completed in Kirtland,

Ohio. According to Joseph Smith's official account of this Pentecostal-like event that followed a week of dedicatory services (27 March–3 April 1836), he and Sidney Rigdon (a counselor to Smith in the church's ultimate governing body, the First Presidency) received a vision of Christ, who accepted the temple as the "House of the Lord," his official dwelling place on earth (see D&C 109:1–5, 12–3, 16; 110:6–9). A series of Old Testament prophets then appeared and conferred upon Smith and Rigdon essential priesthood keys, that is, specific authority to carry out God's will in the latter days. The first of these messengers was Moses, who bestowed upon them "the keys of the gathering of Israel from the four parts of the earth" (D&C 110:11).[7]

The house of Israel officially began to be organized among the Latter-day Saints when Joseph Smith revealed the ceremonies (called ordinances) connected with another sacred temple as it was nearing completion in the 1840s in Nauvoo, Illinois. The "new and everlasting covenant of marriage" (see D&C 131:1–4), solemnized by a ritual "sealing" of husbands and wives and parents and children,[8] was instituted first in the upper room of Joseph Smith's red-brick store in 1842, before the temple was completed.

Before and after the Prophet's martyrdom in 1844, there was considerable anxiety among the Latter-day Saints to complete the Nauvoo Temple so that as many as possible could receive these sacred ordinances. They believed that once they were sealed to one another, neither earth nor hell could prevent them from receiving their promised blessings of exaltation as a covenanted kinship community. The holy order of matrimony entered into through the sealing ordinance became available for worthy Latter-day Saint couples in the Nauvoo Temple from 7 January 1846 until the Mormons were driven from their "city beautiful" and began their monumental exodus to western North America (see D&C 124:22–48).[9]

The Structure of Mormon Identity

If Mormon identity consists in membership in and acceptance of the transcendent meaning of the complementary institutions of the Church of Christ, the kingdom of Zion, and the house of Israel, how is this identity expressed by the Latter-day Saints? Each of these social institutions has a distinctive ritual of membership, code of conduct, sacerdotal order, and concept of salvation. These elements combine systematically to create a complex and profound sense of solidarity among those so identified. I will discuss each of these elements in their respective cultural contexts and then demonstrate briefly some of the major analytical advantages of this interpretive framework for understanding Mormon history.

The Church of Christ

Membership in the Church of Christ is defined by the covenant of baptism and bestowed by the complementary ordinances of "baptism by immersion for the remission of sins" and "laying on of hands [confirmation] for the gift of the Holy Ghost" (Article of Faith 4). The covenant of baptism consists in the promise that church members are "willing to take upon them the name of [Christ], and always remember him and keep his commandments which he has given them." In return, Christ promises that they will "always have his Spirit to be with them" (D&C 20:77). Latter-day Saints renew this covenant weekly by partaking of the emblems (bread and water) of Christ's atoning sacrifice (see D&C 20:77, 79) in the sacrament of the

Lord's supper (commonly referred to as the sacrament), the centerpiece of Mormon Sunday worship services.

The LDS ritual of baptism is performed under priesthood authority. The baptismal candidate, dressed completely in white, is fully immersed in water in similitude of the death and resurrection of Jesus Christ and the spiritual rebirth (symbolic washing away of the sins) of the individual candidate. Baptism is an essential ordinance of salvation, and the entire performance—from the clothing worn and the prayer uttered (see D&C 20:73) to the actions performed and sanctioned by priesthood authority—symbolically represents an ideal spiritual life characterized by complete moral purity and total fidelity to the "still small voice" (D&C 85:6), or the promptings of the Holy Ghost. Such worthiness is required of all who would be saved in the celestial kingdom. Because it is a token of a person's assuming moral responsibility, baptism must be consented to by the prospective member, who must be of the age of accountability (at least eight years old; see D&C 20:71; 68:25–7), understand the difference between right and wrong, and commit to live a life of moral purity and good works (see D&C 20:37). These qualifications must be attested either by a designated full-time missionary (in the case of converts more than eight years old) or by the bishop (in the case of eight-year-old converts), who is the priesthood leader of the local ecclesiastical community.

Confirmation follows baptism. A formal prayer declares an individual officially a member of the Church of Jesus Christ of Latter-day Saints and commands him to "receive the Holy Ghost." The confirmation concludes with spontaneous blessings and counsel pronounced by the officiator, who is a faithful Melchizedek Priesthood holder (the higher spiritual authority in the church) and usually a family member or friend.

The code of conduct enjoined upon members of the

Church of Christ can be summarized as the law of the gospel. This law is grounded specifically in the commandments, beginning with faith in the Lord Jesus Christ and repentance (see Article of Faith 4), which prepare members to receive forgiveness of sins through the atonement of Jesus Christ and the daily companionship of the Holy Ghost. Related commandments include embracing the full range of Christian moral virtues— honesty, integrity, charity, temperance, humility, obedience, compassion, devotion, and so on—in public and private life.

Through the covenant of baptism, members become disciples of Christ. Thus bound to Christ, they also are bound to one another, obligated by covenant to give compassionate service, such as offering comfort in times of trial and mutual support in the gospel (see Mosiah 18:8–11). Preparing their children for baptism through example and moral instruction is one of the essential responsibilities enjoined upon parents in the Church of Christ (see D&C 20:70; 68:25).

Exhortation to maintain this code of conduct is the usual focus of LDS Sunday worship services. The crux of the congregational assembly is the sacrament (the formal weekly renewal of the covenant of baptism), which all faithful members are expected to receive.[10]

Those who violate the covenant of baptism by repudiating the church's code of conduct are subject to ecclesiastical discipline, which may include disfellowshipment or excommunication. The former is a temporary suspension of membership privileges such as partaking of the sacrament, while the latter is a total revocation of formal church ties. Neither sanction is necessarily permanent, and neither prohibits a person from attending, without active participation in, Sunday worship services.[11]

The ecclesiastical order of the church exists to help members realize and preserve gospel ideals in their lives. It consists of programs, quorums, and auxiliaries and is regulated and presided over by the Melchizedek Priesthood, which holds and governs all spiritual keys in the church (see D&C 84:19; 107:18). Priesthood officers oversee all public meetings and all religious activities of the congregation, and they control access to formal spiritual blessings of the church such as ordinations, callings, participation in the sacrament, and membership itself. Specific presiding offices in the priesthood include elder, high priest, bishop, apostle, seventy, and president of the church. Holders of the first three offices of the priesthood preside over an elaborate system of local organization: branches, wards, quorums, auxiliaries, and stakes. Councils of the First Presidency, Twelve Apostles, and Seventy preside over the church as a whole (see D&C 107:21–38).

In short, the Church of Christ embodies the following concepts central to the definition and expression of Mormon religious identity: Jesus Christ is an essential role model for all church members (see 3 Nephi 27:27); the law of the gospel is intended to purify members from all unrighteousness and to prepare them to become holy, like God; the covenant of baptism identifies those who have committed to so order their lives; the central purposes of congregational worship are for members to renew the covenant of baptism through the sacrament and to receive instruction on the proper conduct of their lives according to gospel standards; church members need one another, both during Sunday worship services and throughout the week, in order to better realize these spiritual goals; and the celestial kingdom will include those who have realized the blessings of this covenant and ecclesiastical order in their lives.

The Kingdom of Zion

The ecclesiastical order defined by the Church of Christ does not comprehend all elements of Mormon religious identity. The latter also includes a territorial order called Zion. The quest for Zion in early Mormonism reflected the core Mormon beliefs that the "earth is the Lord's, and the fulness thereof" (Psalm 24:1), that God gave mankind the responsibility to till the earth and take care of His other material creations in accordance with divine commandments (see Genesis 1:26, 28; 2:15; 3:23), that obedience to these commandments would result in the creation of a righteous kingdom on earth acceptable to God, and that Jesus Christ will eventually return to earth to reign personally as King of Zion (see Article of Faith 10) once the full framework has been properly established.[12]

While the biblical model for Mormonism's ecclesiastical order is Christ and the New Testament church, the model for its territorial and socioeconomic order is Enoch and the City of Zion. Founded in ancient times, Enoch's "City of Holiness" (Moses 7:19) was characterized by such righteousness that it was literally removed from mundane existence into heaven, where it became God's "abode forever" (Moses 7:21). Joseph Smith came to see himself as a latter-day Enoch, called of God to establish on earth a city, society, and kingdom characterized by a degree of righteousness sufficient to cause God to restore Zion to earth, in fulfillment of his covenant with Enoch. Once united with heavenly Zion, earthly Zion would be transformed into a celestial kingdom in which those who lived worthy of its eternal glories would live literally in the presence of God (see D&C 76:62; 88:25–9; Article of Faith 10).

Membership in Zion, like that in the Church of Christ, was defined and established by covenant. Zion's covenant was called consecration. The covenant of consecration was established not by a priesthood ordinance per se, but by a formal transaction in which a person desiring to become a citizen of Zion consecrated, or deeded, all of his material possessions to the bishop, God's earthly agent who oversaw Zion's material resources. In return he received from the bishop a stewardship (perpetual-use right) over an inheritance (specified property in Zion). Formal deeds of consecration and stewardship were executed to ratify this covenant between Zion and her inhabitants (see D&C 42:30–9).[13]

Zion's code of conduct was called the law of consecration. This law required that all residents devote their energy, time, and other personal resources to establishing Zion. Work was of prime importance for all residents of Zion. By this means they "magnified" their stewardships, or increased the productivity of their inheritances. As a result, the community's resource base expanded in order to care for each family's dependents. All residents of Zion were also to donate (consecrate) the surplus of their efforts to the general needs of Zion: caring for the poor, the infirm, and the needy; preparing stewardships for Zion's future inhabitants; and establishing new settlements of Zion throughout the earth.[14]

In Mormon scripture some of the most exalted labor of God, angels, and mankind is called work, reflecting the theological importance of this socioeconomic imperative.[15] Thus work was intended to become for the Mormons a kind of public- and community-based devotion during the first six days of the week, while worship was the ideal focus of Sabbath day activity. Just as Mormons sought to glorify God through their Sabbath day worship, they sought to imitate him through their work during the rest of the week.[16]

Complementary values of Zion's territorial order included cooperation, thrift, generosity, responsibility, and sacrifice. These values helped the people overcome the materialistic, individualizing, and competitive tendencies of market economies and secular governments. The ultimate aim was to unify Zion as a heavenly society and make her inhabitants equal in material things so that they could equally qualify for the highest spiritual blessings (see D&C 78:5–6). Joseph Smith's revelations declared unequivocally that if the Saints were not thus united, they could not claim to be God's chosen people (see D&C 38:27).

Bishops held the priesthood authority over Zion's material resources. They were given the keys of judgment to help them determine the righteous use of Zion's wealth and the appropriate consecrations of her residents. If Zion's inhabitants ever violated their covenant of consecration through unrighteous behavior or neglect of their stewardships, they would forfeit their inheritances and be exiled from the kingdom. Their stewardships would then be given to another (see D&C 42:37).

In short, as the Church of Christ established a sacred ecclesiastical order for the Latter-day Saints, so the kingdom of Zion defined their socioeconomic and territorial orders. Zion represented an essential concept of salvation: living in the presence of God. The associated blessings and glories—unity, safety, peace, abundance—were conditional upon residents' making and keeping sacred covenants (consecration) and living according to a prescribed code of conduct within the ubiquitous context of hard work. These efforts were designed to prepare the earth to become a celestial kingdom over which God and Christ will personally reign and which will be inhabited by those people who, along with God's other creations, fill the divine measure of their creation (see D&C 88:17–20, 25–9).

The House of Israel

The third principal dimension of Mormon religious identity is defined in kinship terms: the house of Israel. This ethnic identity binds Mormons together as adopted heirs of God's covenant with Abraham, the third major biblical figure honored by the early Mormons (see Abraham 2:9–11).[17]

Latter-day Saint identity with the house of Israel is established by means of two distinct rituals: patriarchal blessings and temple sealings. Mormon patriarchs possess nonadministrative keys of the Melchizedek Priesthood and a spiritual gift that allow them to bestow blessings upon Latter-day Saints. These blessings identify church members with one or another of the twelve tribes of Israel and grant them insight or counsel regarding the conduct of their lives. Almost always included in a patriarchal blessing is the promise of exaltation in the celestial kingdom, conditional upon one's living according to the covenants entered into and the commandments that person has received.[18]

Formal membership in the house of Israel is officially conferred via the covenant and ritual of sealing. Sealings are performed only in a temple and grant Latter-day Saints adopted kinship status in the house of Israel as full heirs of the blessings of the Abrahamic covenant. The realization of these blessings ultimately depends not on a person's genetic inheritance but on faithfulness to the sealing covenant and its associated commandments. As the Mormon concept of Zion uses territorial imagery to define an earthly religious community and heavenly ideal, so the concept of Israel uses a kinship idiom to express ultimate spiritual realities and relate them to an earthly context.

From the perspective of the house of Israel, the basic social unit in mortality and eternity is the family.[19] Temple sealings bind Latter-day Saints together in conjugal and parental relationships that are intended to have eternal duration. The eternal promise of sealings is conditional upon the sealed persons' faithfulness to one another and their obedience to God's commandments. In fact, only those who have entered into this "new and everlasting covenant of marriage" can become qualified for the highest degree of the celestial kingdom (see D&C 131:1–4). According to a revelation given through Joseph Smith, those who through their faithfulness have this covenant "sealed unto them by the Holy Spirit of promise . . . shall . . . be gods, because they have no end; therefore shall they be from everlasting to everlasting, because they continue; then shall they be above all, because all things are subject unto them. Then shall they be gods, because they have all power, and the angels are subject unto them" (D&C 132:19–20).

One power reserved exclusively for sealed couples in the next life is eternal increase, or the continuation of procreation (see D&C 132:19, 22, 30–1). Thus the covenant community created by the Mormon identity with the house of Israel consists of patriarchal lineages that extend from mankind's first parents, Adam and Eve, to the earth's last generation and then throughout eternity, as sealed couples beget spirit children who will in turn inhabit their own new mortal "worlds without number" (Moses 1:33) in the expanse of never-ending space. Hence gender status and conjugal relations are recognized by Latter-day Saints as eternal, essential characteristics of humankind and as natural and essential for the propagation of the human race and the complete fulfillment of human potential in heaven as on earth.

The code of conduct enjoined upon those who aspire to the blessings and powers encompassed by the house of Israel is comprehended in the law of chastity. Specifically, the law of chastity requires that sexual relations be reserved only for husbands and wives who have been legally bound together in marriage. Implicitly, this law is also a basis for purity and virtue of thought and action in all aspects of social relationships defined by "diffuse, enduring solidarity,"[20] including love, service, caring, righteous parenting, patience, fidelity, harmony, and all other elements of a happy home life.[21]

By Mormon reckoning, sexual intercourse is not only the most distinctive expression of lawful conjugal relations in mortality but also one of a few specific acts by which humans most closely approximate the creative role and power of God. Thus sanctified, procreation is at the center of one of Mormonism's key dimensions of religious identity and at the height of its concept of spiritual progression.[22]

Although Mormons do not ritually sever the genetic links of those who violate their covenants of sealing, sealings can be canceled (made void as regards eternal blessings) for those who repudiate these sacred relationships through unrighteous behavior. Just as excommunicants can be rebaptized into the church on condition of sincere repentance, those whose sealings have been canceled can receive a restoration of temple blessings upon appropriate rehabilitation. However, the process and authority by which persons are rebaptized into the church are neither identical to nor simultaneous with the process and authority of having one's temple blessings restored.[23] Thus the need for at least a structural distinction between the Church of Christ and the house of Israel in Mormon thought.

In summary, eternal family relations extend throughout Mormondom the blessings of Abraham and an identity with the chosen house of Israel, regardless of one's actual genetic inheritance. Membership in the house of Israel and access to its promised blessings are defined by covenant, bestowed by priesthood ordinance, and realized by faithful adherence to a strict moral code. The rituals and relations of Mormonism's kinship order are just as crucial to the expression of a complete spiritual identity as are those of the ecclesiastical and territorial orders of the Latter-day Saints.

Historical Implications of Mormon Identity

The final section of this chapter suggests some of the ways in which Mormon identity, thus conceived, can inform the study of Mormon history.

The Church of Christ

In the latter half of the nineteenth century and throughout the twentieth century, ecclesiastical practices and programs expanded from those introduced during Mormonism's pre-Utah period or evolved in response to later social, cultural, and environmental conditions. This was especially true of local congregations, where auxiliaries for women, youth, and children were organized and expanded into formal churchwide programs. In addition, priesthood quorums became age-graded, with male youth receiving the Aaronic, or preparatory, Priesthood and the Melchizedek Priesthood being reserved for worthy adult males. Instructional and social programs of the church became increasingly influenced by standardized, professional principles and practices.

The church also began constructing meetinghouses that were the spiritual and social center of the local congregation, or ward. As the Mormon practice of patterned settlement was discontinued in the late nineteenth and early twentieth centuries, wards increasingly assumed the social functions and symbolic identity of the geographic communities of Zion. In fact, standard-plan and multifunctional meetinghouses have become the most widespread and dominant physical symbol of a permanent Mormon presence in secular urban and rural environments throughout North America and around the world. The church's meetinghouse construction and maintenance programs have become some of the most extensive in the world and figure prominently in the church's massive annual operational budget.

Missionaries have been sent to virtually every Christian nation and to many other parts of the world to spread the gospel and seek converts. The organization of wards and stakes has spread throughout North America and increasingly on other continents because converts no longer have been encouraged to gather to Zion, but to strengthen the church in their native lands. Church membership, currently nearly ten million, is greater outside than inside the United States. In response, the General Authorities of the church have established extensive transportation, communication, and organizational networks with local congregations in order to further integrate church membership and increase the church's overall operational effectiveness.

The Kingdom of Zion

Although Zion was not established as Joseph Smith had initially envisioned it, and although the covenant of consecration was formally discontinued as a prescribed social practice in Nauvoo,[24] it is instructive to view Mormon history in light of Zion's core ideals and values. Through continued perseverance and hard work, Mormons did eventually establish one of the most extensive and intensive culture regions in North America, whose several hundred settlements largely resembled, though did not precisely imitate, Joseph Smith's plan for Zion.[25]

Within Zion's territorial and socioeconomic order, the Mormons founded effective and extensive social institutions designed to recruit new inhabitants to Zion (proselytizing missions), to develop the earth's natural resources for the benefit of Zion and its citizens (economic missions, cooperative commercial and industrial corporations, welfare projects, and commercial business ventures), to improve the worldly skills and intellect of Latter-day Saints (primary and secondary schools and institutions of higher education, including Brigham Young University), to distribute the material resources of Zion equitably throughout the society (bishops' storehouses, humanitarian services, employment services, and tithing and fast offerings), and to address the psychological, emotional, and social challenges facing Latter-day Saints (LDS Social Services).[26] Mormonism's social programs that were established in the nineteenth century and continue in the present cannot be properly and fully understood outside the religious context of Zion and its covenant and ideal of consecration.

The House of Israel

The institutionalization of plural marriage (or more technically, polygyny) among Mormons in the nineteenth century heightened their distinctive ethnic identity. Although only a minority of rank-and-file Mormons ever entered into the practice, polygyny was certainly portrayed by Mormon leaders as a conjugal ideal and lived as a spiritual imperative.

At the same time, temples were being erected in which couples, either monogamous or polygynous, could be "sealed for time and all eternity." The Endowment House (1855–77) on Temple Square in Salt Lake City performed this function until temples could be completed in strategically located Mormon population centers. At present some fifty temples are in operation throughout the world for the purpose of extending the blessings of Abraham to the entire family of Adam, both living and dead, through the performance of living and proxy temple ordinances.

Although the unique significance and full benefit of temple sealings are wholly realized only in the next life, the church has increasingly tried to sanctify the daily life of nuclear and extended families. With strong encouragement from general church officials, many LDS families hold daily and weekly devotional activities such as family home evening, family prayer, and family scripture study. Extended families organize themselves into family associations for purposes of family history research, proxy performance of temple rituals for deceased ancestors, family reunions, and mutual support in times of need.[27]

Because of their interest in creating eternal family relationships among all God's children—past, present, and future—Mormons have created the most extensive family history library and research network in the world. Many millions of names are currently recorded in vast electronic and microfilm databases. The Family History Library in Salt Lake City contains printed genealogical research materials that are made available to hundreds of thousands of persons interested in tracing their ancestries. In addition, branch family history libraries in numerous locations throughout North America and elsewhere serve countless others by facilitating access to these genealogical resources.[28]

Conclusion

During its first two decades, Mormonism began to develop a simple yet multifaceted and profound religious identity based on fundamental concepts of salvation: that heaven consisted of those who had been purified through Christ's atonement and who enjoyed intimate and enduring familial relationships with others who had been perfected, and that together they lived eternally on a sanctified earth and in the literal presence of God. From this perspective, heaven fulfilled the essential purpose of God's primordial creation: to order the existence of mankind in terms of duties and opportunities in relation to God, other human beings, and the earth so that God might bless the faithful with eternal life and exaltation.

For Mormons the urgency and immediacy of realizing this complex religious order are reflected in the belief that this earth is to be the heaven that God will inhabit with his redeemed Saints and that actual lineal and collateral relatives will constitute its population: "When the Savior shall appear we shall see him as he is. We shall see that he is a man like ourselves. And that same sociality which exists among us here will exist among us there, only it will be coupled with eternal glory, which glory we do not now enjoy" (D&C 130:1–2; see D&C 88:14–47).

The complementary institutions of the Church of Christ, the kingdom of Zion, and the house of Israel enable Latter-day Saints to conform their individual and corporate lives to the heavenly order. Associated with particular membership rituals, codes of conduct, modes of being, and ideal relationships, these institutional orders were established, maintained, and cele-brated through the sacred covenants of baptism, consecration, and sealing, respectively. The complementary dimensions of this religious identity are preserved at the corporate level by priesthood authority. The various orders and keys of the priest-hood define the criteria and regulate the procedures by which individuals gain access to these covenants and their blessings. Duly ordained priesthood officials also oversee the operation of the various religious institutions composed of those who have kept the covenants.

At the individual level, personal righteousness helps pre-serve the order and unity of this religious identity. Mormon commandments, ranging from those given initially to Adam and Eve to those given through the current prophet, emphasize in general terms how Latter-day Saints are to act toward God, other human beings (including oneself), and material resources (including personal possessions). Obedience to these com-mandments in the context of sacred covenants defines personal righteousness and qualifies individuals, whether in mortality or eternity, for the blessings associated with these covenants.

Taken together, the three dimensions of Mormon religious identity—the Church of Christ, the kingdom of Zion, and the house of Israel—are intended to sanctify essential aspects of

Mormon society and give ultimate significance to the daily life of the Latter-day Saints, which is the earthly reflection and temporal approximation of eternal realities that carry with them the promise of salvation. Consequently, time and eternity, man and God, and earth and heaven have come to be related in a complex system of spiritual realities. Although Mormons at best only approximate these spiritual ideals in their daily lives, and although temporal circumstances have altered the specific details of these covenanted communities throughout Mormon history, Mormonism's three-fold foundations are as relevant to Latter-day Saints today as they were in any historical period of the Mormon past.

Notes

An earlier version of this paper was delivered at a meeting of the American Society of Church History in Oberlin, Ohio, in March 1994.

1. See Emile Durkheim, _The Elementary Forms of the Religious Life,_ trans. Joseph Ward Swain (New York: Free Press, 1965), 332–3.

2. See Richard L. Bushman, _Joseph Smith and the Beginnings of Mormonism_ (Chicago: University of Illinois Press, 1984), 143–4.

3. _History of the Church,_ 1:207; see my article "Joseph Smith's Concept of the City of Zion," in _Joseph Smith: The Prophet, the Man,_ ed. Susan Easton Black and Charles D. Tate Jr. (Provo, Utah: BYU Religious Studies Center, 1993), 203–11.

4. See my dissertation, "The Mormon Ideology of Place: Cosmic Symbolism of the City of Zion, 1830–46" (Ph.D. diss., University of Chicago, 1985), 66–79.

5. See _History of the Church,_ 1:196–9.

6. See _History of the Church,_ 1:357–62. Also see my "Mormon Ideology," 94–8; and my "Joseph Smith's Concept," 209–10.

7. See _History of the Church,_ 2:410–36; Milton V. Backman Jr., _The Heavens Resound: A History of the Latter-day Saints in Ohio, 1830–38_ (Salt Lake City: Deseret Book, 1983), 284–309.

8. See Rex Eugene Cooper, *Promises Made to the Fathers: Mormon Covenant Organization* (Salt Lake City: University of Utah Press, 1990), 137–48.

9. See ibid., 153–63.

10. See Gary Witherspoon, "A Structural Analysis of the Symbolic Elements in the Mormon Sacrament" (master's thesis, University of Chicago, n.d.).

11. See *General Handbook of Instructions* (Salt Lake City: The Church of Jesus Christ of Latter-day Saints, 1989), sec. 10, p. 5.

12. See Parley P. Pratt, *Voice of Warning and Instruction to All People* (Salt Lake City: Hawkes Publishing, 1847), 29–63, 89–115. Also see my "Mormon Ideology," 258–76.

13. See Leonard J. Arrington, Feramorz Y. Fox, and Dean L. May, *Building the City of God: Community and Cooperation among the Mormons* (Salt Lake City: Deseret Book, 1976), 15–21.

14. See ibid. and my "Mormon Ideology," 94–8.

15. See, for example, Moses 1:39; 3 Nephi 21:5, 7, 9, 26–8; D&C 4:1–5; 20:11–4; 77:12; 101:20, 64–5, 95, 100–1; 109:5, 23, 59, 78; 124:49–50, 53, 78–9.

16. On the spiritual significance of work in Mormon society, see Mark P. Leone, *Roots of Modern Mormonism* (Cambridge: Harvard University Press, 1979), 43–110; Arrington et al., *Building the City of God,* 337–58.

17. See Cooper, *Promises Made to the Fathers,* 100–31; Gordon Irving, "The Law of Adoption: One Phase of the Development of the Mormon Concept of Salvation, 1830–1980," *BYU Studies* 14 (spring 1974): 291–314.

18. See *Encyclopedia of Mormonism,* s.v. "patriarchal blessings"; Cooper, *Promises Made to the Fathers,* 74–5.

19. See *Encyclopedia of Mormonism,* s.v. "family."

20. This concept of kinship is developed by Meyer Fortes in his *Kinship and the Social Order: The Legacy of Lewis Henry Morgan* (Chicago: Aldine, 1969).

21. See *Encyclopedia of Mormonism,* s.v. "law of chastity."

22. See *Encyclopedia of Mormonism,* s.v. "sexuality"; Lester E.

Bush Jr., *Health and Medicine among the Latter-day Saints: Science, Sense, and Scripture* (New York: Crossroad, 1993), 139–78.

23. See *General Handbook of Instructions*, sec. 10, pp. 12–3.

24. See *History of the Church*, 3:301; 4:93.

25. See Raymond D. Gastil, *Cultural Regions in the United States* (Seattle: University of Washington Press, 1975), 237–42; Milton R. Hunter, *Brigham Young, the Colonizer* (Salt Lake City: Deseret News Press, 1940); Richard V. Francaviglia, *The Mormon Landscape: Existence, Creation, and Perception of a Unique Image in the American West* (New York: AMS Press, 1978); Richard H. Jackson, *The Mormon Role in the Settlement of the West* (Provo, Utah: Brigham Young University Press, 1978).

26. See James B. Allen and Glen M. Leonard, *The Story of the Latter-day Saints* (Salt Lake City: Deseret Book, 1976); Leonard J. Arrington, *Great Basin Kingdom: An Economic History of the Latter-day Saints, 1830–1900;* Arrington et al., *Building the City of God;* Glen L. Rudd, *Pure Religion: The Story of Church Welfare since 1930* (Salt Lake City: The Church of Jesus Christ of Latter-day Saints, 1995).

27. See *Encyclopedia of Mormonism*, s.v. "family life"; "family history, genealogy"; "family home evening"; "family organizations"; and "family prayer." Also see John L. Sorenson, "Ritual as Theology," *Sunstone* (May–June 1981): 11–4.

28. See James B. Allen, Jessie L. Embry, and Kahlile B. Mehr, *Hearts Turned to the Fathers: A History of the Genealogical Society of Utah, 1894–1994* (Provo, Utah: BYU Studies, 1995).

CHAPTER 2

MORMON FUNERAL SERMONS
IN THE NINETEENTH CENTURY

Davis Bitton

All cultures employ rituals in the burial of their dead. The Mormons of the nineteenth century were, on the surface, not strikingly different from many Protestants in their burial rituals. Unlike Catholics and Episcopalians, Mormons were not given to liturgy, nor did they consider pomp and extravagant displays of mourning to be necessary.[1] But this did not mean the avoidance of form. Mormon funeral services included prayers, sermons, music, and sometimes a procession to the cemetery. It is the content of these forms, especially the sermons, that can inform us whether, beneath the outward shell, there was something distinctive about the Mormon way of saying good-bye to the dead. While pursuing a doctorate at the University of California at Los Angeles, John L. Sorenson prepared a study of funeral behavior among several religious groups, and a portion of that study was recently published under

Davis Bitton, emeritus professor of history at the University of Utah, is a past president of the Mormon History Association and served as assistant historian for the LDS Church from 1972 to 1982.

the title "Mormon Funeral Behavior."[2] Other scholars have considered additional aspects of Mormon death and dying,[3] but to my knowledge no one has yet provided an analytical cross section of funeral sermons.[4]

In the process of examining sixty-five complete funeral sermons and summaries or partial accounts of other sermons, I prepared synopses with careful attention given to repetitive themes and scriptural texts. On the basis of this sampling, I offer here a look at the defining features of the Mormon funeral sermon as it became standardized during the nineteenth century. Anyone familiar with Mormon funerals of the twentieth century will, I think, conclude that the continuity of sermon content has been strong. This study, however, concerns the first seventy years of Mormon history.

Eulogy: The Mormon Character Ideal

Most Mormon funeral sermons included, but were not restricted to, reminiscences on the life of the deceased. These sermons were not eulogistic orations of the classical rhetorical tradition, with its standard praise of the noble family heritage, descriptions of extraordinary character in childhood, recitation of heroic virtues such as courage and magnanimity, and peroration urging the auditors to go and do likewise,[5] although, as in so many of our cultural forms, broad features of that tradition lingered. Far removed from the aristocratic estates of Europe, where the great Bossuet could wax eloquent in praise of bravery in battle, largesse, public service, and magnificence of style, the Mormons loved and valued their dead for simpler, more rudimentary virtues. They praised them for having been kind, truthful, unselfish, patient, and cheerful; for having been obedient, dutiful children; or for having given selfless service as parents. Fortitude in the face of life's challenges was also often commended. This naturally required mentioning some of those trials, including, often, the final cause of death.

The most characteristic Mormon virtues seem to have been being *faithful* and *true*. Faithful and true, we ask, to what? At the funeral of Mormon Church president John Taylor in 1887, Elder Heber J. Grant said: "He has been a faithful Latter-day Saint, and no more can be said of any man. Every Latter-day Saint has had the privilege of receiving a testimony of the Gospel, and those of us who live true to that testimony, and that fill up a life of usefulness and do nothing that will rob us of the light of the Holy Spirit, when we come to lay down this body, can have no greater thing said of us than that we have been faithful."[6]

What Elder Grant was praising was steadfastness—unwavering commitment to the restored gospel. In other words, it was more than generalized trustworthiness. To describe someone as faithful and true was to commend that person for fidelity to the gospel or, more specifically, to the baptismal covenant and the later priesthood and temple covenants. The scripturally based adjectives *faithful* and *true* regularly appeared in Mormon funeral sermons from early times to the present.[7]

The opposite adjectives, *unfaithful* and *untrue,* referred to apostates, those once loyal, practicing members of the church who had abandoned the faith and ignored or repudiated their commitments. In secular terminology, the equivalent would be treason. Less dramatic, those who were lax and indifferent concerning their duty were also considered to be unfaithful and untrue. Funerals for Latter-day Saints who had not been faithful and true could be awkward. The speakers would probably mention happy memories or other positive qualities of the deceased, perhaps giving a general statement about the justice of God and the reality of the future life. But such sermons generally were not those that were preserved in printed form.[8]

Because their primary purpose was to comfort the bereaved, Mormon funerals were not occasions to dwell on the deceased's misdeeds or otherwise condemn him or her. At the February 1879 funeral service of Dimmick B. Huntington, a longtime church member who died in good standing, John Taylor said, "I am reminded of an item in Brother Dimmick's written request, desiring that only his good deeds should be spoken of at his funeral, and also of a remark . . . that we should not speak anything but good of our friends whether living or dead." Pursuing that theme, President Taylor gave a scriptural basis for emphasizing the positive—all that is "good and amiable":

> I am really astonished sometimes to witness the hard feelings and rancor that exist among men. They come—I do not know where they come from; yes, I do too, they come from beneath. The fruits of the Spirit of God are love, peace, joy, gentleness, long-suffering, kindness, affection, and everything that is good and amiable. The fruits of the spirit of the devil are envy, hatred, malice, irritableness, everything that tends to destroy mankind, and to make them feel uncomfortable and unhappy. The fruits of the Spirit of God are love and peace, and joy in the Holy Ghost; and the man that says he loves God and hateth his brother, is a liar, and the truth is not in him. I do not care who he may be, or what his name, or where he lives. This is the way I read the Scripture, and the way the Gospel teaches me. "By this shall all men know that ye are my disciples, if ye have love one to another."[9]

At the funeral of William Clayton in December 1879, Joseph F. Smith acknowledged the deceased's faults but minimized them because "they were of that nature that injured nobody perhaps except himself and his own family." He explained that whatever Clayton's faults were, Clayton would have to answer for them in the next life. In urging the surviving family members to emulate the deceased, Elder Smith made a distinction: "Follow in the footsteps of your husband and father, *excepting wherein he may have manifested the weaknesses of the flesh;* imitate his staunch integrity to the cause of Zion, and his fidelity to his brethren; be true as he was true, be firm as he was firm, never flinching, never swerving from the truth as God has revealed it to us."[10]

Abraham H. Cannon, an apostle who died in 1896 at age thirty-seven, was described by Wilford Woodruff as "willing to take a great load upon him, and to do all that he could for the benefit of the Church and of his brethren wherever he has been."[11] According to Joseph F. Smith, second counselor in the First Presidency at the time, Elder Cannon was faithful in the ministry, united with his brethren, patient, and persuasive but never by coercion. President Smith continued:

> I thank God that we have had an Abraham Cannon. I thank God that he was called to the glorious ministry to which he was called. I thank God that he has not polluted it; that he has honored it, that he has maintained his integrity, that he has fought the good fight, that he has kept the faith, and that he has gone home to the Father of light, with whom there is no variableness nor shadow of turning, unsullied, undefiled, honest, virtuous, pure, high-minded and intelligent, with the testimony of the truth rooted and grounded in his heart and in his soul till it was a part of him and he a part of it.

President Smith considered Cannon to be a good role model: "I would to God that all the young men of Zion would follow in his footsteps, would emulate his example, would be as *true and faithful* as he has been, and would eschew evil as he has, and be as industrious as he has been in acquiring knowledge and in fitting and preparing himself for the work of the ministry and for the labor that was imposed upon him in

life, in which he excelled always." ¹² Of course, President
Smith's use of the phrase *true and faithful* was altogether
befitting such a paragon as Abraham Cannon.

One purpose of praising the dead was to urge others to do
likewise. As the eulogist of Samuel H. Smith wrote in 1844,
"When a faithful saint dies, like this, our lamented brother,
calm, faithful and easy, all Israel whispers, as expectants of the
same favor, 'let me die the death of the righteous, and let my
last end be like his.'"¹³ Thus, whereas many sermons urged surviving family members to emulate the virtues of the deceased,
the injunction was also applied more generally to the entire
congregation with the phrases *let us* and *may we.*

At his funeral in 1899, Franklin D. Richards was praised
for his speaking and writing abilities and his "amiable and engaging" personality, yet his other attributes were considered
more important. Richards was described as full of generosity,
charity, forgiveness, and kindness: "During all our long and intimate acquaintance with him we do not remember a single
instance where he spoke unkindly of any one." ¹⁴ These homely
virtues were not manifest only in his small private circle, for he
was devoted to something larger than himself—the cause of the
latter-day work of the gospel. In his leadership positions, he
demonstrated a love of his fellowmen, and he diligently labored
in their behalf.

The Gospel of Comfort

In the course of eulogizing the deceased, speakers often recalled specific experiences in order to evoke fond memories and
thereby involve family members and the rest of the congregation in a collective "reappreciation." Colloquial sermons in the
settlements, those unlikely to be recorded for posterity, may
well have been largely anecdotal, but Mormon funerals have

never been solely devoted to remembrance of the deceased. They were also designed to provide comfort and understanding.

When speaking of the purpose of life and the different stages of existence, Mormon preachers naturally called upon their religious faith. Looking forward in time, they described the spirit world, resurrection, judgment, and eventual reward in one of the three degrees of glory. Noting the death of Samuel H. Smith in 1844, the *Times and Seasons* reported, "The highest point in the faith of the Latter Day Saints, is, that they know where they are going after death, and what they will do, and this gives a consolation more glorious than all the fame, honors and wealth, which the world has been able to heap upon her votaries or ever can."[15] This comment describes and anticipates an invariable feature of Mormon funerals—reference to the continued life of the spirit after death.

According to Mormon theology, the spirit survived the death of the physical body and was released from it. An oft-repeated trope described the disembodied spirit as relieved from suffering, no longer having to endure the tribulations of this "vale of tears." The spirit of the deceased, according to one commonplace expression that communicated reassurance, was "all right."

Drawing upon both the Bible and modern scriptures, the speakers would then elaborate: the spirit was now in paradise. In this realm of the spirit world it joined the many other righteous spirits who had preceded it, a thought that invited scenes of joyous reunion as parents and other departed loved ones welcomed the spirit of the deceased individual.

When someone died at an advanced age, his or her "tilt" toward the other side was sometimes noted; that is, more and more of those people the deceased had known and loved were not on earth but had passed beyond.[16] Even a small child would find loving arms on the other side, but for elderly people the drawing power was strong and natural. They had every reason to welcome the transition to a place where parents, siblings, and most of their friends were already awaiting them.

The Mormon conception of life in paradise was not one of simply basking in eternal glory. Quite early in the history of the church, the immense task of preaching the gospel to the spirits in spirit prison was seen as the primary activity in the spirit world. A scriptural basis for this doctrine was found in premises implicit in the teachings of Jesus Christ—namely, that a just God would not condemn any individual who had had no opportunity on earth to accept the gospel[17]—and in the vicarious work for the dead as revealed through the Prophet Joseph Smith.[18] The work for the dead performed in the Endowment House in Salt Lake City and in the temples on earth had its corollary in the preaching in the spirit world.

The knowledge of missionary activity in the spirit world enabled survivors to envision their departed loved ones as still active and striving in the work of the Lord. It also provided a possible explanation for untimely deaths. The Mormon preachers could have limited their comment on untimely death by observing, as did John Calvin, that by definition the will of God is just, a doctrine that is true enough in abstract terms but does little to comfort the bereaved and promote understanding. Instead, these preachers longed for something more and thought they had a possible explanation in the continued work of the gospel in the spirit world.

For some, the preaching activity, general social environment, and even the surroundings of the spirit world were communicated in dreams and visions. A remarkable example of this was the after-death experience of Jedediah M. Grant. Heber C. Kimball described the experience as follows:

> I laid my hands upon him and blessed him, and asked
> God to strengthen his lungs that he might be easier, and in

two or three minutes he raised himself up and talked for about an hour as busily as he could, telling me what he had seen and what he understood, until I was afraid he would weary himself, when I arose and left him.

He said to me, brother Heber, I have been into the spirit world two nights in succession, and, of all the dreads that ever came across me, the worst was to have to again return to my body, though I had to do it. But O, says he, the order and government that were there! When in the spirit world, I saw the order of righteous men and women; beheld them organized in their several grades, and there appeared to be no obstruction to my vision; I could see every man and woman in their grade and order. I looked to see whether there was any disorder there, but there was none; neither could I see any death nor any darkness, disorder or confusion. He said that the people he there saw were organized in family capacities; and when he looked at them he saw grade after grade, and all were organized and in perfect harmony.[19]

Grant went on to describe the reunion with his wife Caroline, who held in her arms her child who had died on the plains. Buildings, gardens, flowers—everything was glorious and beautiful.

The importance of this personal account lies in its detail and in the fact that it came from a member of the church's First Presidency and was, at the funeral, endorsed by both Presidents Young and Kimball. Similar experiences became part of the lore of later Mormons,[20] and one of the most detailed experiences, that of President Joseph F. Smith, was canonized as scripture in Doctrine and Covenants 138.

One consolation that became a commonplace of Mormon funerals was the continuation not merely of the individual soul but also of the family unit beyond the grave. Despite their profound sorrow, those who survived found comfort and reassurance in the knowledge that they one day would be brought back together as husband and wife, parents and children. Faith in this reunion touched the deepest wellsprings of emotion.

But this could also be a discomfiting doctrine, for what of children who led dissolute lives or were otherwise unworthy of the celestial kingdom? A partial buffer was provided in the idea of possible repentance in the spirit world, but this could not be presented as a kind of carefree second chance. The real answer was the same as that for salvation in general: the promise of joyful family reunion beyond the grave was sure for those who followed Christ and were faithful in all things. Those who did not make the grade had no one to blame but themselves, for they had their moral agency and had been given a fair opportunity to make the right choices. The promise of being together forever with those most dear was a comfort to those nearing death and an inducement for survivors to live worthy of that reward.

Beyond the spirit world, an indeterminate period of existence, was the resurrection of the body and the final judgment. Mormons believed in a universal physical resurrection in which the immortal spirits of all mankind would be united with their glorified and immortal bodies. They did not claim to know how this miracle would occur; they simply pointed to the resurrection of Christ as the prototype and to modern scriptures that verified the reality of the resurrection.

Many funeral sermons stopped early in commenting on the postmortal trajectory of the soul. That the individual survived in spirit and was out of pain might be all that was said; that the deceased would rejoin loved ones was a bonus. Mention that the later physical resurrection was a reality was usually added as a fitting conclusion.

Some sermons, however, drew upon modern revelation to discuss the different degrees of glory. Because it was not of particular comfort to think about the lower degrees, sermons generally concentrated on the celestial, or highest, kingdom, where those who were worthy regained God's presence and, if they qualified for the highest gradation, went on under God to have their own glory and dominion. In funeral sermons this ultimate reward for righteousness was often expressed in less explicit terms, most likely because it would be presumptuous to claim exaltation, for the Lord, after all, was the judge. Thus the general assurance of exaltation in the highest degree of glory was more appropriately conveyed by references to thrones, principalities, powers, dominions, and related expressions.[21] Even the "crown of righteousness" that Paul expected to receive (2 Timothy 4:8) was seen by many Mormons as a symbol of exaltation.

What about the death of infants and children? Before the rise of public health standards and modern medicine, the death of infants and children was common on the American frontier. In 1875 the terrible death of two children, ages six and four, by burning seemed unusually hard to deal with. Wilford Woodruff began the funeral sermon by reading the first chapter of Job, then remarked, "The loss of these little children, taken away as they were, is certainly painful, not only to the parents, but to every person who reflects; and it is a very hard matter for any of us to enter into and appreciate the depth of sorrow which parents feel on occasions like this, it is difficult to bring the matter home to our own hearts unless we have been called to pass through similar affliction and sorrow."[22]

Continuing his remarks, Woodruff made the astounding statement that "there are many things in this world that are far more painful and afflicting than to have our children burned to death." More tragic by far than the death of young children, in Woodruff's view, was the loss of older children "who have gone to the grave disgraced, and a dishonor to themselves and to their parents." After all, he explained, young children were "innocent" and "not in transgression," and although their deaths were "very painful," they were no longer suffering. They would arise unmarred in the resurrection and would rejoin their parents "in the family organization of the celestial world." Because they each had obtained a physical body, they would be resurrected. Elder Woodruff suggested that although we know little about such things, these children who had died so young would be resurrected as children who would then grow to adulthood. Struggling bravely with a difficult assignment, he assured the congregation that God's purposes would be fulfilled and that ultimately all would be made right. "Why our children are taken from us it is not for me to say, for God never revealed it unto me," Elder Woodruff added. "We are all burying them." Of his own thirty children, he reported, "ten of them are buried, all of them young."

The question of "baby resurrection" had been unsettled and even, at times, a bone of contention among some members. A sermon of Joseph Smith, as recorded in longhand, seemed to state that babies would be resurrected but remain of that small stature throughout eternity. In 1873 Orson Pratt challenged the idea head-on: "But I doubt very much in my own mind if those who reported that sermon got the full idea on this subject; and if they did, I very much doubt whether the Prophet Joseph, at the time he preached that sermon, had been fully instructed by revelation on that point, for the Lord has revealed a great many things to Prophets and revelators, and among them to Joseph Smith, the fullness of which is not at first given."[23] Pratt went on to list several reasons why, in his belief, those who died as infants would "grow up to the full stature of manhood or womanhood, after the resurrection."

In 1877 Franklin D. Richards declared that children who died would grow to their full stature after the resurrection and during the millennium. Apparently unaware of Orson Pratt's earlier statement, Joseph F. Smith explained the sequence of this teaching: "The first man I ever heard mention this in public was Franklin D. Richards, and when he spoke of it I felt in my soul: the truth has come out, the truth will prevail. It is mighty and will live; for there is no power that can destroy it. Presidents Woodruff and Cannon approved of the doctrine, and after that I preached it."[24] President Woodruff later recalled hearing Joseph Smith teach this same doctrine.

Because of faith in the overarching plan of life and salvation, mourning presented a kind of paradox. On the one hand, it was natural to shed tears over the departure of dear ones, and no funeral speaker would attempt to deprive the bereaved of that needed emotional outlet. Those left behind would inevitably have great cause to mourn. Yet many funeral sermons also declared mourning to be somehow inappropriate. Knowledge of the gospel plan and certitude of God's mercy and justice should help the survivors realize that all is right. "Let us rejoice," some speakers urged, meaning that for the moment anguish was natural but in the long run should give way to faith in God and his eternal, merciful plan. We do not weep or mourn, said some funeral speakers, "as those who have no hope."[25]

The earliest sermons do not indicate that because the spirit survived and retained its individual identity, it might still be present on earth, even in the very room in which the funeral was held. However, this idea appears in later sermons. For example, at the funeral of Elizabeth H. Cannon in 1882, Wilford Woodruff observed: "Whether her spirit is present witnessing these funeral services, or whether she, on opening her eyes in the spirit world, would say, 'I leave my body for my friends to bury, I must enter upon my mission,' that is something we are not able to speak definitely about. God not having revealed it unto us."[26]

Speaking at the same funeral, Joseph F. Smith was characteristically less tentative. After noting that the lifeless body was present, although "the intelligent and the immortal part [had] gone to God from whence it came," President Smith added, "Not but what she might be present if she desires to be here, and her desire be consistent with the will and pleasure of our heavenly Father; for those who live here in the flesh have a claim upon this earth, and upon the bodies they have occupied while they sojourned here."[27] Elaborating on the nature of angels (who, according to D&C 130:5, "do belong or have belonged" to the earth), the visits to earth of ancient prophets, and the several earthly visits of Jesus Christ, President Smith concluded: "In like manner our fathers and mothers, brothers, sisters, and friends who have passed away from this earth, having been faithful and worthy to enjoy these rights and privileges, may have a mission given them to visit their relatives and friends upon the earth again, bringing from the divine Presence messages of love, of warning, of reproof and instruction to those whom they had learned to love in the flesh. And so it is with Sister Cannon." Although an essential qualifying phrase— *provided it be in accordance with the wisdom of the Almighty*—is present in President Smith's exposition, strong encouragement was being given to the idea that the spirit of the deceased was present at the funeral service and that there could also be visitations by other loved ones from the spirit world.

In short, the consolation of the gospel was that life had meaning and would continue after death and ultimately come to a glorious fulfillment. This idea was the consolation of all Christian preaching expanded upon by Mormon teachings about the preexistence, the spirit world, and the ultimate reward of the faithful.

Funeral Texts

Mormon funeral sermons were not required to start with a scriptural text. Some did, but more typically, scriptural references were incorporated into the sermon. The nonchalance toward having a specific text was once conveyed by President Brigham Young:

> I will not go to the Bible, to the Book of Mormon, nor to the Book of Doctrine and Covenants for my text, for I will give you a text which comprehends the sermon also, so that if I do not dwell directly upon it, I trust that what I say will be true, for it will be incorporated in my text, and the text alone will be a sermon. On this occasion I will say, as on other occasions, blessed are they that hear the Gospel of salvation, believe it, embrace it, and live to all its precepts. That is the text, and a whole sermon in and of itself.[28]

Scriptural language, including phrases and sometimes whole verses, was often included in a sermon without any reference to its source. This language resonated with the congregation, one assumes, and shows the ease with which the early preachers moved into and out of sacred texts. Certain scriptural passages occurred with enough regularity to be considered standard within the funeral preaching tradition:

"Know ye not that there is a prince and a great man fallen this day in Israel?" (2 Samuel 3:38). King David's comment about Abner captured in a few words the feeling of the people whenever a beloved leader died. Robert B. Thompson quoted David's words at the funeral of Joseph Smith Sr. on 15 September 1840.[29]

"The Lord gave, and the Lord hath taken away; blessed be the

name of the Lord" (Job 1:21). Job's statement of submission in the face of great loss could appropriately be repeated at any funeral. When used at the funerals of those who died at a young age or otherwise unexpectedly, the words perhaps implied more than they strictly state. "I do not understand, but I will not renounce my faith in God, who does understand and in whose ultimate justice and mercy I repose my confidence"—such would seem to be the intent of the well-known passage.

"For I know that my redeemer liveth, and that he shall stand at the latter day upon the earth: And though after my skin worms destroy this body, yet in my flesh shall I see God" (Job 19:25–6). In a traditional Christian reading, this passage testifies of both Jesus Christ and the bodily resurrection of the dead.

"Well done, thou good and faithful servant: thou hast been faithful over a few things, I will make thee ruler over many things: enter thou into the joy of thy lord" (Matthew 25:21). These words from the parable of the talents were from the beginning seen as referring to the last judgment. For early Mormons, the word *faithful* and the expression *I will make thee ruler* dovetailed beautifully with the grand truths revealed in Doctrine and Covenants 76 and 88. At the funeral of President John Taylor, a sheaf of wheat bore the inscription *Well done, good and faithful servant.*[30]

"Lord, now lettest thou thy servant depart in peace, according to thy word: For mine eyes have seen thy salvation" (Luke 2:29–30). Simeon pronounced these words, according to Luke's gospel, after holding the infant Jesus in his arms. The Holy Ghost had previously informed him that "he should not see death, before he had seen the Lord's Christ" (Luke 2:26). In the context of a funeral, Simeon's words conveyed the idea that the deceased had lived a full life and had been faithful.[31]

"Jesus said unto her, I am the resurrection, and the life: he that believeth in me, though he were dead, yet shall he live: And whosoever liveth and believeth in me shall never die" (John 11:25–6).

On one hand, this well-known verse provided simple reassurance of the reality of the resurrection. In a strict sense, because all spirits are eternal, they will never die. But this verse conveys something more as well: the indispensable role of Jesus Christ in making possible both resurrection and the *eternal* life that for Mormons meant exaltation in God's highest kingdom. John Taylor elaborated on this concept in 1845:

> There is faith and power connected with the gospel of Jesus Christ, whereby the sleeping dead shall burst the barriers of the tomb as Jesus did. "He that liveth and believeth in me, shall never die." They have begun to live a life that is eternal, they have got in possession of eternal principles. They have partaken of the everlasting priesthood, which is eternal;—without beginning of days or end of years. They have become familiar with eternal things and understand matters pertaining to their future destiny, and are in possession of an exalted glory. They have become familiar with all these things and consequently their life is hid with Christ in God; Christ lives and he in them, and they in him. Though he is dead, he ever liveth to make intercession for us, and all who partake of the same spirit, live to him and for him and to and for eternity, or in eternal glory.[32]

For Taylor, who later became president of the church, Latter-day Saints had an eternal perspective larger and more glorious than that of the rest of the Christian world.

"If in this life only we have hope in Christ, we are of all men most miserable. . . . For as in Adam all die, even so in Christ shall all be made alive. . . . O death, where is thy sting? O grave, where is thy victory?" (1 Corinthians 15:19, 22, 55). All of 1 Corinthians 15 was appropriate for funerals. It essentially insists on the reality of the resurrection, without which life would be meaningless. These particular verses were appreciated for their pithiness.[33]

"I have fought a good fight, I have finished my course, I have kept the faith" (2 Timothy 4:7). If the deceased had been faithful, Paul's memorable words to Timothy seemed a fitting tribute. Indeed, the expression was so familiar that speakers simply inserted it into the sermon without attribution. The next verse (2 Timothy 4:8) completes the thought and seemed highly appropriate for faithful Mormons who had ears to hear: "Henceforth there is laid up for me a crown of righteousness, which the Lord, the righteous judge, shall give me at that day."[34]

"And when he had opened the fifth seal, I saw under the altar the souls of them that were slain for the word of God, and for the testimony which they held" (Revelation 6:9). This verse seemed especially relevant for Mormon missionaries who were murdered while preaching the gospel. This passage and several subsequent verses were read at length by George Q. Cannon at the funerals for Joseph Standing (1879) and John H. Gibbs (1884), both of whom died at the hands of persecutors.[35]

"After this I beheld, and, lo, a great multitude, which no man could number, of all nations, and kindreds, and people, and tongues, stood before the throne, and before the Lamb, clothed with white robes and palms in their hands" (Revelation 7:9). Here was another reference to the righteous souls who worshiped God. As the passage continues, those in the white robes are identified as souls who are "before the throne of God, and serve him day and night in his temple" (Revelation 7:15). In 1845, at the funeral of Caroline Smith, widow of the Prophet Joseph Smith's younger brother William Smith, Orson Pratt began his sermon with this passage.[36]

"Blessed are the dead which die in the Lord from henceforth: Yea, saith the Spirit, that they may rest from their labours; and their works do follow them" (Revelation 14:13). Especially reassuring for those who have been believing and faithful, this passage appears as early as the 1833 funeral of David Johnson in

Kirtland, Ohio.[37] It includes the idea of surcease of earthly burdens and responsibilities and also recognizes the importance of works, which in Mormon parlance meant that beyond resurrection and the simple assurance of continued existence in a resurrected state, individual persons would receive different degrees of reward according to their reception of gospel ordinances and their faithfulness in keeping the commandments.

Most often, however, only the opening words of this passage were quoted: "Blessed are the dead which die in the Lord." The expression could be left without comment, allowing the congregation to draw its own conclusion that the deceased person being honored did so qualify.[38] At the funeral of Daniel Spencer in 1868, President Brigham Young explained the meaning of the phrase *die in the Lord* as follows: "In other words, blessed are those who have received the Priesthood of the Son of God, and have honored it in their lives. Those who have honored their calling and Priesthood to the end die in the Lord, and their works do follow them."[39]

"And I saw the dead, small and great, stand before God; and the books were opened: and another book was opened, which is the book of life: and the dead were judged out of those things which were written in the books, according to their works" (Revelation 20:12). This passage conveyed to the congregation that the dead did survive, for they would be judged. The expression *according to their works,* which did not fit easily with the *sola fide* tradition, was tailor-made for the Mormons, who did indeed proclaim that after the universal resurrection by grace, one's works did determine future status. This verse was also a good starting point for paying tribute to the good deeds of the deceased.

These scriptural passages were not, of course, exclusively Mormon. They are the traditional funeral texts of all Christendom, as any study of patristic or medieval sermons would demonstrate. However, in quoting and expanding on these verses, the

Mormon preachers sometimes gave them a special interpretive twist. Before long, modern scripture was also used in funeral sermons, and of course this provided a framework of meaning unique to the restored gospel. The texts used most often were Alma 40–2 (on the resurrection and the spirit world), Doctrine and Covenants 76 (on the three degrees of glory), Doctrine and Covenants 88 (on the degrees of glory and obedience to law), and Doctrine and Covenants 132 (on exaltation and the possibility of attaining godhood). Doctrine and Covenants 42:46 was also used: "And it shall come to pass that those that die in me shall not taste of death, for it shall be sweet unto them."[40]

Even when the exact words of the traditional biblical passages were not quoted, the ideas contained in them were repeated over and over. The difference in the way Mormons used them was in their placing them in the context of the restored truths of an all-encompassing gospel plan of salvation. It was in relation to that plan that each life found its meaning and purpose.

Conclusion

On occasion, Mormon funeral sermons may have strayed from the norm by awkwardly trying to make a scoundrel appear faultless, speculating too freely about the future, or unknowingly distorting the latter-day doctrine. But such variation apparently was not at all common, for we have no evidence that this was a concern requiring instruction or correction. Thus in my view the examples considered in this chapter are sufficient in number and variety to give a good idea of the nature of Mormon sermons in the late nineteenth century.

Read in the spirit in which they were delivered, these funeral sermons still have power to comfort, explain, and inspire. But what more have we discovered? Were Mormon funerals simply the same as those common throughout the Christian world? Of course there is overlap, but two significant differences should not be overlooked. First, the virtues describing a model Latter-day Saint were not those of a crusader of ascetic. If many of the virtues seem to be innocuously Christian, it is by context that we realize the unique slant or understanding the Mormons placed upon them. Second, after 1850 Mormon preachers drew upon modern scriptures in their funeral sermons, thus amplifying the understanding of the premortal existence, the future life, and the purpose and meaning of the earthly probation. As they did so, these preachers continued to cite biblical passages in support of the plan of salvation as proclaimed by the restored gospel.

Mormon funerals included much that had long been established in Christian usage, but they were Christian funerals with a difference. The repetition of praiseworthy traits in the sermons reveals the Mormon cultural ideal, specifically the ideal individual personality. The funeral sermons expressed the teachings of the restored gospel not abstractly but as reassurance and comfort extended to individuals and families at a time of emotional distress. For Mormons, the universal human experience of grief and the sense of emptiness triggered by death were placed in the context of the merciful plan of the great Creator.

Notes

1. See *Journal of Discourses*, 4:131, 135; 22:355. This compilation of sermons is hereafter abbreviated *JD*.

2. See John L. Sorenson, *Mormon Culture: Four Decades of Essays on Mormon Society and Personality* (Salt Lake City: New Sage Books, 1997), 157–68. For another cross-cultural comparison, see C. Paul Dredge, "What's in a Funeral? Korean, American-Mormon and Jewish Rites Compared," in *Deity and Death*, ed. Spencer J. Palmer (Provo, Utah: BYU Religous Studies Center, 1978), 3–31.

3. For example, M. Guy Bishop and others in "Death at Mormon Nauvoo, 1843–1845" (*Western Illinois Regional Studies* 9 [fall 1986]: 70–83) utilize sextons' reports to analyze causes and ages of death, while Craig R. Lundahl in "The Perceived Other World in Mormon Near-death Experiences: A Social and Physical Description" (*Omega* 12/4 [1981–82]: 319–27) focuses on descriptions of the hereafter. Truman G. Madsen itemizes Mormonism's reassuring teachings about death in "Distinctions in the Mormon Approach to Death and Dying" (in Palmer, *Deity and Death*, 61–76) but provides no historical context. For general orientation, see L. Kay Gillespie, "Death and Dying," in *Encyclopedia of Mormonism*, 1:364–6; and Lester E. Bush Jr., "On Death and Dying," in his *Health and Medicine among the Latter-day Saints: Science, Sense, and Scripture* (New York: Crossroad, 1993), 9–39.

4. Earlier treatments of similar subject matter include M. Guy Bishop, "To Overcome the 'Last Enemy': Early Mormon Perceptions of Death," *BYU Studies* 26/3 (summer 1986): 63–79 (this article is limited to the Nauvoo period, from which almost no funeral sermons survive); Mary Ann Meyers, "Gates Ajar: Death in Mormon Thought and Practice," in *Death in America*, ed. David E. Stannard (Philadelphia: University of Pennsylvania Press, 1975), 112–33; Klaus Hansen, "The Mormon Rationalization of Death," in *Mormonism and the American Experience*, ed. Klaus Hansen (Chicago: University of Chicago Press, 1981), 84–112; and M. Guy Bishop, "The Celestial Family: Early Mormon Thought on Life and Death, 1830–1846" (Ph.D. diss., Southern Illinois University, 1981).

5. On the encomium, see, for example, Aristotle, *Rhetoric*, bk. 1, ch. 9.

6. In *Collected Discourses*, comp. Bryan H. Stuy (1987), 1:49. Hereafter this useful work is abbreviated *CD*.

7. In addition to describing the Savior (see Revelation 19:11), *faithful* and *true* can also apply to his dedicated followers, such as Helaman's stripling warriors (see Alma 53:20–1; 57:26–7; 58:40) and those who endure in righteousness (see D&C 23:16–18; 76:53) and thus will inherit eternal life (see D&C 51:19). An extension of

the scriptural linkage of these terms is seen in the title of Joseph Fielding McConkie's biographical work *True and Faithful: The Life Story of Joseph Fielding Smith* (Salt Lake City: Bookcraft, 1971).

8. One exception is the sermon that John Taylor, president of the Quorum of the Twelve Apostles, delivered on 8 February 1880 at the funeral of a nephew of his by marriage, Joseph M. Cain, a young drunkard. See *JD*, 21:14–22.

9. In *JD*, 20:141.

10. In *JD*, 21:13; emphasis added.

11. In *CD*, 5:169.

12. In *CD*, 5:173; emphasis added.

13. *Times and Seasons* 5 (1 Aug. 1844): 606.

14. George Q. Cannon, in *Juvenile Instructor* 34 (15 Dec. 1899): 770.

15. *Times and Seasons* 5 (1 Aug. 1844): 606.

16. See Brigham Young, in *JD*, 14:227–32.

17. On the equity, mercy, and righteousness of divine judgment, see, for example, Luke 12:48; John 5:25, 30; Romans 2:11–16; 1 Peter 3:18–20; 4:6.

18. See D&C 76:71–5; 137:7–10; JST 1 Peter 3:18–20; 4:6; cf. D&C 138:32–4.

19. In *JD*, 4:135–6. See Lundahl, "Perceived Other World."

20. One example was the out-of-body experience of Brother John J—, in which he observed apostles preaching to many of his progenitors in the spirit world and then had his diseased lungs healed by the angel who conducted him there (see C. C. A. Christensen, "A Glimpse of the Spirit World," *Juvenile Instructor* 28 (1893), 56–7.

21. See Revelation 5:10; 20:6; D&C 76:56; 132:19.

22. In *JD*, 18:30.

23. In *JD*, 16:335.

24. As quoted in Franklin L. West, *Life of Franklin D. Richards* (Salt Lake City: Deseret News Press, 1924), 184.

25. See *JD*, 12:179–82; *CD*, 4:244–52.

26. In *JD*, 22:349.

27. In ibid., 350.

28. In *JD*, 4:129–30.

29. See *Times and Seasons* 1 (Sept. 1840): 171.

30. See *CD*, 1:40.

31. For an example of this application, see *Times and Seasons* 1 (Sept. 1840): 173.

32. *Times and Seasons* 6 (15 Jan. 1846): 1098.

33. See *Times and Seasons* 6 (1 June 1845): 918–20; and *JD*, 18:306–13, 324–35; 22:347–9.

34. For more information on the meaning of crowns and their relationship to the expression *kings and priests,* see Orson Pratt's funeral sermon of 25 July 1852, found in *JD*, 1:290–1. Other direct and indirect citations of *I have fought a good fight* include *JD*, 12:180, 186; 25:285; and *CD*, 1:41–5, 113–14; 5:170–4.

35. See *JD*, 20:244–52; 25:275–80.

36. See *Times and Seasons* 6 (1 June 1845): 918.

37. See *Evening and Morning Star* 2/15 (Dec. 1833): 117.

38. See *JD*, 15:341–7; and *CD* 1:113–14; 5:167–70. An exception is *JD*, 13:75–7, in which Brigham Young explains the meaning of the phrase *die in the Lord.*

39. In *JD*, 13:75.

40. See, for example, *JD*, 10:365–8.

CHAPTER 3

PARLEY P. PRATT AND THE PACIFIC MISSION: MORMON PUBLISHING IN "THAT VERY QUESTIONABLE PART OF THE CIVILIZED WORLD"

David J. Whittaker

Between 1851 and 1855 Parley P. Pratt served twice as president of the Pacific Mission of the Church of Jesus Christ of Latter-day Saints. Although headquartered in the San Francisco area, the mission embraced the Pacific Basin, including South America and the islands of the Pacific from Hawaii to Australia. Central to Parley's approach to missionary work was writing and publishing.[1] During his presidencies Parley issued the first broadside defense of plural marriage in July 1852, one month before the official church announcement of the practice; he authored the first Mormon work published in the Pacific Basin, *Proclamation! To the People of the Coasts and Islands of the Pacific* . . . ; he published the first LDS work in Spanish; and beginning in August 1851 he composed the bulk of

David J. Whittaker, president of the Mormon History Association from 1995 to 1996 and associate professor of history, is curator of Western and Mormon Manuscripts at Brigham Young University's Harold B. Lee Library.

Mormonism's first comprehensive theological work, *Key to the Science of Theology*. In addition to writing defenses of the church for the local press, he actively worked to establish a printing office called the Latter-day Saints' Book Depot for his mission, and he also made plans for publishing the *Mormon Herald*, a newspaper for Latter-day Saints in the California region. This chapter reviews Parley's written approach to his missionary work in the Pacific Basin and suggests its impact on later Mormon publishing, particularly through the work of his successor in publishing, George Q. Cannon.

Background: The Early Publishing

Before his mission to the Pacific area, Parley had firmly established his place in Mormon thought as the church's most important pamphleteer. Almost everywhere he traveled as a missionary after his conversion in 1830, he expressed his thoughts in writing. In 1835 he published the first work of Mormon poetry, and in 1837 in New York he issued his *Voice of Warning*, which in the nineteenth century was the most widely read LDS book aside from the church's canonical works. In 1838 he issued the first detailed reply to an anti-Mormon work, and in 1840 he published a history of the persecutions his people had endured in Missouri. In February 1840 he issued *An Address to the Citizens of Washington*, a concise listing of fundamental LDS beliefs that helped shape the form and content of the basic Mormon missionary tract as well as the better-known Articles of Faith of Wentworth Letter fame.

Serving in England with his fellow apostles in 1840, Parley continued his literary approach to missionary work. As a member of the publishing committee, Parley worked on the Manchester hymnal (his contributions included composing many of the hymns) and on the first British edition of the Book of Mormon, and he was the founding editor of the influential *Latter-day Saints' Millennial Star*. In fact, it was in his Manchester home that Parley established the Latter-day Saints' Book Depot for the British Mission. Later moved to Liverpool, this office established such a good foundation that almost all nineteenth-century LDS publications descended from British editions published under its auspices.

In addition to his work with the *Star*, Parley continued to write tracts. The first Mormon reply to a British anti-Mormon work was Parley's *Plain Facts, Showing the Falsehood and Folly of the Rev. C. S. Bush*. Among his most popular replies were *An Address to the People of England* (five thousand copies), *A Letter to the Queen* (ten thousand copies), and a broadside satire entitled *An Epistle of Demetrius*. . . . His incisive mind, poetic nature, and great popularity and influence led Edward Tullidge to refer to him as "the Isaiah of his people."[2]

After the Prophet Joseph Smith's death in 1844, Parley continued his active involvement as a member of the Quorum of the Twelve Apostles, devoting much time to writing and publishing. He authored the 1845 "Proclamation of the Twelve"[3] and provided key leadership—particularly through his writing—in New York City during the critical months of the succession crisis. He issued "Regulations for the Publishing Department of the Latter Day Saints in the East" in January 1845, a further consolidation of the power of the Twelve in church affairs.[4]

Turning Westward: The First Pacific Mission

Following the 1846–47 westward movement of the church, Parley actively continued in various leadership roles. In 1849 and 1850, for example, he led the Southern Exploring Company into southern Utah.[5] But our story begins in 1851, when

Brigham Young sent him to California, where as president of
the Pacific Mission he would "hold the presidency of all the
islands and coasts of the Pacific."[6]

He left Salt Lake City on 16 March, arrived in Los Angeles
on 16 June, and on 7 July left San Pedro for San Francisco,
where he arrived four days later. He became president of the
San Francisco Branch on 20 July. His letter a few days later to
Brigham Young spoke of the new and dramatic growth that the
gold rush had forced upon the sleepy port of Yerba Buena,
where Latter-day Saints from the ship *Brooklyn* had settled in
1846: "We find a great city here and perhaps one thousand vessels in port. A more central point for spreading the Gospel, and
communicating with all nations I have not found. . . . We have
now an organized Branch here and meetings every Sabbath.
Many inquire after the truth, Books, etc. I think of Publishing
a General Proclamation."[7]

Taking his presidency seriously and sensing the key role this
now dynamic port could play in the future of the church in the
Pacific region, Parley first corresponded with Mormon missionaries already serving on various islands in the Pacific.[8] In
August he called recently repentant and rebaptized Charles
Wandell to accompany John Murdock, whom Brigham Young
had earlier called to be president of the Australian Mission, to
Australia.[9] Because of various problems in the Society Islands,
Parley decided not to send additional missionaries there, but he
did send more missionaries to Hawaii, where the prospects of
success were more favorable.[10]

With these main areas taken care of for the time being, and
perhaps expecting South America to be as fruitful as early Victorian England had been for Mormon missionaries, Parley told
Brigham: "I expect to leave this country for South America
soon; unless I should be able to go to New York, via the Isth-
mus, to get some books printed. . . . I am studying Spanish with

all diligence, and will, I trust, master it in the course of a few months."[11]

Before sailing for Chile, and presumably between Spanish lessons, Parley wrote the first LDS work to be printed in the Pacific region: *Proclamation! To the People of the Coasts and Islands of the Pacific; of Every Nation, Kindred and Tongue.* He gave the manuscript to Murdock and Wandell, who had it published in November 1851 in Sydney, Australia, within a few days of their arrival there.[12] In this tract Parley declared that a new dispensation of the gospel had been revealed and that as a missionary he was charged with declaring it to every nation and people. The text called its readers to repent and be baptized in the name of Jesus Christ. Declaring the apostasy from the primitive Church of Christ, Parley told of a new apostolic authority now held by the Latter-day Saints. Then, in separate sections or chapters, he addressed the "Pagans" (non-Christians), the Jews, and the "Red Man." In the section to Native Americans, he discussed the Book of Mormon and specifically argued that father Lehi and his family came out of Jerusalem, built a ship, crossed the great sea, and landed on the "western coast of America, within the bounds of what is now called Chil[e]."[13] Perhaps it was this view that motivated and directed Parley's own mission there, especially because he strongly believed that 80 or 90 percent of the population of most of the countries of Spanish America were the blood descendants of Lehi.[14]

Parley's mission to Chile was short and unsuccessful. Accompanied by his wife, Phoebe, and Rufus C. Allen, he left San Francisco for Chile on 5 September 1851. They arrived on 8 November, sixty-four days later, at Valparaiso.[15] Initially optimistic, Parley wrote to Franklin D. Richards in Liverpool, England, and ordered a variety of LDS literature that he planned to distribute in Chile.[16] The group stayed in Valparaiso long enough for Phoebe to give birth to a son, Omner, on 30 November, but the boy died five weeks later. On 24 January 1852 they traveled thirty-six miles to the small town of Quillota, where they spent only five weeks before returning to Valparaiso. The limited details that have survived from this period suggest they went to Quillota to rest, to allow Phoebe time to regain her health and to seek divine counsel regarding their future course. In this very Catholic town, missionary work did not seem possible.

Parley's decision to return to Valparaiso was a logical one. The city had become an important commercial center for the western coast of South America, and the California gold rush had made it an important port for shipping foodstuffs to the gold fields. Valparaiso was also an important way station for ships traveling around Cape Horn and on to California. By 1852 probably more than ten thousand Chileans had gone to California in search of gold. Parley very likely had met and even conversed with some of them before his own trip to Chile.[17] But the language barrier, the social and political upheaval, and the dominance of the Roman Catholic Church forced Parley to abandon the first Mormon mission to Chile.[18]

Parley later reported to Brigham Young a conversation he had with a minister of the American Congregational Church: "He said there was no difficulty in landing religious books or papers and circulating the same, although the press is not free to print or publish any religion but the Catholic."[19] Thus Pratt's *Proclamation Extraordinary! To the Spanish Americans*, written in January 1852 but not published until his return to San Francisco, contains a strong critique of Catholicism and an even stronger denunciation of the lack of the religious and press freedoms that Parley had generally enjoyed in the United States.[20]

The group departed for San Francisco on 2 March. During the sixty-three days at sea, Parley had ample time to continue writing and also to reflect. In a letter to Brigham Young written on the return voyage, Parley summarized his work:

> Elder Rufus Allen and myself and Ph[o]ebe sailed from San Francisco September 5, for Chile, S.A., arrived in Valparaiso on the 8th November; from that time to the present has been devoted by us to the study of the Spanish language, and the laws, constitutions, geography, history, character, religion, manners, customs, resolutions, and events of Chile and Peru in particular, and Spanish America in general.
>
> By intense application, I soon became able to read with a degree of understanding and interest in that language. . . .
>
> It is in my heart to translate the Book of Mormon, and some other works and to print the same in Spanish as soon as I have the language sufficiently perfect. As [the cost of] printing is very high in all parts of the Pacific, it may be wisdom to go to England and get some printing and perhaps stereotyping done. . . .
>
> I study the language all day, and think it, and even talk it loud in my sleep, in which I sometimes learn more than in the day. But it is no small work, to become familiar with the entire grammar, words and style of a foreign tongue, so as to write for publication.[21]

He had wanted to visit Peru, but "an empty purse and imperfect tongue" and a "want of books or the means to print them" forced him to reconsider.[22] Parley explained that because he, his wife, and Elder Allen were in the midst of a civil war, still struggling with the language, and often going without proper food, they had decided to return to San Francisco. They arrived there on 21 May 1852.

Recuperating in the Bay area from May to July, Parley issued his *Proclamation!* in Spanish and had his *Proclamation Extraordinary!* printed. When a review of the latter appeared in

a San Francisco newspaper and questioned the morality of
Brigham Young, Parley responded with a broadside dated 13
July 1852: *"Mormonism!" Plurality of Wives! An Especial Chapter, for the Edification of Certain Inquisitive News-Editors, Etc.*
Because the church's official public announcement of plural
marriage was not made in Salt Lake City until 29 August 1852,
he defended the doctrine of plural marriage without admitting
to its actual practice.[23] He left in July for Utah, arriving on 18
October 1852 in the Salt Lake Valley.

The Second Pacific Mission

For the next year Parley busied himself in local matters. He
participated in laying the cornerstones of the Salt Lake Temple
in April 1853, farmed, and in August 1853 was elected to the
territorial legislature. His April 1853 general conference address, "Spiritual Communication," was issued as an eight-page
pamphlet in California, probably in 1854 and after Parley had
returned to San Francisco.[24] During the winter of 1853–54 he
served as a regent of the University of Deseret, worked on a
committee developing the Deseret Alphabet, and continued his
personal writing and study of Spanish.

On 6 April 1854 Parley was appointed to serve a second
mission to California and the Pacific region. He left Salt Lake
City on 5 May and arrived in San Francisco on 2 July. This
second mission, lasting about one year, found him concentrat-
ing on local missionary work (mainly in the San Francisco and
San Jose areas) and on writing and publishing. In his *Autobiography*, written largely during this time, he summarized his
activities: "We now commenced holding meetings, circulating
books, tracts, and in every way we could, to notify and warn the
people. . . . I devoted the time I could spare from the ministry
to writing my history and for the press."[25]

Parley's publishing activities during this second mission fall into three categories: (1) his attempts to establish an LDS press in San Francisco, (2) his efforts to establish an LDS book supply agency for California and the Pacific, and (3) his own writing during this time.[26] In all of these areas, George Q. Cannon would later play an essential role.

The idea of establishing a press for the Pacific was strongly encouraged by Brigham Young, although the issue centered on whether Hawaii or California was a better location. There were compelling reasons for initially selecting Hawaii, including the earlier history of missionary work in the islands, the Book of Mormon legacy in Alma 63 that ties the island peoples to those of that sacred text, and the growing importance of Hawaii in the Pacific region.[27] The acquisition of the press was actually initiated in Hawaii with funds raised there, but circumstances brought it to California.

Once Hawaii was eliminated as the best location for the press, President Young deemed California "a central and influential position" where a press "can print for the islands as well, or better than if located there, which saves the expense of an additional press."[28] The press was shipped from Hawaii and finally arrived in San Francisco, but too late for Parley to use. However, his successor, George Q. Cannon, made good use of it, as will be shown later.[29]

While Parley was working to establish a printing press in California, he was also anticipating the establishment of an LDS bookstore or distribution center by ordering large quantities of LDS publications from Liverpool.[30] In April, before he left the Salt Lake Valley for California, Parley ordered materials from Franklin D. Richards in England. The large order was sent to him in July, and Richards included the invoice in a letter he wrote on 31 August 1854. The order included five hundred copies each of the Book of Mormon, the Doctrine and Covenants, the hymn book, and Lucy Mack Smith's *Biographical Sketches*, three hundred copies each of the Pearl of Great Price and Lorenzo Snow's *Only Way to Be Saved*, two hundred copies each of John Lyon's *Harp of Zion*, Parley's *Voice of Warning*, and Orson Spencer's *Letters*, one hundred copies of Spencer's *Patriarchal Order*, plus a variety of other tracts and periodicals. The total cost of the order came to just over £340, much of which would be left to George Cannon to discharge.[31]

Parley had told Richards that he intended to publish a Mormon newspaper in California, and Richards had responded encouragingly in 1855: "I hail with great pleasure the opening of your book store, and the establishment of the 'Mormon Herald.' I trust that much good will result therefrom and that you may receive that patronage for it that will enable you [to] sustain it and maintain the interest of the work of the Lord in California and the Pacific Mission."[32]

Six months later Richards, who was also Parley's editor and publisher in England during this period, inquired about the newspaper's progress: "I am anxiously awaiting to see a copy of the paper to be published in California, and wish you much success in conducting the same that it may 'Herald' forth in that very questionable part of the civilized world the pure principles of Light and Truth."[33]

Parley's own writing occupied much of his time. In August 1854 a number of returning Hawaiian missionaries arrived in San Francisco, including George Q. Cannon, James Hawkins, Henry Bigler, and William Farrer. Parley invited Cannon to remain in his home, while the other missionaries traveled across the Bay to seek jobs picking potatoes to earn money for the rest of their journey home to Utah. Much of Cannon's time was spent copying Parley's history. By 21 September, four hundred manuscript pages covering Parley's life to July 1840 had been copied.[34] For his work, Cannon was paid fifty dollars and given board.[35] Parley also issued a broadside circular in August, *Repent! Ye People of California!*, which proclaimed his willingness to preach wherever invited as well as advertised his bookstore on Broadway Street.[36]

Parley had begun work on the *Key to the Science of Theology* in August 1851 and had given a manuscript to Franklin D. Richards to take with him to England in 1854. One chapter was printed in the *Deseret News* in November 1852,[37] and the entire volume was finally offered for sale in March 1855.[38] Parley was anxious to see this volume in print; it would be a possible source of income, and it managed to pull together many of the threads of his earlier writings. Writing to his brother Orson in May 1853, Parley announced: "I have completed a Volume of theology which is now ready from the press. It is altogether the choicest and most perfect specimen from my pen."[39] Aware of Parley's anxiety about the volume, Richards wrote him in May 1855 to explain the delay:

> As regards the "Key to Theology" I can readily conceive with what anxiety you have watched for the book, and have much regretted that you should have to wait for it so long. I fully intended to have had the work out and to have forwarded your 2000 Copies to Cal. and the 500 to Utah last fall, but such was prevented by circumstances which I could not control. The manuscript was put into the printers hands directly after my arrival in this country, but he was very unfortunate in having the plates go astray and with them the type on its return from London where the stereotyping had to be done, there being no place in Liverpool where such business is done at all fit for our purpose. This I believe was several times repeated, and to make matters worse he became embarrassed. These untoward and unlooked for circumstances drove the work into our Emigrating Season when it necessarily became a some what secondary matter for reasons I need not inform you of. Furthermore I was

quite unwilling to have the work hurried thro the press
without the opportunity of giving it that careful attention
which I felt assured you expected of me. The book is now
before the public, and when it meets your eye I trust it will
also meet your approval. The sale is rapid and I think another edition will shortly be wanted. In the meantime I am
having the Stereo. plates corrected in such things as most
generally escape detection in first editions. I allude to uni-
formity, orthography, punctuation, etc. In addition to what
corrections I may make there may be still some which you
would wish to introduce after reading the work. If so, I
would submit that it would be very advantageous if they
could be introduced before the plates leave for America.[40]

Richards also was preparing the eighth edition of Parley's
popular *Voice of Warning*, and both works were issued in editions of five thousand copies.[41] Parley's *Key to the Science of Theology* was a publishing event. It was Mormonism's earliest comprehensive treatment of its doctrines. Without the dogmatism
that sometimes characterized his brother Orson's writings, Parley surveyed the broad spectrum of Mormon thought in a style
that invited further contemplation. He discussed the nature of
the Godhead, the origin and destiny of the universe, the restoration of the gospel, the proper channel for mankind's regain-
ing the presence of God, the resurrection, the three degrees of
glory, and the great destiny of exalted men and women as pro-
creative beings in the eternities. Many of these topics he had
written on earlier, but this work allowed him to pull all these
thoughts together in one volume, and it suggests the same process of gathering and assembling that he was using in composing his *Autobiography*. It would be his last book and his greatest
work.[42]

The last chapter of *Key to the Science of Theology*, which has
been altered in the later editions, was on a topic that plagued

Parley's missionary efforts in California: polygamy. His 1852 broadside had addressed the topic, but the issue refused to die, particularly after the official public announcement in August 1852.[43] After a short mission to the San Jose area in October 1854, Parley wrote Brigham Young that "plurality is a choker—some swallow it Bible and all, and others think the Bible is not true."[44] In December he again reported the situation: "We are baptizing a few, from time to time, and the Gospel is being preached in many places. Polygamy meets us everywhere, and we are compelled to satisfy their minds on that first before they can possibly be satisfied with our preaching,—so we have met it in press, and pulpit, and the Spirit of Truth has almost struck them dumb with amazement and wonder. They are silent, and in a quandary, and feel half inclined to openly renounce the bible."[45]

Parley must have been heartened upon receiving a copy of *Defence of Polygamy by a Lady of Utah*, a pamphlet by one of his own plural wives, Belinda Marden.[46] It was one of few published defenses of plural marriage written by women in early Mormonism. Dated 12 January 1854, the pamphlet presumably had been printed by March in Salt Lake City. Parley had received and distributed copies by September, when he wrote to the author: "Your Printed Letter is of world wide notoriety. It has appeared in a number of Newspapers, and finally in the Millennial Star. It convinces or shuts the mouths of all. It is one of the Little entering wedges of a worlds Revolution. A Learned Doctor here, who is a great spiritualist, Borrowed one of the pamphlets, and begs to keep it as a great treasure. The Governors Br. here read it, and remarks that the whole foundation of society was wrong, and needed revolutionizing."[47]

Although California has a twentieth-century reputation for open-ended lifestyles and religious experimentation, Parley was

unable to convince the nineteenth-century inhabitants of that
state to accept his arguments for plural marriage.

Parley P. Pratt's Successor: The Work of George Q. Cannon in San Francisco

By the time Parley left California in June 1855, he had
worked to establish a printing press and a book supply agency
for LDS literature, and he had also made plans to publish a
newspaper in San Francisco. He had set things in motion to accomplish all three, but it was left to George Q. Cannon to bring
them to fruition. In a sense he was Parley's apprentice, and
many of Cannon's publishing projects show Parley's influence.

Parley had written to Brigham Young in February 1855
that the press, papers, and other materials from the islands
would probably reach San Francisco in early April and that
then "there will be nothing to hinder going ahead with printing, both in English and in the Island language, provided Elder
Cannon can return here to help. I see no way to dispense with
him, as he understands both languages, is a practical printer,
and has the Book of Mormon in manuscript in the Island language. . . . We can commence the publication of a 'paper' as
soon as he comes and we can arrange the furniture etc. for
printing." Parley's plans called for "A Book Depot—Press—&
and a well conducted Periodical in this central position."[48] Parley felt that these developments would be a blessing and help
for the cause of Zion. By May he could report, "The press and
paper has arrived in San Francisco to my charge, and is duely
stored, and awaits the action of Bro. Cannon, who I am glad to
learn is coming out to use it."[49] The same letter reported that a
fire had destroyed forty buildings in the city, a fact that probably encouraged Cannon's later choice of a brick building to
house their publishing operation.

Cannon had devoted much of his 1850–54 Hawaiian mission to studying the language and trying to get various LDS works translated and published. Once he had conquered the language, the major project of his Hawaiian mission was to translate into Hawaiian and publish the Book of Mormon.[50] Cannon had completed the first manuscript draft of a translation by 22 July 1853, although he continued rereading and revising it in the months that followed.[51] At a preconference meeting on 5 October, the missionaries in Hawaii focused on the challenge of printing the translation. "The press was the first thing taken into consideration," Cannon noted, "whether we ought to have the Book of Mormon printed by hiring or whether we should purchase a press of our own and publish it and other works necessary for the instruction of the saints." When asked to express his own opinion, Cannon recalled, "I did not consider that my mission was fully filled until I saw the Book of Mormon in press if there was a prospect of it being done in a reasonable time."[52] The group decided to appoint a committee of three (Cannon, Benjamin F. Johnson, and Philip B. Lewis) to adopt measures for procuring a press by subscription. In a conference vote the next day, these actions were sustained by the members.

The committee spent the next several weeks raising money for the purchase of a press, a project greatly assisted by a thousand-dollar interest-free loan in December.[53] On 31 December 1853 Cannon received a batch of letters from home. Particularly important were reports of the publishing activities of his mentor and relative, apostle John Taylor, who was publishing the Book of Mormon and newspapers in French and German.[54] In addition, a letter from Brigham Young encouraged Cannon's publishing effort, although Young advised caution regarding financial matters associated with the enterprise.[55]

The committee initially tried to purchase the press from

California, and in March 1854 they were considering having the translation printed there, but ultimately the press was ordered from Boston.[56] By the time the press reached the islands, the missionaries had moved to California on their way home from their missions. It was this press that Parley Pratt eventually received and stored in San Francisco.

Cannon arrived in San Francisco from Hawaii on 12 August 1854. He worked with Parley for a short time, mostly assisting with the copying of Pratt's autobiography, and then returned to the Salt Lake Valley. His visit there was brief. He married Elizabeth Hoagland on 11 December 1854 and was soon heading back to San Francisco on another mission that was clearly considered a continuation of his first. Following his arrival in California, he wrote an extensive report to Brigham Young, much of which focused on the press and his plans for publishing.[57]

Parley had received and stored the press, type, and paper. Cannon discovered upon examination of the press that a few of the ribs were damaged. He met with apostle Orson Hyde, who was visiting from Carson Valley, Nevada, and who convinced him to procure a suitable building in San Francisco in which to establish a print shop and to delay publishing a newspaper and concentrate his energies on publishing the Hawaiian edition of the Book of Mormon.[58]

Hyde and Cannon found a brick building on Montgomery Street in which they could rent two rooms. The building was owned by Samuel Brannan, and they arranged the rental agreement with his brother. A fireproof brick building was essential because a major fire had recently swept through the wooden structures in the city. After moving their printing material into this building, they were ready to begin the project of printing the Hawaiian edition of the Book of Mormon. There were numerous problems to solve; for example, although English fonts

could be used in the typesetting, Cannon was short of the letters *h* and *k*, which were quite common in Hawaiian.[59]

By the end of August 1855 the first 128 pages had been
printed. In a letter to Cannon, Hyde had given him the liberty
to commence a Mormon newspaper and suggested *The Western
Standard* as a title for it,[60] but Cannon wanted to defer the enterprise until the Book of Mormon was much further along.

By October Cannon was getting bids for the binding of the
Hawaiian edition, and he reviewed the details in a letter to
Brigham Young that same month.[61] By 3 December they had
printed the 464th page of the translation, with just 56 pages to
go, not counting the index, title page, and introductory matter.
Although an anticipated paper shortage threatened to delay the
printing of the final pages,[62] Cannon's attention was beginning
to focus on publishing a newspaper: it would be a boost to their
missionary efforts and would help publicize their printed work.
Cannon was concerned about Californians' deafness to the gospel message and hoped that "if perchance a spirit of inquiry
might be aroused thro' the instrumentality of the press," missionaries would be on hand to preach.[63]

In January 1856 the printing of the Hawaiian edition was
complete. Cannon sent Brigham Young one of the first bound
copies [64] and informed him that he had issued fifteen hundred
copies of a pamphlet in Hawaiian that gave a short history of
the coming forth of the Book of Mormon: "I thought it would
be a good idea to publish something of this kind and prepare
them to comprehend and rightly estimate the Book when they
obtained it."[65]

In the same letter he also forwarded to President Young a
copy of the prospectus for the *Western Standard.* Dated 4 January
1856, the prospectus announced a weekly newspaper that would
be devoted to the interests of the church and "be an exponent

of its doctrines, and a medium through which the public can derive correct information in relation to its objects and progress. Its columns will also contain items of general intelligence and the current news of the day, both foreign and domestic, which from our position, situated in the Queen City of the Pacific, we will be able to obtain at the earliest dates and in ample detail."[66]

The *Western Standard* was issued weekly from 23 February 1856 to 18 November 1857. Its publication occupied much of Cannon's energy and time, and the financial concerns were a major theme in his correspondence with Brigham Young.[67] He sought subscriptions for it in both California and the Mormon settlements, especially in Utah, where he always found the most support for his publication.[68] In September he noted, "We are still striving to create an interest in the minds of men toward the glorious principles of the latter day work," but he felt that "California is a hard country."[69] To give more visibility to his newspaper, he had "a Bulletin board made and fastened to the edge of the sidewalk," and on it he pasted copies of each issue. The printing shop on Montgomery Street, "the most public thoroughfare in the city," was used to great advantage to "publish glad tidings."[70]

The *Western Standard* regularly responded to criticism of the Mormon Church. The paper's masthead announced its philosophy: "To correct Mis-representation we Adopt Self-representation." Cannon responded to other newspaper attacks and the growing publicity of the "Utah Question" in national politics, and he reprinted items from national publications such as *Harper's Magazine* and the *New York Herald,* as well as a weekly price list of various goods selling in San Francisco. The paper regularly reported the activities of LDS missionaries in California, Hawaii, and elsewhere and periodically included the minutes of various regional conferences of the church. In an early issue

William A. Shearman encouraged both the publication and its editor: "Though but <u>one</u> 'Cannon' may you prove an effective, invincible and powerful 'Battery,' which the enemies of the Kingdom shall find it impossible to silence or captivate."[71]

Heeding Brigham Young's specific counsel to give more coverage to several earlier LDS pamphlets, Cannon serialized Orson Pratt's 1848 *Divine Authority; or the Question, Was Joseph Smith Sent of God?* and selections from Orson Spencer's *Letters*.[72]

Cannon's awareness of American literary trends and his growing opposition to reading fiction seems to date from this period. While Cannon was not opposed to all fiction (evidence indicates that he read James Fenimore Cooper during his Hawaiian mission), the tendency of nationally popular fiction to portray Mormons in the most unfavorable light led him to consider most of it either corruptive or a waste of time. Cannon's own publishing business would later try to offer alternatives to Mormon readers, who were increasingly drawn to the novel.[73]

Explaining and defending the practice of plural marriage were demanding more and more of Cannon's time.[74] In December 1856 and January 1857, he noted in his paper the anti-Mormon lectures of John Hyde Jr. Hyde continued his activities against the church in the Bay area through April, which probably encouraged Cannon to print twelve hundred copies of *Scriptural Evidences in Support of Polygamy*, an expansion of Parley Pratt's earlier *Marriage and Morals in Utah*.[75] The additional material in the pamphlet was one of the first examples of a Mormon author using non-Mormon material to defend the unpopular marriage system.[76] Cannon, like Parley Pratt, wanted to print a series of pamphlets on LDS doctrine, but financial limitations continued to prevent this.

Additional frustrations soon presented themselves: "San Francisco seems to be the most difficult of all fields in which to awaken the people," Cannon reported to Brigham Young.[77] In addition, the events leading to the so-called Utah War, which saw the abandonment of many missions outside Utah, forced Cannon to make several decisions. Copies of the Hawaiian edition of the Book of Mormon, for the most part still unbound, were sent to missionaries in the islands who could bind them as needed. As for his own press and printing establishment in San Francisco, Cannon first considered setting up a printing office in Hawaii by using spare items from the California operation. Although Cannon was sure that a newspaper in Hawaii would accomplish much good, the prohibitive costs and general poverty of the members there cautioned against it.

Following instructions from Brigham Young, Cannon began to shut down his printing operation in October 1857, publishing the last issue of the *Western Standard* on 18 November 1857.[78] He tried to sell the printing fixtures but was unable to do so. He and his family left San Francisco on 3 December 1857 and were back in Utah on 19 January 1858.[79]

The Legacy

Cannon was subsequently assigned to other missions. Three years after Parley Pratt's death in May 1857, Cannon was called to the Quorum of the Twelve Apostles; and later, in 1873, he was called to serve as a counselor in the First Presidency of the church. In 1860 he served in the British Mission by assisting with the editing of the *Millennial Star* and with other publishing assignments, including the important decision to establish a church press in Liverpool rather than hire non-Mormon printers.[80] Although the move was the logical outcome of Parley's 1845 publishing statement that centralized Mormon publishing in the hands of the apostles, it was more directly a result of the church's earlier success in California of owning and operating its own printing office under the auspices of Cannon. While in England, Cannon oversaw publication of the second edition of Parley's *Key to the Science of Theology* in 1863, and in 1864 he gathered a variety of items from his earlier newspaper into *Writings from the "Western Standard."*[81]

Cannon's California experience of publicly responding to religious attacks and keenly analyzing and responding to the effect of national political developments on Utah were soon put to further use. Brigham Young assigned him to work with Thomas L. Kane in public and private lobbying activities on the East Coast in behalf of Utah and the Mormons. The full story is yet to be told, but President Young's growing trust of Cannon is evident in his correspondence with both Cannon and Kane.

Following his missions to California and Great Britain, Cannon established his own publishing business, George Q. Cannon and Sons. This enterprise was modeled after Parley's publishing business, which combined religious publications with business interests and ecclesiastical responsibilities. Cannon obviously had in mind Parley's autobiography—a work of literary merit and full of faith-promoting experiences[82]—when he began to issue what was promoted as a "faith-promoting series" in 1879, the first volume of which was Cannon's own personal history of his Hawaiian mission.[83] After Cannon's death in 1901, the LDS Church acquired his printing company and later, in 1919, renamed it Deseret Book Company. It remains the flagship of the LDS Church's publishing interests—and a fitting legacy of Parley P. Pratt's and George Q. Cannon's pioneering efforts to strengthen and defend the church and to help spread the glad tidings of the restoration.

Notes

An earlier version of this paper was presented at the annual meeting of the Mormon History Association in Laie, Hawaii, 11 June 1990.

1. The basic source for the life of Parley P. Pratt is *The Autobiography of Parley Parker Pratt,* ed. Parley P. Pratt Jr. (1874); hereafter cited as *Autobiography.* The first biography of Parley is Reva Stanley, *A Biography of Parley P. Pratt, the Archer of Paradise* (1937). An important overview of Parley as a writer, including a comprehensive chronological listing of his published work, is Peter L. Crawley, "Parley P. Pratt: Father of Mormon Pamphleteering," *Dialogue* (autumn 1982): 13–26. Parley's writings are compiled in *Writings of Parley Parker Pratt,* comp. Parker Pratt Robison (1952); and *The Essential Parley P. Pratt,* with a foreword by Peter L. Crawley (1990). Parley's extensive publishing in early Victorian Britain is detailed in "To 'Hurl Truth Through the Land': Publications of the Twelve," in *Men with a Mission: The Quorum of the Twelve Apostles in the British Isles, 1837–1841,* ed. James B. Allen, Ronald K. Esplin, and David J. Whittaker (1992), 236–66.

2. Edward Tullidge, *Life of Brigham Young; or, Utah and Her Founders* (1876), supplement, 75.

3. His authorship is made clear in a letter to him from Brigham Young, 26 May 1845; original in Special Collections and Manuscripts, Harold B. Lee Library, Brigham Young University, Provo, Utah.

4. Originally published in New York City in *The Prophet* (4 January 1845): 2, these regulations were reprinted in Nauvoo in *Times and Seasons* 6 (15 January 1845): 778.

5. See Stephen F. Pratt, "Parley P. Pratt in Winter Quarters and the Trail West," *BYU Studies* 24 (summer 1984): 373–88; Rick J. Fish, "The Southern Utah Expedition of Parley P. Pratt, 1849–1850" (master's thesis, Brigham Young University, 1992); and Donna T. Smart, "Over the Rim to Red Rock Country: The Parley P. Pratt Exploring Company of 1849," *Utah Historical Quarterly* 62 (spring 1994): 171–90.

6. See Parley P. Pratt to Addison Pratt, 26 July 1851, and Parley P. Pratt to King Kamehameha, 26 July 1851, both in Pratt, *Autobiography,* 429–31. The *Millennial Star* 11 (1 August 1849): 232, citing the First General Epistle of the First Presidency, noted that Parley

had been assigned "a mission to the Western Islands." In a letter dated 8 July 1849 and sent from Salt Lake City to his brother Orson, Parley noted: "I don't know when I shall be sent away. I am studying the Spanish language, and preparing for Spanish America" (*Millennial Star* 11 [15 November 1849]: 343).

7. Parley P. Pratt to Brigham Young, 25 July 1851, Brigham Young Collection, Correspondence File, Historical Department, Archives Division, the Church of Jesus Christ of Latter-day Saints, Salt Lake City, Utah (hereafter cited as LDS Church Archives). Unless otherwise noted, all manuscripts cited are from the Brigham Young Collection in this repository.

8. A useful history of the earliest LDS missions is S. George Ellsworth, *Zion in Paradise: Early Mormons in the South Seas* (1959).

9. See Parley Pratt to Brigham Young, 28 August 1851.

10. See R. Lanier Britsch, *Unto the Islands of the Sea: A History of the Latter-day Saints in the Pacific* (1986), 3–20, 93–110; and his *Moramona: The Mormons in Hawaii* (1989).

11. Parley P. Pratt to Brigham Young, 28 August 1851.

12. The full story is told in Peter L. Crawley, "The First Australian Mormon Imprints," *Gradalis Review* (Brigham Young University) 2 (fall 1973): 38–51. See also my "Early Mormon Pamphleteering" (Ph.D. diss., Brigham Young University, 1982), 275–81, 463–7.

13. Parley P. Pratt, *Proclamation! To the People of the Coasts and Islands of the Pacific; of Every Nation, Kindred and Tongue* (1851). The text was printed in *Millennial Star* 14 (18, 25 September 1852): 465–70, 481–5, and republished in Madras, India, in August 1853 by Richard Ballantyne.

14. See, for example, Pratt, *Autobiography,* 447 (Parley P. Pratt to Brigham Young, 13 March 1852).

15. For the best sources on this mission, see Pratt's journal, Special Collections and Manuscripts, Harold B. Lee Library, Brigham Young University; and his papers in LDS Church Archives. Some of the most important documents are cited in his *Autobiography,* 433–52. Secondary sources include Stanley, *A Biography of Parley P. Pratt,* 243–71 (see n. 1); A. Delbert Palmer, "Establishing the L.D.S.

Church in Chile" (master's thesis, Brigham Young University, 1979),
2–57; and F. LaMond Tullis, "California and Chile in 1851 as Experienced by the Mormon Apostle Parley P. Pratt," *Southern California
Quarterly* 67 (fall 1985): 291–307.

16. See Parley's 24 November 1851 letter in *Millennial Star* 14
(15 February 1852): 54–5.

17. See Palmer, "Establishing the L.D.S. Church in Chile," 4–8,
24–5.

18. Mormon missionaries did not return to Chile until the 1950s.
Chile has since become one of the most successful LDS missions in
South America.

19. Pratt, *Autobiography*, 445.

20. See *Proclamation Extraordinary! To the Spanish Americans*
(1852). This sixteen-page tract has two-column pages, with the text
in Spanish in the left columns and in English in the right columns.
The English portion has been reprinted in *Writings of Parley Parker
Pratt*, 150–62. The pamphlet was dated as having been written in
January 1852 in Valparaiso, Chile. An interesting discussion of the
problems with the Spanish translation, specifically arguing that the
style and quality of the translation changes on page 8, is in Palmer,
"Establishing the L.D.S. Church in Chile," 34–5. A curious bibliographical note explains that the first Mormon imprint in New
Zealand apparently was a short work by Parley P. Pratt, although the
title page of the work attributed it to Joseph F. Smith. This item—
Good Tidings, or the "New and Everlasting Gospel" (1875?)—was actually a reprint of a four-page tract issued by the Millennial Star Office in Liverpool, England, in about 1874 by Joseph F. Smith. But
the text for the tract came from Parley's essay "The Gospel, Illustrated in Questions and Answers," *Millennial Star* 1 (June 1840):
25–8.

21. Parley P. Pratt to Brigham Young, 13 March–29 April 1852.
Minor spelling and punctuation changes have been made.

22. Pratt, *Autobiography*, 447–8 (Parley P. Pratt to Brigham
Young, 13 March 1852).

23. Reprints of this work are in Stanley, *A Biography of Parley P.*

Pratt, 254; and in *The Essential Parley P. Pratt*, 169–71. For a larger
context see my article "The Bone in the Throat: Orson Pratt and the
Public Announcement of Plural Marriage," *Western Historical Quarterly* 18 (July 1987): 293–314. See also the extract from Parley's diary
in Holdaway Stanley and Charles L. Camp, eds., "A Mormon Mission to California in 1851," *California Historical Society Quarterly* 14
(March, June 1935): 59–73, 175–82.

    24. See Parley P. Pratt, *Spiritual Communication* (1854?). Also
see *Journal of Discourses*, 1:6–15; *Millennial Star* 27 (11, 18 February
1865): 89–94; 105–9.

    25. Pratt, *Autobiography*, 458–9.

    26. In this essay I ignore Parley's writings in California newspapers. For a sample of his material published in the San Francisco
Chronicle and *Alta California*, see *Millennial Star* 17 (31 March
1855): 198–200, which includes Parley's 26 January 1855 cover letter to the editor of the *Millennial Star*. Parley told Brigham Young in
February 1855: "I am still able to work upon the public mind
through the public <u>press</u>. The <u>California Chronicle</u> has never failed
to publish any article from my pen" (Pratt to Young, 15 February
1855). Parley's frustrations with other newspaper editors is expressed
in his 16 June 1855 letter to Brigham Young, which reveals his
awareness that *any* publicity is better than none.

    27. The larger context, including history of the movement of
various missionary groups into the Pacific Basin, is described in
Arrell Morgan Gibson and John S. Whitehead, *Yankees in Paradise:
The Pacific Basin Frontier* (1993).

    28. Brigham Young to Parley P. Pratt, 19 August 1854, Parley P.
Pratt Collection, LDS Church Archives. See Brigham Young to Parley
Pratt, 19 September 1854, Parley P. Pratt Collection, LDS Church
Archives. In February 1855 Parley was anticipating establishing "A
<u>Book Depot</u>—<u>Press</u>—& and well conducted Periodical in this central position [which] will, by the aid & blessing of God, be a blessing, & a help to the cause of Zion" (Pratt to Young, February 1855).
In this same letter Parley said that he was anticipating the arrival of
George Q. Cannon, who would take charge of the printing.

For the historical context of Pratt's California missions, see Hubert Howe Bancroft, *History of California*, vol. 23 in *The Works of Hubert Howe Bancroft* (1888); Kevin Starr, *Americans and the California Dream, 1850–1915* (1973), 49–109; and Sandra Sizer Frankiel, *California's Spiritual Frontiers: Religious Alternatives in Anglo-Protestantism, 1850–1910* (1988).

Studies of the early Mormon experience in California include Eugene E. Campbell, "History of the Church of Jesus Christ of Latter-day Saints in California, 1846–1946" (Ph.D. diss., University of Southern California, 1952); Kenneth Wayne Baldridge, "A History of Mormon Settlement of Central California with Emphasis on New Hope and San Francisco, 1846–1857" (master's thesis, College of the Pacific, 1956); Richard O. Cowan, "The Mormon Church in the California Gold Rush" (master's thesis, Stanford University, 1958); Eugene E. Campbell, "The Mormon Gold-Mining Mission of 1849," *BYU Studies* 2 (autumn 1959–winter 1960): 19–31; Annaleone D. Patton, *California Mormons by Sail and Trail* (1961); and Richard O. Cowan and William E. Homer, *California Saints: A 150-Year Legacy in the Golden State* (1996).

One of the earliest Mormon entrepreneurs in California was Samuel Brannan, who included a printing press in his business ventures. His *California Star* was important in announcing and advertising the discovery of gold but is not considered a Mormon printing operation in this essay. A short sketch of his early press is in Douglas S. Watson, "Herald of the Gold Rush—Sam Brannan," *California Historical Society Quarterly* 10 (September 1931): 298–301. See also Paul D. Bailey, *Sam Brannan and the California Mormons* (1959).

The larger context of the emerging non-Mormon printing enterprises in California is described in Carl I. Wheat, *Pioneers: The Engaging Tale of Three Early California Printing Presses and Their Strange Adventures* (1934); Charlotte P. Lambert, *Printing in California, 1846–1856* (n.d.); Hugh S. C. Baker, "A History of the Book Trade in California, 1849–1859," *California Historical Society Quarterly* 30 (June, September 1951): 97–115, 249–67, 353–67; L. Wesley Norton, "'Like a Thousand Preachers Flying': Religious Newspapers on the Pacific Coast to 1865," *California Historical Society Quarterly* 56 (fall 1977): 194–209; and Robert D. Harlan, "Printing for an Instant City: San Francisco at Mid-Century," in *Getting the Books Out: Papers of the Chicago Conference on the Book in 19th-Century America*, ed. Michael Hackenberg (1987), 137–64.

29. See Philip Lewis to Parley P. Pratt, 17 March 1855, Pratt Collection, LDS Church Archives. The press had arrived in San Francisco in April 1855, just as Parley was preparing to return to Utah.

30. The role of Liverpool in early Mormon publishing and distribution is surveyed in my "Early Mormon Pamphleteering," *Journal of Mormon History* 4 (1977): 35–49. See also Peter L. Crawley and David J. Whittaker, *Mormon Imprints in Great Britain and the Empire, 1836–1857* (1987).

31. See Franklin D. Richards to Parley P. Pratt, 31 August 1854, Pratt Collection, LDS Church Archives. This approach was typical of Parley; he recommended the same course to the missionaries on their way to Australia, as seen in the 30 August 1851 letter by Charles Wandell in *Millennial Star* 13 (15 November 1851): 349–50. According to his *Autobiography* (p. 474), Parley sent sets of the books he had ordered and received from Liverpool to his wives and several of his children on his forty-eighth birthday, 12 April 1855.

32. Franklin D. Richards to Parley P. Pratt, 25 May 1855, in Pratt Collection, LDS Church Archives.

33. Franklin D. Richards to Parley P. Pratt, 6 October 1855, in Pratt Collection, LDS Church Archives.

34. See Parley P. Pratt to Brigham Young, 21 September 1854. The *Autobiography* was not published until 1874, almost two decades after Parley's death in 1857. Edited by the family, it still awaits a full study. Steven Pratt has prepared a lengthy analysis of the work, a copy of which he has shared with me, but it remains unpublished. An interesting account by one who traveled with Parley and heard him reading portions of his history to an assembled group is the 11 October 1856 entry in the journal of Isaiah Coombs, LDS Church Archives. In a 9 May 1853 letter to William Patterson, Parley, in the midst of writing his history, provided a humorous, pithy, and concise

overview of his life. See Pratt Collection, Outgoing Correspondence, LDS Church Archives. Also see Parley's discussion of his history in his 23 August 1854 letter to George A. Smith, George A. Smith Collection, LDS Church Archives.

35. Cannon discusses his work with Pratt in the third and last volume of his Hawaiian mission journals, Cannon Collection, LDS Church Archives. Parley's comments are in his own journal, April 1854–November 1854, Pratt Collection, LDS Church Archives.

36. See Pratt, *Autobiography*, 460; and *Writings of Parley P. Pratt*, 150.

37. Chapter 16 was reprinted in the *Millennial Star* 15 (30 July 1853): 500–3.

38. See *Millennial Star* 17 (31 March 1855): 208. The *Star* had earlier announced that the work was "in press" (16 [29 July 1854]: 472–4).

39. Parley P. Pratt to Orson Pratt, 24 May 1853, Parley P. Pratt Collection, LDS Church Archives. See Parley P. Pratt to Brigham Young, 18 May 1853, Parley P. Pratt Collection, LDS Church Archives.

40. Franklin D. Richards to Parley P. Pratt, 25 May 1855, LDS Church Archives. This letter provides good detail on when and where various copies of *Key to the Science of Theology* were shipped. Publishing and distribution information on this work can be traced in the "European Mission Publication Accounts, Ledgers and Account Journals," LDS Church Archives. See especially vol. 1 of the ledgers and vol. 9 of the account journals.

41. See the invoice dated 29 August 1855, folder 14, Pratt Collection, LDS Church Archives. Richards charged a 20 percent commission for editing and publishing *Key*, and a 10 percent commission for the same work on the eighth edition of *Voice of Warning*.

42. The events leading up to his death on 13 May 1857 are treated in Steven Pratt, "Eleanor McLean and the Murder of Parley P. Pratt," *BYU Studies* 15 (winter 1975): 225–56. George Q. Cannon's *Western Standard* 2 (3, 17 July 1857) noted and editorialized on Pratt's death.

43. The details are discussed in my article "The Bone in the Throat: Orson Pratt and the Public Announcement of Plural Marriage" (see n. 23).

44. Parley P. Pratt to Brigham Young, 25 October 1854.

45. Parley P. Pratt to Brigham Young, 18 December 1854. See Parley P. Pratt to Brigham Young, 6 June 1855. In a 29 December 1855 letter, Young counseled Parley: "I observe in some of the papers you challenge to meet a convention of able men on the subject of Plurality. I think there is no chance of them meeting you; but if they should so much the better, pure principles will then stand a fair chance for investigation."

46. For more information on Belinda Marden and the pamphlet, see my "Early Mormon Polygamy Defenses," *Journal of Mormon History* 11 (1984): 53–7. See also Benjamin F. Johnson, *Why the "Latter Day Saints" Marry a Plurality of Wives* (1854), which was written for the Hawaiian mission, published by the Excelsior Printing Office in San Francisco in May and June 1854, and then distributed in Hawaii. For a discussion of the Johnson tract, see my "Early Mormon Polygamy Defenses," 50–3.

47. Parley P. Pratt to his family, 21 September 1854, LDS Church Archives. Photocopy in my possession. Richard Burton, the British explorer and visitor of holy cities, thought enough of Belinda Marden's pamphlet to print it in his *City of the Saints* (1863), 484–93. Parley P. Pratt's *Marriage and Morals in Utah* (1856), an address read before a joint session of the Utah Territorial Legislature in Fillmore City on 31 December 1855, was reprinted in *Deseret News* 5 (16 January 1856): 356–7. See its later expansion by George Q. Cannon in *Scriptural Evidences in Support of Polygamy* (1856), which carried the subtitle *Being an Address Entitled Marriage and Morals in Utah . . . And a Protestant Minister's Arguments from the Bible in Favor of Polygamy. Extracted from the Work of Rev. D. O. Allen.* Cannon indicates in his 3 January 1857 letter to Brigham Young that he printed twelve hundred copies.

48. Parley P. Pratt to Brigham Young, February 1855. Parley was later assigned to preach and publish in the eastern United States and

possibly to assist John Taylor with the LDS newspaper *The Mormon* in New York City. See letter of First Presidency to Parley P. Pratt, 10 September 1856, LDS Church Archives.

49. Parley P. Pratt to Brigham Young, 18 May 1855.

50. The details of this endeavor are traceable in Cannon's Hawaiian mission journals, 3 vols. (October 1849–August 1854), LDS Church Archives. See also Cannon, *My First Mission* (1879), the first book of the "Faith-Promoting Series." The Cannon journals after August 1854 are in the LDS Church Archives, but they are currently restricted. For secondary biographical information on Cannon, see the George Q. Cannon series by Joseph J. Cannon, in *Instructor* (January 1944 to November 1945). A useful compilation of material is Jerreld L. Newquist, comp., *Gospel Truth: Discourses and Writings of George Q. Cannon* (1987). See also Lawrence R. Flake, "George Q. Cannon: His Missionary Years" (doctor of religious education diss., Brigham Young University, 1970).

51. He had carefully read through the manuscript twice by January 1854. See his Hawaiian mission journal, vol. 3, 31 January 1854.

52. See Cannon's Hawaiian mission journal, vol. 2, 5 October 1853.

53. The details are in Cannon's Hawaiian mission journal, vol. 3, 18 November and 2 December 1853. In a letter dated 20 November 1853 to Brigham Young, Cannon had explained why there was no possibility of getting others to print the translation.

54. See John Taylor to George Q. Cannon, 29 May 1853, as cited in Cannon's journal, vol. 3, 31 December 1853.

55. See Brigham Young to George Q. Cannon, 30 September 1853.

56. See Cannon's Hawaiian mission journal, vol. 3, 20 March and 26 May 1854.

57. See George Q. Cannon to Brigham Young, 27 July 1855.

58. Throughout the project Cannon was assisted by Joseph Bull and Matthew F. Wilkie. David H. Cannon and William H. Shearman were later a part of these early Mormon publishing efforts in San

Francisco. A photograph of the whole group appears in *Improvement Era* (April 1959): 239.

59. See the detailed discussion in George Q. Cannon to Brigham Young, 27 July 1854. See also George Q. Cannon to Parley P. Pratt, 21 October 1855.

60. See George Q. Cannon to Brigham Young, 31 August 1855.

61. See George Q. Cannon to Brigham Young, 1 October 1855.

62. See George Q. Cannon to Brigham Young, 3 December 1855.

63. Ibid.

64. See *Ka Buke a Moramona* (1855), the Hawaiian edition of the Book of Mormon. Most of the three thousand copies were left unbound. The first bound copies had a red binding; about two hundred of these had been bound by September 1856. The problems and cost of getting the work bound are discussed in Cannon's letters to Brigham Young dated 26 May and 27 September 1856 and 31 August 1857. Cannon tells Young that most of the volumes are unbound and describes his plans to send the printed sheets to the missionaries in Hawaii, who could get them bound as they were needed. The existence of a variety of bindings suggests that this practice was followed, though it is impossible to determine how many of these books were bound in Hawaii. For Young's positive reaction upon receiving a bound volume, see Brigham Young to George Q. Cannon, 3 April 1856.

65. George Q. Cannon to Brigham Young, 26 January 1856. See Brigham Young to George Q. Cannon, 4 November 1856. The eight-page Hawaiian tract was dated San Francisco, 27 December 1855, and was titled *He Olelo Hoolaha*. The title in English is *A Word of Instruction to All Hawaiians Who Love the Truth*. It was printed on the same press that would print the *Western Standard*.

66. Parley P. Pratt, "Prospectus of the Western Standard," LDS Church Archives. A useful short history of the newspaper is Jerreld L. Newquist, "The Western Standard" *Improvement Era* (April 1959): 238–9, 274–82. Brigham Young's letter to Cannon, dated Fillmore, Utah Territory, 3 January 1856, had given him the approval

to publish the paper. In the introduction to his *Writings from the Western Standard* (1864), Cannon explained the relationship between his *Western Standard* and Parley Pratt's planned *Mormon Herald*, for which Parley had issued a prospectus (vi–xi).

67. See, for example, George Q. Cannon to Brigham Young, 27 September 1856.

68. In his 26 May 1856 letter to Brigham Young, Cannon reported 146 subscriptions. By September he had more than 800 subscriptions in Utah Territory, as reported in his 27 September 1856 letter to Young. For a list of his agents, most of them in Utah, see the early issues of the *Western Standard*.

69. George Q. Cannon to Brigham Young, 27 September and 26 May 1856.

70. George Q. Cannon to Brigham Young, 27 September 1856.

71. William A. Shearman, letter, 29 March 1856, in *Western Standard* 1 (15 March 1856): 3. Orson Hyde voiced similar sentiments in the next issue.

72. Orson Pratt's tract appeared on the front page of six issues of *Western Standard* 1 (21 June–26 July 1856), and Orson Spencer's work appeared therein beginning with the 6 September 1856 issue. For Young's specific counsel, see Brigham Young to George Q. Cannon, 29 April 1856.

73. Cannon's earliest feelings about fiction reading are in *Western Standard* 2 (1 September 1857). For his later expressions, see "Select Your Reading," *Juvenile Instructor* 1 (15 August 1866); *Conference Reports* (5 October 1897): 38–40; and "Editorial Thoughts: What Do You Read?" *Juvenile Instructor* 34 (1 January 1899): 22–3. That Cannon helped shape Brigham Young's own views on these matters is suggested in Stephen Kent Ehat, "How to Condemn Noxious Novels," *Century 2* (Brigham Young University student publication) 1 (December 1972): 36–48. Cannon was too early to see the development of the important literary frontier in such contemporary writers as Mark Twain and Bret Harte in California. See Franklin D. Walker, *San Francisco's Literary Frontier* (1939); and Lawrence R. Flake, "The Development of the *Juvenile Instructor* under George Q.

Cannon and Its Functions in LDS Religious Education" (master's thesis, Brigham Young University, 1969).

74. See George Q. Cannon to Brigham Young, 3 January 1857.

75. For information on the activities of John Hyde Jr. in both Hawaii and California, see Lynne Watkins Jorgensen, "John Hyde, Jr., Mormon Renegade," *Journal of Mormon History* 17 (1991): 120–44. Two issues of the *Western Standard* (22, 29 November 1856) had printed accounts of Hyde's activities in Hawaii. Cannon's editorial on Hyde's anti-Mormon lectures in central California appeared in *Western Standard* 1 (29 November 1856): 2. John Hyde published *Mormonism: Its Leaders and Designs* in the summer of 1857, and the next year he completed an anti-Mormon novel that was never published. The manuscript of the unpublished novel is in Special Collections and Manuscripts, Harold B. Lee Library, Brigham Young University.

76. See George Q. Cannon to Brigham Young, 3 January 1857. Also see Brigham Young to George Q. Cannon, 31 January 1857. "Marriage and Morals in Utah" was printed in *Western Standard* 1 (10 May 1856): 1. Much of what was added in *Scriptural Evidences* was material from Rev. David O. Allen, *India, Ancient and Modern* (1856). This material, "A Protestant Minister's Arguments from the Bible in Favour of Polygamy," was published in *Millennial Star* 19 (3 October 1857): 636–40 and in other LDS publications as noted in my "Early Mormon Polygamy Defenses," 61–2 and n. 57.

77. George Q. Cannon to Brigham Young, 19 May 1857.

78. Cannon details his 30 October 1857 activities in a letter to Brigham Young. He indicated in a 7 October 1857 letter to Young that he had boxed and shipped the printed sheets of the Book of Mormon to Hawaii.

79. For the later history of the printing press, see Brigham Young to Dwight Eveleth, 4 September 1858.

80. The story is told in my "Early Mormon Pamphleteering," 35–49.

81. Cannon explained this project in his 9 February 1864 letter to Brigham Young.

82. See Taunalyn Ford Rutherford, "'Properly Presented': The

Autobiography of Parley P. Pratt" (master's thesis, Brigham Young University, 1995); and R. A. Christmas, "The Autobiography of Parley P. Pratt: Some Literary, Historical and Critical Reflections," *Dialogue* (spring 1966): 33–43.

83. The first title in this series designed "for the instruction and encouragement of young Latter-day Saints" and published in Salt Lake City by the Juvenile Instructor Office was George Q. Cannon's *My First Mission* (1879). The inspirational volumes (nearly all of which were focused on biographical narratives of missionary work) were offered in a serious attempt to provide positive alternatives to the pulp fiction that was pouring out of American publishing houses of the period. Young readers were cautioned to watch what they read, and they were warned that "fiction dulls perception and impairs the memory" (preface to *Scraps of Biography*, bk. 10 [1883]).

CHAPTER 4

THE RISE AND DECLINE OF THE LDS INDIAN STUDENT PLACEMENT PROGRAM, 1947–1996

James B. Allen

In 1975 Dan George, a Swinomish Indian chief from British Columbia, addressed a group of Latter-day Saint educators and LDS Indian student placement service personnel in Yakima, Washington. There he depicted both the grandeur of his heritage and the dilemma of his times. Reflecting on the changes he had seen during his lifetime, Chief George lamented the impact of the "rushing tide" of modernism on the cultural dignity of his people:

> I was born when people loved all nature and spoke to it as though it had a soul. . . .
>
> [But] then the people came. More and more people came. Like a crushing, rushing wave they came, hurling the years aside. And suddenly I found myself a young man in the midst of the twentieth century. I found myself and my people adrift in this new age, not part of it.

James B. Allen is emeritus professor of history at Brigham Young University and a senior research fellow at the university's Joseph Fielding Smith Institute for Church History.

We were engulfed by its rushing tide, but only as a captive eddy, going round and round. On little reservations, on plots of land, we floated in a kind of gray unreality, ashamed of our culture that you ridiculed, unsure of who we were or where we were going, uncertain of our grip on the present, weak in our hope of the future. . . .

And now you hold out your hand and you beckon to me to come across the street. Come and integrate, you say. But how can I come? . . . How can I come in dignity? . . . I have no gifts. What is there in my culture you value? My poor treasures you only scorn.

. . . Somehow I must wait. I must delay. I must find myself. I must find my treasure. I must wait until you want something of me, until you need something that is me. Then I can raise my head and say to my wife and family, "Listen, they are calling. They need me. I must go."

Then I can walk across the street and hold my head high, for I will meet you as an equal. I will not scorn you for your seeming gifts, and you will not receive me in pity. Pity I can do without; my manhood I cannot.[1]

As the words of Chief George so eloquently reveal, Native Americans throughout the United States and Canada have faced a cruel dilemma in the twentieth century: how to maintain their cultural dignity and, at the same time, gain the education and training they need to compete in the very different and brutal world that has engulfed them. The LDS Indian student placement service (ISPS) was an attempt by the Church of Jesus Christ of Latter-day Saints to help address that problem among its members. It was also the focus of considerable controversy and conflicting interpretation, ranging from angry criticism on the part of Native American groups who felt it undermined their youth's awareness of and appreciation for their heritage to high praise from Mormon participants and others who believed that it accomplished its goal of preparing Native

American youth to better meet the challenges of the modern world and value their cultural legacy. The motives of those who founded the program, the selfless efforts of numerous individuals and families who put so much into trying to make it work, the experiences (both good and bad) of students in the program, the program's strengths and weaknesses, the various efforts to evaluate its results, the legal considerations that affected it, the reasons for its demise—all these are part of an engrossing and highly important episode in the history of both the LDS Church and many Native Americans.

The story of the ISPS cannot be separated from its larger American context, which includes a variety of efforts by the federal government to "Americanize" Native Americans.[2] This meant, in effect, replacing their "old ways" and cultural traditions with all the attributes of America's economic and social system, a goal that in essence was at the heart of the late-nineteenth-century reservation system,[3] the ill-fated General Allotment Act of 1887, and the failed attempt at "termination"[4] in the 1950s.

Throughout the nineteenth century, white Americans often justified removing Native American children from their homes, forcibly if necessary, for the purpose of educating and "civilizing" them.[5] The government established day schools on reservations, but it also set up boarding schools, sponsored a foster home program, and encouraged adoption by white families, all of which took children off the reservations.[6] The most controversial institutions were the boarding schools, usually located long distances from the reservations. Some parents, concerned about the economic future of their children, assented to their enrollment in these schools, while others objected strenuously but could do little about it. Overenthusiastic Indian agents, often anxious to fill quotas and protect the annual federal appropriations, sometimes literally kidnapped the children of reluctant families and forced them to the schools. Talayesva, a Hopi formerly enrolled in the Keams Canyon boarding school, described an annual "student roundup." Agency police rode in and surrounded his village, he said, "with the intention of capturing the children of the hostile families and taking them to school by force. They herded us all together at the east edge of the mesa. Although I had planned to go later, they put me with the others. The people were excited, the children and mothers were crying and the men wanted to fight."[7]

The treatment received at boarding schools was often unusually cruel,[8] and students were constantly reminded that something was wrong with their heritage and that they were there to be purged of it. Obviously, such strategy did nothing for their feelings of self-worth or cultural pride. In 1936 Helen John, a six-year-old Navajo who later became the catalyst for the LDS Indian placement program, found herself in a boarding school in Tuba City, Arizona. There she saw firsthand how damaging these institutions could be to ethnic pride. When two boys were caught speaking Navajo, the principal washed out their mouths with soap, saying, "You know that what I am doing is to show you what we think of your talking Navajo. I'll just wash those words right out." At least one teacher wondered silently, "How can we teach these children to love the words we teach them when we show disdain for the only meaningful words they know?" But most had the attitude of the principal—the Navajo language, along with the culture it represented, had to go.[9] Nevertheless, the continuing hope for a better education led many Native American families to place them in a variety of off-reservation programs, including the LDS program.

There is another historical context, however, for the origin of the ISPS. It consists of several elements, including Latter-day Saints' religious commitment to the idea that the Native Americans were a choice people whom they had an obligation to help. It also included the special commitment of a loving and powerful church leader, Spencer W. Kimball, the tragic economic problems of the Navajo in the mid-1940s, and the determination of a sixteen-year-old Navajo girl.

As chairman of the LDS Church's Committee on Indian Relationships, Spencer W. Kimball developed a deep appreciation for the history and culture of Native Americans. He believed that a new day was dawning for them and that the Latter-day Saints were destined to play a role in the accomplishments of that day. "The difference between them and us is opportunity," he frequently said.[10]

Elder Kimball reproved church members for their lack of understanding concerning Native Americans and their reluctance to help them. In a particularly pointed address at BYU in 1953, he pleaded with Latter-day Saint to overcome their seeming hypocrisy:

> . . . I want to tell you that, above all the problems the Indian has, his greatest one is the white man—the white man, who not only dispossessed him, but the white man who has never seemed to try to understand him—the white man who stands pharisaically above him—the white man who goes to the Temple to pray and says, "Lord, I thank thee that I am not as other men are."—The white man is his problem. . . .
>
> My young brothers and sisters, . . . I plead with you to accept the Lamanite as your brother. I ask not for your tolerance—your cold, calculating tolerance; your haughty, contemptible tolerance; your scornful, arrogant tolerance; your pitying, coin-tossing tolerance. I ask you to give them what they want and need and deserve: opportunity and your fraternal brotherliness and your understanding; your warm and glowing fellowship; your unstinted and beautiful love; your enthusiastic and affectionate brotherhood.[11]

When the Navajo were placed on the reservation in 1868, they numbered ten thousand people. Eighty years later they had grown to sixty-four thousand. One of their chief means of livelihood was raising sheep, but as both the human and sheep populations increased, the grasslands were practically destroyed. Families were forced to go farther and farther away, sometimes many miles, just to graze their sheep. As children were assigned to watch and drive the sheep, the work became a family enterprise.

In 1935 the federal government responded to the erosion problem by beginning a massive stock reduction program on the reservation. From the standpoint of Navajo families, this solution was a disaster because their sheep were their total means of livelihood. The impact on Helen John's family was devastating—they were reduced to poverty. It was under these circumstances that Helen's parents "voluntarily" took her to the boarding school in Tuba City, where she attended until she was twelve.

In 1947 a severe drought added to the problems of the Navajo, and it appeared that the coming winter would be one of freezing and starvation. This potential tragedy led Spencer W. Kimball to write at least two sharply critical news articles[12] and to do considerable work in behalf of the Navajo. Convinced that adequate education was the only way for Native Americans to deal effectively with their own problems, he excoriated the national government for its years of violating its 1868 Navajo treaty, and he put special emphasis on the lack of schools. The Navajo population included approximately twenty-four thousand children, but nineteen thousand of them were still without schools. Seventy-five percent of the Navajo people were illiterate, he said, compared with 1.5 percent illiteracy among U.S. whites. "Why such deprivation for the people whom we replaced?" Elder Kimball lamented. "Can graver injustices be found in any land?"[13]

In the spring of 1947 Helen John and her family were in the vicinity of Richfield, Utah, along with many other Navajo people, hiring out to sugar beet farmers.[14] Helen asked her father, Willie John, if she could stay in Richfield to go to school once the family had left. Willie refused, telling her that she needed no more of the *Bilagaanas'* (white men's) education and that she should be proud to be a Navajo. Hurt, Helen ran across the field to the home of Amy Avery, for whom she and her family were working. Amy heard her crying and invited her in. They talked, Helen explained what she wanted, and the two even prayed together. Amy then telephoned Golden Buchanan, who had just been appointed coordinator for Indian affairs in the Sevier Stake of the LDS Church, and told him she had the first case for him—a girl who wanted to go to school. Buchanan told Amy to keep in touch with her.

The John family returned to Richfield in October, and Helen went to see Amy as soon as she could. Amy taught Helen and her family about Mormonism while they tried to figure out a way for her to attend school. Meanwhile, Buchanan decided there must be a way to get a family to take her in so she could go to school. He even wrote to Spencer W. Kimball about his idea. Two days later at about eight o'clock in the evening, Elder Kimball showed up on Buchanan's doorstep. After dinner he asked the Buchanans to take Helen into their home—not as a servant girl or a guest, but as a member of the family. After considerable soul-searching that night, the family agreed. Elder Kimball emphasized that although this arrangement was not part of an official church program, he wanted to see it tried out because he could see a great future possibility.

The next morning was cold and snow had fallen during the night, yet the Navajo were out early in the frozen fields, topping beets. Buchanan found Helen there at work and invited her to stay with his family while she went to school in Richfield. Helen accepted without hesitation—this was what she had been dreaming of and, in her own way, praying for. She also had her parents' permission.

The Buchanans worked hard to help Helen feel welcome, and Helen tried equally hard to adjust to the new Bilagaana way of living. The Buchanans also arranged for a few other children to be taken into other homes. It was not long before the Buchanans were forced to make what might be interpreted as the first harsh screening decision of the placement program. Helen had left them for a while, but she returned with two girls who spoke no English at all. The Buchanans knew that education and adjustments were difficult enough for people like Helen, but they felt that with the language handicap the girls would simply not be able to survive in school. Wanting to avoid what could have been a social disaster, the Buchanans sent them home to Arizona.[15]

These beginnings reflect at least three important aspects of the placement program as it later developed. First, from the standpoint of the Navajo students, this was an opportunity to break out of the poverty and ignorance they saw around them and to begin making more positive contributions to their own people. Second, Willie John's initial reaction demonstrated that the Native Americans had mixed attitudes—some believing with young Helen that such a program was best for their people in the long run, others fearful that it would lead to cultural genocide. Third, the motives of the local church leaders and foster families who began the program were generally selfless. When Amy Avery first called Golden Buchanan about Helen, it was not with the idea that here was a new convert to be made, but that here was a young woman who needed help. The same desire motivated Spencer W. Kimball.

Despite the potential problems inherent in placement programs, many Native American families were not as reluctant as Willie John to get their children involved. Helen's success, in fact, prompted a number of them to approach church leaders with the request that their children also be placed.[16] The program grew more rapidly than Buchanan had anticipated, and by the 1953–54 school year sixty-eight students had been placed, including a few in southern California, Idaho, and Oregon.

When Buchanan left Richfield to become president of the Southwest Indian Mission, Miles Jensen took his place. Foreshadowing the work of the later reception centers, Jensen provided transportation from the reservation, and his wife usually took the children into her home, bathed them, fed them, and lodged them for their first night away from their families. At this early stage of the program, most of the children involved were not members of the church.[17]

According to Clarence R. Bishop, the apparent success of the trial program in terms of benefits to the children "exceeded the fondest dreams of those involved."[18] Elder Kimball watched carefully and reported the results to the First Presidency and the Council of the Twelve Apostles. Church leaders were well enough impressed that in July 1954 they made it an official church program. In a letter to seven stake presidents in the areas most affected, the First Presidency suggested a few firm guidelines. Latter-day Saint families were not to be pressured into participating in the program; rather, the decision to participate must be completely of their own free will. They were also to understand that no child was to be considered "a mere guest," nor a servant, though "he or she would be expected to assume such responsibilities of service as all children ought to have and share." Moreover, foster families must be willing to assume financial responsibilities, because most Native American families had no means to provide all that was needed.[19] In addition, participating students must be Latter-day Saints. The major goals of the placement program were to help LDS students gain the education they needed to succeed in the modern world and to help them understand and live more fully the religious principles of the church.

In order to protect its legal status, the program was placed under the Social Service Department of the church's Relief Society, which was already a licensed agency for placing children. This also meant that each child placed in a foster home would be assigned to a social worker as part of that worker's regular caseload.[20]

In the fall of 1955 enrollment jumped from 68 to 253 children. By that time a reception center had been established in Richfield. The church chartered buses to bring the children to the center, where they received food, medical examinations, baths and shampoos (including disinfectants), and chest x-ray examinations. They were then introduced to their foster families, who were given an extensive orientation before they were allowed to take the children home. As the program expanded, reception centers were established in several places, often using the facilities of LDS stake centers. It was a bit overwhelming for some, especially the younger children. For many it was a time of fear, apprehension, crying, and wanting to go home.

The program did not get off the ground without some problems and complaints.[21] One concerned the nature of recruitment. As soon as the program became an official church program, missionaries on the reservations were assigned as recruiters. It was practically inevitable that they would use the program as a proselytizing tool, for the opportunity to enroll their children into the program might induce some families to join the church. This practice led to serious public relations problems until it was eliminated in 1972.

In 1956 the Bureau of Indian Affairs (BIA) began to receive complaints from the Hualapai Indians in Arizona. The Hualapai charged that, among other things, the placement program was used for proselytizing, it alienated children from parents, it took children from reservations when education was available in their own communities, and the social workers were guilty of poor casework practices. As a result, an important meeting was held in Kanab, Utah, in March 1957. In attendance were representatives of the church, Utah and Arizona governments, and the BIA. The meeting ended with a new spirit of understanding and cooperation, a feeling of general support for the program once it had been fully explained, and the church's agreeing to improve some administrative aspects of the program. The problem of proselytizing was also discussed. The church agreed that caseworkers would go to the reservation and interview children and their families with respect to qualifications. Missionaries still helped recruit, but caseworkers made the final decision for acceptance, not missionaries.[22]

In the long run, using the placement program as a proselytizing tool was of questionable religious value, at least for those families who joined the church mainly to qualify their children for the program. Some families did little or nothing more to become familiar with church programs.[23] One former placement student who later served as a missionary on a reservation said that missionaries had quotas to meet and that they baptized children to go on placement just to fill their quotas. "I learned," he reported, "that a lot of the kids were baptized just to go to school. . . . As a result, a lot of the kids that were on Placement would go home and [not] have anything to do with the Church. . . . You hear of all these hundreds of people that are members of the Church. . . . The only reason that they're on the records is because they went on Placement. We run into a lot of them even now that say, 'Oh, I used to be LDS.'"[24]

In the 1950s and 1960s the number of students in the program grew and various administrative refinements were made.[25] In 1969 a major change came in the administration of all church social services when a new administrative entity, the

Unified Social Services, was created. It became the umbrella for the Relief Society adoption services, the Youth Guidance Program, and, inevitably, the ISPS. In 1973 this entity became a separate legal corporation known as LDS Social Services.

The ISPS expanded into Arizona (1962), the Northwest (1963), Canada (1964), Idaho (1965), and Oklahoma (1966).[26] At its height it operated also in Wyoming, Montana, and North and South Dakota.[27] The vast majority of students were Navajo, but by the end of the 1960s, students from at least sixty-three tribes in the United States and Canada had participated in the program.[28] At its peak in 1970 and 1971 it served approximately five thousand students.

The success or failure of the Indian placement program depended on the foster families as well as the preparation and attitudes of the students. There were numerous stresses and strains, usually connected with the problem of crossing cultural barriers. Some foster families gave up in just a few months, others after the first year. Some never fully understood their foster children. Others loved the experience, had a positive impact on the Native American children who came to live with them, and were pleased to take more. A few anecdotal examples help illustrate some of the problems, achievements, failures, and successes of the program and also illustrate some of the conclusions reached by the professional evaluations that are discussed later in the chapter.

When interviewed about their experiences, former placement program students frequently mentioned the initial trauma and homesickness they felt as they left home for the first time in their lives. Audrey Boone, for example, remembered when her mother took her and her sisters to the social services office in Salt Lake City for their initial interview. A social worker asked the children all kinds of questions. The students didn't realize they were being interviewed in order to help the social worker determine with whom they should be placed, so they were taken aback when the potential foster families soon entered the waiting room ready to take those who had been assigned to them.[29] Boone reported this discomforting first meeting: "I had all kinds of confused feelings in my mind and heart. I was angry, mad, and sad all at the same time. I didn't really know what to think. I didn't know what was going to happen next.

"As I was looking at the families, I picked out a family that I thought I wouldn't want to be with. I was hoping and wishing I wouldn't be with them. I had no social interaction. I didn't meet them. I just looked at them and thought, 'I don't want to be with that family.' It ended up that I was matched with that family. I didn't say much on the ride home. I've never told them what I was thinking about at the time."[30]

Most students had initial adjustment problems. Vanta Quintero, who began the program in Provo, Utah, in the seventh grade, cried for two weeks. Despite everything her foster parents tried to do, she was inconsolable until her real parents came from Fort Apache, six hundred miles away, and took her home. The next year, however, she went back.[31]

Edouardo Zondajas was not prepared for some aspects of white Mormon family life, including taking baths, going to bed early, wearing pajamas (instead of just sleeping in the clothes he had worn all day), brushing teeth, and eating breakfast. He was also deeply homesick. But he held it inside—too proud to cry or in any way let his foster family know how he felt. One day his foster brother was playing in their room with a watch Edouardo's father had given him. He tossed it to Edouardo, but it fell on the floor. Nothing was broken, but to the homesick youngster "it was a good excuse to let go." He burst out crying, blaming it on his foster brother's dropping the watch. His foster parents came to see what was wrong, and after they left he

heard the father say, "But it was just a watch. There's no big deal
about that." He later felt, however, that his foster mother "saw
through what was going on."[32]

In the long run, Zondajas profited from the program and
gave it a positive evaluation.[33] After graduating, he became a
volunteer with LDS Social Services in the Omaha area, working with other students in the program. As a result of that experience, he was critical of the program when it raised the age
requirements. While he realized that some students may have
been a bit too young, he nevertheless thought that limiting the
program to high school students had serious drawbacks. "By
the time a lot of these kids are fourteen or fifteen years old, they
are living on their own," he said. "Some of them are pregnant.
They are using drugs or alcohol. It is essentially too late." He
thought that ages ten through twelve were just about right, for
that was when students were most impressionable. "More often
than not," he said, "they [then] fall into the wrong group." He
further explained: "Some of these kids are not getting the kind
of family life and support that is necessary for them to be successful. I thought at least the Placement Program was giving
some of those kids a chance. I have just been involved with so
many kids that deserved a chance at the age of twelve. These
twelve-year-old kids are already babysitting their younger
brothers and sisters over the weekend while their mom's out
getting drunk and spending the welfare check. They don't have
anything to look forward to. . . . [But] I've seen a lot of kids that
were given that chance and were able to take advantage of it."[34]

Some of the problems associated with placement became
apparent the moment the Cox family first met Virgil. From
Virgil's perspective, getting off the bus that day was a rude dis-
appointment. He had expected to meet the foster family with
whom he had lived the previous two years, but instead he saw
the Coxes. Stunned, he said nothing as he was piled into the car

with the rest of the kids and driven home. "What's the matter with your head?" Kay Cox asked herself. "What have you gotten yourself into? He doesn't even speak English." But when she showed Virgil his bed, he suddenly spoke the feelings that had been devastating him all the way home. "Why didn't my other foster parents like me? What did I do?" He then cried himself to sleep.[35]

The story had a happy ending, but not until both Kay and Virgil had gone through some difficult times. Virgil's early experience in school demonstrated both the unfortunate attitude many whites still had toward Native American children and a foster mother's determination to prove them wrong. Virgil did poorly the first two months, but whenever Kay asked that books be sent home so she could help him learn to read, Virgil's teacher refused. One night Virgil sobbed out that the teacher told him simply not to try—he wasn't capable of doing the work. Angered, Kay marched into the offending teacher's classroom, took Virgil out, put him in another classroom taught by a friend, and warned her friend of her impending wrath if Virgil did not remain there. The principal, of course, objected that Kay could not do what she had just done, but she did it anyway. Her attitude was exactly opposite that of the racist principal, who said, "Why are you trying so hard with this kid? Don't you know he's an Indian? He can't learn." But with his new teacher's willing cooperation, Virgil brought books home, and with Kay's help he learned quickly. When he graduated from high school a few years later, Virgil was the only Sterling Scholar scholarship finalist in the entire graduating class.[36]

A marvelous example of the intercultural benefits of the program came many years later when Virgil's son, Paul, became one of the Coxes' foster children. As described by Kay Cox: "Toward the end of his first year, Paul did a hoop dance in his school program. I was able to teach it to him; his dad had taught it to me. It was the long way around for Navaho culture, but Paul loved it; and I loved being able to show him how."[37]

Fortunately for the students, many foster families had attitudes toward Native American culture much like those of the Coxes. They had no desire to wean their foster children away from the best traditions of their fathers—only away from the ills associated with poverty and debasing lifestyles such as drunkenness. According to Emery Bowman, "My foster parents basically pushed me back into the Navajo tribe, Navajo tradition." His foster mother told him, "To be Navajo is to be greatly religious. To understand the Navajo tradition and the Navajo religion is very complex. So learn it."[38] Another student, who became an educator, opined that "the kids that go on the Placement Program for some reason search more about their culture. . . . It seems to me that the ones that stay at home are kind of ashamed about their culture. . . . I think the kids that . . . go on the Placement Program hang on to their culture better and respect their culture."[39]

An abundance of such anecdotal material provides important insight into the personal side of the Indian placement program. Beyond this, however, numerous evaluations conducted in the 1970s and early 1980s looked more systematically at results. They were mostly master's theses and sociological surveys, as well as some opinion surveys. As summarized by Grant Hardy Taylor in 1981, they indicated that the ISPS provided "a better social, spiritual, cultural, and educational opportunity than the other options available to Indian youth."[40] Taylor did not report, however, on one 1976 thesis that surveyed the attitudes of Navajo community leaders and concluded that the church needed to improve its public relations regarding the program.[41]

Several studies based on sociological data were generally positive in their results. When compared with nonplacement students, for example, ISPS students had stronger LDS commitments and better reading skills, and they were more likely to go to college. With respect to scholastic achievements, they also compared favorably with students who were not Native Americans.[42] Nevertheless, survey results sometimes conflicted. Anthropologist Martin Topper studied a group of twenty-five Navajo children over a period of four years and concluded that separation from tribe and family caused emotional stress.[43] He was no doubt correct, though how serious the problem was and how long lasting the effects remained open for debate. He also reported that twenty-three out of the twenty-five dropped out of the program before graduation, leaving the impression that few students attained this educational goal. However, as will be discussed shortly hereafter, a later and more thorough survey produced a more positive picture.

One study had some especially interesting things to say about caseworkers. The extent to which caseworkers were willing and able to relate to Native Americans had much to do with successful student adjustment. Three criteria for the ideal caseworker were (1) prior residence on a reservation, (2) extended yearly visits to the reservation, and (3) person-to-person conferences outside the foster home not less than once a month. Significantly, the students did not ask that caseworkers be permissive.[44]

In a doctoral dissertation completed in 1981, Grant Hardy Taylor studied Native American students at BYU and compared those who had been on the placement program with those who had not. He found that students with placement experience tended to begin college earlier and to finish more semesters, though placement experience seemed to make no significant difference in grade point average. He also reached a number of conclusions that demonstrated the religious value of the program. Students with ISPS experience were much more likely to go on LDS missions and to marry in the temple.[45] Such conclusions are not surprising, but their implications must be modified by the data collected when BYU sociology professors Bruce A. Chadwick, Stan L. Albrecht, and Howard W. Bahr asked different kinds of questions. In 1981 they conducted the most thorough and sophisticated study of the program ever made. The study was funded by the church's Presiding Bishop's Office, and the findings were reported publicly five years later. Still later, Chadwick and Albrecht further refined and explicated them.[46] Some of their conclusions are summarized below.

A continuing goal of the ISPS was that students return to their foster families each year until they graduated from high school. However, about 40 percent of them dropped out of their own accord, usually because of illness at home. Another 15 percent left at the request of their parents, who for various reasons required their help at home. About 8 percent were sent home by their foster families and not invited to return, half because of changes in family circumstances and the other half because of conflict between participants and members of the foster families. Another 2 percent left for miscellaneous reasons. The result was that only about one-third of the students remained in the program long enough to graduate. At the same time, various federal vocational programs that required participation of a year or less and did not call for high school graduation reported completion rates ranging from 20 to 70 percent. In that context the Indian student placement program, which called for several years of participation and resulted in 34 percent high school graduation, was actually quite remarkable.[47] Equally significant was the fact that even after dropping out of the program, placement students went on to finish high school in significantly larger numbers than the control group (which consisted of friends of placement students who had not gone on placement). Eighty-two percent of ISPS participants eventually graduated, compared with 45 percent in the control

group studied.[48] In addition, the ISPS seemed to have excep-
tional success in encouraging post–high school training.
Among those former participants who were age twenty-five or
older at the time of the survey, 52 percent had obtained at least
one year of college, as opposed to 21 percent of the control
group.[49]

In terms of economic security, the results of the placement
program were not as impressive. Those who participated had
higher rates of employment, and more of them were in occupations considered more prestigious (29 percent were employed
in managerial or professional occupations, compared with only
5 percent of the control group), but the results were not statistically significant enough to be conclusive. In some respects,
the investigators reported, participation in the program en-
hanced the economic status of those in the survey, while in
other respects it did not. Nevertheless, they concluded that
"none of the economic indicators showed that the participants
were worse off than the controls." In addition, the longer students remained in the program, the more likely they were to be
employed and to earn high incomes.[50]

The investigators came to other surprising conclusions
about the overall social impact of the program. There was no
statistically significant difference, for example, with respect to
marital stability—that is, divorce rates. Similarly, "contrary to
expectations, the marriage of participants were neither more
happy nor more enduring than those of the control group."[51] In
other areas of social adjustment, results were mixed, though
with most participants, especially those who remained in an
off-reservation environment, the results were generally more
positive than those of the control group. The longer participants stayed on the placement program, the more likely they
were to marry. Participants involved themselves with friends
and neighbors more frequently than did nonparticipants, and

they also joined more organizations. The two groups showed no great differences, however, in voting behavior, either in national or tribal elections. Most surprising was the difficulty participants seemed to have with the law. During a selected five-year period, 25 percent were arrested, compared with only 12 percent of the control group. This was partially explained, however, by the fact that only 21 percent of the participants continued to live on the reservation after completing the program, while 65 percent of the control group lived there after high school graduation. Those living off the reservation were simply at greater risk of being apprehended by law enforcement officers.[52]

The question of ethnic identity, so important to critics of the program, was carefully investigated by Chadwick, Albrecht, and Bahr, who found that the program indeed had some effect. When asked to what degree they felt "Indian" or "white," 7 percent of the participants identified themselves as "mostly white" or "totally white," compared to none among the control group. At the other end of the scale, 70 percent of the participants, as compared with 83 percent of the controls, considered themselves "totally Indian" or "mostly Indian." Ninety-one percent of both groups felt that they "completely fit in" or "fit in pretty well" with most Native Americans, though the percent of controls who felt that they fit in completely was twice that of the participants. Conversely, 85 percent of the ISPS group and 80 percent of the controls also saw themselves fitting in "completely" or "pretty well" with most whites, with only 10 percent of the participants and 8 percent of the controls saying that they completely fit in. The differences were not statistically significant, leading the investigators to express surprise that control group members felt they fit into white society just as well as the participants.[53]

Significantly, the study turned up no evidence of the severe psychological trauma often attributed to participation in the placement program. The investigators also noted that serious "maladaptive behaviors," such as suicide attempts and excessive drug or alcohol abuse, did not occur any more frequently in the lives of participants than in those of their control group. In contrast, they said, "participation was associated with higher general happiness and a stronger perception of being at ease in the white world," though there was a "modest lessening of Indian identity."[54]

The program was impressively successful so far as its educational goals were concerned, but the record was less impressive when it came to religiosity. Surprisingly, although Chadwick, Albrecht, and Bahr found that participation in the homes of strong LDS families strengthened religious belief, they reported no statistically significant behavioral difference between the participants and the control group with respect to such behavior as making financial contributions and praying (though in terms of raw figures participants contributed more and prayed more often). Neither were there substantial differences regarding the use of tobacco and alcohol (items forbidden by the LDS Church's revelation known as the Word of Wisdom), though participants refrained more readily from the use of peyote. Students who stayed on the placement program longer, however, were more likely to follow the Word of Wisdom as adults. Participation in the program increased the likelihood that young Native Americans would marry in an LDS temple rather than obtain a civil marriage. The rate of temple marriage was seven times higher among participating LDS students than among those who did not participate. In general, however, the investigators concluded that participation in the placement program "had only a minor effect on the religiosity of the Indian students and that the longer time spent on placement made only a small difference."[55]

Chadwick, Albrecht, and Bahr also studied the program's impact on the relationship between children and their natural families. The two major reasons given by parents for sending their children to foster LDS homes were the same reasons the church maintained the program: to help them obtain a better education and to help them learn more about their LDS faith. The results, so far as the parents were concerned, were overwhelmingly positive: 82 percent reported a favorable effect on their families, and only 13 percent reported any negative consequences. Religiosity improved, education benefited the children, and younger siblings profited from the experiences of their older brothers and sisters. When asked if they would place their child in the program if they had it to do over again, 88 percent of the natural parents said yes.[56]

The impact on white foster families was another matter. In 20 percent of the cases, disagreement over how to handle a child led to strains in husband-wife relationships. Twenty-five percent of the children reported that it caused strains between them and their parents, and a third indicated that their relationships with their natural brothers and sisters suffered. Many parents agreed. Nevertheless, most foster families praised the program. The most frequently mentioned reason was the "enduring warm relationship that was developed with the Indian child." Many said they had grown personally, gained greater patience, and valued their exposure to a different culture. Eighty-five percent said they would do it again. In summary, said the investigators, "the foster family members experienced very real costs by taking in a placement child. For the majority of both parents and children, however, the overall experience was good."[57]

Despite the positive results and the strong approval of the Native American families involved in the program, criticism mounted. The censure was clearly related, at least in part, to continuing disapproval of foster homes in general, and it was certainly affected by the rising militance and pride among some Native Americans. Though boarding schools continued, by the 1970s an increasing number of children were being placed in foster homes or adopted. In 1974 an estimated 25 to 35 percent of all Native American children were in foster homes or other institutions, most of which did nothing to help preserve their native heritage.[58] Most of those who promoted these many programs were undoubtedly well-meaning, but Manuel P. Guerrero, a Native American attorney writing in 1979, expressed in particularly strong terms the feeling of many Native Americans concerning the cultural immorality of such a policy. "This wholesale separation of Indian children from their families ranks among the most tragic and destructive aspects of contemporary life," he declared. "State intrusion in parent-child relationships within the Indian culture impedes the ability of the tribe to perpetuate itself and is ultimately an unjustified coerced assimilation into the larger society."[59] Such feelings led to widespread criticism of any program designed to take children away from their families, whether state sponsored or not, including the LDS Indian placement program.

The long-standing concern for what was happening to children involved in such programs finally gave rise to the Indian Child Welfare Act of 1978. That year one hundred thousand children were involved in various placement programs.[60] Nearly twenty-seven hundred were enrolled in the LDS placement program.[61] The new law gave the tribes, rather than the federal government or the states, complete jurisdiction in child custody cases. It also provided that placement in foster homes could be done only with the consent of the parents. As originally proposed, the act would have made it nearly impossible for the ISPS to continue, but a major lobbying effort on the part of the church resulted in an amendment that protected the program.[62]

The cultural memory of the boarding school and the continuing problems associated with student placement in foster homes and adoption programs no doubt contributed to the fact that many Native Americans looked askance at the ISPS. The criticism took various forms. Some charged, especially in the early days of the program, that it was a thinly disguised tool for proselytizing. Others argued that the program left Native American students in a "potentially destructive cultural limbo,"[63] for it destroyed their identity with their native culture, caused deep emotional problems, and alienated children from their natural families. Still others charged Mormons with hypocrisy, claiming they would accept only the best and the brightest into the program.[64]

In 1972 enrollment in the LDS Indian placement program began to drop, and it was cut almost in half by the end of the 1970s. About 2,500 students were enrolled each year until 1984, when the program went into another fairly dramatic decline. By 1992 the program served only about 350 to 400 students, and by 1996 it had virtually come to an end.[65]

The phaseout was related to several factors. One was a 1972 decision by church leaders to withdraw missionaries as recruiting agents. Another was that in 1984 the church limited the program to children ages eleven to eighteen primarily because of the "greater accessibility of educational opportunities for younger children near their homes."[66] The program then dropped off one grade each year until it got to the point that only high school students, ninth grade and above, were accepted.[67] Finally, in 1992 the state of Utah began to enforce a rule that required nonresident students to pay out-of-state tuition that averaged about $2500 (depending on which school district was involved).[68] This prohibitive cost made it difficult for students from reservations outside the state to come to Utah. An exemption was made for the 1992–93 school year, and those already in the program were allowed to graduate from Utah schools.

The church gave some thought to expanding the program outside Utah, but the increasing accessibility of schools on or near the reservations and the apparent improvement in facilities and educational opportunities made such an effort seem counterproductive. Instead, officials at LDS Social Services hoped that strengthening the church's social programs on the reservations would help accomplish the religious and social goals inherent in the former placement program.

Thus ended a unique chapter in the story of Native Americans in the LDS Church. It began with the yearning for education of a sixteen-year-old Navajo girl, along with the desire of an LDS apostle and many local church members to help her and others like her. Adopted in 1954 as an official church program, it expanded to a peak in the 1970–71 school year with some five thousand students in ten western states and parts of Canada. No matter how successful the program may have been, however, it was vulnerable to criticism, for the previous history of boarding schools, foster homes, and adoption programs for Native Americans had created an atmosphere of mistrust of any such program operated and controlled by white society. To some it looked too much like simply another manifestation of traditional efforts to Americanize the Indians and eliminate their distinctive cultural heritage. Some white Mormons were no doubt completely unfamiliar with Native American culture and were therefore incognizant of what being taken away from their natural families for most of the year, several years in a row, might do to young children in the placement program. Others, however, were very much aware of the potential problems, and most foster families made commendable efforts to accomplish the educational and religious aims of the program and at the same time help their foster children maintain appreciation for their native heritage. In the end, the Indian student placement service performed exceptionally well in achieving the major goal it began with—to provide better educational opportunities for LDS Indian children. It also played an important role in enhancing their religious faith, though it contributed somewhat less to permanently changing religious behavior. In that regard, participants who did not return to the reservations seemed to fare better than those who did.[69] This is certainly not surprising, but it highlights the continuing social realities faced by Native Americans as they continued to live in two worlds at the same time. Nevertheless, educational opportunity on and near the reservations continued to improve, and this eventually made the placement program less essential. For this and other reasons, the church gradually phased out the program, and by 1996 it was a thing of the past. Meanwhile, LDS Social Services increased its efforts to help out in other ways on the reservations. Working in cooperation with the tribes and other agencies, this and other programs could help bring Native Americans even closer to fulfilling the dream of Chief George: "Then I can walk across the street and hold my head high, for I will meet you as an equal. I will not scorn you for your seeming gifts, and you will not receive me in pity."[70]

Notes

1. Chief Dan George, "My People, the Indians," *Dialogue* (winter 1985): 130–1.
2. For a general overview of American Indian policy and its

problems, see Alvin M. Josephy Jr., *The Indian Heritage of America* (New York: Knopf, 1968); Arrell Morgan Gibson, *The American Indian: Prehistory to the Present* (Lexington, Mass.: D. C. Heath, 1980); Francis Paul Prucha, *United States Indian Policy: Historical Essays* (Lincoln: University of Nebraska Press, 1981); and Francis Paul Prucha, *The Great Father: The United States Government and the American Indians,* 2 vols. (Lincoln: University of Nebraska Press, 1984).

    3. See Gibson, *American Indian,* 426–8.

    4. The "termination" policy was an effort to end all federal relations with the Indian tribes.

    5. See Manuel P. Guerrero, "Indian Child Welfare Act of 1978: A Response to the Threat to Indian Culture Caused by Foster and Adoptive Placements of Indian Children," *American Indian Law Review* 7 (1979): 51–77.

    6. At the end of the nineteenth century the federal government was appropriating nearly $2 million annually for the operation of 148 boarding schools and 225 day schools that accommodated more than twenty thousand Native American children. See Gibson, *American Indian,* 432.

    7. Ibid., 434.

    8. See Guerrero, "Indian Child Welfare Act," 52.

    9. This experience is recorded in Neil J. Birch, "Helen" (copy of unpublished manuscript in possession of David J. Whittaker), 16–8.

    10. Spencer W. Kimball, "The Lamanites Are Progressing," *Improvement Era* (June 1953): 435.

    11. Spencer W. Kimball, "The Lamanite" (address to BYU student body, Provo, Utah, 15 Apr. 1953), in *Speeches of the Year, 1952–53* (n.p., n.d.), 10–1.

    12. See Spencer W. Kimball, "U.S. Breaks Navajo Pact, Church Leader Charges," *Deseret News* (28 Nov. 1947): 76–8; and "Deaf Ears Meet Appeal of Indians for Schools," *Deseret News* (29 Nov. 1947): 120–4. See also Spencer W. Kimball, "The Navajo . . . His Predicament," parts 1 and 2, *Improvement Era* 51 (Feb. 1948): 210–2; (Apr. 1948): 252–3, 255.

13. Spencer W. Kimball, "U.S. Breaks Navajo pact," 6.

14. The summary of Helen's stay and the beginning of the program is based on chap. 3 of Clarence R. Bishop, "Indian Placement: A History of the Indian Student Placement Program of the Church of Jesus Christ of Latter-day Saints" (master's thesis, University of Utah, 1967); Birch, "Helen"; and Neil J. Birch, "Helen John: The Beginnings of Indian Placement," *Dialogue* (winter 1985): 119–29.

15. To conclude the story of Helen, she enrolled in the seventh grade. Although she did well in school, she dropped out two years later. Nevertheless, she eventually went to beauty school, received an operator's license, and worked in New Mexico. She also joined the LDS Church and went on a mission. She later married a returned missionary in the Salt Lake Temple, and the couple had four children. At age fifty she finally graduated from high school, having attended night school at South High in Salt Lake City. Three of her children filled missions, and all four were active in the church. So far as the goals of the placement program were concerned, Helen achieved them all.

16. See Bruce A. Chadwick and Stan L. Albrecht, "Mormons and Indians: Beliefs, Policies, Programs, and Practices," in *Contemporary Mormonism: Social Science Perspectives,* ed. Marie Cornwall, Tim B. Heaton, and Lawrence A. Young (Urbana: University of Illinois Press, 1994), 292.

17. See Bishop, "Indian Placement," 39, quoting from a 17 November 1966 interview with Miles Jensen.

18. Bishop, "Indian Placement," 42.

19. Letter from Stephen L Richards and J. Reuben Clark Jr., 10 August 1954, as cited in ibid., 43–4. It was sometimes a financial burden on the foster families, but in 1960 they received a little relief. Work by members of Utah's congressional delegation resulted in an Internal Revenue Service policy that allowed an income tax exemption of up to fifty dollars for each month a placement student was maintained in a home. See ibid., 75.

20. Initially the program was called the Boarding Care Program. The Relief Society developed means for evaluating both the students

who wanted to participate in the program and the potential foster families. Beginning in the fall of 1954, clear rules concerning placements were adopted: the students must be members of the LDS Church; they must each have a physical examination before being placed; each must be of school age (i.e., six years or older); legal consent must be obtained from the natural parents; and special consideration would be given to those who had "some knowledge of the English language." See "Regulations for Boarding Care of Indian Children," cited in Bishop, "Indian Placement," 48.

21. Some members of the church continued to take children into their homes independently of the church program. Because this could cause legal problems, in 1955 the church encouraged them to stop (see ibid., 54–5). Another problem arose because many students wanted to go home for Christmas vacation. This raised grave concerns about the dangers of travel (the church neither provided the transportation for such midyear travel nor had any way of supervising it) and increased homesickness and therefore a potentially higher dropout rate. As a result, in 1956 the Indian Student Placement Committee recommended that only those students who were willing to stay the entire school year should be encouraged to return to the program.

22. See Bishop, "Indian Placement," 61–2. Caseworkers were to be sure that both parents and students were members of the church and that the children were participating with the full consent of their parents. Robert Gottlieb and Peter Wiley, in their book *America's Saints: The Rise of Mormon Power* (New York: Putnam's, 1984), refer to this as a promise to stop using the program for proselytizing purposes, though the agreement as reported by Bishop was not quite that (see p. 164). Gottlieb and Wiley also say that the promise was "a meaningless concession given the reasons for starting the program in the first place and the nature of Mormon family life, with its constant emphasis on the teaching of correct doctrine" (ibid.). Again, they probably exaggerate if they are implying that the reasons for starting the program included proselytizing. The program did, however, clearly include teaching the gospel, though that was confined to

church members. There is no evidence that the original intent of the program was missionary related. At a follow-up meeting in Kanab a year later, a much more cooperative spirit pervaded, and there was little opposition voiced to the program.

23. Kay H. Cox, for example, writes of the father of one of her foster sons, who, "being a Church member in name only, . . . didn't understand Primary graduation or various Church achievements, but he accepted gratefully the chances his children now had that he had missed" (Kay H. Cox, *Without Reservation* [Salt Lake City: Bookcraft, 1980], 35).

24. Jimmy H. Benally, interview by Odessa Neaman, transcript, 18 July 1990, LDS Native American Oral History Project, Charles Redd Center for Western Studies, Brigham Young University, 7.

25. These improvements are outlined in chapters 4–6 of Bishop, "Indian Placement." One important change came in 1964, when the Indian placement program was given its own director who reported directly to the church's Committee on Indian Relationships, chaired by Spencer W. Kimball. The first director was Clarence R. Bishop.

26. See ibid., 77–8.

27. At one point, students from Oklahoma were being placed with Mormon families in Denver, Colorado, and some from North Carolina were being placed in Atlanta, Georgia. See David A. Albrecht, interview by author, tape recording, Sandy, Utah, 3 September 1992.

28. See Bishop, "Indian Placement," 97, for a listing.

29. Kay H. Cox makes an interesting observation on the evolution of this process: "It might be well to note that in the early days of the placement program, foster parents were introduced to a small group of students and given information about each child. The parents were then taken aside and asked, 'Which child is yours?'

"Whether by inspiration or personal commitment, when these choices were made, they seemed to be more permanent. Those with Ph.D.'s felt this was such an unprofessional method that it was dropped in favor of caseworkers' choosing and placing. I suppose it is more professionally regimented, but inspiration and personal commitment suffer, and with them, many placements" (Cox, *Without Reservation*, 26).

30. Audrey Boone, interview by Malcolm T. Pappan, transcript, 6 April and 11 April 1990, LDS Native American Oral History Project, Charles Redd Center for Western Studies, Brigham Young University, 2.

31. As she was preparing to graduate from high school in 1965, Quintero reported: "I can truthfully say it was worth it—all the tears and sacrificing from everyone involved have been well worth it. . . . If I could pray for anything I would like, it would be that more Indian children could be given those same opportunities that I have been blessed with" (Vanta Quintero, "My Happiest Year," *Relief Society Magazine* 52 [Oct. 1965]: 735).

32. Edouardo Zondajas, interview by Malcolm T. Pappan, transcript, 7 April 1990, LDS Native American Oral History Project, Charles Redd Center for Western Studies, Brigham Young University, 3–4.

33. See ibid. The program's value, he said, was "getting a sense of family life." He felt that he had a good upbringing in his own family, but in the placement program he saw a different kind of structure. "There is one family in particular that I have patterned my family after," he said. "I'd like to think that I do some of the same things that this family did. I guess that's probably the most positive aspect of the Placement Program. I was able to be involved in the type of family setting that I want to pattern my own family after" (7).

34. Ibid., 8.

35. See Cox, *Without Reservation*, 1.

36. See ibid., 4.

37. Ibid., 117.

38. Emery Bowman, interview by Deborah Lewis, transcript, 27 January 1990, LDS Native American Oral History Project, Charles Redd Center for Western Studies, Brigham Young University, 13.

39. James Lee Dandy, interview by Jessie L. Embry, transcript, 2 October 1990, LDS Native American Oral History Project, Charles Redd Center for Western Studies, Brigham Young University, 10–1.

40. Grant Hardy Taylor, "A Comparative Study of Former LDS Placement and Non-Placement Students at Brigham Young University" (Ph.D. dissertation, Brigham Young University, 1981), 14. These studies are more fully summarized by Taylor in earlier pages. The opinion surveys he looked at included LeRoi Gardner Barclay Jr., Gary L. Wade, and Arland L. Welker, "A Study of Graduates of the Indian Student Placement Program of the Church of Jesus Christ of Latter-day Saints" (master's project, University of Utah, 1972); G. T. Lindquist, "The Indian Student Placement Program as a Means of Increasing the Education of Children of Selected Indian Families" (master's thesis, Utah State University, 1970); Robert E. Leach, "Interstate Compact Study Showing Positive Parental Attitudes toward LDS Social Services' Indian Student Placement Services" (1977); and Wasatch Opinion Research Corporation, "Indian Student Placement Service Evaluation: Opinion Survey Phase I" (1979). Those that he classified as "evaluative" included Clarence R. Bishop, "An Evaluation of the Scholastic Achievement of Selected Indian Students Attending Elementary Schools in Utah" (master's thesis, Brigham Young University, 1960); B. P. Cundick, Linda Willson, and Douglas K. Gottfredson, "Changes in Scholastic Achievement and Intelligence of Indian Children Enrolled in a Foster Placement Program," *Developmental Psychology* 10 (1974): 815–20; Bruce H. Higley and Larry L. Adams, "A Study of American Indian Students at Brigham Young University" (1972); George P. Lee, "A Comparative Study of Activities and Opinions of Navajo High School Graduates among Four Selected School Models" (Ph.D. diss., Brigham Young University, 1975); Robert Dean Smith, "Relationships between Foster Home Placement and Later Acculturation Patters of Selected American Indians" (master's thesis, Utah State University, 1968); and Linda O. Willson, "Changes in Scholastic Achievement and Intelligence of Indian Children Enrolled in a Foster Placement Program" (master's thesis, Brigham Young University, 1973).

41. See Howard Rainer, "An Analysis of Attitudes Navajo Community Leaders Have toward a Religion Sponsored Program Based upon Membership of That Faith and Amount of Information At-

tained" (master's thesis, Brigham Young University, 1976). For a more recent study, based on interviews with former participants of the placement program, see Tona J. Hangen, "A Place to Call Home: Studying the Indian Placement Program," *Dialogue* (spring 1997): 53–69.

42. See Taylor's summary of Higley and Adams, "American Indian Students," in his "Comparative Study," 11–2.

43. See Martin D. Topper, "Mormon Placement: The Effects of Missionary Foster Families on Navajo Adolescents," *Ethos* 7 (summer 1979): 142–60; and Bruce A. Chadwick, Stan L. Albrecht, and Howard M. Bahr, "Evaluation of an Indian Student Placement Program," *Social Casework* 67 (Nov. 1968), 516.

44. See Dorothy Jensen Schimmelpfennig, "A Study of Cross-Cultural Problems in the L.D.S. Indian Student Placement Program in Davis County" (Ph.D. diss., University of Utah, 1971), 81.

45. See Taylor, "Comparative Study," 43–59.

46. See Chadwick, Albrecht, and Bahr, "Evaluation," 515–24; and Chadwick and Albrecht, "Mormons and Indians," 287–309.

47. See Chadwick, Albrecht, and Bahr, "Evaluation," 517; and Chadwick and Albrecht, "Mormons and Indians," 295.

48. See Chadwick and Albrecht, "Mormons and Indians," 295.

49. Chadwick, Albrecht, and Bahr, "Evaluation," 518, table 2.

50. See ibid., 518–9; and Chadwick and Albrecht, "Mormons and Indians," 296–8.

51. Chadwick and Albrecht, "Mormons and Indians," 298.

52. See Chadwick, Albrecht, and Bahr, "Evaluation," 519–20; and Chadwick and Albrecht, "Mormons and Indians," 298–300.

53. See Chadwick and Albrecht, "Mormons and Indians," 302.

54. Ibid., 303. In their earlier article, these same investigators noted that two-thirds of the participants believed that their placement experience actually made them feel closer to their Native American heritage than they would have been without it. There was no indication, they said, that the program itself was the cause of a significant decline in identification with that heritage. See Chadwick, Albrecht, and Bahr, "Evaluation," 521.

55. Chadwick and Albrecht, "Mormons and Indians," 308.

56. See Chadwick, Albrecht, and Bahr, "Evaluation," 523.

57. Ibid., 524.

58. See Guerrero, "Indian Child Welfare Act," 53. For a nice summary of various off-reservation educational programs for Native Americans in the 1960s, see chap. 1 of Bishop, "Indian Placement."

59. Guerrero, "Indian Child Welfare Act," 53.

60. See Coleen Keane, "'Where Have All the Children Gone?' Controversy over Native Child Placement by Mormon Church," *Wassaja* 9 (Sept./Oct. 1982): 13.

61. See Taylor, "Comparative Study," appendix, 90.

62. Lobbyists included the Washington law firm of Wilkinson, Cragun, and Barker; Utah's congressional representative Gunn McKay; David A. Albrecht, the director of the LDS Social Services Agency in Washington, D.C.; and George P. Lee (see Albrecht, interview; and Gottlieb and Wiley, *America's Saints,* 166). Lee, thirty-five years old, was a full-blooded Navajo and the son of a medicine man. He had gone through the placement program as a youth, received a doctorate in education from BYU, and had become president of a small church college in Arizona. In 1975 he became a General Authority of the LDS Church when he was sustained as a member of the First Quorum of the Seventy. He had the ability to plead eloquently for his people before both Mormons and non-Mormons. The testimony of such a Native American in favor of the amendment was no doubt most persuasive.

63. Gottlieb and Wiley, *America's Saints,* 165.

64. These and other criticisms are summarized briefly in Gottlieb and Wiley, *America's Saints,* 164–5.

65. The few remaining students, who stayed in the program so they could graduate from high school, included ten to fifteen in Utah, fifteen to twenty in Idaho, and three or four in Arizona (see Albrecht, interview); Albrecht, telephone interview by author, 7 Sept. 1996).

66. See "LDS Alter Indian Policy," *Deseret News* (9 Mar. 1984): B–1.

67. See David A. Albrecht, "A Conversation about Changes in

the Indian Student Placement Service," *Ensign* (Oct. 1985): 76; Albrecht, interview.

68. This resulted from an interesting lawsuit brought against the Washington County School District in 1990 by Raindancer Youth Services, Inc. This organization brought Native American students from New Mexico and Arizona to St. George, where they received free public education just as the students on the LDS placement program did. But the schools became overcrowded, and in 1990 school officials said they would not provide any more such education unless each student paid the required out-of-state tuition. Raindancer then brought suit, showing that 450 students in the LDS program throughout Utah and another 100 students in a boarding school program in Sevier County were receiving free education. Raindancer demanded equal treatment. In a settlement worked out in 1992, the church agreed not to bring in any more out-of-state students. As a result of the settlement, it was also anticipated that boarding school programs in Sevier and San Juan Counties would close. See Marrianne Funk, "Settlement May Spell End of Two Programs," *Deseret News* (30 Sept. 1992): B–1, 2.

69. David A. Albrecht recalled that one administrator noted that, in general, those who remained off the reservation retained LDS religious commitment and lifestyles better than those who did not (telephone interview by author, 8 Sept. 1996).

70. George, "My People, the Indians," 131.

CHAPTER 5

MORMON INTRUDERS IN TONGA: THE PASSPORT ACT OF 1922

R. Lanier Britsch

On 29 June 1922 the Legislative Assembly in the island kingdom of Tonga enacted a law that prohibited all members of the Church of Jesus Christ of Latter-day Saints from entering that country.[1] This event occurred after considerable discussion and debate among governmental officials in Tonga, Fiji, Great Britain, and the United States. This study reviews the Latter-day Saint exclusion issue as it relates to the historical development of Christianity in Tonga, including sectarian relationships and government involvement in ecclesiastical affairs, the official attitude of the U.S. government regarding the Latter-day Saints and polygamy, and the United Kingdom's official actions toward the Latter-day Saints.

A Prevailing Intolerance

LDS Church history provides many examples of the relationship of governments to a minority religious organization,

R. Lanier Britsch is professor of history at Brigham Young University and former director of the university's David M. Kennedy Center for International Studies.

examples that have invariably caused crisis situations in the Mormon movement.[2] The most serious of these crises occurred between 1882, when the first Edmunds Act outlawing polygamy was passed, and the outbreak of World War I. As before, the church during this period was the recipient of much abuse. Even LDS Church leaders' banning of polygamy did little at first to reduce public hostility. The effects of the polygamy problem went beyond the bounds of the United States and extended into Great Britain[3] and her protectorates. Although the attitude of most Americans toward the Latter-day Saints and their beliefs mellowed after the outbreak of World War I, intolerance prevailed elsewhere. At the conclusion of World War I, for example, the LDS Church had considerable difficulty obtaining permission from the British Foreign and Home Offices for its missionaries to enter Great Britain. Through pressure from the U.S. State Department, the problem was finally resolved in England in June 1920,[4] but it remained a sensitive issue in Australia, New Zealand, and Tonga.

To understand the Tongan government's position against the Mormons, it is necessary to know the background of Tonga's religious history. "The Church history of Tonga," wrote Charles W. Forman, "has been the most turbulent of all the Pacific Islands."[5] Yet Tonga has made greater attempts to preserve unity than any other island territory. Perhaps it was the desire to preserve unity at one time and to restore it at another that moved the government to take action to stop the growing influence of the Latter-day Saints.

The first successful Christian mission to Tonga was under Wesleyan Methodist leadership. After two abortive attempts to gain converts, the first by the London Missionary Society (LMS) in 1797 and the second by Walter Lawry in 1822, John Thomas and John Hutchison finally succeeded in an effort that began in 1826. By 1829 seven converts had been baptized, and on 7 August 1831[6] Chief Tāufaʻāhau of Haʻapai submitted to baptism, taking the Christian name George and becoming a close ally of the missionaries. Tonga was nominally Christianized by the 1840s.[7]

Even before Chief Tāufaʻāhau was baptized, an important decision had been made concerning missionary jurisdiction in Tonga and other nearby areas. To prevent competition between the LMS, which was operating in the area, and the Wesleyan Missionary Society, representatives of the two groups met in 1830 and arrived at an agreement.[8] Samoa, they decided, would henceforth be an LMS area, while Tonga and Fiji would be the responsibility of the Wesleyans. The religious groups that arrived later—first the Roman Catholics and then the Seventh-day Adventists, Anglicans, and Latter-day Saints—were considered intruders.

Political matters led to Tāufaʻāhau's becoming the paramount chief, or *Tuʻi Kanokupolu*, in 1845, then king of the Vavaʻu group, and finally, after difficult times that included three wars, the last of which ended in 1852, king of the whole of Tonga. He took the title King George Tupou (posthumously known as Tupou I) and reigned until his death in 1893.

The Christianization of Tonga was a disruptive force from the beginning, affecting virtually all aspects of life. The old sociopolitical structure was based on patterns of power that were undermined by the acceptance of the new religion, leaving chiefs worried and uncertain about the extent of their authority. King George recognized these problems early in his reign; in fact, in 1838, before he became king of Tonga, he issued a legal code designed to solve them. His efforts to clarify and improve Tonga's legal structure continued through several stages, culminating in 1862 with a more extensive and clearly written code. The code contained a clause that emancipated the people, who virtually had been the slaves of the chiefs. It also set up a parliament (the Legislative Assembly) consisting of (1) the cabinet ministers, (2) seven nobles who were elected by their hereditary peers, and (3) seven representatives of the common people. Missionary influence was evident throughout the code: a recently arrived missionary named Shirley W. Baker had been the king's principal adviser while the document was being drafted.

In November 1875 a constitution was promulgated. The result of considerable discussion among the king, leading government officials, and missionaries, particularly Shirley Baker,[9] it was an important and progressive document. But Article V, which granted complete freedom of religion and religious toleration, became a point of contention and misunderstanding within the dominant Wesleyan Church and also among various denominations and church divisions.

The most painful discord began in January 1885, when ties with the Wesleyan Conference in Sydney were broken and the *Siasi Uesiliana Tau'atāina 'o Tonga,* the Free Wesleyan Church of Tonga (Free Church of Tonga), was established.[10] Historian Elizabeth Wood Ellem explains the affair:

> The converts of the Wesleyan Mission between 1826 and 1885 were supporters of the Tu'i Kanokupolu (the title that has since become synonymous with sovereign), just as the converts to Catholicism were the supporters of the Tu'i Tonga, rival of the Tu'i Kanokupolu. After the death of the last Tu'i Tonga and the withdrawal of foreign funds from the Wesleyan Mission, the Tu'i Kanokupolu King George Tupou (posthumously known as Tupou I) sought to establish himself as head of the church, just as he had established himself as head of the state. Tupou I's request to the parent church in Australia for a greater degree of independence was acceded to, except in one particular: the parent church would not agree to Tupou selecting and appointing the President of the Conference of the newly independent

branch of the Wesleyan Church of Australasia. In 1885, therefore, Tupou broke from the parent church completely, and founded his own church . . . commonly known as the Free Church of Tonga.[11]

During his later years, George Tupou I came increasingly under the influence of Shirley Baker, who had been appointed prime minister and who had held several other important offices. Before the events of the mid-1880s, Baker had a falling-out with his Wesleyan colleagues in Tonga and Sydney. He argued that Tongan moneys were being sent out of the country, that the king was thus losing control of these moneys, and that the British were planning to use the Wesleyan Church as a means of taking possession of Tonga.[12]

The Reverend Jabez Bunting Watkin (born in Lifuka, Ha'apai), a longtime friend of Baker and a coworker in the Wesleyan Church, became president of the Free Church of Tonga. He held that position until 1924, when at age eighty-seven he was discharged by Queen Sālote.[13] By that time, what had started as the king's church had come under the influence of "chiefs of intermediate rank," most of whom were opposed to the queen. As a result, the royal house had difficulty controlling the church it had founded.[14]

The ecclesiastical break in 1885 brought bitter feelings. The king wanted all Tongans to leave the Wesleyan congregation and to show their loyalty to him by joining the new church. But religious convictions were strong, and a small but vocal minority refused to make the move. Persecution finally persuaded the loyal Wesleyans to join the Free Church, but some individuals in high positions remained faithful to the old church. Baker deprived eleven notables of their titles and dismissed them from office.[15]

By September 1885 matters had calmed down, but the relative peace was broken when in 1887 a group of escaped prisoners attempted to assassinate Baker. The attempt failed, but the attack was blamed on the Wesleyan Church. J. Egan Moulton, head of the Wesleyan Church, described the results: "After weeks of suffering—a veritable reign of terror, during which churches and colleges were closed—all who remained faithful to the Wesleyan Church in Tonga, Ha'apai, and Vava'u were exiled to Fiji. Ninety noble souls."[16] Basil Thompson recorded that two hundred people were shipped out of the country.[17] Among the exiles was the daughter of the king.

This time Baker had gone too far. On 5 July 1890 the British high commissioner for the western Pacific stepped in and ordered him off the islands. Six days later the new premier granted amnesty for acts of conscience committed by the Fiji exiles and others during the period of struggle.[18]

Only a year and ten days after Baker was deported, Latter-day Saint missionaries Brigham Smoot and Alva J. Butler arrived at Tongatapu. They immediately arranged for an interview with the aging Tongan king, George Tupou I, who "gave them permission to preach to the people." His people, King George said, were "free to join whichever church suited them best." However, he quickly changed his mind. On the same day that the Mormons visited the king, representatives of both the Free Church of Tonga and the Wesleyan Church paid the king a special visit and reportedly asked him to "banish the Mormons."[19] Within two weeks an order was issued to deport the two missionaries.

Why the missionaries were allowed to stay in the country for three or four months before the order was rescinded is not clear. It may have been because of the protests of the American vice-consul at Apia, Samoa, who demanded that the LDS missionaries be permitted to proselytize just as the other missionaries had been allowed to do. For the time being this ended the conflict between the Latter-day Saints, the Tongan government, and the two opposing sects. Other LDS missionaries arrived, and an active proselytizing effort ensued. Progress was so slow, however, that the mission was closed six years later, in 1897. There had been only sixteen baptisms.[20]

Ten years later, in 1907, LDS missionaries returned to Tonga. This second effort proved more fruitful than the first, and soon additional missionaries were assigned to Tonga. In 1916 Willard L. Smith, a missionary serving with his wife, Jenny, in Samoa, was called to preside over the newly organized Tongan Mission. Although missionary numbers in Tonga were not large (only eight to twelve) during Smith's four-year tenure, the mission there saw modest success. By the time of his departure in 1920, 820 Tongans had been baptized into the church.

From the moment Smith began his new assignment in 1916, he began asking LDS Church authorities in Salt Lake City to send more missionaries. His requests were not easily met, however, because the British government refused to issue the necessary visas.[21] Initially the cause was World War I and the complications it provoked, but when the war ended in November 1918, the British continued to exclude LDS missionaries from Tonga. Senator Reed Smoot, a member of the LDS Church's Quorum of the Twelve Apostles, protested to the U.S. Department of State about the ban. The State Department forwarded its concurring view to London, and the issue was finally resolved in June 1920, when Great Britain agreed once again to grant visas to LDS missionaries.[22] In the meantime, Latter-day Saints destined for Tonga had found it possible to enter that land through Vava'u via American Samoa.[23] When Willard Smith and his wife left Tonga in the spring of 1920, his replacement, M. Vernon Coombs of Canada, because he was a resident of a British Commonwealth country, had no difficulty obtaining a permanent visa.

One of the reasons Smith wanted more missionaries was

because of his, and later Coombs's, commitment to education as a means of helping the people. It was also a productive means of proselytizing. The first LDS missionaries in Tonga had organized several elementary schools, and further educational efforts were begun when missionary work recommenced in 1907. By 1920 two schoolhouses had been constructed, but they only partially represented the total educational effort of the church. Each pair of elders taught a school in the village where they were stationed. Coombs considered the schools "the very life of our missionary endeavor," and by the end of 1921, formal government approval for the schools had been obtained.[24]

Almost concurrently with their educational successes, however, came trouble. Antagonism against the Latter-day Saints flared in the Ha'apai group during September 1921, when the local officials, using the pretext of an influenza epidemic, denied them the right to hold a conference. The decision was clearly an act of religious discrimination: the Wesleyans and the Free Church of Tonga had been allowed to hold meetings even larger than the LDS conference at the very time the latter had been scheduled.[25] At the same time, in late 1921, the government rejected an application to lease property[26] on which a mission house at Lifuka, Ha'apai, was to be constructed. When Coombs asked Prince Tungī, minister of lands, for an explanation, he was informed that the government was considering a proposal to exclude Latter-day Saints from entering Tonga. Until that matter was resolved, the government would grant no more leases to the LDS Church.[27]

Unknown to the LDS missionaries, excluding Latter-day Saints from Tonga had first been considered in international circles during the fall of 1919—two years before the missionaries suspected anything—when Laverne Clarke, the wife of an LDS missionary in Tonga, applied for an entry visa.[28] When her application reached Tonga, it was rejected by officials who explained to the British consul and agent Islay McOwan that "it is not considered advisable to allow any more members of the Mormon Church to come to Tonga." Moreover, explained Premier Tuʻi Vakanō, when the seven missionaries already in Tonga left, no replacements would be allowed. Two denominations, he believed, were all that were needed.[29]

McOwan found the government's proposed action unacceptable. Unless better reasons were forthcoming, McOwan told Tuʻi Vakanō, he could not defend such a course to the British high commissioner, the official with final authority over passports. Tuʻi Vakanō confessed that he was not able to bring any specific charge against the Latter-day Saints, but he repeated rumors that LDS missionaries in England were exporting "numbers of young girls to . . . America." Besides, he noted, "other civilized nations" were not favorably inclined toward the Mormons.[30]

Late in February 1920 the Tongan government repealed its decision about Laverne Clarke, stating that she could now enter Tonga. Her husband's residence in Tonga was the expressed reason for allowing one last Mormon to enter the country. But considerable time passed before Mrs. Clarke's application was formally approved by London,[31] because First Viscount Alfred Milner, secretary of state for the British colonies, delayed action until the entire Mormon visa question was resolved. The government reached a decision in June 1920, but Milner did not grant Mrs. Clarke's request until August. By then her husband's remaining term in Tonga was so short that she did not join him there.[32]

The Exclusion Law of 1922

It seems strange that even though the British government had decided to allow LDS missionaries into the United Kingdom, this decision was not applied to Tonga. Instead, the British

Foreign Office instructed the British Passport Control Office in New York not to grant visas to LDS missionaries bound for Tonga. Word of this decision did not reach Tonga until late February 1921, but by then it was obvious to Tuʻi Vakanō and his cabinet that the British action was ineffective. Determined missionaries were avoiding the New York Passport Control Office and entering Tonga from Canada, Fiji, and American Samoa. To close these gaps, Tongan authorities proposed to handle the problem themselves. Tuʻi Vakanō requested British permission to pass a law banning LDS missionaries as undesirable immigrants. "They can hardly be looked on as Christians, and therefore religious liberty would not apply to them," he explained.[33] The British government seemed to agree. As Winston Churchill, the colonial secretary, expressed: "After consultation with His Majesty's Ambassador at Washington, the Secretary of State for Foreign Affairs considers that no objections are likely to be raised by the United States Government to the exclusion of these missionaries from Tonga, on the understanding that the contemplated legislation is to be confined to the exclusion of those who may wish to enter in the future and not to the expulsion of those who already reside in the islands."[34]

With that encouragement, Tongan leaders acted quickly. On 29 June 1922 the Legislative Assembly enacted legislation prohibiting Latter-day Saints from entering Tonga, imposing a £100 fine, deportation, or both on violators. Latter-day Saints already in Tonga, however, would be allowed to remain there.[35] The new law went into effect on 18 July, but fortunately for the LDS mission, another missionary couple, Lawrence Leavitt and his wife, Mary, arrived just before the deadline. They were the last LDS missionaries to enter the country for more than two years.

The exclusion law naturally caused serious problems for the LDS Church. Because church leaders call laymen as full-time "ministers of the gospel" for a relatively short time and keep a cycle of replacements coming, the breaking of that cycle threatened to quickly eliminate the mission. During the two years following the enactment of the law, Coombs saw his mission staff dwindle to a total of five foreign (that is, American and Canadian) missionaries. Had he not called Tongans to act as missionaries, conversions to the church would have ceased. Two American missionaries had died of typhoid fever at Pangai, several others had left because of elephantiasis, one departed because of a hernia, and another left because he was "a complete physical wreck." Still others left because of financial or domestic complications at home.[36]

The steady decline of the missionary force was a strain on Coombs and the Tongan members. As the elders finished their missions and departed, the schools, which had been conducted at virtually every location where missionaries lived, were consolidated, until by early 1924 only one school remained open in each island group. There were other problems as well. On Tongatapu, Coombs was responsible for nine branches or congregations. Travel between these units was usually by horseback, or, for Mrs. Coombs, in a horse-drawn carriage. Travel between the Tongan islands was most commonly by small sailboats. However, as word spread of the legal status of the Latter-day Saints, missionaries found it virtually impossible to hire boats and boatmen. Coombs vividly described the growing persecution of the Latter-day Saints: "We have been stoned out of houses, in Ha'apai the natives will absolutely not allow us to ride in their boats. In Vava'u the natives politely requested us to leave their houses, and the natives everywhere have informed us that they are strictly forbidden to converse with a Mormon missionary."[37]

The open criticism and public cursing of missionaries and their work were heaviest during the summer of 1923. Discouraged, Coombs complained to LDS Church president Heber J.

Grant that only two church members in Haʻapai had faith
strong enough to stand any test. Furthermore, Coombs doubted
there were more than thirty members with strong faith among
the thousand members in the mission.[38] This frankness did not
serve Coombs's interests, for in November 1923 Grant suggested the possibility of closing the Tongan mission and bringing everyone home. Before Coombs could reply, other troubles
arose and were reported to Salt Lake City.

Among Coombs's most serious concerns during the early
part of 1924 was moral laxity among members. Several incidents of sexual immorality were reported far and wide and
greatly hindered the Mormon cause. A severe blow came when
a Tongan missionary couple had disagreements and the wife
"slept several nights with another young man."[39] Coombs had
counted this pair among his select thirty faithful.

The missionaries did not criticize the Tongans individually,
but they did believe that certain cultural traits created problems. They found the Tongans "emotional and passionate" and
difficult to influence with "cold reason and hard fact." "They
are all good people," Coombs wrote to the First Presidency,
"and take very active parts, observe the tithing law, observe the
Word of Wisdom [health law], and contribute liberally to our
various functions, but simply cannot leave the opposite sex
alone."[40]

Efforts to Repeal a Discriminatory Law

Why the exclusion law was passed was at first a mystery to
LDS Church members and missionaries alike. Through careful
probing, Coombs pieced together most of the Legislative Assembly debate several months before he succeeded in acquiring
a transcript of the proceedings. According to his informants,
the Latter-day Saints were accused of teaching and practicing

polygamy, teaching the people to be disobedient and disrespect-
ful to government authorities, claiming to belong to *the* church
of Jesus Christ, claiming to be saints, and being rude. As the
months passed, the list of accusations grew.[41]

The transcript of the debate, which Coombs finally acquired in December 1923, revealed that polygamy was the
main issue. But there were others: "Disturbances are caused by
this church," and "Many of their religious doctrines clash with
the doctrines of other churches which have been brought to
Tonga."[42] Coombs never could discover why the polygamy issue was raised in Tonga when the practice, which had been
abandoned by the church in 1890, had never been taught in the
islands. From discussions with friends in the expatriate community, he tentatively concluded that outside antagonists—
that is, non-Tongan ministers of the Wesleyan Church and the
Free Church of Tonga—were the source of the problem.

Coombs concluded that there were only three possible approaches to getting the law repealed.[43] One, which proved
fruitless, was to pressure the British high commissioner to
countermand the law, but he did not have authority to veto
Tongan legislation. Another tactic was to persuade the Legislative Assembly that the law was unconstitutional or was based
on false information. A third approach, in which Coombs did
not have much confidence because he was not aware of the efforts being made in this avenue, was through the U.S. State
Department.

The legislative approach was slow and difficult. Paperwork
was time consuming, and Coombs was sure he suffered an un-
fair disadvantage. "To make matters worse," he observed in
February 1923, "the native members of the Legislative Assembly are nearly all the local pastors in their respective village, of
the Free Church of Tonga and the Wesleyan Church. These
Pastor-Legislators know that their cause is lost if they give us an

open deal; they close in on us and will sit tight until outside pressure compels them to alter their movements."[44]

Ironically, serious problems were brewing between the four thousand members of the Wesleyan Church and the seventeen thousand who followed the Free Church of Tonga. According to Coombs, these problems arose in late 1922 when the young Queen Sālote, at that time in New Zealand, was informed that the Reverend J. B. Watkin, the head of the Free Church of Tonga, had refused to reveal how the annual monetary collection was expended. "Does the Free Church belong to you or me?" the queen asked Watkin.[45]

As early as 3 November 1922 Coombs was aware of the problems brewing between the two factions. He could see no outcome more likely for the two groups, considering their similar interests, than unification. This was especially probable because Queen Sālote, the nominal head of the Free Church of Tonga, was greatly influenced by her husband, Prince Uiliami Tungī, a Wesleyan. More important was their united objective of solidifying their joint rule of Tonga. But unification took some time to accomplish. In an effort to influence her people to unite, Queen Sālote made a trip to the northern islands. When she left in early December 1923, she instructed Watkin not to hold the annual monetary collection. However, he incurred her wrath by making the collection anyway, and matters became increasing heated until April 1924, when Queen Sālote discharged Watkin from his post.[46] Serious clashes between Wesleyans and members of the Free Church led to physical violence. According to Coombs, the immediate result for many Tongans was a lack of confidence in those two sects and greater interest in the Mormons.

In the meantime, developments outside Tonga raised no small stir. Unknown to Coombs, considerable attention was being paid to the exclusion law in Washington, D.C., London, Suva, and Apia. Also unknown to Coombs, British consul Islay McOwan was being informed of these developments as they took place outside Tonga. As the complexion of the British position toward the LDS Church changed, McOwan assumed a more friendly attitude toward the Latter-day Saints.

At this point it is helpful to trace the sequence of events relating to the Mormon exclusion issue as they occurred in the international diplomatic sphere after the exclusion law was passed on 29 June 1922.

On 9 August 1922 Quincy F. Roberts, U.S. vice-consul in Apia, Samoa, sent a telegram to Secretary of State Charles Evans Hughes, informing him of the passage of the discriminatory law in Tonga. Roberts had been informed of these events by John Q. Adams, LDS mission president in Samoa. Hughes forwarded a copy of Roberts's telegram to Senator Reed Smoot, who informed LDS Church president Heber J. Grant of the exclusion law.

Meanwhile, Roberts had acted on the matter without instructions from Washington. On 28 August 1922 he sent letters of protest to the prime minister of Tonga, to British high commissioner Cecil Hunter Rodwell, and to McOwan in Tonga. He complained of prejudice; reminded the concerned parties of the U.S.-Tonga Treaty of 1900, which allowed missionaries of all faiths into the country; and defended the "good morals" of the Latter-day Saints Roberts had known in Samoa. He asked Rodwell and McOwan to use their influence to change the Tongan law,[47] but the high commissioner said he did not "feel justified in interfering with the Tongan Government in the matter."[48]

In late 1922 President Grant asked Senator Smoot to take further action. When Smoot queried Secretary Hughes on the matter, Hughes responded by telegraphing Roberts in Apia and instructing him to submit an official protest to the Tongan government. Roberts did as he was instructed.[49]

In February 1923 President Grant once again encouraged Smoot to do what he could to solve the problem and sent him a letter from Coombs describing the problems in Tonga. Smoot forwarded the letter to Hughes and pressed him to use the "good offices of the State Department" to "induce the Kingdom of Tonga to repeal the Tongan Passport Act of 1922." Three days later, on 13 March 1923, Hughes told Smoot that he had telegraphed Roberts in Apia and was waiting for a telegraphic report.[50] Within a week Roberts reported that he not only had protested the exclusion law by first mail after becoming aware of the problem, but also had again complained to the Tongan government according to the instructions he received on 27 November 1922. On 14 February 1923 he had once again requested that the premier of Tonga permit Latter-day Saints to enter the kingdom. When he received no reply, Roberts requested an answer by telegraph, but he received an evasive response. It is apparent that Quincy Roberts was diligent in pursuing the exclusion issue with the Tongan government.

The Tide Begins to Turn

On 26 March 1923 a frustrated Hughes entreated George Harvey, the U.S. ambassador in London, "to endeavor to obtain a favorable decision." When Smoot learned of this action, he wrote to Ambassador Harvey with a personal plea for help. Harvey informed Lord Curzon, the secretary of state for foreign affairs, concerning the status of Latter-day Saints in Tonga and asked that any discrimination against them because of their faith be removed.[51] In response, the next dispatch from the British colonial office to the high commissioner in Suva con-

tained the duke of Devonshire's observation that Churchill's
instructions on the matter "had reference only to Mormon
Missionaries" and that the provisions of the Passport Act of
1922 "relate to Mormons generally."[52] The duke, secretary of
state for the colonies, had uncovered a flaw in the act that
would allow Britain to reconsider its actions without embar-
rassment. McOwan appears to have accepted the duke's observation as a cue to act in a friendly manner toward the Latter-day
Saints in Tonga.

Coombs knew nothing of this high-level string pulling, but
on 25 June 1923 he had his first helpful encounter with
McOwan. Coombs had previously sought McOwan's assistance
on the exclusion matter but had received a cool response. On
this occasion two things appeared to Coombs to have brought a
change in McOwan's attitude: Coombs carried a British Commonwealth passport, and Coombs convinced McOwan that
Latter-day Saints were not polygamists. Coombs must have
driven his points home effectively, for at the end of the meeting
McOwan offered to sponsor petitions to repeal the exclusion
law in the Legislative Assembly and pass on such petitions to
the British high commissioner in Suva.[53] But McOwan did not
let the matter rest there. He also invited Coombs to play golf
with him (an act that publicly announced McOwan's approval
of Coombs), encouraged other Europeans to sign Coombs's petitions, and invited Coombs and his wife, LaVera, to be guests
of honor at a special dance where the queen and her consort
were in attendance.[54]

Coombs became convinced that petitions were the best approach to the problem. For many months he worked on his case,
enlisting the help of several able Tongans. He spent hundreds of
hours writing petitions and finding people to sign them. During June 1924 Coombs submitted to the government a total of
five documents arguing that on the basis of Articles IV and V of

Tonga's constitution, the Latter-day Saint exclusion law was unconstitutional.[55] Coombs spoke with Chief Justice H. C. Stronge about the LDS Church's position on the matter but found that Stronge held a different interpretation of the laws.

The question of repealing the Latter-day Saint exclusion law was brought before the Tongan Legislative Assembly on 3 July 1924. The final debate was surprisingly short. Two Tongans, Siosaia Mataele and Finau Fisiihoi, a Tongan lawyer, both members of the Legislative Assembly, presented the LDS position before the assembly. The three most vocal Tongan opponents of the repeal petition were Prince Tungī, the new Tu'i Vakanō, and Chief Ata. Coombs expected Chief Justice Stronge to oppose the repeal, but to Coombs's surprise Stronge supported the Latter-day Saints. "My views of the Mormons during the last two years have undergone a complete change," he explained. According to Coombs, he also said that "he had learned that the evidence on which he had condemned the Mormons was false and erroneous."[56] In view of the squabble between the Free Church and the Wesleyans, it was difficult for him to see what harm the Latter-day Saints could do. In his opinion they conducted themselves as peacefully as most other Tongans.

Stronge's change of attitude gave Coombs his first hint that the LDS position on the exclusion issue might prevail. Before the morning session ended, five more speeches were given in favor of the repeal petition. Shortly after lunch, however, it was proposed to refer the issue to the Privy Council. If this had happened, the Latter-day Saints almost certainly would have lost, for only two known friends of the church served on the Privy Council. Fortunately, this motion was defeated.

Victory for the Church

The matter was then put before the assembly for a vote. When the tally was counted, the vote stood at eleven in favor of repealing sections seven through nine of the 1922 Passport Act, with eight dissenting votes. Coombs and the Mormons had won.[57]

The irony of this outcome was that even though Coombs had carefully enlisted the support of many friends, gathered as many Latter-day Saints as was possible for a "show of force," skillfully written a set of arguments using the Tongan constitution as the basis,[58] and personally talked to many government officials to try to change their minds, the law was repealed not so much because Coombs had fought his case well, but because of the problems between the Wesleyans and the members of the Free Church of Tonga. "The trouble between the Tongan Free Church and the Wesleyan Church," Coombs concluded, "has caused intense feeling among all people. All the nobles, except one, . . . are with the Queen and the Wesleyan Church. The representatives . . . are generally against the Queen and the Wesleyan Church and hence will readily support any cause objectionable to the Queen and nobles. The representatives, to a man, voted to grant our petition; two nobles, the Governor of Ha'apai and two members of the Privy Council also voted for us."[59]

When Coombs received the official notice of the repeal, he sent a telegram to Salt Lake City informing President Grant of the good news. In his enthusiasm he also expressed his hope that the first three of twelve needed missionaries would be on their way immediately. To his dismay, on 25 October 1924 Coombs received a letter from the First Presidency congratulating him on the "splendid accomplishment" but informing him of a tentative decision to withdraw missionaries from Tonga. Church leaders in Utah felt that the sacrifice of time and money in Tonga was out of proportion to the results obtained. Because Anthony W. Ivins, a counselor in the First Presidency, was visiting Hawaii, a final decision would not be made until his return. This meant that, at least for the time being, no new missionaries would be dispatched to Tonga.

The next day, Coombs posted a letter containing his most profound expressions of affection for the Tongan people and the mission: "But oh, Brethren, if it is not too late, let me plead for my people. This is the hardest proposition that I have ever faced in my life, and Brethren, I would rather lay down my life for them than to run off and leave them leaderless. They are my people, I have made my greatest sacrifices for them and have used my God-given talents in their behalf; I have bought them with seven years of my youth. I have rejoiced when they have rejoiced and have gone down in sorrow with them. I do not want to persuade you against your better judgement, but if we could have only four missionaries we could, at least, hold our own."[60] Coombs also told the presidency of recent increases in church attendance and better adherence to commandments, and he reminded them of a newly completed chapel. Perhaps his strongest argument was that the Latter-day Saints had a reputation as quitters because they had already left Tonga once before, in 1897.

Coombs's moving letter had the desired effect. On 28 November 1924 the First Presidency wrote, "We are in receipt of your letter of October 26 containing a very earnest appeal for the continuation of the Tongan mission and have decided that it shall continue." Missionaries would be sent "at once." Coombs did not receive this letter until 14 February 1925. By that time most of the problems of the mission had been resolved.[61] The previous August, Coombs had leased a large plot of ground for a school at Mua, to be called Makeke, after he had received word that a new missionary couple was on their way. By then the Latter-day Saints numbered almost twelve hundred. Coombs and his wife continued in their positions until June 1926, when they were released to go home.

Conclusion

At the end of 1995 Tonga had approximately forty thousand Latter-day Saints living in 138 wards and branches composing thirteen stakes. One Tongan in every three is LDS, and thousands more Tongan Latter-day Saints are in Australia, New Zealand, the United States, and elsewhere. This is remarkable considering the hurdles that were placed in the church's path during the period considered in this paper.

The first hurdle was the general attitude of disapproval toward the Latter-day Saints in both Tonga and Great Britain following World War I. That unpopularity opened the door for the Tongan legislature to pass the Latter-day Saint exclusion act. The situation was further complicated by problems caused by the split within the Tongan churches and the relationship of various factions to those churches and to the queen. The ramifications of these events made Coombs's efforts to get the law changed more complex than even he understood. He was convinced that legal and legislative practices common to the Western world could be used to solve the problem, but in retrospect it is clear that pressure from an outsider would not work. The problem and its solution were local matters that were secondary to other issues the Tongans were fighting about.

Fortunately for Coombs, when British officials in England were willing to allow a prejudicial law to be passed against the Latter-day Saints, officers of the U.S. government in Samoa

and Washington, D.C.—Roberts and Hughes, respectively—
were dedicated to rectifying what they believed was an improper and illegal situation. The eventual support from British
representatives such as Islay McOwan also manifested a more
evenhanded attitude than was shown by officials in England.

Finally, had it not been for the determination and tenacity
of M. Vernon Coombs to seek the repeal of a hostile law and
then to set passionately before the LDS Church leaders a strong
case for continuing the Tongan mission, LDS membership
among the Tongan people likely would be only a fraction of its
current number. One man made a significant difference. It is
hard to imagine what course history might have taken had
Coombs not been the man he was. How small the hinge on
which events turn. Coombs's efforts to reopen Tonga to Latter-
day Saint missionaries and his heartfelt pleading to the First
Presidency changed the history of the church in that land.

Notes

1. The little island kingdom of Tonga is located about twenty
degrees south of the equator in the Southwest Pacific. This 269-
square-mile multi-island nation enjoys a pleasant climate similar to
that of Hawaii. The principal islands support a relatively large population; two-thirds of Tonga's more than one hundred thousand residents live on the island of Tongatapu alone. The population has
more than tripled since the 1920s. For information on the general
history and background of Tonga, see Alfred H. Wood, *A History
and Geography of Tonga* (Wodonga, Victoria, Australia: Border
Morning Mail, 1972); Noel Rutherford, ed., *Friendly Islands: A History of Tonga* (Melbourne: Oxford University Press, 1977); and Ian C.
Campbell, *Island Kingdom: Tonga Ancient and Modern* (Christchurch:
Canterbury University Press, 1992).

2. See Leonard J. Arrington, "Crisis in Identity: Mormon Responses in the Nineteenth and Twentieth Centuries," in *Mormonism
and American Culture,* ed. Marvin S. Hill and James B. Allen (New

York: Harper and Row, 1972), 168–84. For general background on
the Mormon polygamy issue, see James B. Allen and Glen M.
Leonard, *The Story of the Latter-day Saints,* 2nd ed. rev. and enl. (Salt
Lake City: Deseret Book, 1992).

3. See Malcolm R. Thorp, "The Mormon Peril: The Crusade
against the Saints in Britain, 1910–1914," *Journal of Mormon History* 2 (1975): 69–88.

4. See Malcolm R. Thorp, "The British Government and the
Mormon Question, 1910–1922," *A Journal of Church and State* 21
(spring 1979): 305–23.

5. Charles W. Forman, "Tonga's Tortured Venture in Church
Unity," *Journal of Pacific History* 13/1–2 (1978): 3.

6. See Harold G. Cummins, ed., *Sources of Tongan History: A
Collection of Documents, Extracts, and Contemporary Opinions in
Tongan Political History, 1616–1900* (Nuku'alofa, Tonga: Tupou
High School, 1972), 58.

7. See ibid., 52–93; see also Sione Latukefu, "King George
Tupou I of Tonga," in *Pacific Island Portraits,* ed. James W. David-
son and Deryck Scarr (Canberra: Australian National University
Press, 1976), 55–75; Martin Jarrett-Kerr, *Patterns of Christian Accep-
tance: Individual Response to the Missionary Impact, 1550–1950*
(London: Oxford University Press, 1972), 171–88; and Noel
Rutherford, *Shirley Baker and the King of Tonga* (Honolulu: Univer-
sity of Hawaii Press, 1996). A useful summary of the advent of
Christianity in Tonga is found in chapters 3 and 4 of Alan R.
Tippett, *People Movements in Southern Polynesia: Studies in the Dy-
namics of Church-Planting and Growth in Tahiti, New Zealand,
Tonga, and Samoa* (Chicago: Moody Press, 1971).

8. See Tippett, *People Movements,* 78–9, 111–26. Tippett has
carefully reconstructed the elements of the comity agreement in the
Tonga-Samoa area. See also Richard Lovett, *The History of the London Missionary Society, 1795–1895* (London: Oxford University
Press, 1899), 1:284–5.

9. See Noel Rutherford, "George Tupou I and Shirley Baker," in
Friendly Islands, ed. Rutherford, 157–63.

10. See note 8 above.

11. Elizabeth Wood Ellem, "Sālote of Tonga and the Problem of National Unity," *Journal of Pacific History* 18 (July 1983): 165.

12. See Rutherford, "George Tupou I," 163–9; Mark Vernon Coombs, journal, 1920 to August 1926, typescript, 113, Historical Department, Archives Division, the Church of Jesus Christ of Latter-day Saints, Salt Lake City, Utah (hereafter cited as LDS Church Archives).

13. See J. E. Curruthers, *Memories of an Australian Ministry* (London: n.p., 1922), 146–9.

14. Ellem, "Sālote," 165.

15. See Rutherford, *Shirley Baker,* 169–70.

16. J. Egan Moulton Jr., "Tonga," in *A Century in the Pacific,* ed. James Colwell (London: n.p., 1914), 432.

17. See Basil Thompson, *The Diversions of a Prime Minister* (London: n.p., 1894), 16.

18. See Cummins, *Sources of Tongan History,* 385–6.

19. Coombs, journal, 113–4. See Ermel J. Morton, *Brief History of the Tongan Mission of The Church of Jesus Christ of Latter-day Saints* (n.p.: Fiji Times Press [1968?]), 1.

20. See Morton, *Tongan Mission,* 7–10.

21. See Harold G. Reynolds (mission secretary) to Willard L. Smith, 1 September 1917, President's Correspondence, 1916–1925, Tongan Mission, LDS Church Archives (hereafter cited as President's Correspondence).

22. See Reed Smoot, Cumulative Correspondence, Special Collections, Harold B. Lee Library, Brigham Young University, Provo, Utah (hereafter cited as Smoot Correspondence).

23. See Thorp, "British Government," 305–23; see also Reynolds to Smith, 5 March 1920, President's Correspondence.

24. M. Vernon Coombs to First Presidency of the Church of Jesus Christ of Latter-day Saints, 22 December 1920, President's Correspondence; see also Coombs, journal, 53; Coombs to Junius F. Wells (Church Historian's Office), 8 November 1921, President's Correspondence. Wells was assistant Church historian.

25. See Coombs, journal, 78–83.

26. The landholding system of Tonga is rather unusual. All land is the property of the crown, but it is divided into large estates assigned to hereditary nobles. There is no privately owned land in the kingdom. Tongans and foreigners can lease land, but this is subject to the approval of the cabinet. The cabinet does not have to approve leases that are transferred from one holder to another, and it was this type of arrangement that appealed to Coombs when he was seeking land for a school.

27. See Coombs to Heber J. Grant, 24 January 1922, President's Correspondence. In this correspondence Coombs quotes a letter from U. M. Umafuke, acting minister of lands in Tonga. See also Coombs, journal, 117.

28. See Lord Milner (secretary of state for the colonies) to Cecil Hunter Rodwell (high commissioner for the western Pacific), 6 October 1919; and Roger Greene to Islay McOwan, 5 January 1920. Both letters are held by Records and Historical Services, Foreign and Commonwealth Office, Milton Keynes, England (hereafter cited as FCO).

29. See Tuʻi Vakanō to McOwan, 13 November 1919, FCO; and Tuʻi Vakanō to McOwan, 18 December 1919, FCO.

30. McOwan to Tuʻi Vakanō, 18 November 1919, FCO; see Tuʻi Vakanō to McOwan, 18 December 1919, FCO.

31. See Tuʻi Vakanō to Vice-Consul Masterton, 25 February 1920, FCO; and Rodwell to Milner, 24 March 1920, FCO.

32. See Milner to Rodwell, 12 August 1920, FCO; and Foreign Office to Passport Control Office, New York, 18 August 1920, FCO.

33. Tuʻi Vakanō to McOwan, 6 April 1921, FCO.

34. Winston Churchill to Rodwell, 19 December 1921, FCO. It is not clear from the records whether the British ambassador in Washington, D.C., actually contacted the U.S. State Department on this matter, or if they did, at what level discussion took place. Considering the response of Secretary Charles Evans Hughes when he

learned about passage of the law, it appears doubtful that he was contacted about the proposed legislation. His involvement in the matter will be mentioned later.

35. See *Tongan Government Gazette* (18 July 1922): 113. See also "Annual Financial and Statistical Reports of the Missions of The Church of Jesus Christ of Latter-day Saints, 1922," LDS Church Archives; and translation of "Transcript of Minutes of the Legislative Assembly," 30 June 1922 (22 December 1923), President's Correspondence.

36. See Coombs to First Presidency, 13 February 1924, President's Correspondence.

37. Coombs to Heber J. Grant, 30 June, 4 August 1923, President's Correspondence.

38. Coombs to Grant, 14 July 1923, President's Correspondence.

39. Coombs to First Presidency, 26 January, 13 February 1924, President's Correspondence.

40. Ibid., 13 February 1924.

41. See Coombs, journal, 118. Because much social disruption was caused when the native practice of polygamy was stopped in Tonga in the 1830s and 1840s, it is not surprising that this practice was at the head of the list of complaints against the Latter-day Saints.

42. Translation of "Transcript of the Minutes of the Legislative Assembly of Tonga," June 30, 1922, President's Correspondence. This problem was considered a serious one by Prince Tungī long before the legislative debate took place. In a 1921 interview with Prince Tungī, Elder David O. McKay of the LDS Church's Council of the Twelve Apostles asked him, "Upon what grounds do you object to our missionaries?" Prince Tungī replied, "The other churches were here first and their ministers think that you are taking too many of their people away from them" (Coombs, journal, 120).

43. Coombs was misinformed concerning the power of the high commissioner (as was the U.S. vice-consul in Apia): the high commissioner's authority did not extend beyond consultation and

advice, and he could not invalidate the passport law even if he deemed it desirable to do so.

44. Coombs to Grant, 16 February 1923, President's Correspondence.

45. Ibid., 28 December 1922, President's Correspondence; see also Coombs, journal, 122.

46. See Coombs, journal, 156, 188–9.

47. See Quincy F. Roberts to Tu'i Vakanō, 28 August 1922, FCO; see also Roberts to Rodwell, 28 August 1922, FCO; Roberts to McOwan, 28 August 1922, FCO; Roberts to Charles Evans Hughes, 31 August 1922, FCO and Smoot Correspondence.

48. McOwan to Rodwell, 7 September 1922. See Rodwell to McOwan, 11 September 1922, FCO; and Roger Greene to Roberts, 20 October 1922, FCO.

49. See Roberts to Hughes, 21 March 1923; and Hughes to Smoot, 19 December 1922, Smoot Correspondence.

50. See Smoot to Hughes, 10 March 1923; see also Hughes to Smoot, 13 March 1923, Smoot Correspondence.

51. See Hughes to Smoot, 26 March 1923; Smoot to George Harvey, 11 April 1923, Smoot Correspondence; Harvey to Secretary of Foreign Affairs, 13 April 1923, FCO; Foreign Office to Post Wheeler, 29 May 1923, FCO.

52. Duke of Devonshire to Rodwell, 12 June 1923, FCO. The duke's full name was Victor Christian William Cavendish, the ninth duke of Devonshire.

53. See Coombs, journal, 139–40.

54. See ibid., 143–4, 194–5.

55. See Cummins, *Sources of Tongan History*, 193.

56. Coombs, journal, 196.

57. See ibid., 194, 196–7.

58. Coombs argued his case under three general headings. He pointed out that on constitutional grounds the exclusion law was not legal because (1) the section did not affect all classes equally, (2) it

was retrospective in its ultimate effect, and (3) it was provocative of discrimination against the Latter-day Saints.

59. "Annual Financial and Statistical Reports of the Missions of The Church of Jesus Christ of Latter-day Saints, 1924," LDS Church Archives.

60. Coombs to First Presidency, 26 October 1924, President's Correspondence.

61. The internal squabbles between the Free Church of Tonga and the Wesleyan Church were not having a direct bearing on the LDS mission, unlike the time when Prince Tungī considered the LDS Church a threat to Tongan unity. The conflict between the Free Church and the Wesleyan Church had calmed down when the elderly Watkin died on 23 January 1925, leaving the Free Church without its most enthusiastic supporter and leader. At the time of his death, Watkin had been head of the Free Church of Tonga for forty years and a missionary in Tonga for fifty-nine years.

ELUCIDATING THE BOOK OF MORMON

NEPHITE KINGSHIP RECONSIDERED

Noel B. Reynolds

While previous attempts to understand Nephite kingship
have emphasized perceived continuities with Old Testament
Davidic monarchy and its rituals, I would like to expand this
effort by calling attention to discontinuities that point to the
uniqueness of the Nephites' situation. Lehi clearly aligned himself with the tradition of purists that believed it necessary to go
out of Egypt or even Jerusalem when these societies were dominated by evil to find a place where they could serve God in
righteousness. The evils of a corrupt Jerusalem were closely associated with the corruptions of the Judahite regime. Nephi
pointedly chose not to teach his descendants the ways of the
Jews, while preserving for them the writings of Israel's prophets.[1] But not all Lehi's children accepted his preference for righteousness and hardship in the desert to wealth and comfort in
the great city. Laman and Lemuel and their adherents saw

*Noel B. Reynolds is professor of political science at Brigham Young Uni-
versity and president of the Foundation for Ancient Research and Mormon Studies.*

nothing wrong with the public morality of Jerusalem's Jews as justified by their adherence to the forms of the law of Moses.

In this paper I will extend and update my previous efforts to understand the political dynamic of the Book of Mormon by looking at four themes or issues that can be developed from the text itself. The first section is an expansion of earlier treatments of the contradictory Nephite and Lamanite political ideologies that informed relations between these two groups across their thousand-year history. The second section explores the historical possibility that Nephi may never have been anointed king of the Nephite people, an issue that suggests a need to reassess the character of Nephite kingship. The third section brings together the many ways in which Nephi implicitly and explicitly compares himself to Moses, illuminating the Nephite regime by pointing to a preferred older and even more authoritative model of Israelite rulership. The final section offers an interpretation of the crucial confrontation between Nephi and his jealous brothers in 1 Nephi 17, in which Nephi represents Laman and Lemuel as having committed themselves to his rulership, even according to the rituals of their own preferred Judahite model. Together these four studies may help us better understand the character of the Nephite regimes and the degree to which they continued ancient Israelite patterns or purposely diverged from them in innovative ways.

The Political Argument of the Small Plates

The political subtext of Nephi's writings has been identified previously.[2] Through a thousand years of Nephite history, both Nephite dissidents and Lamanite invaders accused Nephite rulers of usurping the right to rule that belonged to Laman and Lemuel, the elder sons of Lehi, and to their descendants (see Alma 54:17). For the aggrieved parties, the offense arose from a series of incidents when Nephi "took the lead of their journey in the wilderness," while crossing the sea, and again "in the land of their first inheritance" when he led a small group away— "robbing" them of the brass plates and the right of ruling Lehi's descendants (see Mosiah 10:12–16). Nephi himself reports their complaint: "Our younger brother thinks to rule over us; and we have had much trial because of him; wherefore, now let us slay him, that we may not be afflicted more because of his words. For behold, we will not have him to be our ruler; for it belongs unto us, who are the elder brethren, to rule over this people" (2 Nephi 5:3). Nephi's separate colony came under Lamanite attack in his own lifetime, during the same period in which he was writing the small plates (see 2 Nephi 5:28–34); and he had been shown in vision the future demise of his own descendants at the hands of the Lamanites (see 1 Nephi 12:19–23).[3] In view of these circumstances, Nephi's followers and descendants desperately needed a justification of the legitimacy of their own government to counter the ideology of the Lamanites and even Nephite dissidents.

Although Nephi's primary purpose in writing was "to persuade our children, and also our brethren, to believe in Christ, and to be reconciled to God" (2 Nephi 25:23), a secondary purpose appears to have been to demonstrate for all time that his ruling position in the family of Lehi was legitimate. Nephi had seen the future and knew that the integrity of Nephite society would depend on the ability of his descendants to understand and believe in the correctness of the religious and political institutions and traditions that defined their independence from the Lamanite regimes.

The authority of Nephi and his successors was established on three grounds. First, the Lord had chosen Nephi for the role and designated him "a ruler and a teacher over [his] brethren" (1 Nephi 2:22). The angel of the Lord had personally informed

Laman and Lemuel of this divine appointment, explaining that the reason they had not been chosen was "because of [their] iniquities" (1 Nephi 3:29). Nephi's role as leader seemed divinely confirmed on various occasions when he was filled with the power of God (see 2 Nephi 1:26–7). Second, Laman and Lemuel had acquiesced to Nephi's role as ruler and teacher, going to him for explanations of Lehi's vision and bowing down before him on several occasions (see 1 Nephi 7:20; 15:1–16:5; 16:24; 17:55). Third, father Lehi had formally given to Nephi the leadership and even his first blessing (if the eldest son did not hearken to Nephi), commanding the brothers not to rebel against Nephi anymore, for the Spirit of the Lord was in him and "opened his mouth to utterance that he could not shut it" (see 2 Nephi 1:24–9). The implicit argument of the small plates is that Laman and Lemuel knew on various occasions that Nephi's authority to rule was from God and that they acknowledged this in word and deed on those occasions. Consequently, their ultimate rebellion against Nephi and their accusations that he was a usurper were based on intentional lies that denied their own experience and broke their own solemn agreements.

Nephi's small-plates account emphasizes the miraculous experiences by which Laman and Lemuel were brought at certain points to know the truth of Lehi's and Nephi's teachings and the power of the Lord by which they spoke. Indeed, it was ultimately the Spirit of the Lord in them that legitimized their ruling position to their own satisfaction. By contrast, Laman and Lemuel justified their claims to authority on the familiar ground of an inherited right to rule, which fit well with the Davidic or Judahite monarchical tradition of their own times. Nephi asserted instead a prophetic calling and appointment evidenced by the power of God given to him and appealing to the older Israelite tradition featuring similar events in the lives of Joseph, Moses, and Samuel. It was a contest between the claims of inherited royal right and divine prophetic calling, a contest that necessarily put religious claims at the center of the dispute. Specifically, the revelation of Christ to Lehi and Nephi was inextricably linked to Nephi's political claims. The two claims to authority were based on the same revelations. The logic was simple: if God had chosen Nephi, as Nephi and Lehi claimed, then Christ would come as prophesied. But by classic *modus ponens* implication, the reverse was also true: if Nephi's prophecies of Christ were false, so were his claims to divine authority to rule. Thus the Nephite dissidents who would reject these prophecies would simultaneously reject the legitimacy of their own political regime. For example, four hundred years after Nephi's time, the apostate Zoramite Ammoron begins his letter to the Nephite leader Moroni with the familiar accusation that "your fathers did wrong their brethren, insomuch that they did rob them of their right to the government when it rightly belonged unto them" (Alma 54:17). The letter concludes in a similar vein, preceded by a different accusation— that Ammoron's ancestor Zoram was "*pressed* and brought out of Jerusalem" (verse 23). Moreover, Ammoron in effect denies the god that Moroni accuses him of having rejected (see verse 21).

The small plates were written late in Nephi's life. He began writing them thirty years after leaving Jerusalem (see 2 Nephi 5:28–30), completed only twenty-seven chapters ten years later (see verse 34), and finished his writings and turned them over to his younger brother Jacob fifteen years after that (see Jacob 1:1). The aforementioned political issues were fully developed before this record was undertaken. The need to justify and legitimate the Nephite political regime was both clear and pressing.

The small plates report a series of events that cumulatively make it clear why Nephi could rightfully lead Lehi's posterity. When Lehi first led the family into the wilderness at God's command, Laman and Lemuel murmured, regretting the loss of their wealthy position in Jerusalem. They were "like unto the Jews who were at Jerusalem, who sought to take away the life of [Lehi]" (1 Nephi 2:13). But Nephi did not rebel, and upon seeking the Lord in prayer, he was visited by the Spirit and told that he would "be made a ruler and a teacher over [his] brethren" (see verses 16–22). Again directed by God, Lehi sent his sons back to Jerusalem to obtain the lineage records and scriptures held by Laban. Laman and Lemuel refused, but Nephi accepted the call and led his brothers in that quest, succeeding alone after their initial group efforts failed. In the process an angel of God appeared to the four brothers, interrupting Laman and Lemuel's physical beating of the younger two and informing them of Nephi's future position as their ruler and teacher (see 1 Nephi 3).

Lehi again sent his sons back to Jerusalem, this time to enlist Ishmael and his family so that Lehi's sons might have wives. The mission succeeded: the Lord softened Ishmael's heart, and he and his family accepted Lehi's prophetic call to flee Jerusalem (see 1 Nephi 7:5). But they were not far into the journey before the rigors of desert travel brought Ishmael's sons and Laman and Lemuel to their citified senses. Grasping the seriousness and seeming insanity of this life-changing flight, they made a stand and insisted on returning to the good life in Jerusalem and the protection of the Judahite regime there. Angered by Nephi's exhortations to be faithful to their mission, they seized and bound him with the intention of leaving him to die. But God intervened again, miraculously loosing Nephi from his bands (see 1 Nephi 7). The rebellion was quelled, and the reader is now alerted to the tension between those who put their trust in the Judahite regime and the prosperous life in Jerusalem and those who accept the cries of various prophets denouncing Jerusalem for its wickedness and announcing its imminent destruction.

Lehi was given a remarkable vision and great understanding of God's saving plan for his children, the report of which left Laman and Lemuel questioning and doubting (see 1 Nephi 15:7). Nephi, however, sought clarification in prayer and was carried by the Spirit of the Lord to a high mountain where he was shown the same vision, or perhaps a more extensive version of it, which later enabled him to explain many things to his questioning brothers (see 1 Nephi 10:1–16:5). Thus Nephi became their teacher, at their own request, when they told him "the Lord maketh no such thing known unto us" (1 Nephi 15:9). During their subsequent wilderness travels a food crisis occurred, and Nephi was divinely guided to find the wild game that saved their lives (see 1 Nephi 16:18–32). Ishmael's death triggered another crisis in which Laman and Lemuel again enlisted Ishmael's sons in a plot to kill both Nephi and Lehi. Laman and Lemuel resented their sufferings in the wilderness and felt that Nephi, the younger brother, had usurped the position of ruler and teacher and "thought to make himself a king and a ruler over us, that he may do with us according to his will and pleasure" (see verses 35–8). This early murmuring formulated the basic elements of the Lamanite tradition that lasted a thousand years. The threatening disaster was averted when "the voice of the Lord came and did speak many words unto them, and did chasten them exceedingly" (verse 39). This incident provides a glimpse of both the corruption and the perverse attraction of the Davidic monarchy that empowered kings to "do with [their subjects] according to [their] own will and pleasure" (verse 38). Rather than seeing this as a reason to condemn wicked Jerusalem and its corrupted monarchy, Laman and Lemuel saw it as a motivation to assert their own rights to rule against Nephi's divine appointment.

After spending nearly a decade crossing the Arabian Peninsula and then arriving at a fertile oasis on the southern coast,

Nephi received the command to build a ship with his brothers'
help. Again Laman and Lemuel rebelled, and angered by
Nephi's exhortations and call to repentance, they moved to kill
him by throwing him "into the depths of the sea" (1 Nephi
17:48). Again, miraculously, Nephi was filled with the power of
God to such an extent that the older brothers were frightened
into obeying him, and they "fell down before [Nephi], and
were about to worship [him]" (verse 55).

Finally, while the company crossed the ocean, the impious
revelries of Laman and Lemuel led Nephi, in his tenuous role as
ruler and teacher, to rebuke and admonish them, an act they responded to by binding him with cords. But God again quelled
their rebellion, this time with a storm that threatened to capsize
the ship. After several days, and faced with the prospect of such
a death, they released Nephi, who by praying gained relief from
the storm and power to guide the ship directly to the promised
land (see 1 Nephi 18). The hand of God in these events was not
hidden; he openly appointed and supported Nephi against his
older brothers, who clearly deserved their demotion and hu-
miliations. Lehi, the only possible source for their own claimed
authority, affirmed Nephi's claims over theirs and enjoined
them on his deathbed not to rebel against Nephi but to obey
him (see 2 Nephi 1:24, 28). And so it was that, in Nephi's
words, "the words of the Lord had been fulfilled unto my brethren, which he spake concerning them, that I should be their
ruler and their teacher. Wherefore, I had been their ruler and
their teacher, according to the commandments of the Lord,
until the time they sought to take away my life" (2 Nephi
5:19).

The Question of Nephi's Kingship

Some time after the arrival in the promised land, Nephi led
those who would follow him away from the land of their first

inheritance and into the wilderness, to a place that they called Nephi, according to the wish of his people, who also "did take upon them to call themselves the people of Nephi" (see 2 Nephi 5:8–9). Nephi reports that after they had settled themselves, established defenses and an economy, and even built a temple, his people "would that I should be their king. But I, Nephi, was desirous that they should have no king; nevertheless, I did for them according to that which was in my power" (2 Nephi 5:18).

Second Nephi 5 provides several major insights into the Nephite regime. The chapter opens with a description of the resurgent conflict between Nephi and his older brethren in the land of their first inheritance. Like Moses and his father, Lehi, before him, Nephi was warned by the Lord that he "should depart from them and flee into the wilderness, and all those who would go with [him]" (verse 5). We already know from 1 Nephi 17 that Nephi endorsed Joshua's account of the conquest of Canaan in which there was no compromise with the local population: "And after they had crossed the river Jordan he did make them mighty unto the driving out of the children of the land, yea, unto the *scattering them to destruction*" (verse 32). This conquest had come only after the Lord had, "because of their iniquity," straitened the sometimes rebellious Israelites "with his rod" (verse 41; see verses 31, 42). But after centuries in their promised land, the Israelites had "become wicked, yea, nearly unto ripeness," and Nephi knew the day was coming "that they must be destroyed" and "led away into captivity" (verse 43). In Nephi's record, Laman and Lemuel's complaint that "it would have been better that [the women] had died before they came out of Jerusalem than to have suffered these afflictions" (verse 20) implicitly evokes comparison between Laman and Lemuel and the complaining Israelites who told Moses that "it had been better for us to serve the Egyptians, than that we should die in the wilderness" (Exodus 14:12).[4] Laman and Lemuel are also like the wicked Jews at Jerusalem who sought Lehi's life and accommodated themselves to that same comfortable lifestyle that puts personal comfort ahead of rigorous righteousness. Nephi makes it clear that the general principle involved cuts against the unrighteous, whether they be pagans or Israelites: "Behold, the Lord esteemeth all flesh in one; he that is righteous is favored of God. . . . [The Lord] raiseth up a righteous nation, and destroyeth the nations of the wicked. And he leadeth away the righteous into precious lands, and the wicked he destroyeth" (1 Nephi 17:35, 37–8). This tradition of separating the righteous from the wicked continued strong in Nephite culture. For example, centuries later Alma called the Nephites to "come ye out from the wicked, and be ye separate, and touch not their unclean things; . . . [for] the names of the wicked shall not be mingled with the names of my people" (Alma 5:57).

Second Nephi 5 can also be read as a summary account of Nephi's reign because it recounts the Nephites' founding as a separate people at the Lord's command, their faithfulness to "the commandments of the Lord in all things" (verse 10), their economic fortunes as a people, the list of sacred objects in their ruler's possession, their defense measures, their city and temple building, the establishment of their teachers and priests, and the variety of official records that had been written. In this sense it resembles Benjamin's testament in Mosiah 1–6 on the occasion of Mosiah's coronation and also the testament of Moses as presented in Deuteronomy.

Clearly, Nephi had been the ruler and would continue in that role. What is left unclear is whether he ever finally accepted the formal designation and rights of a king, or whether his reluctance in this regard was as emphatic as that of Alma, the repentant priest-leader who, when "the people were desirous that Alma should be their king," replied in chiastic form:

A Behold, it is not expedient that we should have a king;
  B for thus saith the Lord:
    C Ye shall not esteem one flesh above another,
    C' or one man shall not think himself above another;
  B' therefore I say unto you
A' it is not expedient that ye should have a king.

(Mosiah 23:7)

Obviously, Alma was more determined in this matter than was Nephi. Alma's adamant refusal to be king, no doubt greatly reinforced by the evils suffered under King Noah, soon led to the abandonment of traditional kingship as practiced among the larger Nephite society. Nephi himself could not have been so implacably opposed to monarchy, for he personally consecrated his own successor a king. But even Alma believed that monarchy was beneficial "if it were possible that ye could always have just men to be your kings" (Mosiah 23:8). Nephi had not known "the iniquity of king Noah and his priests" (verse 9), so his reluctance was based on more personal reservations.

The odd, and even problematic, aspect of Nephi's story is that he gives no account of his own anointing as king over the Nephite people. How was he chosen? By whom was he anointed? The proper ritual installation of a king is the most obvious historical justification for his legitimate rule, yet Nephi passes over this in silence. Modern readers have generally assumed that Nephi was the first and founding king in a four-hundred-year succession of Nephite monarchs, but the evidence for this is problematic. Nephi's silence on this score, in a writing that carefully marshals every available argument for the legitimacy of his rule, raises serious questions about this assumption.

If Nephi never recorded his own kingship as a fact, where do we as modern readers get the idea that he was the first Nephite king? Several statements, which upon reflection turn out to be ambiguous, seem to have led to this widespread assumption. The germ of this idea is first planted in the reader's mind by Laman and Lemuel's accusation that Nephi has monarchical ambitions. Whereas Nephi quotes the Lord and an angel to affirm to his readers that he will be made "a ruler and a teacher" over his brethren (see 1 Nephi 2:22; 3:29), Laman and Lemuel on one occasion distort this phrasing to mean that Nephi intends to "make himself a *king* and a ruler over us" (1 Nephi 16:38). While we cannot know for sure whether the term *king* derives originally from their own imaginations and ambitions, reflecting more what they would have thought had they been in Nephi's position, or whether it reflects actual language Nephi used, the term does not seem to accurately reflect Nephi's way of thinking or writing about these matters. Indeed, Nephi's language attributes the term not to what he said but to Laman and Lemuel's speculation about his intentions: "he has *thought* to make himself a king and a ruler over us" (1 Nephi 16:38). We should also remember that the terms *king* and *ruler* are not equivalent terms; the latter is much broader and could also apply to a judge or a leader. For example, Moses appointed "rulers of thousands, and rulers of hundreds, rulers of fifties, and rulers of tens" (Exodus 18:21). King Mosiah instituted a system of ruling judges to replace the kingship (see Mosiah 29:41). The phrase *a king and a ruler* is first applied officially to Nephi's successor (see Jacob 1:9).

It may be that Nephi answers the kingship question for us in the comment "I did for [my people] according to that which was in my power" (2 Nephi 5:18). Was it in Nephi's power to make himself a king? Nephi had led his people from place to place and through the wilderness. He had established a people, provided for their defense, consecrated priests and teachers, taught them the material arts, and even built a sanctuary or temple for their worship of God. But all of these things could be done by a prophet-ruler without the additional prerogatives of royal rule. We cannot conclude from what Nephi did for his people that he had taken the monarchical role. Moses, who was not a king, had done all this and much more.

Before dying, Lehi may have structured a situation in which Nephi could not become a king under any recognized model. Lehi was God's prophet and the ruler of his own people and could therefore have chosen a king to rule in his stead, as Samuel had done for Israel anciently. But Lehi was not inspired in that direction. Rather, he chose to perpetuate the status quo, making one final appeal to his rebellious older sons to accept the younger Nephi's leadership. Lehi promised these sons his "first blessing," appropriate to their firstborn status, if they would follow Nephi, who spoke by the power of the Spirit of God. Otherwise, the first blessing would go to Nephi (see 2 Nephi 1:24–9). But who would adjudicate? Who would decide who had the rightful claim to the first blessing? It was an impossible situation. Each party was left to judge its own cause. Nephi judged his brothers not to have accepted his leadership—they were plotting to assassinate him—and, being divinely warned of the plot, struck off on his own. The conflict would never be adequately resolved between their descendants.

The legitimacy of Nephi's position as ruler of the Nephite people was, from an objective standpoint, firmly established: he was chosen by God, he was blessed with the spirit of prophecy, and he had plausible claim to his father's first blessing.[5] But could he anoint himself king? Not by any known precedent. So he did for his people "according to that which was in [his] power" (2 Nephi 5:18). As the recognized prophet, it was within his power to anoint kings as his successors. While this Israelite model may explain Nephi's reluctance or even inability to assume the monarchical role, it apparently posed no obstacle for the first Lamanite kings or for Zeniff's son Noah. The

Lamanites seem to have installed a very different system—one of tributary kings appointed by the superior monarch, not by a prophet (see Mosiah 24:2–3), more like the system that appears to have prevailed in ancient Mesoamerica. At no time do we see the Nephites using a multilayered or federal system with subordinate kings.

While it becomes clear in the Book of Mormon that centuries later the kingship is always passed down to descendants of Nephi in preference to any of the people of Zarahemla (see Mosiah 25:13), Jacob's account of the succession gives no hint that rulership passed from Nephi to a son or even to a brother or other close relative, as the patterns of Nephite and Lamanite kingship would later require and as Israelite kingship had previously established. Rather, Nephi "anointed *a man* to be a king and a ruler over his people now, according to the reigns of the kings" (Jacob 1:9). The phrasing of Jacob's sentence can be read as indicating that in this anointing Nephi was initiating "the reigns of the kings."

This passage, written by Nephi's younger brother Jacob some time after the succession it describes and possibly even many decades after Nephi's death, can be read quite differently, depending on whether the reader assumes that Nephi was the first Nephite king. If one does not make that assumption, Jacob's reference to "the reigns of the kings" becomes retrospective and divides the reign of Nephi from those of his successors, who were kings. Nephi was revered and loved "exceedingly" by his people for "having been a great protector" of them and for "having labored in all his days for their welfare" (Jacob 1:10)—but no mention is made of his having been their king. Compare the emphasis on kingship in comparable passages describing Kings Mosiah$_1$, Benjamin, and his son Mosiah$_2$. In honor of Nephi, the people called his successors "second Nephi, third Nephi, and so forth, according to the reigns of the kings. . . , let them be of whatever name they would" (verse 11). The text gives us no indication that the first Nephi was also a king. Jacob survived several of Nephi's successors and in his subsequent writing turns first to iniquities that arose among the people "under the reign of the second king" (verse 15), who, according to the chronology suggested in verse 11, would be the king known as third Nephi. This interpretation also maintains and separates these unfortunate events at a more plausible distance from the righteousness described during Nephi's reign.

Passages that might be read as indicating that Nephi had served his people in the monarchical role state twice that on the large plates "should be engraven an account of the reign of the kings" (1 Nephi 9:4) and that the small plates contain an account of Nephi's "reign and ministry" (1 Nephi 10:1). We should not make anything of the word *reign*, which evidently is used as a synonym for *regime*, as it is when Mormon chronicles the commencement of "the *reign* of the judges" and the ending of "the *reign* of the kings over the people of Nephi" (Mosiah 29:44, 47). One subscribing to the view that Nephi was a king might ask how, if this was not the case, Nephi could have known there would be kings, for he himself had declined acclamation to that position. But knowledge of the future seems to be doubly implied in 1 Nephi 9:4, where Nephi uses the plural term *kings* twice; and even if he was the first king, no successor appeared until fifteen or even twenty-five years after he wrote this line. The phrase *should be engraven* also refers to the future. It is thus reasonable to assume that 1 Nephi 9:4 is based on Nephi's prophetic knowledge of the future, for to his great sorrow, he had been shown the fate of his own people and the Lamanites (see 1 Nephi 12:1–3). This interpretation—that 1 Nephi 9:4 refers to the future reign of kings and does not imply Nephi's kingship—seems reinforced by Nephi's statement of the future of the two records he initiated: "Wherefore,

I, Nephi, did make a record upon the other plates, which gives an account, or which gives a greater account of the wars and contentions and destructions of my people. And this have I done, and commanded my people what they should do after I was gone; and that these plates should be handed down from one generation to another, or from one prophet to another, until further commandments of the Lord" (1 Nephi 19:4).

Another sentence that might seem to be an indication of Nephi's kingship occurs in Jacob's first recorded address to the Nephites. Jacob provides *bona fides* for his sermonizing by citing his own ordination and his "having been consecrated by . . . Nephi, unto whom ye look *as a king* or a protector, and on whom ye depend for safety" (2 Nephi 6:2). But even here Jacob does not say Nephi was king, only that he was looked upon *as* a king. The ambiguity of the characterization is further emphasized by Jacob's provision of an alternate characterization—"or a protector." We are reminded of Oliver Cromwell, who as Lord Protector of England exercised most of the powers we associate with the monarchy. It may also be worth noting that the conjunction *or* is sometimes used in the Book of Mormon to supply a corrected or improved word choice. Writers in metal did not have erasers.

Scholars have recognized that Jacob's sermon (2 Nephi 6–10) contains the typical elements of a covenant speech and that some features link it to the Israelite autumnal festivals. For example, because such speeches were sometimes associated with coronations, John W. Welch speculates that Jacob's speech might have been selected for inclusion at this point in the small plates because it was delivered at the coronation of Nephi.[6] John S. Thompson points out that while the ten-year time span between the events in 2 Nephi 5 and the beginning of Jacob's sermon in chapter 6 makes this connection uncertain, it is still useful to see Jacob's sermon as characteristic of the annual festi-

val and covenant renewal speech.[7] This point remains equally
valid whether or not Nephi was actually coronated. The chief
models for such covenant renewal texts (Joshua 24, Exodus 19–
24, and Deuteronomy) are all premonarchical. The covenant is
with the Lord, and the primary purpose of the sermon is to point
the people to him, the true king. Jacob's use of Isaiah in 2 Nephi
7–8 emphasizes this point. Whether or not the sermon was delivered at the coronation of Nephi or at some annual renewal or
festival, it is likely that it set a pattern for the Nephites by fully
integrating a festival required by the law of Moses with the gospel of Jesus Christ as revealed to Nephi and Jacob. The new and
old covenants function seamlessly together, with the implied
blessing of the revered Isaiah. This text must have been considered a milestone in Nephite thought and ritual and therefore
deserved to be included in the sacred history of that people.

While Nephi may not have been formally installed as a
king, he clearly performed the important functions that his
people associated with kingship. They were familiar with kingly
rule because of their memory of the Old World order, their
knowledge of the brass plates accounts of the kingdom of
Judah, and their experiences with the Lamanite monarchies—
which receive some descriptive attention later in the book—
and whatever other unmentioned peoples the Nephites might
have known as geographical neighbors. If, as John L. Sorenson
has so ably argued, the Nephite homeland was in Mesoamerica,
the Nephites would have been surrounded by monarchical societies.[8] Consequently, Nephi's role would have been best explained to outsiders in the language of kingship, even though
he may have declined to appoint himself to that position.

The widespread assumption that Nephi was a king cannot
be supported conclusively from a reading of the text. If anything, the Book of Mormon text may tilt against that assumption, and at best the textual support for Nephi's kingship is

ambiguous. In what follows, I will examine the background of tradition and expectations from Israel and Judah that would have provided important context for Nephi's beliefs, actions, and statements for whatever additional probabilities these might provide for or against Nephi's kingship. What we will see is that Nephi's writings implicitly appeal to patterns of Israelite rulership that could provide precedent for his rule without the formality of a royal anointing. The systematic and extensive character of this appeal as it is embedded in the text suggests that Nephi needed this kind of precedent, which in turn suggests that he was not an anointed monarch.

Monarchy in Ancient Israel

Ancient Israel, as described in the biblical record, was plagued with ambivalence about the role of human kings. By all accounts, Israel was founded under the direction of prophet-rulers who were called by God and who could not rightfully pass their position on to their sons. For a long interim Israel was ruled at least intermittently by judges who seemed to have operated with much more limited powers than those enjoyed by neighboring monarchs. Kingship was unequivocally and problematically introduced at the time of Saul. In the centuries after Moses, Israel had no earthly king. Rather, the Lord (Yahweh) was Israel's king: "I am the Lord, your Holy One, the creator of Israel, your King" (Isaiah 43:15). All Israelites owed their full allegiance to him. Righteousness was equated with obedience to his commandments. And he was their king by covenant, made with all the people at Sinai: "Moses commanded us a law, as a possession for the assembly of Jacob. Thus the Lord became king in Jesh'urun, when the heads of the people were gathered, all the tribes of Israel together" (Deuteronomy 33:4–5 Revised Standard Version).[9]

The people's demand that Samuel provide them with a human king was not interpreted so much as a rejection of him as prophet-ruler or judge as it was a rejection of the Lord as their king: "It is not you they have rejected, but they have rejected me as their king. As they have done from the day I brought them up out of Egypt until this day, forsaking me and serving other gods, so they are doing to you" (1 Samuel 8:7–8 New International Version). Both Samuel and the Lord were offended, but the Lord instructed Samuel to acquiesce to the popular request and to anoint as king the man whom the Lord would select (see verses 8–10). In spite of the clearly articulated evils that kingship would bring on Israel (see verses 10–18), the Lord gave his divine sanction to the people's requested monarchy, establishing it with a prophetic anointing, miraculous events, and the provision of "regulations of the kingship," which were explained to the people, written on a scroll, and deposited in a sacred place "before the Lord" (1 Samuel 10:25 NIV).

Israelite history provided the Nephites with multiple models of rulers, including the prophet-rulers—Moses, Joshua, Samuel, and the other judges—and the royal dynasty of David, who had also been selected by God through his servant Samuel to replace the wayward Saul. By the time of Mosiah$_1$ and Benjamin, when the Nephites and Mulekites merged in Zarahemla, Nephite kingship had reabsorbed the priestly and prophetic functions. Mosiah$_1$ and Benjamin served both as prophets and kings. They received marvelous revelations in the service of their people, and there was every expectation that their eldest sons would inherit the kingship. But the gap in the record (due to the loss of 116 manuscript pages) deprives us of any adequate explanation of how the functions of prophets and kings came to be recombined. Clearly, Nephi had separated them before his death. The political rule, including custodial responsibility for maintaining the large plates, was assigned to a man he had chosen and anointed to be king, while the prophetic and priestly duties were passed, with the small plates, to Nephi's younger brother Jacob, and from him possibly to his descendants, down to the time that they turned the plates over to Mosiah.[10] The mere fact that the Nephites had become monarchists seemed to facilitate their peaceful merger with the people of Zarahemla, whose ancestor was Mulek, a son of Zedekiah, king of Judah. For reasons not mentioned in the Book of Mormon, neither this Davidic ancestry nor prior possession of the land was sufficient grounds for Zarahemla to be selected as king over the newly joined peoples.

Nephi seems to have served his people as a Moses or a Samuel. The fact that he composed the small plates near the end of his life in such a way as to repeatedly call attention to this comparison could be taken as strong evidence that he did not formally assume the kingly office. It may likewise be significant that Nephi's small plates make no positive references or allusions to David or Solomon. The most direct references to them are by Jacob, who blames David and Solomon for their abominable practice of having many wives and concubines. In the next verse, Jacob pointedly cites the sins of the Jews in Jerusalem as the Lord's reason for leading Lehi out of that land so that he "might raise up . . . a righteous branch from the fruit of the loins of Joseph" (see Jacob 2:24–5). Lehi and Nephi repeatedly justified their flight from Jerusalem in similar terms, though Laman and Lemuel insisted that Jerusalem was a righteous city and that their father was tragically mistaken to abandon it for the wilderness. Other references to the Davidic dynasty in the Book of Mormon are incidental and have no implications for the issues under consideration here.

Nephi's extensive quoting from Isaiah serves this same political agenda quite nicely, for Isaiah was a southern prophet who accepted the Davidic tradition only insofar as the monarchy operated faithfully within the theology of Zion as understood by the traditional Jerusalem cult, which saw Yahweh as Israel's only king and the one in whom total reliance must be placed for protection. Ben C. Ollenburger distinguishes the political traditions of David and Zion.[11] In his analysis of Isaiah he finds the political sensibility and rhetoric to be thoroughly rooted in the ultimate and pervasive kingship of Yahweh: "How beautiful upon the mountains are the feet of him that . . . saith unto Zion, Thy God reigneth!" (Isaiah 52:7).[12] By the time of the Assyrian conquest, Isaiah saw Israel's king and the Jerusalem establishment as the enemies of Zion, who refuse to trust in Yahweh and who forge a protective alliance with Egypt, rejecting their true king in the process. As Ollenburger further argues, "There is precious little evidence from chapters 1–39 that Isaiah based any hope for salvation on Yahweh's promises to the Davidic house." Accordingly, Isaiah criticized "the practice of kingship in Judah since it [was] arrogant in its refusal to accord Yahweh his exalted status."[13] Judah chose to rely on armaments and foreign alliances rather than trust in Yahweh (see Isaiah 2:8; 7:9; 28:16; 30:1–5, 16; 31:1–3).[14]

The similarity between the ancient exodus of Israel from Egypt and the experience of Lehi and his people was explicitly recognized by Nephi at the time and by Limhi and Alma in later centuries (see 1 Nephi 17:19–44; Mosiah 7:19–20; Alma 36:28–9).[15] Thus both Lehi and Nephi can be seen as Moses figures. This comparison has been developed by previous writers[16] and can be extended significantly with the following composite list that focuses specifically on Nephi as a Moses figure. As I have demonstrated elsewhere, it is reasonable to believe that the version of Genesis available to the Nephites in the brass

plates was similar to the version in the Joseph Smith Translation.[17] Accordingly, I will include some comparisons from that
text as well. While there are enormous differences in the experiences of Moses and Nephi, the mature Nephi chose to tell his
story in such a way that more than twenty explicit and implicit
points of comparison stand out.

1. Both Moses and Nephi fled into the wilderness after killing
   a public figure who is portrayed as repressive or even crimi-
   nal. Their flight prevented their being detected (see Exodus
   2:11–15; 1 Nephi 4:18, 38).

2. Moses was "caught up into an exceedingly high mountain"
   to receive comprehensive revelation that would both
   ground and guide his prophetic career (Moses 1:1). Nephi,
   after praying to know the things his father had seen, was
   also "caught away . . . into an exceedingly high mountain"
   where he received this same kind of fundamental revelation
   (1 Nephi 11:1).

3. As a result of these great visions, both Moses and Nephi
   prophesied a future scattering and destruction of their own
   people because of wickedness. Both also prophesied a latter-
   day restoration of their people (see Deuteronomy 4:26–31;
   1 Nephi 12:19–23; 13:30; 34–42).

4. Moses spoke with and even saw God face-to-face (see Exodus 33:11; Numbers 12:8; Moses 1:2, 31). The "Spirit of
   the Lord" that caught Nephi up into the mountain and
   narrated the first part of his vision may well have been Jesus
   Christ. This identification is suggested when the guide van-
   ishes without explanation—at the very point in the narrative when Jesus Christ appears in the vision—and is replaced for the remainder by an unnamed angel as narrator

(see 1 Nephi 11:1, 12, 21). In a later recounting, which seems to be an expansion of part of this same vision, Nephi reports how the voices of both the Father and the Son spoke to him in alternation to provide detailed doctrinal explanation for the baptism of Jesus by John (see 2 Nephi 31: 4–15). Either this same experience or some other is implied when Nephi reports that Jesus "hath redeemed my soul from hell" (2 Nephi 33:6), phrasing used by Lehi in conjunction with the further claim to have "beheld his glory" (2 Nephi 1:15). This interpretation is reinforced by use of the same language a third time when Lehi, in blessing his son Jacob, says he knows that Jacob is redeemed and has beheld the Redeemer's glory (see 2 Nephi 2:3–4). Moreover, Nephi notes that Isaiah had seen the Redeemer, "even as I have seen him" (2 Nephi 11:2).

5. It should be noted of both Moses and Nephi that their respective calls to be God's prophet and the leaders of his people were unexpected in terms of high birth, office, or other social or natural distinction. Moses was a refugee from Egypt and a shepherd in Midian. Nephi was the fourth son of Lehi and a refugee from Jerusalem (see Moses 1:6, 26; Exodus 3:1; 1 Nephi 2:19–24).

6. In their founding visions, both Moses and Nephi were shown the future peoples of the world and the Lord's purposes for them (see Moses 1:8, 27–30; 1 Nephi 11–14).

7. Both Moses and Nephi were major figures in leading people out of wicked places, Egypt and Jerusalem (see Exodus 3:10; 12:51; 1 Nephi 2; 1 Nephi 17:43). Though Nephi did not lead Lehi's family in their original exodus, he appears to have been the leader when they returned the second time

to Jerusalem and led Ishmael's family from there to Lehi's wilderness camp (see 1 Nephi 7). He was clearly in charge as they built the ship and crossed the ocean.

8. Moses invoked the power of God to lead his people miraculously across the Red Sea (see Exodus 14:13–22). Similarly, with divine direction and aid, Nephi led his people in building a ship and crossing the sea, during which crossing his prayers persuaded the Lord to end the typhoon and carry them safely on their journey (see 1 Nephi 17–18). The language Nephi used to describe this incident evokes Moses' parting of the Red Sea: "There arose a great storm, yea, a great and terrible tempest, and we were driven back upon the waters for the space of three days" (1 Nephi 18:13). Moses relates, "And all that night the Lord drove the sea back with a strong east wind" (Exodus 14:21 NIV).

9. Both Moses and Nephi led their people safely to a promised land (see Numbers 13; Deuteronomy 1; 1 Nephi 19:25). The difference is that Moses was not permitted to enter.

10. The wilderness travels of Moses and Nephi and their peoples also are described with several general and specific similarities. For example, both entailed years of difficult desert conditions, and in both cases the people suffered and murmured against their leaders, thinking fondly of the more comfortable lives they had left behind. The children of Israel lamented, "It had been better for us to serve the Egyptians, than that we should die in the wilderness" (Exodus 14:12), whereas, Laman and Lemuel proclaimed that "it would have better that [the women] had died before they came out of Jerusalem than to have suffered these afflictions" (1 Nephi 17:20).[18]

11. These murmurings became severe on several occasions in both exodus stories, to the point that there was an apparent attempt on Moses' life at least once, and on Nephi's life several times (see Exodus 17:4; Numbers 14:5–10; 1 Nephi 7:16; 16:37; 17:48; 2 Nephi 5:3).

12. The stories of murmuring often end with some form of reconciliation taking place between God and those involved after his power is manifested in a divine act (see, for example, Exodus 17:1–7; Numbers 14–16; 20:1–13; 21:5–9; 23; 1 Nephi 3:28–31; 7:6–22; 17–18).

13. Both Moses and Nephi were accused of usurping leadership and being driven by thoughts of self-promoted grandeur. The rebels Korah, Dathan, and Abiram asserted the holiness of the congregation of Israel and asked Moses and Aaron, "Wherefore then lift ye up yourselves above the congregation of the Lord?" and accused Moses of bringing them into the wilderness to make himself "altogether a prince over" them (Numbers 16:3, 13). When attempting to stop a fight between two Hebrews, "[Moses] asked the one in the wrong, 'Why are you hitting your fellow Hebrew?' The man said, 'Who made you *ruler and judge* over us?'" (Exodus 2:13–14 NIV; emphasis added). Like the Israelites who challenged the rulership of Moses, Laman and Lemuel accused Nephi of thinking to make himself "a king and a ruler" over them (1 Nephi 16:38).

14. In each account the Lord provided divine means for guiding the people through the wilderness. For ancient Israel this was in the form of a pillar of light by night and a cloud by day (see Exodus 13:21–2). For Lehi's party it was the Liahona (see 1 Nephi 16:10, 16, 28–31; 18:21–2).

15. Both accounts tell how starvation was averted when food was provided through divine intervention (see Exodus 16:2–16; 1 Nephi 16:30).

16. In the Exodus account, when Moses came down from Sinai with the tablets, "his face was radiant, and they were afraid to come near him" (Exodus 34:29–30 NIV). Similarly, when Nephi was threatened by his brothers, he was "filled with the power of God" and warned them not to touch him lest God smite them and they "wither even as a dried reed" (1 Nephi 17:48), whereupon they were afraid to touch Nephi "for the space of many days" (verse 52). This incident was resolved when the Lord told Nephi to touch his brothers that he might shock them. Being physically shaken by this touch, they acknowledged that it was "the power of the Lord" that had shaken them (see verses 53–5).

17. Moses and Nephi furnished their people with founding texts that provided religious and prophetic guidance for centuries. The five books of Moses have their parallel in Nephi's large and small plates. These texts established the record-keeping traditions that enabled the people to benefit from centuries of recorded prophecy and religious history.

18. Moses and Nephi both built sanctuaries. The tabernacle of Moses provided the basic model for Solomon's Temple, which in turn was the model for Nephi's temple in the Western Hemisphere (see Exodus 25–7, 36–9; 2 Nephi 5:16).

19. Moses consecrated his brother Aaron and Aaron's sons to be priests with authority to administer religious matters for the Israelites (see Exodus 28–9; Leviticus 8; Numbers 8). Likewise, Nephi consecrated his brothers Jacob and Joseph to "be priests and teachers over the land of [his] people" (2 Nephi 5:26).

20. Moses gave Israel the Ten Commandments and the law of Moses as given to him by God on Sinai (see Exodus 20:2–17). Similarly, Nephi provided his people with a new law that was given to him by God. Nephi received the gospel, or "doctrine of Christ" (2 Nephi 31:2), from the Father and the Son as they spoke to him on the mountain and explained that repentance, the baptisms of water and of fire and the Holy Ghost, faith in Jesus Christ, and enduring to the end are prerequisites to receiving eternal life (see 2 Nephi 31).[19] Furthermore, Nephi explicitly taught his people that this new law superseded the law of Moses, which they would need to observe only until Christ came into mortality (see 2 Nephi 5:10; 11:4; 25:24–7).[20]

21. Just as Moses "laid his hands" on Joshua to be his successor as leader of Israel (Deuteronomy 34:9), so Nephi anointed a man to be king and ruler after him (see Jacob 1:9). Nephi's spiritual role was passed on to his brothers Jacob and Joseph, who had been "consecrated priests and teachers of this people, by the hand of Nephi" (Jacob 1:18).

While some of these parallels are weaker than others, the obviousness and importance of the strong ones support the view that Nephi included all of them intentionally. Many of these comparisons between Nephi and Moses could be drawn between Moses and Lehi as well. But this correlation further emphasizes Nephi's role as a Moses, because the small plates show that Nephi inherited the role of his father. After Lehi, only Nephi could be counted on to carry out the essential missions commanded by the Lord during the wilderness travels of Lehi's band of exiles. And by the time they reached the ocean, the Lord gave the commandment to build the ship directly to Nephi.

This transition of leadership is clearly demonstrated in 2 Nephi. For example, Lehi explicitly recognized the Lord's blessing of Nephi to become the leader of his people (see

2 Nephi 1:24–9), and charge of Lehi's youngest children, Jacob and Joseph, was passed to Nephi, who was to care for them in place of Lehi (see 2 Nephi 2:3; 3:25). A pattern of events then unfolds, showing Nephi in the prophet-leader role played by Lehi in 1 Nephi and his younger brother Jacob assuming the role of teacher first held by Nephi. The Lord warned Nephi to take those who would follow him and depart from his brethren, who were plotting to kill him, and flee into the wilderness (see 2 Nephi 5:4–5), echoing the earlier divine warning to Lehi to leave Jerusalem (see 1 Nephi 2:1–2). As in 1 Nephi, where Nephi receives the same visions his father received, in 2 Nephi Jacob also sees those same things in vision (see 2 Nephi 6:8–9). Both Moses and Lehi are types for Nephi. How could the legitimacy of his rule be more solidly established?

The Uncoronation of Nephi

I have already pointed out the oddity of the absence of any reference in the Book of Mormon to Nephi's coronation and official installation as a king. Now I would like to explore the possibility that Nephi told the story of the building of the ship in such a way as to evoke the sense of a coronation in the tradition of the Davidic kings, a tradition that, ironically, would have required Laman and Lemuel, supporters of the Judahite model of monarchy, to be faithful servants of their king Nephi. In this way the story is a linchpin in Nephi's case for the legitimacy of Nephite government.

In an earlier paper, I discussed how all of 1 Nephi can be understood as two parallel structures, each built around three stories that are directly paired with each other.[21] For instance, obtaining the brass plates is the central story of the first half of 1 Nephi, an episode that parallels the story of the building of the ship in the second half. Significantly, each of these stories is also structured as a long and elaborate chiasm. The brass plates story focuses on the most egregious example of Laman and Lemuel's murmuring—that being immediately after they were rebuked and taught by an angel. The ship-building story focuses on Nephi's only detailed response to that murmuring, and the chiastic structure of this story testifies of its importance and probable role in the oral tradition of the early Nephites.

> A Nephi is summoned to the mountain, where he speaks to the Lord (17:7).
>> B Nephi is told to construct a ship after the manner the Lord will show him (17:8).
>>> C The Lord shows Nephi where to find ore to make tools (17:10).
>>>> D The Lord will miraculously bless them in the wilderness so they will know it was he who delivered them. Nephi keeps the commandments and exhorts his brethren to faithfulness (17:12–15).
>>>>> E Nephi's brethren murmur against him and withhold their labor from him (17:17–18).
>>>>>> F Nephi is exceedingly sorrowful (17:19).
>>>>>>> G Nephi's brethren present the details of their case against him and their father (17:19–21).
>>>>>>>> H Nephi's brethren defend the Jews of Jerusalem for their righteousness (17:22).
>>>>>>>>> I Although the Lord by miracles led "our fathers," the Israelites, out of Egypt and through the wilderness to the promised land, they hardened their hearts and reviled against both Moses and God (17:23–30).
>>>>>>>>>> J God blesses the righteous and destroys the wicked. He "esteemeth all flesh in one." Whoever is righteous is favored of the Lord (17:31–5).

J' The Lord blesses the righteous and de-
stroys the wicked. He loves whoever will
have him to be their God (17:36–40).

I' Even though the Lord loved "our fathers,"
covenanted with them, led them out of
Egypt, and straitened them by miraculous
means in the wilderness, still they hard-
ened their hearts and reviled against both
Moses and God (17:40–2).

H' Nephi prophesies the destruction of the Jews
of Jerusalem for their wickedness (17:43).

G' Nephi presents the case against his brethren
(17:44–6).

F' Nephi's soul is rent with anguish (17:47).

E' Nephi's brethren are angry with him, but he
commands them not to withhold their labor from
him (17:48–9).

D' The Lord miraculously shocks Nephi's brethren so
they will know the Lord is their God. Nephi tells
them to obey specific commandments (17:53–5).

C' The Lord shows Nephi how to work timbers for the
ship (18:1).

B' Nephi builds the ship after the manner the Lord has
shown him (18:2).

A' Nephi often goes to the mount to pray to the Lord (18:3).
(1 Nephi 17:7–18:4)

The Lamanite complaint against Nephi's ruling authority
can be answered indirectly by these stories, which Nephi tells in
such a way that Laman and Lemuel's actions refute the
Lamanite ideology. All great literature recognizes the tension
between speech and deed as well as the priority of deed as an
indicator of truth. This tension creates ironic insights into
truth. The events recounted in 1 Nephi 17 are crafted so as to
evoke several kinds of rituals known to every Israelite. These

evocations refute Laman and Lemuel's account of those same events and reinforce Nephi's account, making chapter 17 a kind of political tract and as such one of the most potent elements of 1 Nephi. For example, ancient Israelite year-rites presented the king in a duel with the powers of evil, with his life at stake. At the end he was acclaimed the ruler of the new age. Coronation rituals were associated with these events.[22] In 1 Nephi 17 this classic ritual is suggested unmistakably in the descriptive framework of the story that begins with the dramatic attempt of Laman and Lemuel to kill Nephi by throwing him into the depths of the sea and that ends with their falling down before Nephi to worship him (see verses 48, 55).

John A. Tvedtnes has abstracted a general account of the ancient Israelite Feast of Tabernacles, a celebration that was associated with coronations, which are reported in less complete form at different points in the Old Testament.[23] In the five items that follow, I note the correspondences between the ritual elements of the Feast of Tabernacles as identified by Tvedtnes and many aspects of Nephi's account in 1 Nephi 17:7–18:4:

1. The ritual takes place at a cultic site. Nephi's account begins and ends with the reference to a mountain where Nephi goes to communicate with God (see 1 Nephi 17:7; 18:3). In lieu of a temple—often thought of as "the mountain of the Lord"—ancient Israelites resorted to the sanctuary of a mountaintop for worship and other matters of ritual significance.

2. The ritual address of the leader commonly included eight elements, seven of which are directly present or alluded to more vaguely in Nephi's speech—or are implied in the framing context of his speech—to his brothers in 1 Nephi 17:23–47: *(a)* the law of Moses (verse 22) and the blessings and cursings associated with it (verses 35, 38); *(b)* an exhortation

to love, fear, and serve God (verses 15, 44–7, 49–52); *(c)* a recounting of God's deliverance of the fathers, particularly from Egypt (verses 23–35, 41–2); *(d)* reference to God's role as creator and source of all good things (verse 36); *(e)* a call to assist the needy (verses 20–1); *(g)* a blessing to the people (verses 53–4); and *(h)* additions as particularly needed (verses 35–43).

Of the items on Tvedtnes's list, only *f,* the "Paragraph of the King," is missing in Nephi's speech. If the occasion for his speech was not an actual coronation, then of course that paragraph would not have been included. I only want to point out how the passage evokes a coronation for the Israelite mind. Yet by the time this story was written, Nephi, the aging Nephite ruler, was the living exemplar of the requirements laid out and stipulated in Deuteronomy 17:14–20. For example, he was "a brother Israelite" (verse 15 NIV) who did not take many wives (as far as the text reveals), and he did "not accumulate large amounts of silver and gold" (verse 17 NIV). Rather, he was careful to study and follow the God-given law and did not consider himself better than his brothers or use his position to build personal power or wealth.

3. God covenants with the people that if they will obey him they will be prosperous and live long in the land (1 Nephi 17:13–14, 35–40) and receive other blessings not duplicated in 1 Nephi 17.

4. The people in turn covenant to be God's servants and to obey him (1 Nephi 17:15). The ruler's speech is written down (as Nephi does in his record). Other symbolic acts occur that are not mentioned in 1 Nephi 17, nor does the passage contain allusions to other activities typically associated with the

festival: building an altar, making sacrifices, expressing joy through music and dance, or the blowing of trumpets.

5. The coronation ritual additionally stressed that God is the true king (1 Nephi 17:39) and that he chooses the earthly king (verse 44), who must be approved by the people (verse 55), anointed, and given charge (verse 53).

It appears that in addition to suggesting these rituals, the account of Nephi's shipbuilding was also written so as to evoke the famous passage in which the kingship is passed from David to his son Solomon, in the context of instructions to Solomon for building the temple (see 1 Chronicles 28–9). The divine charge for Solomon to build the temple is couched in a divine reassurance that David and Solomon are a divinely blessed royal dynasty that will last forever (see 1 Chronicles 28:4–8). The instructions for the building were given to David "by the spirit" (see verses 12, 19), and the Lord provided him with willing and skillful workers (see verse 21). David encouraged Solomon, reassuring him that the Lord would not fail him but would bless him to finish the work (see verse 20). All the Israelites came forward to give rich contributions for the building of the temple (see 1 Chronicles 29:6–9) and "bowed low and fell prostrate before the Lord and the king. . . . Then *they acknowledged Solomon son of David as king a second time,* anointing him before the Lord to be ruler and Zadok to be priest. So Solomon sat on the throne of the Lord as king in place of his father David. He prospered and all Israel obeyed him. All the officers and mighty men, as well as all of *King David's sons, pledged their submission* to King Solomon" (1 Chronicles 29:20, 22–4 NIV; emphasis added).

Similarities and contrasts call attention to the role of Laman and Lemuel as subjects to Nephi and simultaneously to their deep unwillingness to accept that role, even though it was mandated by God, conditional upon their own faithfulness. Just as the Lord showed David and Solomon how to build their temple, he also showed Nephi how to build his ship (see 1 Nephi 17:8). The Lord also provided Nephi with laborers, but they were initially unwilling to labor (see verse 18). They criticized both Nephi and his father, and they certainly did not buy into any notion that Nephi and his descendants should be their rulers. The Lord blessed Nephi to be able to complete the work, even filling him with a powerful spirit to compel his brothers' cooperation. Ultimately, Laman and Lemuel "fell down before [Nephi]" (verse 55) and were about to worship him; they virtually acclaimed Nephi king because of the undeniable power of God. Thus, in his record Nephi ingeniously invoked the Davidic model of inherited rulership (which Laman and Lemuel used to legitimate their own political claims) to present the historical moment in which they acclaimed him! So even though they rejected Nephi's appeal to the models of Moses and Samuel and turned to the Davidic dynasty for validation of their political claims, their conduct on the occasion just described further legitimated Nephi's leadership role.

Because all of Lehi's descendants knew they had come from the land of Jerusalem far away across the western sea, an inescapable question arises: how did they obtain a ship to come to their new land? The tradition of the Lamanites apparently did not deal with this question, for the answer would have been fatal to that tradition. Thus their tradition focused on charges of usurpation against the Nephites. On the other hand, Nephi's account of how the ship was built, like the account of acquiring the brass plates, must have been a centerpiece in the Nephite tradition. In fact, both of these accounts deal with inescapable historical questions: the plates exist; their origin must be explained. The Nephites are in a new world; that transoceanic voyage needs to be explained. The historical account in each case vindicates Nephi's legitimate authority as a ruler and teacher over his brethren, as does Laman and Lemuel's attempt to worship him—an action that essentially acclaimed his leadership in the manner of the Israelites with David and Solomon. From a modern viewpoint, the fact that Laman and Lemuel—and not Nephi—admired Judahite monarchy only intensifies the condemnation of their later rebellions. In Nephi's account they are refuted by their own actions, standards, and ideology, as well as by his.

Conclusion

The political subtext of Nephi's writings is even richer and more pervasive than previously realized. Nephi's justification of his and all subsequent Nephite rule consists in showing that he was appointed ruler and teacher by God; that Laman and Lemuel themselves knew and, on occasion, accepted that; and that father Lehi had officially endorsed that arrangement in his final blessings. Nephi further identified his rule with Moses and the earlier nonmonarchical model of Israelite government, while his two brothers appear to have preferred the kingly rule of the Davidic dynasty and its pattern of inherited kingship. A close reading of the text with this background in mind raises serious and systematic doubts about whether Nephi was actually ever installed as a king. If he was not, the first generation of Nephites lived under a prophet-leader like Moses or Samuel and did not move to kingship until the end of Nephi's life. As later Nephite kings made clear, they had not adopted the attitudes of Lamanite kings and did not see themselves as "entitled to the gratitude and obedience of the populace"; rather, they saw themselves "acting as an agent of superior command," as agents of God, who was the true king of this people by covenant.[24]

Because Laman and Lemuel and their heirs could make no credible claim to such divine appointments, they claimed that the right to rule was a matter of inheritance and that they, as the eldest sons, were rightfully entitled to it.[25] Subsequent centuries of Nephite and Lamanite struggles testify to the foresight and importance of Nephi's early efforts to provide a justification for the Nephite regime by calling attention to premonarchical models from ancient Israel and demonstrating repeatedly the Lord's direct involvement in its formation, in spite of the contrary efforts and views of Lehi's oldest sons.

Notes

The author gratefully acknowledges the essential contributions of his research assistant, Victoria Andrews, a graduate student at Union Theological Seminary, and of FARMS for the funding that made her assistance in this project possible. Several individuals have provided important commentary and criticism that have enriched and hopefully strengthened this paper, including especially John W. Welch and, appropriately, John L. Sorenson. While their comments have been most helpful, the conclusions advanced herein remain my own.

1. "For I, Nephi, have not taught them many things concerning the manner of the Jews; for their works were works of darkness, and their doings were doings of abominations" (2 Nephi 25:2).

2. See my article "The Political Dimension in Nephi's Small Plates," *BYU Studies* 27/4 (1987), 15–37. John L. Sorenson noted the similarity between Nephi's writings and the lineage histories of the Guatemalan highland Indians that were used to confer "legitimacy and sanctity on the rulers" (see his *An Ancient American Setting for the Book of Mormon* [Salt Lake City: Deseret Book and FARMS, 1985], 50–1). See Sorenson's extended comparison of these histories with the Book of Mormon in his "The Book of Mormon as a

Mesoamerican Record," in *Book of Mormon Authorship Revisited: The Evidence for Ancient Origins*, ed. Noel B. Reynolds (Provo, Utah: FARMS, 1997), 391–521.

3. Richard L. Bushman develops this Lamanite ideology further in the context of the full range of Lamanite relationships with the Nephites (see his "The Lamanite View of Book of Mormon History," in *By Study and Also by Faith: Essays in Honor of Hugh W. Nibley*, ed. John M. Lundquist and Stephen D. Ricks [Salt Lake City: Deseret Book and FARMS, 1990], 2:52–72).

4. All biblical references are to the King James Version unless otherwise noted.

5. Nephi provides almost no information on Sam. He does say that Lehi blessed Sam to share the inheritance of Nephi (see 2 Nephi 4:11), but it is not clear how Lehi's first blessing applies specifically to Sam. Lehi includes Sam with the older brothers when he tells them, "If ye will hearken unto [Nephi] I leave unto you a blessing, yea, even my first blessing. But if ye will not hearken unto him I take away my first blessing, yea, even my blessing, and it shall rest upon him" (2 Nephi 1:28–9). Of the sons listed in this promise, only Sam hearkened to Nephi. Did he thereby receive the first blessing and not Nephi? In the absence of other clarification or evidence, I assume that Nephi in his terse report did not intend to imply that Sam had inherited a birthright that would include the right to rule.

6. See John W. Welch, "The Temple in the Book of Mormon," in *Temples of the Ancient World*, ed. Donald W. Parry (Salt Lake City: Deseret Book and FARMS, 1994), 328, 334–6.

7. See John S. Thompson, "Isaiah 50–51, the Israelite Autumn Festivals, and the Covenant Speech of Jacob in 2 Nephi 6–10," in *Isaiah in the Book of Mormon*, ed. Donald W. Parry and John W. Welch (Provo, Utah: FARMS, 1998), 124–7.

8. See, generally, Sorenson, *Ancient American Setting*.

9. Most Bible translations and commentaries agree that Yahweh is the subject of verse 5, although the KJV calls Moses king. No other texts refer to Moses in monarchical terms.

10. See Jarom 1:2; Omni 1:11; Words of Mormon 1:10.

11. See Ben C. Ollenburger, *Zion, the City of the Great King: A Theological Symbol of the Jerusalem Cult* (Sheffield, England: JSOT Press, 1987).

12. Isaiah 52:7 is invoked several times in the Book of Mormon (see 1 Nephi 13:37; Mosiah 12:21; 15:14; 3 Nephi 20:36).

13. Ollenburger, *Zion*, 125, 131.

14. See ibid., 131.

15. It is interesting to note that Laman and Lemuel, although they rejected Nephi's identification of Jerusalem with oppressive Egypt, seem to have clearly understood the implied comparison of their situation to ancient Israel (and thus the comparison of Lehi and Nephi to Moses). This is evident when they affirm the righteousness of the people of Jerusalem: "We know that the people who were in the land of Jerusalem were a righteous people; for they kept the statutes and judgments of the Lord, and all his commandments, according to the law of Moses; wherefore, we know that they are a righteous people; and our father hath judged them, and hath led us away" (1 Nephi 17:22).

16. See S. Kent Brown, "The Exodus Pattern in the Book of Mormon," *BYU Studies* 30/3 (1990): 111–26; my "Political Dimensions," 33–4; and George S. Tate, "The Typology of the Exodus Pattern in the Book of Mormon," in *Literature of Belief: Sacred Scripture and Religious Experience*, ed. Neal E. Lambert (Provo, Utah: BYU Religious Studies Center, 1981), 245–62.

17. See my "The Brass Plates Version of Genesis," in *By Study and Also by Faith*, ed. Lundquist and Ricks, 2:136–73.

18. Compare Exodus 2:14; 5:21; 15:11; 16:3; Numbers 14:2; 20:3; 1 Nephi 3:28; 7:6, 16–19; 16:20, 38; 17:20–2.

19. I interpret the events detailed in 2 Nephi 31 as an expanded version of the vision Nephi reported earlier in 1 Nephi 11. See my "The Gospel of Jesus Christ as Taught by the Nephite Prophets," *BYU Studies* 31 (summer 1991): 34.

20. While it has been convincingly demonstrated that the Nephite lists of crimes (compare Mosiah 2:13 and Alma 23:3) reflect the law of ancient Israel, it is not really clear what Nephi means by

"the law of Moses." He could mean more or less than students of the Old Testament might expect (see, for example, John W. Welch, "Series of Laws in the Book of Mormon" [FARMS, 1987]).

21. See diagrams and more complete explanations of this structural analysis in my "Nephi's Outline," *BYU Studies* 20 (winter 1980): 131–49, which is conveniently reprinted in Noel B. Reynolds, ed., *Book of Mormon Authorship: New Light on Ancient Origins* (Provo, Utah: Religious Studies Center, 1982; reprint, Provo, Utah: FARMS, 1996), 53–74. The chiasm included in the present study updates my analysis published earlier.

22. See Hugh W. Nibley, *An Approach to the Book of Mormon* (Salt Lake City: Deseret Book and FARMS, 1988), 296.

23. See John A. Tvedtnes, "King Benjamin and the Feast of Tabernacles," in *By Study and Also by Faith*, 2:220–1.

24. George E. Mendenhall, *The Tenth Generation: The Origins of the Biblical Tradition* (Baltimore: Johns Hopkins University Press, 1973), 30. See chap. 1, "Early Israel as the Kingdom of Yahweh," for an excellent description of the differences in Israelite theories of kingship.

25. The Lamanite kings and their tributary Nephite king Noah, who have not been examined in this study, seem to be styled on the common model rejected in Nephite tradition and, like King David's successors, dissolved religion into politics (see ibid., 16). But that is a story for another day.

CHAPTER 7

NEPHI AND HIS ASHERAH: A NOTE ON 1 NEPHI 11:8–23

Daniel C. Peterson

A stylized tree with obvious religious significance already occurs as an art motif in fourth-millennium Mesopotamia, and, by the second millennium B.C., it is found everywhere within the orbit of the ancient Near Eastern oikumene, including Egypt, Greece, and the Indus civilization. The meaning of the motif is not clear, but its overall composition strikingly recalls the Tree of Life of later Christian, Jewish, Muslim, and Buddhist art.[1]

Given the presence of the "sacred tree" throughout the ancient Near East—one leading archaeologist says that "the familiar tree of life [was] one of the oldest and most widespread motifs in ancient Near Eastern art and iconography"[2]—we are scarcely surprised to find tree imagery prominently displayed in the Book of Mormon, an ancient text rooted in the eastern Mediterranean.[3] Thus, for instance, in order to illustrate profound lessons about the nature and cultivation of faith, Alma

Daniel C. Peterson, associate professor of Islamic studies and Arabic at Brigham Young University, is chairman of the board of trustees for the Foundation for Ancient Research and Mormon Studies and editor of the journal FARMS Review of Books.

the Younger discusses a metaphorical seed that, if nourished and cultivated, will grow into the salvific tree of life.[4] And one of the most famous incidents in the Book of Mormon involves Nephi's vision of the tree of life, which was an expanded repetition of the similar vision given earlier to his father, Lehi. I will contend in this paper that a crucial element of Nephi's vision reflects a signification of the sacred tree that is unique to the ancient Near East and that, indeed, can only be fully appreciated when the ancient Canaanite and Israelite associations of that tree are borne in mind.

First, of course, we need to review a portion of Nephi's experience, as it is preserved in the Book of Mormon:

> And it came to pass that the Spirit said unto me: Look! And I looked and beheld a tree; and it was like unto the tree which my father had seen; and the beauty thereof was far beyond, yea, exceeding of all beauty; and the whiteness thereof did exceed the whiteness of the driven snow.
>
> And it came to pass after I had seen the tree, I said unto the Spirit: I behold thou hast shown unto me the tree which is precious above all.
>
> And he said unto me: What desirest thou?
>
> And I said unto him: To know the interpretation thereof. . . . (1 Nephi 11:8–11)

Since Nephi's wish—expressed at the specific request of his guide—was to know the meaning of the tree that had been shown to his father, and that he himself now saw, we would expect the Spirit to answer Nephi's question. However, the guide's response to Nephi's question is hardly what we would have anticipated:

> And it came to pass that he said unto me: Look! And I looked as if to look upon him, and I saw him not; for he had gone from before my presence.
>
> And it came to pass that I looked and beheld the great

city of Jerusalem, and also other cities. And I beheld the city of Nazareth; and in the city of Nazareth I beheld a virgin, and she was exceedingly fair and white.

And it came to pass that I saw the heavens open; and an angel came down and stood before me; and he said unto me: Nephi, what beholdest thou?

And I said unto him: A virgin, most beautiful and fair above all other virgins.

And he said unto me: Knowest thou the condescension of God?

And I said unto him: I know that he loveth his children; nevertheless, I do not know the meaning of all things.

And he said unto me: Behold, the virgin whom thou seest is the mother of the Son of God, after the manner of the flesh.

And it came to pass that I beheld that she was carried away in the Spirit; and after she had been carried away in the Spirit for the space of a time the angel spake unto me, saying: Look!

And I looked and beheld the virgin again, bearing a child in her arms.

And the angel said unto me: Behold the Lamb of God, yea, even the Son of the Eternal Father! (1 Nephi 11:12–21)

Then, immediately and, to many readers, no doubt unexpectedly, the Spirit asks Nephi precisely the question that Nephi himself had put to the Spirit only a few verses before:

Knowest thou the meaning of the tree which thy father saw? (1 Nephi 11:21)

Strikingly, in view of the seeming irrelevance of the vision of Mary to the original question about the significance of the tree—for the tree is nowhere mentioned in the angelic guide's response—Nephi himself now replies that, yes, he knows the proper reply to his own question.

And I answered him, saying: Yea, it is the love of God, which sheddeth itself abroad in the hearts of the children of men; wherefore, it is the most desirable above all things.

And he spake unto me, saying: Yea, and the most joyous to the soul. (1 Nephi 11:22–3)

How has Nephi come to this understanding? Clearly, the glimpse given to Nephi of the virgin mother with her child is the answer to his question about the meaning of the tree. Indeed, it is evident that in some sense the virgin *is* the tree. This is apparent from the structure of the pericope, of course, but also in the parallel descriptions given of the tree and the virgin. Just as she was "exceedingly fair and white," "most beautiful and fair above all other virgins," so was the beauty of the tree "far beyond, yea, exceeding of all beauty; and the whiteness thereof did exceed the whiteness of the driven snow."[5] In one sense, therefore, the fruit of the tree—which was "desirable to make one happy" (1 Nephi 8:10), "desirable above all other fruit" (verses 12, 15), "most sweet, above all that [Lehi] ever before tasted" (verse 11), and which "filled [his] soul with exceedingly great joy" (verse 12)—is clearly the fruit of Mary's womb, Jesus.[6] Moreover, it is evident that the mere sight of the virgin, by herself, leaves Nephi still a bit bewildered. It is only when she appears with a baby and is identified as "the mother of the Son of God" that he grasps the meaning of the tree.

The question to be treated in this paper is, Why would Nephi, without any explicit direction from his guide, have seen an immediate connection between a tree and the virginal mother of a divine child? In other words, how, without any real explanation, would he recognize a depiction of Mary and Jesus as an elucidation of the meaning of a beautiful tree? In order to answer that question, I believe we must examine a facet of the history of ancient Israelite worship that has become much clearer only in the light of very recent research.

Asherah, Consort of El

It is apparent, on archaeological and other grounds, that the cultural and religious distance between Canaanites and Israelites, though it did exist, was considerably smaller than scholars once thought. (Michael D. Coogan says it clearly: "Israelite religion [was] a subset of Canaanite religion.")[7] For one thing, absolute monotheism itself, supposedly the chief claim to uniqueness and the foremost virtue of the Abrahamic religions, seems to have developed relatively late (perhaps as late as the Babylonian exile) in both popular and official Hebrew circles.[8] "Monotheism," declares Mark Smith, "was hardly a feature of Israel's earliest history."[9] Monolatry, the worship of only one god, "grew out of an early, limited Israelite polytheism that was not strictly discontinuous with that of its Iron Age neighbors."[10] In fact, says Professor Smith, "texts dating to the Exile"— in other words, to the period immediately following the departure of Lehi and his family from Jerusalem—"are the first to attest to unambiguous expressions of Israelite monotheism."[11]

In their attempts to better understand the beliefs of the ancient Israelites, modern scholars have been greatly helped by extrabiblical documents and artifacts that have been recovered from the soil of the Near East. For many years, there had been little beyond the Bible itself for them to study. The situation has changed, however, and dramatically so. Beginning in 1929, for example, the discovery of the Ugaritic texts at Ras Shamra, in Syria, revolutionized our understanding of Canaanite religion in general, and of early Hebrew religion in particular.

The god El was the patriarch of the Canaanite pantheon. Concerning the title *ʾēl ʿōlām,* Harvard's Frank Moore Cross Jr. noted: "We must understand it . . . as meaning originally 'ʾEl, lord of Eternity,' or perhaps more properly, 'ʾEl, the Ancient One.' The mythological tablets of Ugarit portray ʾEl as a greybeard, father of the gods *('ab bn 'ilm)* and father of man *('ab 'adm)*."[12] However, observed Professor Cross, "it seems clear that no later than the fourteenth century B.C. in north Syria, the cult of 'El was declining, making room for the virile young god Ba'l-Haddu."[13] Similarly, it now seems clear that, as with the Canaanites, "the original god of Israel was El." In the earliest Israelite conception, father El had a divine son named Jehovah or Yahweh.[14] Indeed, there were a *number* of "sons of El."[15] Gradually, however, the Israelite conception of Yahweh absorbed the functions of El and, by the tenth century B.C., had come to be identified with him.[16]

For the purposes of the present essay, one of the most important things to emerge from these texts was the definitive demonstration of the existence in Canaanite religion, long denied by many earlier authorities, of a goddess called Asherah.[17] She was, in fact, the chief goddess of the Canaanite pantheon. She was the wife of El, who was the patriarch and chief god of the Canaanites, and the mother and wet nurse of the other gods, the sons of El. Just as El was called "father of the gods" and "procreator of the generations of the gods," Asherah was the "mother of the gods" and "the one giving birth to the gods." Thus the gods of Ugarit could collectively be called "the family of [or 'the sons of'] El" or the "sons of Asherah."[18] Not unexpectedly, in this light, Asherah was widely regarded as a goddess of fertility.[19] And, just as she was the mother of the gods, she was connected with the birth of earthly royal heirs and could be metaphorically considered to be their mother as well.[20]

She had a center of worship in the Canaanite coastal city of Tyre and seems to have had a uniquely strong tie with the city of Sidon, at least in the period following Lehi and Nephi's departure from the Old World, and probably before.[21] This is interesting because Lehi, a man whose family origins appear to lie in the north of Palestine and who evidently came from a trading background, "seems to have had particularly close ties with Sidon (for the name appears repeatedly in the Book of Mormon, both in its Hebrew and Egyptian forms), which at that time was one of the two harbors through which the Israelites carried on an extremely active trade with Egypt and the West."[22] Intriguingly, too, Asherah's title *Elat* ("goddess") persists to this day in the name of a major Israeli coastal resort and in the Israeli name for the Gulf of Aqaba.[23]

Indeed, "Asherah . . . was the earliest female deity known to have been worshiped by the Children of Israel," over a period extending at least from the conquest of Canaan to the fall of Jerusalem in 586 B.C.—the time of the departure of Lehi and his family from the Old World.[24] Ancient Israelite women, for instance, were sometimes buried in "Asherah wigs." Furthermore, two upright pillars, a relatively large one and a smaller one, have been found in the sanctuary of the Israelite temple at Arad, which dates to the ninth century B.C. At least one leading authority on the archaeology of ancient Palestine believes that they stood, respectively, for Yahweh and Asherah. To choose another example, at Taanach, near Megiddo, evidence suggests that images of the Queen of Heaven, perhaps Astarte but probably Asherah, were mass produced. And these very common terracotta figurines, of which thousands have now been found at Israelite sites, were not just a rural phenomenon. More of them have now been found in the Jerusalem area than in the countryside.[25] Summarizing the evidence, William Dever writes of the figurines that "most show the female form nude, with exaggerated breasts; occasionally she is depicted pregnant or nursing a child." But there is one significant difference between the figurines from Israelite sites and those recovered from pagan Canaanite locations: the lower body of the Israelite figurines lacks the explicit detail characteristic of the Canaanite objects; indeed, the area below the waist of the Israelite figurines is typically a

simple plain column. Whereas the pagan Canaanite objects depict a highly sexualized goddess of both childbearing and erotic
love, in the Israelite figurines the aspect of the *dea nutrix*, the
nourishing or nurturing goddess, comes to the fore. As Professor Dever writes, "The more blatantly sexual motifs give way to
the nursing mother."[26]

Scholarly opinions are divided about whether Asherah was
a foreign goddess who had become fully assimilated into Israelite worship, or whether she was indigenous to original Hebrew
belief.[27] For the limited purpose of this paper, though, her origins are of little consequence. Over a period of many years,
worship of her seems to have been popular among all segments
of Israelite society.[28] Few careful readers of the Old Testament
will have missed the fact that Asherah was venerated in the
countryside.[29] She was worshiped in Israel under the judges,[30]
and she was important in later Hebrew urban centers as well.
Although 1 Kings 3:3 reminds readers that King Solomon
"loved the Lord," he brought Asherah into Jerusalem, probably
sometime after 1000 B.C. The famous tenth-century Israelite
offering stand found at Taanach, not far from Megiddo, links
Asherah and Yahweh, and J. Glen Taylor argues that it is evidence of an actual "cult" of the two, a cult that once flourished
"at a large-scale cultic centre which perhaps functioned under
(at least indirect) royal administrative sanction during the reign
of Solomon."[31]

After the separation of the states of Israel and Judah, King
Ahab and his Phoenician-born queen, Jezebel, daughter of
"Ethbaal, king of the Sidonians," installed Asherah in their
capital city, Samaria, where, as David Noel Freedman observes,
"around 800 B.C.E., the official cult of Yahweh included the
worship of his consort Asherah."[32] She seems to have remained
comfortably ensconced there until Israel fell to the Assyrians in
721 B.C.

But the veneration of Asherah was hardly restricted to the often-denigrated northern kingdom.[33] In the south, in Judah, Solomon's son, Rehoboam, introduced her into the temple—meaning, presumably, that he erected some sort of sacred symbol (sometimes referred to in the lowercase as "an *asherah*" or "the *asherah*") that represented the goddess Asherah. Asa and Jehoshaphat removed Asherah from the temple, but Joash restored her, whereupon the great reforming king Hezekiah removed her again, along with the so-called Nehushtan, which 2 Kings 18:4 describes as "the brasen serpent that Moses had made." Subsequently, although he failed to restore the Nehushtan, King Manasseh reinstalled Asherah in the Jerusalem temple, where she remained until the reforms of King Josiah, who reigned from roughly 639 to 609 B.C. So visible was Asherah still in the period just prior to the Babylonian captivity that Lehi's contemporary, the prophet Jeremiah, felt obliged to denounce the worship of her.[34] In other words, an image or symbol of Asherah stood in Solomon's Temple at Jerusalem for nearly two-thirds of the period of its existence, certainly extending into the lifetime of Lehi and perhaps even into the lifetime of his son Nephi.[35]

By the time of Israel's Babylonian exile and subsequent restoration, however, opposition to Asherah was universal in Judaism.[36] Indeed, the developing Israelite conception of Yahweh seems, to a certain extent, to have absorbed her functions and epithets, much as it had earlier absorbed those of Yahweh's father, El.[37] In a certain sense, therefore, Asherah disappeared from the history of Israel and subsequent Judaism.[38] In the text of the Bible as we now read it, hints of the goddess remain, but little survives that would enable us to form an accurate or detailed understanding of her character or nature.[39] As William Dever sums it up:

The "silence" regarding Asherah as the consort of Yahweh, successor to Canaanite El, may now be understood as the result of the near-total suppression of the cult by the 8th–6th century reformers. As a result, references to "Asherah," while not actually expunged from the consonantal text of the MT [Masoretic Text], were misunderstood by later editors or reinterpreted to suggest merely the shadowy image of the goddess. In this "innocent deception," they were followed by the translators of the Septuagint, the Vulgate, the Targumim, and the King James and most other modern versions, including the Revised Standard. Indeed, by the time of the Mishna the original significance of the name "Asherah" had probably been forgotten, not to be recovered until the goddess emerged again in the texts recovered from Ugarit.[40]

Steve A. Wiggins agrees, maintaining that the reformers actually suppressed information regarding Asherah from the Bible as we now have it.[41] The biblical texts must be read, Saul Olyan says, with their filtering through the Deuteronomists kept fully in mind, for they used purposeful distortion to make their case.[42] (Manfried Dietrich and Oswald Loretz may not be entirely off the mark when they refer to the work of the Deuteronomists as *Kriegspropaganda,* or "war propaganda.")[43]

So what are we to make of Asherah? Does the opposition to venerating her, as expressed and enforced by the Deuteronomists and the reforming Israelite kings, indicate that she was a foreign and evil pollution of the legitimate Hebrew religion? Not necessarily. Recall that Hezekiah removed both the asherah and the Nehushtan from the temple at Jerusalem. The Nehushtan was not a pagan intrusion; it was "the brasen serpent that Moses had made," which had been carefully preserved by the Israelites for nearly a millennium until Hezekiah, offended by the idolatrous worship of "the children of Israel [who] did burn incense to it" (2 Kings 18:4), removed it and destroyed it.[44] In other words, the Nehushtan had an illustrious pedigree entirely within the religious world of Israel, and there is no reason to believe that the asherah was any different in this respect.[45] Indeed, it should be recalled that Manasseh brought the asherah back to Yahweh's temple in Jerusalem, but not the Nehushtan.

Sherlock Holmes once solved a case because of a dog that, contrary to all expectation, did not bark. What is striking in the long story of Israel's Asherah is the identity of those who did not oppose her. No prophet appears to have denounced Asherah before the eighth century B.C.[46] The great Yahwist prophets Amos and Hosea, vociferous in their denunciations of Baal, seem not to have denounced Asherah,[47] and the Elijah-Elisha school of Yahwist reformers do not appear to have opposed her. Although 400 prophets of Asherah ate with Jezebel along with the 450 prophets of Baal, Elijah's famous contest with the priests of Baal, while dramatically fatal to them, left the votaries of Asherah unmentioned and, evidently, untouched. "What happened to Asherah and her prophets?" asks David Noel Freedman. "Nothing."[48] In subsequent years the ruthless campaign against Baal inspired by Elijah and Elisha and led by Israel's Jehu left the *asherah* of Samaria standing. Baal was wholly eliminated, while the veneration of the goddess actually outlived the northern kingdom.[49]

Belief in Asherah seems to have been a conservative position in ancient Israel; criticism of it was innovative. Saul Olyan, noting that "before the reforming kings in Judah, the asherah seems to have been entirely legitimate,"[50] argues that ancient Hebrew opposition to Asherah emanated entirely from the so-called Deuteronomistic reform party, or from those heavily influenced by them. Other factions in earliest Israel, Olyan says, probably thought that worshiping her was not wrong and may well have worshiped her themselves.[51] (The book of Deuteronomy is usually associated with the reforms of the Judahite king Josiah in the seventh century B.C., and many scholars believe that it was actually written during that period.) Writing of the common goddess figurines to which we have already alluded, William Dever remarks, "As for the notion that these figurines, whatever they signified, were uncommon in orthodox circles, the late Dame Kathleen Kenyon found a seventh-century B.C. 'cult-cache' with more than three-hundred-fifty of them in a cave in Jerusalem, not a hundred yards from the Temple Mount."[52] (It should be kept in mind that a date for these figurines in the seventh century B.C. makes them at least near contemporaries of Lehi.)

What was Asherah's role in early Israelite religious belief? As one might have predicted, given what we have already said about the history of Canaanite and Israelite religion, "Asherah may have been the consort of El, but not Yahweh, at some early point in Israelite religion."[53] Gradually, however, as the concept of Yahweh began to absorb the attributes of Yahweh's father, El, Israelite imaginations seem also to have granted to Yahweh the wife and consort of his father.[54] "It is well-known," remarks André Lemaire, who lays out the argument clearly despite his rejection of it, "that in Israelite religion Yahweh replaced the great god El as Israel's God. If Yahweh replaced El, it would seem logical to suppose that under Canaanite influence asherah replaced Athirat [Asherah], and that, at least in the popular religion of ancient Israel if not in the purer form of that religion reflected in the Bible, asherah functioned as the consort or wife of Yahweh."[55]

Professor Lemaire's skepticism notwithstanding, Saul Olyan is probably correct in asserting that the view of Asherah as a divine consort, the wife of Yahweh, is gaining ground among scholars of ancient Israelite religion.[56] "That some in Judah saw his consort as Asherah is hardly any longer debatable," declares Thomas Thompson.[57] "Asherah was a goddess paired with El, and this pairing was bequeathed to Israelite religion by virtue of the Yahweh-El identification."[58] Asherah seems to have been regarded as Yahweh's consort in both state and public religion in the northern kingdom of Israel and in the southern kingdom of Judah.[59]

Important support for this contention has come from two recent and very controversial archaeological finds in Palestine. The first is Khirbat al-Qūm, a site about eight miles west of Hebron and roughly six and a half miles east-southeast of Lachish in the territory of ancient Judah. The paleo-Hebrew inscriptions at Khirbat al-Qūm can be dated to the eighth century B.C,[60] and whatever their other disagreements about them, scholars agree that they represent at least a strand of the popular religion of their time.[61] The second is Kuntillat 'Ajrūd, perhaps the southernmost outpost of the kingdom of Judah, which served as either a fortress or a caravansary (or both) and is situated on the border between the southern Negev and the Sinai peninsula, not far from the road that linked Gaza and Elat. (It is approximately forty miles south of Kadesh-Barnea on a hill beside the Wādī Qurayya.) The archaeological ruins at this location, reflecting influences from the northern kingdom of Israel, date to the late ninth or early eighth century B.C.,[62] which would place them in the reign of Jehoahaz, king of Israel, the son and successor to the militant anti-Baalist Jehu.[63]

The inscription at Kuntillat 'Ajrūd, written in red ink on the shoulder of a large *pithos* (clay vessel), seems to refer to "Yahweh of Samaria and his Asherah." On the other side of the *pithos* is a drawing of a tree of life.[64] The tomb inscription at Khirbat al-Qūm also appears to mention "Yahweh and his asherah" (where some sort of cultic object is intended) or, less likely, "Yahweh and his Asherah" (where the reference may be directly to a goddess-consort). With these finds explicitly in

mind, the eminent archaeologist William G. Dever has contended that "recent archeological discoveries provide both texts
and pictorial representations that for the first time clearly identify 'Asherah' as the consort of Yahweh, at least in some circles
in ancient Israel."[65] Raphael Patai declares that they indicate
that "the worship of Asherah as the consort of Yahweh ('his
Asherah'!) was an integral element of religious life in ancient
Israel prior to the reforms introduced by King Joshiah [Josiah] in
621 B.C.E."[66] David Noel Freedman concurs: "Our investigation
suggests that the worship of a goddess, consort of Yahweh, was
deeply rooted in both Israel and Judah in preexilic times."[67]

At one stage of Hebrew religion, Yahweh appears to have
been regarded as "the patriarch of all the gods, as the universal
progenitor" of the heavenly "host"[68]—a role he probably inherited from his father, El. (Yahweh may originally have been
numbered as one of the host, perhaps even worshiped as such—
albeit as the sun, the most important among them.)[69] The "host
of heaven," in turn, were associated with the stars and heavenly
bodies but were also described as heavenly councilors, and an
increasing number of scholars believe that they were equivalent
to the gods of surrounding Canaanite faiths.[70] Thus, John Day
argues, just as the Ugaritic goddess Asherah was the wife of El
and the mother of the gods, the Israelite Asherah, consort of the
chief Hebrew deity, was the mother of the divine children of
God.[71] In other words, at the creation of the earth, "when the
morning stars sang together, and all the sons of God shouted
for joy" (Job 38:7), Asherah appears to have been there too,
among her children.[72] Furthermore, as among the Canaanites,
Asherah was also associated with earthly human fertility and
human childbirth.[73] A Hebrew incantation text found in
Arslan Tash in upper Syria, dating from the seventh century
B.C. (the period just prior to Nephi's vision), appears to invoke
the help of the goddess Asherah for a woman in delivery.[74]

For our present purposes, though, we need to focus more precisely on the nature of the veneration that the Israelites paid to the divine consort. What was the asherah that stood in the temple at Jerusalem and in the Israelite capital at Samaria? Some controversy attends this question. Asherah seems to have been associated with trees.[75] The tenth-century cultic stand from Taanach, a site located five miles southeast of Megiddo at the southern edge of the plain of Esdraelon, features two representations of Asherah, first in human form and then as a sacred tree. Asherah *is* the tree.[76] Perhaps we should think again, here, of the Israelite goddess figurines: it will be recalled that their upper bodies are unmistakably anthropomorphic and female, but their lower bodies, in contrast to those of their pagan Canaanite counterparts, are simple columns. William Dever suggests that these columnar lower bodies represent tree trunks.[77] And why not? Asherah "is a tree goddess, and as such is associated with the oak, the tamarisk, the date palm, the sycamore, and many other species. This association led to her identification with sacred trees or the tree of life."[78] The rabbinic authors of the Jewish Mishnah (compiled around 200 A.D.) explain the asherah as a tree that was worshiped.[79]

Asherah's symbol may have been a living tree, or a sacred grove of some sort, but scholarly consensus seems to be growing behind the proposition that the lowercase asherah was most commonly a carved wooden image, perhaps some kind of pole. Unfortunately, since the image was wooden, little if any direct archaeological evidence for it has survived.[80] But we know from the biblical evidence that it could be planted (see Deuteronomy 16:21) so that it stood up (see 2 Kings 13:6), but that it could also be pulled down (see Micah 5:13), cut (see Exodus 34:13), and burned (see Deuteronomy 12:3). Very probably it symbolized a tree, and it may itself have been a stylized tree.[81] It was not uncommon in the ancient Near East for a god or goddess to be essentially equated with his or her symbol,[82] and Asherah seems to have been no exception: Asherah was both goddess *and* cult symbol. She *was* the tree.[83]

The menorah, the seven-branched candelabra that stood for centuries in the temple of Jerusalem, supplies an interesting parallel to all this: Leon Yarden maintains that the menorah represents a stylized almond tree. He points to the notably radiant whiteness of the almond tree at certain points in its life cycle and reminds his readers of the perennial association of the tree of life with light (pointing in this context even to the burning bush, from which Yahweh chose to address Moses at Sinai). It is fascinating, therefore, to see Yarden argue that the archaic Greek name of the almond *(amygdale,* reflected in its contemporary botanical designation as *Amygdalis communis),* almost certainly not a natively Greek word, is most likely derived from the Hebrew *em gedolah,* meaning "Great Mother."[84]

"The Late Bronze Age iconography of the asherah would suggest," writes Mark Smith, "that it represented maternal and nurturing dimensions of the deity."[85] Raphael Patai has called attention to the parallels between Jewish devotion to various female deities and quasi deities over the centuries, commencing with Asherah, and popular Catholic veneration of Mary, the mother of Jesus.[86] Interestingly, it appears that Asherah, "the mother goddess par excellence," may also, paradoxically, have been considered a virgin.[87] The Punic western goddess Tannit, whom Saul Olyan has identified with Israelite-Canaanite Asherah, the consort of El, the mother and wet nurse to the gods, was depicted as a virgin and symbolized by a tree.[88] It may be recalled, in this context, that an eleventh-century cardinal, saint, and doctor of the Roman Catholic Church, Peter Damian, declared that, as the Virgin Mary matured, she came to have such beauty and charm that God himself was filled with passion for her. It was to her, he says, that God sang the Song of

Solomon, and when his business with angels and men left him fatigued, she was the golden couch upon which he lay down to take his rest. Two centuries later, another cardinal, the important Franciscan philosopher and ascetic St. Bonaventure, went so far as to label Mary "the spouse of the Eternal Father," an expression that would be echoed in 1399 by Christine de Pisan, who also termed Mary the "Queen of Heaven"—the same title given to the goddess of ancient Israel[89]—and attached her to the Trinity itself.[90]

It should by now be apparent why Nephi, an Israelite living at the turn of the seventh and sixth centuries before Christ, would have recognized in the otherwise unexplained image of a virginal mother and her divine child an answer to his question about a marvelous tree and, derivatively, a profound statement about the depth of God's love for humankind. The association in 1 Nephi of the New Testament's Mary with the tree of life is not without parallel in the ancient Near East. The Coptic version of The Apocalypse of Paul, a document that probably originated in Egypt in the mid-third century of the Christian era, relates a vision of the great apostle that, in this detail at least, strikingly resembles the vision of Nephi: "And he [the angel] showed me the Tree of Life," Paul is reported to have said, "and by it was a revolving red-hot sword. And a Virgin appeared by the tree, and three angels who hymned her, and the angel told me that she was Mary, the Mother of Christ."[91] But Nephi's vision goes even further, *identifying* Mary with the tree. This additional element seems to derive from precisely the preexilic Palestinian culture into which, the Book of Mormon tells us, Nephi had been born.

That Mary, the virgin girl of Nazareth, was not literally Asherah, "the lonely goddess of ancient Israelite religion"[92]— that she was, as Nephi's guide carefully stressed, simply "the mother of the Son of God, *after the manner of the flesh*"[93]—is, for the purpose of this discussion, almost certainly irrelevant. Religious thinkers of later Judaism, after all, could discern Asherah in other feminine personages, both historical and mythical. In sixteenth-century Safed, for instance, the Kabbalist Moses Cordovero understood Asherah to be identical with the Matronit-Shekhina of Kabbalistic Judaism.[94] In fact, various Kabbalistic thinkers identified the Shekhina, the deified feminine personification of God's presence, with the historical, mortal women Sarah, Rebekah, Rachel, and Leah.[95] Similarly, in a rather skewed parallel to the image of Mary in 1 Nephi, the third-century-A.D. murals of the Mesopotamian Dura-Europos synagogue depict the Shekhina as a nude woman holding the infant Moses, a quasi-divine child, in her arms.[96] There is evidence, too, that Asherah was occasionally linked to biblical Eve by ancient Hebrews.[97] For that matter, in rabbinic Judaism even the ordinary Jewish wife could be and was viewed as the "earthly representative of the Shekhina," the divine consort of God.[98] But Mary, far more perfectly and precisely than any of these other earthly "Asherahs," was the mortal typification of the wife of the Heavenly Father and the mother of his Son.

Indeed, as ancient Christianity developed, the image of Mary seems to have assimilated goddesses from beyond the Hebraic tradition, as well. Consider, for example, the Greek and Anatolian goddess Artemis (Diana), who was associated with childbirth, with the fertility of humans and animals, and, particularly in the Peloponnesus, with the fruitfulness of trees, and whose carefully guarded virginity only partially obscures her apparent origins as a mother goddess.[99] The area near Ephesus, in modern Turkey, was once strongly associated with Artemis. Her great temple stood there, one of the wonders of the ancient world (see Acts 19:23–41). Today, however, little remains of her shrine beyond a marshy pit and a single melancholy column upon which large migratory birds like to roost.

Even so, tens of thousands of pilgrims still go to Ephesus each
year to visit the purported home of the Virgin Mary in the hills
above the city. Legends of her arrival at Ephesus in the company of Luke the evangelist, and of her lengthy sojourn there in
the care of the apostle John, can be dated back to very nearly
the time when the temple of virgin Artemis was destroyed.

Asherah and Biblical Wisdom

As a final (but, I hope, useful and instructive) exercise, we
will examine a passage in the Bible that seems, in view of the
discussion we have just brought to a provisional conclusion, to
yield several interesting parallels to the visions of Lehi and Nephi.

Biblical scholars recognize a genre of writing, found both in
the canonical scriptures (e.g., Job, Proverbs, Ecclesiastes, the
Song of Solomon) and beyond the canon, that they term "wisdom literature." Among the characteristics of this type of writing, not surprisingly, is the frequent use of the term *wisdom*.
But also common to such literature, and very striking in texts
from a Hebrew cultural background, is the absence of typically
Israelite or Jewish themes, such as the promises to the patriarchs, the story of Moses and the exodus, the covenant at Sinai,
and the divine promise to David. There is, however, a strong
emphasis on the teaching of parents, and especially on the instruction of the father.[100] Careful readers will note that all of
these characteristics are present in the accounts of the visions of
Lehi and Nephi as they are given in the Book of Mormon.

The Bible identifies two chief earthly sources of wisdom. It
is said to come from "the East," which is almost certainly to be
understood as the Syro-Arabian desert, and from Egypt.[101]
(The book of Job, for example, is set in "the East" and lacks
much if any trace of peculiarly Israelite or Hebrew lore.)[102] This
is reminiscent of the twin extra-Israelite influences—Egypt and

the desert—that the Book of Mormon and recent Latter-day
Saint scholarship have identified for the family of Lehi and
Nephi.[103] It may be significant that a section of the book of
Proverbs (31:1–9) claims to represent "the words of Lemuel"—
using a name that not only occurs among the sons of Lehi but
also is perfectly at home in the Arabian desert.

Certain other motifs common to wisdom literature are also
typical of the Book of Mormon as a whole.[104] For example,
both the canonical and extracanonical wisdom books are much
concerned with the proper or improper use of speech.[105] The
book of Proverbs warns against the dangerous enticements of
"the strange woman, even . . . the stranger which flattereth with
her words," and advises us to "meddle not with him that
flattereth with his lips."[106] "Flattering" and "cunning words,"
generally used for evil purposes and with an implication of deceit, are also a recurring concern of the Nephite record.[107] Another consistent theme in both the Book of Mormon and Near
Eastern wisdom literature is the notion that wisdom or justice
or righteousness brings prosperity, while folly or wickedness
leads to suffering and destruction.[108] The vocabulary of Proverbs 1–6, which stresses learning, understanding, righteousness, discernment, and knowledge, is obviously relevant to important elements of the Book of Mormon in general, and of the
visions of Lehi and Nephi in particular.[109] Similarly, Proverbs
3:1–12 focuses on our need to "hear" inspired wisdom, as well
as on the promise of "life" and our duty to trust in the Lord
rather than being wise in our own eyes.[110] Each of these admonitions can also be documented abundantly throughout the
text of the Book of Mormon—notably Nephi's repeated invita-
tion to us to put our trust in the Lord rather than in "the arm of
flesh."[111] In Nephi's vision of the tree of life, the "great and spacious building" symbolizes the wisdom and pride of the world,
which shall fall.[112]

But among the interesting correspondences between ancient Near Eastern wisdom literature and the Book of Mormon, one is of special interest for the present paper. Wisdom itself is represented in Proverbs 1–9 as a personified female.[113] Indeed, here and elsewhere in ancient Hebrew and Jewish literature, Wisdom appears as the wife of God, which can hardly fail to remind us of ancient Asherah.[114] She may even have played a role in the creation: "The Lord by wisdom hath founded the earth," says Proverbs 3:19.[115] "Like the symbol of the asherah, Wisdom is a female figure, providing life and nurturing."[116] In fact, as Steve A. Wiggins observes of Asherah herself, "She is Wisdom, the first creature of God."[117] The classical text on this subject is found in Proverbs 8:22–34:

> The Lord possessed me in the beginning of his way, before his works of old.
>
> I was set up from everlasting, from the beginning, or ever the earth was.
>
> When there were no depths, I was brought forth; when there were no fountains abounding with water.
>
> Before the mountains were settled, before the hills was I brought forth:
>
> While as yet he had not made the earth, nor the fields, nor the highest part of the dust of the world.
>
> When he prepared the heavens, I was there: when he set a compass upon the face of the depth:
>
> When he established the clouds above: when he strengthened the fountains of the deep:
>
> When he gave to the sea his decree, that the waters should not pass his commandment: when he appointed the foundations of the earth:
>
> Then I was by him, as one brought up with him: and I was daily his delight, rejoicing always before him;
>
> Rejoicing in the habitable part of his earth; and my delights were with the sons of men.

Now therefore hearken unto me, O ye children: for
blessed *[ashre]* are they that keep my ways.
Hear instruction, and be wise, and refuse it not.
Blessed *[ashre]* is the man that heareth me.

The use of the Hebrew word *ashre* in this connection—
from the same root *('shr)* that underlies the word *asherah*—is
probably significant.[118] "Happy *[ashre]* is the man that findeth
wisdom" (Proverbs 3:13). (A similar wordplay may be going on
behind the word *happy* in 1 Nephi 8:10, 12, and perhaps even
behind *joy* and *joyous* in 1 Nephi 8:12 and 11:23.)[119] Another
noteworthy fact is that "the 'tree of life,' which recalls the asherah,
appears in Israelite tradition as a metaphorical expression for
wisdom." Indeed, Mark Smith sees Proverbs 3:13–18 as "a con-
spicuous chiasm" in which the essentially equivalent "inside
terms" are *ḥokmāh* (wisdom) and *'eṣ-hayim* (a tree of life).[120]
The apocryphal book of Ecclesiasticus, which is also known as
Wisdom of Ben Sira, uses various trees to symbolize Wisdom
(24:12–19). "Wisdom is rooted in the fear of the Lord," says
Ecclesiasticus 1:20 (New English Bible), "and long life grows
on her branches." "She is a tree of life to them that lay hold
upon her: and happy *[me'ushshar]*[121] is every one that retaineth
her" (Proverbs 3:18). Similar imagery can be found elsewhere
in the Bible as well, including passages where wisdom is the
explicit or implicit topic of discussion:

Blessed *[ashre]* is the man that walketh not in the counsel of the ungodly, nor standeth in the way of sinners, nor
sitteth in the seat of the scornful.

But his delight is in the law of the Lord; and in his law
doth he meditate day and night.

And he shall be like a tree planted by the rivers of water,
that bringeth forth his fruit in his season; his leaf also shall
not wither; and whatsoever he doeth shall prosper.

The ungodly are not so: but are like the chaff which the
wind driveth away.

Therefore the ungodly shall not stand in the judgment,
nor sinners in the congregation of the righteous.
For the Lord knoweth the way of the righteous: but the
way of the ungodly shall perish.[122]

Several parallels between the language of Proverbs 1–9 and
the language of the visions in 1 Nephi will be apparent to careful readers. Note, for example, in Proverbs 3:18, quoted above,
the image of "taking hold," which recalls the iron rod of Lehi
and Nephi's visions.[123] The New English Bible version of Proverbs 3:18 speaks of "grasp[ing] her" and "hold[ing] her fast"—
in very much the same way that Lehi and Nephi's visions speak
of "catching hold of" and "holding fast to" the rod of iron. Proverbs 4:13 advises us to "take fast hold of instruction; let her not
go: keep her; for she is thy life." Apocryphal Baruch 4:1 declares that "all who hold fast to [Wisdom] shall live, but those
who forsake her shall die." "He who holds fast to her will gain
honour," says the likewise apocryphal Ecclesiasticus 4:13.[124]
Both the advice of Proverbs and the images of Lehi's dream,
furthermore, are expressly directed to youths, to sons specifically or to children.[125] ("O, remember, my son," says Alma
37:35, echoing this theme, "and learn wisdom in thy youth;
yea, learn in thy youth to keep the commandments of God.")
Both Proverbs and 1 Nephi speak constantly in the imagery of
"ways," "paths," and "walking" and warn against "going astray,"
"wandering off," and "wandering in strange roads."[126] Proverbs
3:17 declares that "her [Wisdom's] ways are ways of pleasant-
ness, and all her paths are peace." In subsequent Nephite tradition, King Benjamin speaks of "the Spirit of the Lord" that
"guide[s] . . . in wisdom's paths" (Mosiah 2:36), and Mormon
laments "how slow" people are "to walk in wisdom's paths"
(Helaman 12:5).

Proverbs has Wisdom describing her words as "plain," an
attribute that is lauded repeatedly throughout 1 Nephi, notably

in the narrative of Nephi's vision, and throughout 2 Nephi.[127]
The phrase *plain and precious,* recurrent in Nephi's account of
his experience with the angelic guide,[128] could serve as an excellent description of biblical "Wisdom," surpassed in its aptness
only by the phrasing *plain and pure, and most precious* in
1 Nephi 14:23. In Proverbs 8:19 Wisdom declares, "My fruit is
better than gold, yea, than fine gold."[129] "She is more precious
than rubies," says Proverbs 3:15, "and all the things thou canst
desire are not to be compared unto her." "Wisdom," declares
Ecclesiasticus 4:11, "raises her sons to greatness." Similarly,
Lehi and Nephi's tree was "precious above all" (1 Nephi 11:9)—
"a tree, whose fruit was desirable to make one happy" (1 Nephi
8:10), "desirable above all other fruit" (1 Nephi 8:12, 15; compare 11:22). Accordingly, no price is too high to pay, if it will
bring us to attain wisdom. "I say unto you," Alma the Younger
remarked to the poor among the Zoramites in the context of a
discussion centering on a seed and on the tree of life that could
be nourished out of it, "it is well that ye are cast out of your
synagogues, that ye may be humble, and that ye may learn wisdom" (Alma 32:12). Confident in the quality of what she has to
offer, Wisdom invites others to partake:

> Wisdom crieth without; she uttereth her voice in the
> streets:
> She crieth in the chief place of concourse, in the open-
> ings of the gates: in the city she uttereth her words.[130]

> Doth not wisdom cry? and understanding put forth her
> voice?
> She standeth in the top of high places, by the way in the
> places of the paths.
> She crieth at the gates, at the entry of the city, at the
> coming in at the doors.[131]

> She hath sent forth her maidens: she crieth upon the
> highest places of the city.[132]

She is not alone, however. True to his roots in ancient Israel, Lehi taught that "it must needs be that there was an opposition; even the forbidden fruit in opposition to the tree of life; the one being sweet and the other bitter" (2 Nephi 2:15). (The fourth-century Coptic Manichaean psalmbook contrasts "the King of Light who is the tree of life" to "the Darkness which is the tree of death.")[133] This doctrine of divinely ordained opposites is well documented in wisdom literature.[134] Thus, in Proverbs, readers are told of two contradictory "ways"—that of the foolish and that of obedience to wisdom—and Lady Wisdom is contrasted repeatedly with her antagonist, "the strange woman" or "whorish woman," who is certainly "forbidden" to the righteous.[135] (Likewise opposed to the truth of God is Nephi's striking image, given to him in the same vision as the tree of life, of "the mother of abominations," "the whore of all the earth," which fights against the saints.)[136] Lady Wisdom and the "whorish woman" are, in fact, competitors:

> A foolish woman is clamorous: she is simple, and knoweth nothing.
> For she sitteth at the door of her house, on a seat in the high places of the city,
> To call passengers who go right on their ways:
> Whoso is simple, let him turn in hither: and as for him that wanteth understanding, she saith to him,
> Stolen waters are sweet, and bread eaten in secret is pleasant.
> But he knoweth not that the dead are there; and that her guests are in the depths of hell.[137]
> Now is she without, now in the streets, and lieth in wait at every corner.[138]

Furthermore, for all her exalted status, Wisdom must face "scorners," which must surely remind the reader of 1 Nephi of those in "the large and spacious building" who point the finger of scorn at the saints coming forward to partake of the tree of life.[139] This building seems, as we have already noted, to represent a human alternative to the true wisdom, the divine wisdom of God: Nephi records that it symbolizes "the world and the wisdom thereof" (1 Nephi 11:35).

While Wisdom holds out the promise of great blessings to those who accept and listen to her, she predicts disaster for those who reject her teaching:

> But ye have set at nought all my counsel, and would none of my reproof:
> I also will laugh at your calamity; I will mock when your fear cometh;
> When your fear cometh as desolation, and your destruction cometh as a whirlwind; when distress and anguish cometh upon you.
> Then shall they call upon me, but I will not answer; they shall seek me early, but they shall not find me:
> For that they hated knowledge, and did not choose the fear of the Lord:
> They would none of my counsel: they despised all my reproof.
> Therefore shall they *eat of the fruit* of their own way, and be filled with their own devices.
> For the turning away of the simple shall slay them, and the prosperity of fools shall destroy them.
> But whoso hearkeneth unto me shall dwell safely, and shall be quiet from fear of evil.[140]

Wisdom represents life, while the lack of wisdom leads to death.[141] (Perhaps the juxtaposition of a living and nourishing tree in 1 Nephi with the inanimate structure from which the worldly lean out to express their disdain is intended to make this point.) "For the upright shall dwell in the land, and the perfect shall remain in it. But the wicked shall be cut off from the earth, and the transgressors shall be rooted out of it."[142] "For whoso findeth me findeth life," Wisdom says in Proverbs

8:35–6, "and shall obtain favor of the Lord. But he that sinneth against me wrongeth his own soul: all they that hate me love death." The sinner, in fact, falls into the clutches of the "whorish woman," the rival to Lady Wisdom: "For her house inclineth unto death, and her paths unto the dead. None that go unto her return again, neither take they hold of the paths of life."[143] "O how marvelous are the works of the Lord," exclaims the Book of Mormon's Ammon₁, "and how long doth he suffer with his people; yea, and how blind and impenetrable are the understandings of the children of men; for they will not seek wisdom, neither do they desire that she should rule over them!" (Mosiah 8:20).[144] Similarly, Ecclesiasticus 4:19 says of Wisdom and of the individual who "strays from her" that "she will desert him and abandon him to his fate." In Lehi's vision, those who rejected the fruit of the tree "fell away into forbidden paths and were lost" (1 Nephi 8:28) or "were drowned in the depths of the fountain" (1 Nephi 8:32). "Many were lost from his view, wandering in strange roads" (1 Nephi 8:32). It was for fear of this possible outcome that, after partaking of the fruit of the tree, Lehi was "desirous that [his] family should partake of it also" (1 Nephi 8:12). In a parallel vein, Ecclesiasticus 4:15–16 tells us that Wisdom's "dutiful servant . . . will possess her and bequeath her to his descendants."

In 1 Nephi 8:13–14, Lehi's tree is associated with a river and spring of water. "The symbols of fountain and tree of life are frequent" in wisdom literature too.[145] Nephi himself, in 1 Nephi 11:25, actually equates the "tree of life" with "the fountain of living waters," "which waters," he relates, "are a representation of the love of God." "And I also beheld," he continues, "that the tree of life was a representation of the love of God."

And, truly, there can be no greater illustration of God's care for his children than this: "For God so loved the world, that he gave his only begotten Son, that whosoever believeth in him should not perish, but have everlasting life."[146] The inclusion in 1 Nephi of an authentically preexilic religious symbol that could scarcely have been deduced by the New York farmboy Joseph Smith from the Bible—especially given his severely limited knowledge of that book in the late 1820s, when he was translating the golden plates[147]—suggests that the Book of Mormon is, indeed, an ancient historical record. And that, in turn, suggests that God did, indeed, so love the world that he gave his Only Begotten Son to save us. The Book of Mormon is, as it claims to be, a second witness for Christ.

Notes

William J. Hamblin, Paul Y. Hoskisson, Dana M. Pike, Matthew Roper, and John A. Tvedtnes furnished several interesting references and, with Deborah D. Peterson, offered useful comments on earlier drafts of this essay. Of course, the author alone is responsible for the paper's arguments and conclusions.

So that there will be no mistake about my position, let me briefly speak rather more personally: This essay should not be misinterpreted as a brief for theological or ecclesiological innovation within the Church of Jesus Christ of Latter-day Saints. Members of that church have long understood and accepted the idea of a divine Mother in Heaven. If further information or instruction relating to her is to be made public, my conviction is that this will come through revelation to the proper authorities, not through agitation nor even, in any significant way, through scholarship. Unless and until revelation dictates otherwise, I believe that we are to stay within the bounds set by our canonical scriptures on this matter. I suspect that the ancient notion of Asherah as the wife of El reflects true doctrine, albeit frequently garbled and corrupted. I suspect, furthermore, that it was such garbling and corruption that impelled the Deuteronomistic reformers, whom I believe to have been inspired, to oppose and suppress the veneration of Asherah, just as they opposed and suppressed the veneration of the Nehushtan of Moses. My suspicions are not, however, essential to the fundamental thesis of this paper, which is simply that the representation, by a tree, of a divine consort bearing a divine child—to us a rather unexpected juxtaposition—was intelligible to Nephi because, whatever his personal opinion of Asherah may have been, such symbolism was familiar to him.

1. Simo Parpola, "The Assyrian Tree of Life: Tracing the Origins of Jewish Monotheism and Greek Philosophy," *Journal of Near Eastern Studies* 52/3 (1993): 161. Another useful treatment of the theme can be found in Geo Widengren, *The King and the Tree of Life in Ancient Near Eastern Religion* (Uppsala, Sweden: Lundequistska Bokhandeln, 1951). Asko Parpola discusses the tree of life motif as it appears in the ancient Indus River valley (see his *Deciphering the Indus Script* [New York: Cambridge University Press, 1994], 256–71). In his book *The Tree of Life: Image for the Cosmos* (New York: Thames and Hudson, 1974), Roger Cook supplies many images of the motif, from ancient times to the contemporary period. John S. Crawford, in "Multiculturalism at Sardis" (*Biblical Archaeology Review* 22/5 [September/October 1996]: 44), features a photograph of a terra-cotta flask found at an early-fifth-century-A.D. Christian site in modern-day Turkey. It is decorated with a cross from which branches and leaves grow, obviously intended to suggest a tree of life.

2. William G. Dever, *Recent Archaeological Discoveries and Biblical Research* (Seattle: University of Washington Press, 1990), 153. On p. 160 Professor Dever notes the popularity of the tree of life image on ancient Israelite seals (i.e., engraved gemstones used in signet rings) and on ivory furniture inlays. In conversation, my Assyriologist colleague Paul Hoskisson tells me that he doubts that the tree of life actually existed in Mesopotamia—or, at least, that iconographic materials without literary explanations (and, he says, we have none) cannot establish by themselves that it did. He thinks, rather, that the tree was West Semitic, which, if true, would still certainly be compatible with the argument advanced in this paper. For further references on the sacred tree, see Manfried Dietrich and Oswald Loretz, *"Jahwe und seine Aschera": Anthropomorphes Kultbild*

in Mesopotamien, Ugarit und Israel: Das biblische Bilderverbot (Münster: UGARIT-Verlag, 1992), 178 n. 32.

3. The motif is American, no less than Mediterranean. Linda Schele sketches the centrality of the sacred tree as an iconographic theme in pre-Columbian Mesoamerica and includes numerous illustrations in her study "The Olmec Mountain and Tree of Creation in Mesoamerican Cosmology" (in Jill Guthrie, ed., *The Olmec World: Ritual and Rulership* [Princeton: Art Museum, Princeton University Press in association with Harry N. Abrams, 1995], 104–17). David Freidel, Linda Schele, and Joy Parker, in their book *Maya Cosmos: Three Thousand Years on the Shaman's Path* (New York: William Morrow, 1993), discuss the "World Tree" at length. Those who have visited the ancient Mexican site will recall that both the Temple of the Cross and the Temple of the Foliated Cross at Palenque are adorned, in the words of Michael D. Coe (*The Maya*, 3rd ed. [New York: Thames and Hudson, 1984], 99), with "a branching world-tree (which bears an astonishing resemblance to the Christian cross) surmounted by a quetzal bird." Allen J. Christenson, a Latter-day Saint Mesoamericanist, surveys the subject in his article "The Sacred Tree of the Ancient Maya," *Journal of Book of Mormon Studies* 6/1 (1997): 1–23. According to Kevin Locke, a prominent student and exponent of the culture of the Lakota (Sioux) people who was interviewed in the newsletter of the Bahá'í International Community, "The central prayer of the Lakota is to be sheltered under the 'Tree of Life'" (*One Country* 8/2 [July–September 1996]: 10).

4. See Alma 32. The famous allegory of the olive tree, found in Jacob 5, may also be related to this motif. For extended discussions of that chapter, see Stephen D. Ricks and John W. Welch, eds., *The Allegory of the Olive Tree: The Olive, the Bible, and Jacob 5* (Salt Lake City: Deseret Book and FARMS, 1994). Erich Neumann's book *The Great Mother: An Analysis of the Archetype* (trans. Ralph Mannheim [Princeton: Princeton University Press, 1983], 50–2, 70), although seriously marred by arrant Jungianism, contains an interesting discussion of seeds and growth that could be used to relate Alma 32 to the subject of the present paper.

5. In Lehi's vision of the tree, his attention was specifically on the fruit, which was "white, to exceed all the whiteness that I had ever seen" (1 Nephi 8:11). Such language occurs elsewhere in the Book of Mormon as well. Echoing Nephi's vision of "the tree which is precious above all," Alma says of his own "tree springing up unto everlasting life" that its fruit "is most precious, . . . sweet above all that is sweet, . . . white above all that is white, yea, and pure above all that is pure" (Alma 32:41, 42). This fruit is also described as precious in 1 Nephi 15:36 (to which we should probably compare Jacob 5:61, 74). Alma describes Mary as "a precious and chosen vessel" (Alma 7:10). The adjectives under consideration here seem to form a kind of conceptual complex. Moroni's hope is that his unbelieving readers may yet repent and "be found spotless, pure, fair, and white . . . at that great and last day" (Mormon 9:6). The whiteness mentioned here, by the way, is no more to be taken in a racial sense than is the ancient Arabic expression *iswadda wajhuhu* ("His face became black"), which denotes sorrow or shame, or the statement of the Qur'an that, at the last day, the faces of the righteous will be white while those of the wicked will be black (see 3:106–7; compare 39:60; 75:22–4; 80:38–42; see also 16:58; 43:17).

6. Compare Luke 1:42. The well-known Coptic Manichaean psalmbook, which dates perhaps to the fourth Christian century in Egypt, likewise seems to identify Christ with the notably sweet fruit of a sacred tree. See C. R. C. Allberry, ed., *A Manichaean Psalm-Book, Part II* (Stuttgart: W. Kohlhammer, 1938), 134, 155, 158, 171, 176, 185.

7. Michael D. Coogan, "Canaanite Origins and Lineage: Reflections on the Religion of Ancient Israel," in *Ancient Israelite Religion: Essays in Honor of Frank Moore Cross*, ed. Patrick D. Miller Jr., Paul D. Hanson, and S. Dean McBride (Philadelphia: Fortress Press, 1987), 115. Compare Dever, *Recent Archaeological Discoveries*, 121, 128, 166.

8. For the relative recentness of absolute Hebrew monotheism, see Baruch Halpern, "'Brisker Pipes Than Poetry': The Development of Israelite Monotheism," in *Judaic Perspectives on Ancient Israel*, ed.

Jacob Neusner, Baruch A. Levine, and Ernest S. Frerichs (Philadelphia: Fortress Press, 1987), 77–115; Raphael Patai, *The Hebrew God-
dess*, 3rd ed. (Detroit: Wayne State University Press, 1990), especially
pp. 27, 30, and 35 (where Patai observes that some non-monotheistic
materials have been edited out of the Bible as we have it today);
Lowell K. Handy, "The Appearance of Pantheon in Judah," in *The
Triumph of Elohim: From Yahwisms to Judaisms*, ed. Diana Vikander
Edelman (Grand Rapids, Mich.: Eerdmans, 1996), 27–43; Erhard S.
Gerstenberger, *Yahweh—the Patriarch: Ancient Images of God and
Feminist Theology*, trans. Frederick J. Gaiser (Minneapolis: Fortress
Press, 1996), 2–3, 13, 35, 82, 86, 92, 136; and Jon D. Levenson,
Sinai and Zion: An Entry into the Jewish Bible (San Francisco:
HarperSanFrancisco, 1987), 58–65. Many other references could be
given. On the cultural similarities between Canaanites and Hebrews,
see Patai, *Hebrew Goddess*, 31, 35, 40 (on the temple); Mark S. Smith,
*The Early History of God: Yahweh and the Other Deities in Ancient
Israel* (San Francisco: Harper & Row, 1990), xxii, 1, 3, 4, 25; and
William Dever, "Is the Bible Right After All?" interview by Hershel
Shanks, *Biblical Archaeology Review* 22/5 (September/October
1996): 31–4. According to Professor William G. Dever, in a lecture
at Brigham Young University on 14 February 1997, as yet unpub-
lished Israelite inscriptions from Kuntillet ʿAjrūd mention four gods:
Yahweh, Baal, Asherah, and El.

    9. Smith, *Early History of God*, 154.

    10. Ibid., 156.

    11. Ibid., 152. Compare Dever, *Recent Archaeological Discoveries*,
165, 166.

    12. Frank Moore Cross Jr., "Yahweh and the God of the Patri-
archs," *Harvard Theological Review* 55 (1962): 240.

    13. Ibid., 234; compare 241–2; Conrad E. L'Heureux, *Rank
among the Canaanite Gods: El, Baʿal, and the Rephaʾim* (Missoula,
Mont.: Scholars Press, 1979), 29–70, 72.

    14. See Smith, *Early History of God*, 7; and Margaret Barker, *The
Great Angel: A Study of Israel's Second God* (Louisville: Westminster/
John Knox Press, 1992). Compare Larry W. Hurtado, *One God, One*

Lord: Early Christian Devotion and Ancient Jewish Monotheism (Philadelphia: Fortress Press, 1988).

15. See, among the many references that could be given on this subject, Halpern, "'Brisker Pipes Than Poetry,'" 85; John Day, "Asherah in the Hebrew Bible," *Journal of Biblical Literature* 105/3 (1986): 387 and n. 9; and Peter Hayman, "Monotheism—a Misused Word in Jewish Studies?" *Journal of Jewish Studies* 42 (spring 1991): 1–15. Significant evidence can be found in Deuteronomy 32:8–9, where the Septuagint's "children/sons of God" disagrees with the Masoretic text's "children of Israel." The Septuagint's reading has recently been confirmed by a fragment from Qumran (see Emanuel Tov, *Textual Criticism of the Hebrew Bible* [Minneapolis: Fortress Press, 1992], 269, 365). One thinks also of Job 1:6 and 2:1, to say nothing of Psalm 29 (in its original Hebrew), Psalm 82, and Micah 4:5.

16. See Smith, *Early History of God*, xxiii, xxvii, 8–11, 15, 21, 22, 23, 163; Patai, *Hebrew Goddess*, 133; Cross, "Yahweh and the God of the Patriarchs," 253–7; Otto Eissfeldt, "El and Yahweh," *Journal of Semitic Studies* 1 (1956): 25–37; J. A. Emerton, "The Origin of the Son of Man Imagery," *Journal of Theological Studies* 9 (1958): 225–42; and Dietrich and Loretz, *"Jahwe und seine Aschera,"* 86, 93, 101, 118, 134, 146–7, 149, 157; further references to this viewpoint are given by L'Heureux, *Rank among the Canaanite Gods*, 57–9. Halpern seems to dissent on this matter, albeit unconvincingly (see his "'Brisker Pipes Than Poetry,'" 88), and Herbert Niehr summarizes the majority view but appears vaguely to disapprove of it (see his "The Rise of YHWH in Judahite and Israelite Religion," in *Triumph of Elohim*, ed. Edelman, 45). On the common motif of the withdrawal of the elder gods, see Patai, *Hebrew Goddess*, 128; and Halpern, "'Brisker Pipes Than Poetry,'" 80. Many more references could be given, but they would be beyond the scope of the present discussion.

17. See Day, "Asherah in the Hebrew Bible and Northwest Semitic Literature," 385–7, 398; Steve A. Wiggins, "The Myth of Asherah: Lion Lady and Serpent Goddess," *Ugarit-Forschungen: Internationales Jahrbuch für die Altertumskunde Syrien-Palästinas* 23 (1991): 384;

and Steve A. Wiggins, *A Reassessment of "Asherah": A Study according to the Textual Sources of the First Two Millennia B.C.E.* (Kevelaer: Butzon und Bercker, 1993), 192, which suggests that the name *Asherah* means "holy place" or "sanctuary."

18. See J. C. de Moor, "ʾashērah," in *Theological Dictionary of the Old Testament*, ed. G. Johannes Botterweck and Helmer Ringgren (Grand Rapids, Mich.: Eerdmans, 1974), 1:439. On Asherah as divine wet nurse, see Wiggins, *Reassessment of "Asherah,"* 26, 27, 71, 76, 89, 190; on her maternal aspect, see pp. 37, 71, 89.

19. There is, moreover, evidence that she was a chief goddess among the Akkadians and Sumerians and at Ebla, and that she received worship as mother of the gods among the Amorites and Hittites. For this and for the attributes of Asherah alluded to earlier, see Saul M. Olyan, *Asherah and the Cult of Yahweh in Israel* (Atlanta: Scholars Press, 1988), 39, 57 n. 82, 58 n. 88, 61; Patai, *Hebrew Goddess*, 36, 37, 38, 54, 55, 58–9, 61, 119–20, 122; compare 23, 24; de Moor, "ʾashērah," 1:439; Wiggins, "Myth of Asherah," 392; Day, "Asherah in the Hebrew Bible," 385–7, 391; and Wiggins, *Reassessment of "Asherah,"* 150–2. Extant evidence for Asherah appears earliest in ancient Mesopotamia and, somewhat thereafter, in South Arabia (see Wiggins, *Reassessment of "Asherah,"* 2, 132–50, 153–63).

20. See Wiggins, *Reassessment of "Asherah,"* 27, 71, 108–10, 131, 190. On p. 147 Wiggins cites the Babylonian personal name *Ashratum-unnī* ("Ashratum [= Asherah] is my mother").

21. See John Wilson Betlyon, "The Cult of ʾAšerah/ʾElat at Sidon," *Journal of Near Eastern Studies* 44/1 (1985): 53–6. Compare de Moor, "ʾashērah," 1:440; and Day, "Asherah in the Hebrew Bible," 387–8. Patai notes that the goddess Astarte had apparently replaced Asherah in Sidon by the fourth century B.C. (see his *Hebrew Goddess*, 56). Perhaps the two were assimilated. Like Asherah, of course, Astarte was a fertility goddess (see ibid., 57, 59–60).

22. Hugh Nibley, *An Approach to the Book of Mormon*, 3rd ed. (Salt Lake City: Deseret Book and FARMS, 1988), 47; compare 84, 88–9, 92, 98; and Hugh Nibley, *Lehi in the Desert; The World of the Jaredites; There Were Jaredites* (Salt Lake City: Deseret Book and FARMS, 1988), 12, 23–4.

23. See Patai, *Hebrew Goddess*, 37–8, 41, 42, 55; Smith, *Early History of God*, 6; Day, "Asherah in the Hebrew Bible," 387; and Wiggins, *Reassessment of "Asherah,"* 29, 30, 32, 35 n. 71. "Athirat [Asherah] of the two Tyres" seems to be identical with "Elat of the Sidonians" (Wiggins, "Myth of Asherah," 388). Lehi and his party very likely passed through or by Elat on their journey from Jerusalem to the land of promise (see the map in Lynn M. Hilton and Hope Hilton, *In Search of Lehi's Trail* [Salt Lake City: Deseret Book, 1976], 22–3). Qurʾān 53:19–23, incidentally, refers to three goddesses, daughters of Allāh (whose name or title is manifestly cognate with *El* or *Elohim*), one of whom is Allāt (compare 6:100; 16:57; 37:149). Some Qurʾānic commentators allegedly identify another of the daughters with a sacred tree, but I have not yet confirmed this.

24. See Patai, *Hebrew Goddess*, 34; compare Dietrich and Loretz, *"Jahwe und seine Aschera,"* 120. In *Reassessment of "Asherah"* (149), Wiggins notes that the goddess was known in Palestine during the Amarna period (fourteenth century B.C.).

25. The immediately foregoing information comes from Professor Dever's 14 February 1997 lecture at Brigham Young University. See also J. Glen Taylor, *Yahweh and the Sun: Biblical and Archaeological Evidence for Sun Worship in Ancient Israel* (Sheffield: JSOT Press, 1993), 58–9; and Gerstenberger, *Yahweh—the Patriarch*, 66. On the Arad temple, see Dever, *Recent Archaeological Discoveries*, 139–40. In his lecture, Professor Dever noted a lion figure found at the base of an offering table at Arad. Asherah was often associated with lions (and was called "the Lion Lady").

26. Dever, *Recent Archaeological Discoveries*, 157–9. The objects are pictured in figs. 57 and 58, on pp. 158–9.

27. Patai maintains Asherah's foreign origin in *Hebrew Goddess* (31–2, 38, 45, 52). Smith (*Early History of God*, xxiii, 80–1, 146), Olyan (*Asherah and the Cult of Yahweh*, 4–7, 9, 13–14, 18, 22, 88), Saul M. Olyan ("The Cultic Confessions of Jer 2,27a," *Zeitschrift für die alttestamentliche Wissenschaft* 99 [1987]: 259), and Taylor (*Yahweh and the Sun*, 183) appear to argue that, in some sense, she was natively Israelite. As will be seen later (see below), both Canaanites and Israelites associated Asherah with childbirth. Thus, Leah's

exclamation at the birth of a child she significantly named Asher, recorded in Genesis 30:13, may reflect a very early Hebrew devotion to the goddess: "Happy *[be-asheri]* am I, for the daughters will call me blessed *[isheru-ni]*."

28. See Patai, *Hebrew Goddess*, 39; and Thomas L. Thompson, "The Intellectual Matrix of Early Biblical Narrative: Inclusive Monotheism in Persian Period Palestine," in *Triumph of Elohim*, ed. Edelman, 119 n. 13.

29. See Patai, *Hebrew Goddess*, 47, 52.

30. See Smith, *Early History of God*, 6, 145.

31. J. Glen Taylor, "The Two Earliest Known Representations of Yahweh," in *Ascribe to the Lord: Biblical and Other Studies in Memory of Peter C. Craigie*, ed. Lyle Eslinger and Glen Taylor (Sheffield: JSOT Press, 1988), 566. For a relatively complete discussion of the find at Taanach, see Taylor, *Yahweh and the Sun*, 24–37 (focus on Asherah on pp. 28–9; photographs at plates 1a–1d). Dever also discusses the Taanach stand, which, among other things, bears an image of the tree of life (see his *Recent Archaeological Discoveries*, 134–6, 137, fig. 40).

32. David Noel Freedman, "Yahweh of Samaria and His Asherah," *Biblical Archaeologist* 50/4 (December 1987): 248. See Niehr, "Rise of YHWH," 57, 59.

33. See Edelman, "Introduction," 19; and Handy, "Appearance of Pantheon in Judah," 27–43.

34. Jeremiah 2:27 condemns the veneration of Asherah, carefully switching the roles of mother and father in an act of mockery. See Olyan, "Cultic Confessions of Jer 2,27a," 254–9.

35. Brian Schmidt reportedly thinks that an image of Yahweh himself may have stood in the temple at Jerusalem, at least during the period subsequent to Nephi's departure from the city (see Diana V. Edelman, "Tracking Observance of the Aniconic Tradition through Numismatics," in *Triumph of Elohim*, ed. Edelman, 223 n. 118). Pictorial representations of an anthropomorphic or partially anthropomorphic Yahweh are not unknown in antiquity. See, for example, Taylor, "Representations of Yahweh"; Brian B. Schmidt, "The Aniconic Tradition: On Reading Images and Viewing Texts," in *Tri-*

umph of Elohim, ed. Edelman, 75–105; Gerstenberger, *Yahweh—the Patriarch*, 33–4; and Edelman, "Aniconic Tradition," 185–225. On images of Yahweh among the ancient Israelites, see also Taylor, *Yahweh and the Sun*, 109; and Dietrich and Loretz, *"Jahwe und Seine Aschera,"* 100–3, 106–10, 112–17, 163.

36. This summary of Asherah's history among the Hebrews relies upon Patai, *Hebrew Goddess*, 39, 41–2, 45–50; Smith, *Early History of God*, 80, 94; Olyan, *Asherah and the Cult of Yahweh*, 19, 70–2; W. G. Dever, "Asherah, Consort of Yahweh? New Evidence from Kuntillet ʿajrūd," *Bulletin of the American Schools of Oriental Research* 255 (1984): 31; and de Moor, "ʾashērah," 1:444. These sources provide abundant biblical references. Patai argues that Ezekiel saw the image of Asherah in the Jerusalem temple in 592 B.C., only a few years before Jerusalem's destruction and the Lehite departure (see his *Hebrew Goddess*, 50–2). Dever asserts that Asherah was worshiped in Israel down to the end of the monarchy (see his *Recent Archaeological Discoveries*, 164, 166; compare Wiggins, *Reassessment of "Asherah,"* 125).

37. See Smith, *Early History of God*, 98, 161–3; compare Gerstenberger, *Yahweh—the Patriarch*, 92, 136.

38. In another sense, of course, she never vanished at all. That is the whole point of Raphael Patai's fascinating book, *Hebrew Goddess* (see n. 8).

39. See Wiggins, *Reassessment of "Asherah,"* 130.

40. Dever, "Asherah, Consort of Yahweh?" 31. See his *Recent Archaeological Discoveries*, 123–4, 166; and his "Is the Bible Right After All?" 36–7. Diana V. Edelman, in her introduction to *The Triumph of Elohim* (16–17, 18, 19–20), also discusses the possible suppression in the Old Testament of information relating to early Hebrew views of God and the gods (especially as it relates to Asherah), as does Lowell K. Handy in "Appearance of Pantheon in Judah," 30.

41. See Wiggins, *Reassessment of "Asherah,"* 105. A Book of Mormon parallel may be found at Alma 37:21–34, where the prophet Alma advises his son Helaman to suppress certain information about Jaredite secret combinations, lest it prove seductive to his audience.

42. See Olyan, *Asherah and the Cult of Yahweh*, 10–13, 73. He

points specifically to what he regards as their false claim that Asherah was the consort, not of El or of Yahweh, but of Baal (see pp. 38, 39, 61, 65, 73, 74; compare Wiggins, *Reassessment of "Asherah,"* 93–4). Freedman hypothesizes that Yahweh took Asherah over as a consort from Baal following Elijah's victory over Baal's priests (see his "Yahweh of Samaria and His Asherah," 249). Olyan denies that Asherah was ever the consort of Baal, contending rather that the Deuteronomist reformers created this relationship as part of their polemic against her veneration among the Israelites, in order to render her guilty by association (see his "Cultic Confessions of Jer 2,27a," 258). Wiggins agrees that, in the Ugaritic texts, Asherah is never presented as either the consort or even the close associate of Baal, but is solely the consort of El (see his "Myth of Asherah," 383–94). Indeed, although many scholars of the Bible would agree with Lynn Clapham that it assigns Asherah to Baal, Wiggins denies even this (see Lynn Clapham, "Mythopoeic Antecedents of the Biblical World-View and Their Transformation in Early Israelite Thought," in *Magnalia Dei, the Mighty Acts of God: Essays on the Bible and Archaeology in Memory of G. Ernest Wright,* ed. Frank Moore Cross, Werner E. Lemke, and Patrick D. Miller Jr. [Garden City, N.Y.: Doubleday, 1976], 117).

43. Dietrich and Loretz, *"Jahwe und seine Aschera,"* 120. On pp. 117–18 they argue against the "objectivity" of the biblical writers.

44. The Book of Mormon alludes repeatedly to the "brazen serpent" of Moses without a trace of condemnation. In fact, it is described as a symbol of Christ (see Helaman 8:14–15; compare Alma 33:19–22; 2 Nephi 25:20), just as the Savior himself uses it in John 3:14–15. (It is tempting to speculate that, in the asherah and the Nehushtan, we may have temple symbols of a divine mother and son.)

45. Taylor contends that both the Nehushtan and the asherah were "Yahwistic icons" (see his *Yahweh and the Sun,* 183).

46. See Smith, *Early History of God,* 80; compare Wiggins, *Reassessment of "Asherah,"* 96, 101, 106, 128. According to Wiggins, pp. 126–8, possible denunciations of Asherah at Isaiah 17:8, 27:9,

Jeremiah 17:2, and Micah 5:13 (= English 5:14) are all later additions to the texts.

47. See Olyan, *Asherah and the Cult of Yahweh*, 9, 73; and Smith, *Early History of God*, 80. See, however, Patai, *Hebrew Goddess*, 53 (Patai, in turn, is opposed by Day, "Asherah in the Hebrew Bible," 404–5); and Freedman, "Yahweh of Samaria and His Asherah," 248–9. Many years ago Julius Wellhausen proposed a reading of Hosea 14:9 (= English 14:8) that would refer to Asherah. For a recent discussion of the status of the debate, see Dietrich and Loretz, *"Jahwe und seine Aschera,"* 110–12, 173–82.

48. Freedman, "Yahweh of Samaria and His Asherah," 248. The story is recounted in 1 Kings 18:1–46. See also Patai, *Hebrew Goddess*, 42–3, 45, 46; and Olyan, *Asherah and the Cult of Yahweh*, 17.

49. See 2 Kings 10:18–28; 13:6; see also Olyan, *Asherah and the Cult of Yahweh*, 4; Patai, *Hebrew Goddess*, 43–6; and Smith, *Early History of God*, 80.

50. Olyan, *Asherah and the Cult of Yahweh*, 73.

51. See ibid., 3–4, 9, 13–14, 22, 33, 43, 73, 74; Smith, *Early History of God*, 150; Olyan, "Cultic Confessions of Jer 2,27a," 257; and Halpern, "'Brisker Pipes Than Poetry,'" 83. Olyan notes "what were evidently the close associations between Jeremiah and the Deuteronomistic school" ("Cultic Confessions of Jer 2,27a," 258). I suspect, by the way, that Lehi and his posterity could be classed with the Deuteronomists; their philosophy of history is a major clue in this direction but is the subject for another paper. So we would not expect a Deuteronomistic text like the Book of Mormon to praise Asherah nor, perhaps, even to mention her explicitly. But we can reasonably expect contemporaries of the controversies about her to understand the symbolic idiom in which they were carried out, and it is the thesis of this paper that Nephi did just that.

52. Dever, *Recent Archaeological Discoveries*, 159.

53. Smith, *Early History of God*, 89.

54. This is the contention, for instance, of Day ("Asherah in the Hebrew Bible," 393).

55. André Lemaire, "Who or What Was Yahweh's Asherah?" *Biblical Archaeology Review* 10/6 (1984): 46.

56. See Olyan, *Asherah and the Cult of Yahweh,* xiv, 74; and Dever, "Is the Bible Right After All?" 37.

57. Thompson, "Intellectual Matrix of Early Biblical Narrative," 119 n. 10.

58. Smith, *Early History of God,* 19; compare 89, 92–3; and Olyan, *Asherah and the Cult of Yahweh,* xiv.

59. See Olyan, *Asherah and the Cult of Yahweh,* 29, 33–4, 38, 74.

60. See Lemaire, "Who or What Was Yahweh's Asherah?" 42, 44; André Lemaire, "Les inscriptions de Khirbet el-Qūm et l'asherah de YHWH," *Revue biblique* 84 (1977): 602–3 (compare pp. 596, 597); Ziony Zevit, "The Khirbet el-Qūm Inscription Mentioning a Goddess," *Bulletin of the American Schools of Oriental Research,* no. 255 (1984): 39; Olyan, *Asherah and the Cult of Yahweh,* 23; and Day, "Asherah in the Hebrew Bible," 394. Incidentally, the personal names appearing in the Khirbat al-Qūm inscription are, as Zevit points out, those of Yahwists, or worshipers of Yahweh (p. 46). Lemaire ("Les inscriptions de Khirbet el-Qōm et l'asherah de YHWH," 597–9) provides a good verbal description of the Khirbat al-Qūm find, accompanied by a photograph on p. 600 and a much clearer line drawing on p. 598. A good illustration also appears in Dever, *Recent Archaeological Discoveries,* 149, fig. 50. See also the discussions in Dietrich and Loretz, *"Jahwe und seine Aschera,"* 93–5, and Wiggins, *Reassessment of "Asherah,"* 166–71.

61. See Lemaire, "Les inscriptions de Khirbet el-Qūm et l'asherah de YHWH," 608; Lemaire, "Who or What Was Yahweh's Asherah?" 44, 51; and Freedman, "Yahweh of Samaria and His Asherah," 246–9.

62. On northern influences at Kuntillat ʿAjrūd, see Zeʾev Meshel, "Did Yahweh Have a Consort?" *Biblical Archaeology Review* 5/2 (1979): 32; and Lemaire, "Who or What Was Yahweh's Asherah?" 44. For the results of recent radiocarbon dating, see an unsigned news item on the subject in *Biblical Archaeology Review* 22/4 (July/ August 1996): 12; compare Olyan, *Asherah and the Cult of Yahweh,* 32; Day, "Asherah in the Hebrew Bible," 392; Dietrich and Loretz,

"Jahwe und seine Aschera," 95; and Wiggins, *Reassessment of "Asherah,"* 171–81. Judith M. Hadley, "Kuntillet ʿAjrūd: Religious Centre or Desert Way Station?" *Palestine Exploration Quarterly* 125 (1993): 115–24, persuasively argues that the ruins are those of a caravansary rather than of a shrine or fortress.

63. See Freedman, "Yahweh of Samaria and His Asherah," 248.

64. See Meshel, "Did Yahweh Have a Consort?" 31 (pictured on p. 32); Dever, "Asherah, Consort of Yahweh?" 26–7 (illustration on p. 26); and Day, "Asherah in the Hebrew Bible," 391–2. Another image on the *pithos* is that of a cow licking her suckling calf, which Dever suggests may be related to the fact that the chief epithet of the head of the Canaanite pantheon was "Bull El" (see his "Asherah, Consort of Yahweh," 27–8). In *Recent Archaeological Discoveries* (140–9), Dever discusses the find at Kuntillet ʿAjrūd and includes illustrations (for "Bull El," see pp. 130–1 and figs. 33, 34). In an unfortunately still-unpublished paper, my colleague Paul Hoskisson argues that the golden calf of Exodus was chosen to represent Yahweh because he was the son of "Bull El" (compare Taylor, *Yahweh and the Sun*, 31 n. 2). A figurine of a bull, perhaps representing "Bull El," is pictured in Dever, "Is the Bible Right After All?" 34.

65. Dever, "Asherah, Consort of Yahweh?" 21; compare p. 30. See also Olyan, "Cultic Confessions of Jer 2,27a," 257, 259; and Dever, "Is the Bible Right After All?" 37. Intriguingly, Meshel suggests that one of the figures on the *pithoi* at Kuntillat ʿAjrūd may be a drawing of Yahweh himself (see his "Did Yahweh Have a Consort?" 27, 31). More recently, Schmidt, in "The Aniconic Tradition: On Reading Images and Viewing Texts" (75–105), presents an extended argument for the identification of the two figures as Yahweh and Asherah. Gerstenberger, in *Yahweh—the Patriarch* (33–4) concurs.

66. Patai, *Hebrew Goddess*, 52–3; compare Gerstenberger, *Yahweh—the Patriarch*, 33–4.

67. Freedman, "Yahweh of Samaria and His Asherah," 249; compare Day, "Asherah in the Hebrew Bible," 392; and Niehr, "Rise of YHWH," 54–5, 59.

68. Halpern, "'Brisker Pipes Than Poetry,'" 85. Halpern includes

references.

69. See Taylor, *Yahweh and the Sun*, 74 n. 4, 99–111, 116, 171, 172 (where the Deuteronomists are said to have rejected the worship of the heavenly host), 174, 175, 183 and nn. 2–3, 201 and nn. 2–3, 203, 257–60 (to the exilic period, and even beyond).

70. See Deuteronomy 4:19; 17:3; 2 Kings 17:16; 21:3, 5; 23:4, 5; 2 Chronicles 33:3, 5; Nehemiah 9:6; Psalm 33:6; 148:1–5; Isaiah 34:4; 45:12; Jeremiah 8:2; 19:13; 33:22; Daniel 8:10; Zephaniah 1:5. Compare Halpern, "'Brisker Pipes Than Poetry,'" 94, 100, 111 n. 44, and throughout.

71. See Day, "Asherah in the Hebrew Bible," 387, 399–400.

72. See Proverbs 8:22–34. This image that is emerging from very recent scholarship—an enthroned God who sits with his consort in the midst of a divine council composed of his children, who are linked with the sun and moon and stars—sheds fascinating light on Lehi's vision as it is recorded in 1 Nephi 1:9–11. That account describes "One descending out of the midst of heaven," whose "luster was above that of the sun at noon-day" and who was followed by twelve others whose "brightness did exceed that of the stars in the firmament" and who then, together, "came down and went forth upon the face of the earth." Clearly, this refers to the Savior, Jesus Christ, and his twelve apostles. (Taylor, throughout his book *Yahweh and the Sun*, argues for an ancient link between Yahweh or Jehovah [whom Latter-day Saints identify as the premortal Jesus Christ] and the sun.) Read in light of recent biblical scholarship, however, the account of Lehi's vision also appears to imply notions of the premortal existence and the literally divine lineage of humanity that are often presumed to have arisen only in the later doctrinal development of Mormonism.

73. See Dever, "Is the Bible Right After All?" 36; and Patai, *Hebrew Goddess*, 39, 52.

74. Cited in Patai, *Hebrew Goddess*, 39; but see the skeptical remarks of Wiggins (*Reassessment of "Asherah,"* 182–4). On p. 182, though, Wiggins appears willing to acknowledge the possibility of

Philistine veneration of the goddess at Ekron (Tel Miqne) during the same period.

75. See Patai, *Hebrew Goddess*, 49; and Day, "Asherah in the Hebrew Bible," 397. During his lecture at Brigham Young University on 14 February 1997, Professor William G. Dever displayed photographs of many ancient Israelite pendants depicting Asherah with a tree.

76. See Taylor, "The Two Earliest Known Representations of Yahweh," 558–60, 565 n. 19; and Taylor, *Yahweh and the Sun*, 29. A photograph of the cultic stand (unfortunately backwards) appears in Paul J. Achtemeier et al., eds., *Harper's Bible Dictionary* (San Francisco: Harper and Row, 1985), 1012. Dever also alludes to Asherah's connection with the "sacred tree" (see his "Asherah, Consort of Yahweh?" 27). See also de Moor, "ʾashērah," 1:441–3, wherein de Moor suggests that the stylized image of a tree came to replace an actual asherah-tree in the ancient cult of the goddess. Wiggins, in *Reassessment of "Asherah"* (13), cites the work of V. L. Piper, who contends that ancient Hebrews would have seen a reference to Asherah in the tree of life mentioned in the story of the Garden of Eden.

77. William G. Dever, lecture at Brigham Young University, 14 February 1997.

78. Wiggins, "Myth of Asherah," 383, with references to the relevant literature. On the tamarisk as a sacred tree, see Dietrich and Loretz, *"Jahwe und seine Aschera,"* 30; compare Olyan, "Cultic Confessions of Jer 2,27a," 256; and Day, "Asherah in the Hebrew Bible," 398, 400. Ancient goddesses were frequently associated with trees. Consider Babylonian Ishtar, for instance, who was linked with human fertility and with a sacred (palm) tree. The Greek goddess Leto seems to have been related to Ishtar and may have been a "Great Asiatic Mother" goddess. She was also probably a goddess of vegetation and was associated with trees—specifically with a sacred palm tree (see David R. West, "Some Minoan and Hellenic Goddesses of Semitic Origin," *Ugarit-Forschungen: Internationales Jahrbuch für die Altertumskunde Syrien-Palästinas* 23 [1991]: 377–9). The Sumerian "Queen of Heaven and Earth," the goddess Inanna (= Babylonian

Ishtar), was associated with—and perhaps, in a sense, even identified with—a "*huluppu*-tree" originally planted by the Euphrates (see Diane Wolkstein and Samuel Noah Kramer, *Inanna: Queen of Heaven and Earth* [New York: Harper and Row, 1983], 5–9, 137–46). Hugh Nibley discusses the association of goddesses with trees in ancient Egypt (see his *The Message of the Joseph Smith Papyri: An Egyptian Endowment* [Salt Lake City: Deseret Book, 1975], 166–7). See also Leon Yarden, *The Tree of Light: A Study of the Menorah, the Seven-Branched Lampstand* (Uppsala, Sweden: Skriv Service AB, 1972), 44. Lemaire and Parpola supply several images of sacred trees in ancient Near Eastern art (see Lemaire, "Who or What Was Yahweh's Asherah?" 48–9; and Parpola, "The Assyrian Tree of Life," 161–208). Perhaps significantly in this context, in her article "The Olmec Mountain and Tree of Creation" (see n. 3), Linda Schele argues that ancient Mesoamerican rulers were frequently viewed as the personification or embodiment of the "world tree," which was itself (at least at Teotihuacan) equivalent to the "Great Goddess." Widengren notes the identification of the king (and eventually of the Messiah) with the tree of life in ancient Mesopotamia and in the Hebrew Bible (see his *The King and the Tree of Life*, 42–58). In a private communication to me dated 11 November 1996, John A. Tvedtnes contends that the tree of life represents Christ himself (Yarden indicates that this identification is common, especially in medieval literature; see his *Tree of Light*, 42). Tvedtnes may well be correct; certainly the evidence shows that the tree was interpreted in this way in late antiquity and the Middle Ages. But this does not, in and of itself, rule out an identification with a female divine consort, nor does it necessarily rule out the assumption of this paper that the *fruit* of Nephi's tree symbolizes Christ. Powerful symbols like the tree of life can be, and generally are, polyvalent. As we have seen, in Mesoamerica and the ancient Near East the sacred tree could represent both goddess and mortal male, sometimes simultaneously. The Manichaean psalmbook, which, as we saw in note 6 identifies Christ with the fruit of the tree, identifies him elsewhere with the tree in its entirety (see Allberry, *Manichaean Psalm-Book*, 66, 116). Allen J. Christenson observes that "in ancient Maya inscriptions, the human soul was called *sak nik' nal* ('white flower thing'), referring to the white flowers of the ceiba tree" ("Sacred Tree of the Ancient Maya," 11; see 22 n. 13). Even today, the huge and impressive ceiba is revered by the Maya as a manifestation of the sacred world tree.

79. See Day, "Asherah in the Hebrew Bible," 397–8, 401–4, and references supplied there. (The rabbis do not point to any particular type of tree but include grapevines as well as pomegranate, walnut, myrtle, and willow trees and argue that the wood and fruit of such trees must not be used.) Lemaire argues that, although Asherah was a goddess in Canaanite religion, the word *asherah* in biblical materials and ancient Hebrew inscriptions refers *only* to a sacred tree or, perhaps, to a grove of such trees (see his "Les inscriptions de Khirbet el-Qōm et l'asherah de YHWH," 603–7; and his "Who or What Was Yahweh's Asherah?" 42–51). Ziony Zevit defends the idea that the asherah of the inscription refers to a divine person, as do most if not all of the other materials on the subject cited in this paper (see his "The Khirbet el-Qōm Inscription Mentioning a Goddess," *Bulletin of the American Schools of Oriental Research*, no. 255 [1984]: 39–47). Even Lemaire suggests that the asherah was in the process of hypostatization as a truly independent divine being during Hebrew biblical times (see his "Les inscriptions de Khirbet el-Qōm et l'asherah de YHWH," 608; and his "Who or What Was Yahweh's Asherah?" 51).

80. See Wiggins, *Reassessment of "Asherah,"* 92.

81. See ibid., 94–5, 101, 109, 129 (with rabbinic references); Patai, *Hebrew Goddess*, 38–9, 42, 45, 48; Smith, *Early History of God*, 81–5; Olyan, *Asherah and the Cult of Yahweh*, 1–3 (which suggests a date palm as the most likely botanical candidate); Meshel, "Did Yahweh Have a Consort?" 31; Freedman, "Yahweh of Samaria and His Asherah," 247; Day, "Asherah in the Hebrew Bible," 392, 397, 406; de Moor, "ʾashērah," 1:441–3; and Gerstenberger, *Yahweh—the Patriarch*, 27–8, 32 (which points to the existence of symbols of both masculine and feminine deities in early Israelite shrines). The personified female figure of the Sabbath in later Judaism is associated with a "sacred apple orchard" (see Patai, *Hebrew*

Goddess, 270–3). The Old Testament is rather unclear in its treatment of the asherah, except to associate it with pagan worship. This unclarity is heightened by the fact that, in virtually every one of the forty instances where *asherah* and its variants occur, the Greek Septuagint translation gives us *groves* (αλσος, αλση).

82. Levenson suggests that the oak associated with the temple at Shechem in Joshua 24:26–8 was a sacred tree (see his *Sinai and Zion*, 34, 36). On pp. 20–1 he hypothesizes that Yahweh himself was symbolized by a tree.

83. See Olyan, *Asherah and the Cult of Yahweh*, 26, 28, 31–2; W. L. Reed, "Asherah," in *The Interpreter's Dictionary of the Bible*, ed. George Arthur Buttrick (Nashville: Abingdon, 1962), 1:250–2; de Moor, "ʾashērah," 1:441; Day, "Asherah in the Hebrew Bible," 408; and Dietrich and Loretz, *"Jahwe und seine Aschera,"* 82–5, 99. Reed allows for the possibility that the Septuagint has been misinterpreted and that its Greek terminology refers to a wooden cultic object rather than to literal groves (see his "Asherah," 1:250). But early rabbinic commentaries also rendered *asherah* as "grove" (see Lemaire, "Who or What Was Yahweh's Asherah?" 50). There are four exceptions. In Isaiah 17:8 and 27:9, the Septuagint renders the term as "tree" (dendra), and in two other instances (2 Chronicles 15:16; 24:18) it mistakenly identifies *asherah* with a quite distinct goddess, Astarte. The Latin Vulgate follows the Septuagint, using the renderings "wood" *(lucus)* or "grove" *(nemus)* and the proper name "Ashtaroth." The King James Version is based on the readings of the Septuagint and the Vulgate and, on this issue, follows them into error. This can easily be seen in such passages as Judges 3:7 (where the reference is clearly to some sort of personal being or beings, analogous to Baal) and in 2 Kings 23:6 (where the removal of an entire grove of trees seems somewhat far-fetched). Joseph Smith could not have derived an accurate notion of the nature of the asherah from the King James Bible.

84. Yarden, *Tree of Light*, 44–7, 103–6. Widengren, in *The King and the Tree of Life* (62–7), agrees that the menorah is a stylized tree, as does Levenson, who also connects it with the burning bush of

Sinai (see his *Sinai and Zion*, 20–1). For the Egyptian Manichaeans who used the Coptic psalmbook, the tree of life symbolized "the King of Light" (see Allberry, *Manichaean Psalm-Book*, 66).

85. Smith, *Early History of God*, 84; compare Wiggins, *Reassessment of "Asherah*," 37, 71, 89; and Neumann, *Great Mother*, 48–50, 52, 241–3. The Mesoamerican sacred tree was also associated with creation, birth, life, and a primordial mother goddess (see Schele, "Olmec Mountain and Tree of Creation," 110).

86. See Patai, *Hebrew Goddess*, 20, 116, 139–40, 151–2, 199, 265, 280.

87. The quotation is from Olyan, *Asherah and the Cult of Yahweh*, 57 n. 82; compare Olyan, "Cultic Confessions of Jer 2,27a," 259.

88. See Olyan, *Asherah and the Cult of Yahweh*, 56–61, 65–7. Olyan acknowledges, on p. 56, that some have identified Tannit as Anath precisely because of her alleged virginity. John Day is among those (see his "Asherah in the Hebrew Bible," 397). Things often get a bit muddled because of the tendency in antiquity to confuse and blend deities. On this tendency consult Olyan, *Asherah and the Cult of Yahweh*, 10–11. Patai notes the frequent confusion of Asherah and Astarte (see his *Hebrew Goddess*, 37, 41); compare Day, "Asherah in the Hebrew Bible," 400; see also n. 21 above. The goddess Anath was "virginal and yet wanton . . . chaste and promiscuous," and, like Asherah, she was wet nurse to the gods (see Patai, *Hebrew Goddess*, 61; compare p. 120, where the Greek goddess Hera is adduced as a parallel; see also Smith, *Early History of God*, xix, 164; Olyan, *Asherah and the Cult of Yahweh*, 45–6; and de Moor, "ʾashērah," 1:439). Chastity, promiscuity, and motherliness were combined in many ancient Near Eastern goddesses, including the Sumerian virgin and lover Inanna, who can be equated with Mesopotamian Ishtar and Anath, and the Persian Anahita (see Patai, *Hebrew Goddess*, 136–8, 140, 146–7). Inanna characterized herself as possessing "truth" and "deceit," "forthright speech" and "slanderous speech," "treachery" and "straightforwardness" (see Wolkstein and Kramer, *Inanna*, 16–17). The late Jewish goddess figure Matronit is simultaneously virgin,

lover, and mother, as is the personified Sabbath of some Jewish lore (see Patai, *Hebrew Goddess*, 140–3, 146–7, 154, 159, 203–4, 218–220, 249, 252–3, 257–70). On the notion of the virgin-mother, see Neumann, *Great Mother*, 104, 196–7, 267, and for the general phenomenon of contradictory attributes residing in the same goddess, see pp. 12, 21–2, 38, 45, 50, 52, 65–7, 72, 75, 80–1. "Albright, Cross, Stadelmann, and many other commentators have long pointed out an extraordinary, almost bewildering fluidity in the conception of many Northwest Semitic deities, seen in the overlap in their roles, their tendency to coalesce and split off, and even their ability to combine opposites. El-Asherah are paralleled by Baal-Anat. Anat is both wife and sister to Baal; perpetual virgin and mother-figure; goddess of love and of war" (Dever, "Asherah, Consort of Yahweh?" 28; compare de Moor, "ʾashērah," 1:439–41, 444; Day, "Asherah in the Hebrew Bible," 389). Cross remarks that "there is a basic syncretistic impulse in Near Eastern polytheism which tends to merge gods with similar traits and functions" (see his "Yahweh and the God of the Patriarchs," 235).

89. See Jeremiah 44:17–19, 25; compare Halpern, "'Brisker Pipes Than Poetry,'" 83. Day, in his article "Asherah in the Hebrew Bible" (386), cites a Mesopotamian reference to the goddess Ashratum—whose name students of Semitic languages will immediately recognize as an almost certain equivalent to the familiar *Asherah*—as *kallat shar shamī*, "bride of the king of heaven."

90. See Patai, *Hebrew Goddess*, 280. Qurʾān 5:116 denounces a Christian trinity consisting of Allāh (whose name or title, as noted previously, is cognate with *El* or *Elohim*), Mary, and Jesus. Compare the implicit argument of 5:75. Intriguingly, according to Wiggins (*Reassessment of "Asherah,"* 154, 163), ancient South Arabia knew a divine father/mother/son triad in which Asherah was the mother.

91. See Ernest A. Wallis Budge, *Egyptian Tales and Romances: Pagan, Christian and Muslim* (London: Thornton Butterworth, 1935), 280. Compare the versions of the Apocalypse of Paul (chapters 45–6), based on Greek and Latin texts, in J. K. Elliott, *The Apocryphal New Testament* (Oxford: Clarendon Press, 1993), 639–40, and in

Montague Rhodes James, *The Apocryphal New Testament* (Oxford: Clarendon Press, 1924), 549–50, where the connection between the virgin and the tree is perhaps a bit less direct.

92. The phrase is from Wiggins, "Myth of Asherah," 384.

93. 1 Nephi 11:18.

94. See Patai, *Hebrew Goddess*, 152. In support of this, it might be noted that the Kabbalistic divine mother was sometimes pictured, just like her predecessor, Asherah, as a wet nurse (see ibid., 127).

95. See ibid., 128, 145–6, 275. Wiggins notes the association of the goddess Asherah with human women (see his *Reassessment of "Asherah,"* 37).

96. See the discussion in Patai, *Hebrew Goddess*, 219, 282–94.

97. See Olyan, *Asherah and the Cult of Yahweh*, 71 n. 4.

98. See Patai, *Hebrew Goddess*, 272–5.

99. See *The Oxford Classical Dictionary*, ed. N. G. L. Hammond and H. H. Scullard, 2nd ed. (Oxford: Clarendon Press, 1970), 126–7. Those familiar with her statue at Ephesus will have little trouble seeing Artemis in the role of a wet nurse as well.

100. Roland E. Murphy describes the characteristics of wisdom literature, giving abundant references (see his *The Tree of Life: An Exploration of Biblical Wisdom Literature*, 2nd ed. [Grand Rapids, Mich.: Eerdmans, 1996], 1–4, 103).

101. See, for example, 1 Kings 4:29–34; Job 1:3; compare Murphy, *Tree of Life*, 23–5, 175, 195. An ancient Egyptian text dating from roughly the time of Lehi, entitled "The Instruction of Amenemope," seems to have a very close relationship to Proverbs 22:17–24:22. It is partially translated in James B. Pritchard, ed., *Ancient Near Eastern Texts Relating to the Old Testament*, 3rd ed. (Princeton: Princeton University Press, 1969), 421–5.

102. See Murphy, *Tree of Life*, 33.

103. See 1 Nephi 1:2; and Nibley, *Lehi in the Desert; The World of the Jaredites; There Were Jaredites*, 34–42.

104. To the extent that it may be validly linked with wisdom literature at all, the Book of Mormon clearly resembles most the admonitory style, as it is sketched in Murphy, *Tree of Life*, 7–9.

105. See Murphy, *Tree of Life*, 22.
106. Proverbs 2:16 (compare 6:24; 7:5, 21–3); 20:19 (compare 12:6; 26:28; 29:5). See also Psalm 5:9; 12:2; 78:36.
107. See, for example, 2 Nephi 28:22; Jacob 7:2, 4; Mosiah 7:21; 9:10; 10:18; 11:7; 26:6; 27:8; Alma 20:13; 30:47; 46:5, 7, 10; 50:35; 52:19; 61:4; Helaman 1:7; 2:4–5; 13:28; 3 Nephi 1:29; 7:12; Ether 8:2. Daniel 11:21 nicely summarizes a frequent effect of flattery in the Book of Mormon.
108. See Murphy, *Tree of Life*, 15, for this theme in the ancient Near East. The notion is omnipresent in the Book of Mormon. Although the Deuteronomistic biblical tradition, which also stresses the connection of righteousness with prosperity, is obviously not to be identified with the wisdom tradition, a number of scholars have pointed out points of contact between the two (see ibid., 194–6). Likewise, the Book of Mormon bears evidence of unmistakable Deuteronomistic influence. But that is a subject for another paper.
109. "Discernment" is mentioned in Alma 32:35 in a discourse on the tree of life that is manifestly connected to the tree that Lehi and Nephi had seen.
110. Compare Proverbs 26:12.
111. 2 Nephi 4:34; 28:31.
112. See 1 Nephi 11:35–6.
113. See Proverbs 1:20–1; 4:5–9, 13; 7:4; 8:1–3, 22–36; 9:1–3. The Hebrew term translated as "wisdom," *ḥokmāh*, is, of course, a feminine noun. For Proverbs 1–9 as a literary unit or subdivision within the book as a whole, see R. A. Dyson and J. McShane, "Proverbs," in *A New Catholic Commentary on Holy Scripture*, ed. Reginald C. Fuller (Nashville: Thomas Nelson, 1975), 500; Carole R. Fontaine, "Proverbs," in *Harper's Bible Commentary*, ed. James L. Mays, (San Francisco: Harper and Row, 1988), 495, 497; J. Terence Forestell, "Proverbs," in *The Jerome Biblical Commentary*, ed. Raymond E. Brown, Joseph A. Fitzmyer, and Roland E. Murphy, 2 vols. (Englewood Cliffs: Prentice-Hall, 1968), 1:496; Charles G. Martin, "Proverbs," in *The International Bible Commentary*, ed. F. F. Bruce (Grand Rapids, Mich.: Zondervan, 1986), 658. Murphy (*Tree of*

Life, 133–49 and throughout) offers a useful discussion of "Lady Wisdom."

114. Patai supplies references that I do not have space here to discuss (see his *Hebrew Goddess*, 97–8). Proverbs 7:14 advises its audience to take Wisdom as a sister or kinswoman.

115. There are, of course, no uppercase or lowercase letters in biblical (or any other) Hebrew.

116. Smith, *Early History of God*, 95.

117. Wiggins, "Myth of Asherah," 383.

118. See Smith, *Early History of God*, 95.

119. If so, the language of the plates must be Hebrew, or something like it. Compare Genesis 30:13.

120. See Smith, *Early History of God*, 95; compare Proverbs 11:30; 15:4.

121. Again, from the root *'shr.*

122. Psalm 1:1–6.

123. Compare Proverbs 4:13 and 1 Nephi 8:24, 30; 15:24.

124. Cited here and elsewhere from the Revised English Bible.

125. Compare Proverbs 1:4, 8, 10, 15; 3:1, 11, 21; 4:1, 3, 10, 20; 5:1, 7–8, 20; 6:1, 3, 20; 7:1, 7; 1 Nephi 8:12–18.

126. See Proverbs 1:15, 19, 20; 2:1, 8, 9, 12, 13, 15, 18–20; 3:6, 12, 17, 23; 4:11, 12, 14, 18–19, 26–7; 5:5, 6, 8, 21, 23; 6:12, 23; 7:8, 12, 25, 27; 8:2, 13, 20, 32; 9:6. Compare the "paths" (1 Nephi 8:20–3, 28) and "ways" (1 Nephi 8:23, 30–1) and "roads" (1 Nephi 8:32) of Lehi's vision. Compare also Psalm 1:1–6, quoted earlier. Ecclesiasticus 4:17 takes a somewhat different view, suggesting that Wisdom tests her neophyte devotee: "At first she will lead him by devious ways."

127. See Proverbs 8:6–9; compare 1 Nephi 13:26–9, 32, 34–40; 14:23; 2 Nephi 4:32; 9:47; 25:4; 26:33; 33:5–6.

128. See 1 Nephi 13:26, 28, 29, 32, 34, 35, 40. The only place outside of Nephi's vision where any version of the phrase *plain and precious* occurs within the Book of Mormon is 1 Nephi 19:3.

129. Compare Proverbs 3:14; 8:11, 19; also 2:4; Job 28:12–28; Wisdom of Solomon 7:8; 8:5.

Daniel C. Peterson

130. Proverbs 1:20–1.

131. Proverbs 8:1–3.

132. Proverbs 9:3.

133. Allberry, *Manichaean Psalm-Book*, 66.

134. See, for example, Wisdom of Ben Sira 33:7–15; 42:15–43:33; and Murphy, *Tree of Life*, 103.

135. For the two "ways," see Proverbs 1:32–3; 10–15. Compare Murphy, *Tree of Life*, 103. On the "strange woman," see Proverbs 2:16–19; 5:3–23; 6:24–35; 7:4–27; 9:13–18; and Murphy, *Tree of Life*, 194. Neumann sees "the character of enchantment leading to doom"—an apt description of the "whorish woman"—as a separable component of the archetypal mother goddess (see his *Great Mother*, 81). Patai (*Hebrew Goddess*, 25) cites and echoes Neumann. Against Neumann's overall theory, though, Wiggins discounts "the connection of Asherah with the amorphous 'mother goddess.' Asherah is the mother of the gods at Ugarit, not *The Great Mother*. . . . She does not appear in the role of a cosmic mother of all living. This very concept is now becoming increasingly rejected in the studies of European prehistory. It is ironic that this concept is slowest to give way in the ancient Near East, where it began" ("Myth of Asherah," 392; emphasis in the original). In a remarkable illustration of the joining of opposite characteristics in the character of a single "goddess," some Jewish thinkers have linked Proverbs's wanton woman with the Shekhina (see Patai, *Hebrew Goddess*, 150).

136. 1 Nephi 14:9–17.

137. Proverbs 9:13–18.

138. Proverbs 7:12.

139. As in Proverbs 1:22; 3:34; compare 9:6–8, 12; 1 Nephi 8:26–7, 33; 11:35.

140. Proverbs 1:25–33. For the promise of safety to those who hearken to Wisdom, see Proverbs 3:25. Prosperity in the Book of Mormon is often prelude to disaster.

141. On wisdom equated with life, see Proverbs 3:2, 18, 22; 4:4, 10, 13, 22; 6:23–35; 8:35–6; 9:6–11. On unwisdom as the way to death, see Proverbs 2:18; 5:5; 7:22–3, 26–7; 9:18.

142. Proverbs 2:21–2.

143. Proverbs 2:18–19. Recall the much-mocked language of Lehi in 2 Nephi 1:14, where he speaks of "the cold and silent grave, from whence no traveler can return." Critics have claimed that Joseph Smith plagiarized the thought from Shakespeare—as if the idea were not rather obvious and attested from all over the ancient world, including here in Proverbs.

144. Note the feminine pronoun used here to refer to wisdom.

145. Murphy, *Tree of Life*, 29 (with references). See Widengren, *The King and the Tree of Life*. Proverbs 5:15–18 also mentions waters and rivers.

146. John 3:16.

147. For information suggestive of Joseph Smith's lack of direct contact with the Bible during the translation of the Book of Mormon, see John A. Tvedtnes and Matthew Roper, review of "Joseph Smith's Use of the Apocrypha," by Jerald Tanner and Sandra Tanner, *FARMS Review of Books* 8/2 (1996): 330–2. Dictating her memoirs, his mother recalled that, as a boy of eighteen (i.e., in 1823 or 1824) young Joseph "had never read the Bible through in his life." Moreover, "he seemed much less inclined to the perusal of books than any of the rest of our children," although he was "far more given to meditation and deep study" (Lucy Mack Smith, *Joseph Smith and His Progenitors* [Independence: Herald House, 1969], 92).

CHAPTER 8

A SINGULAR READING: THE MĀORI AND THE BOOK OF MORMON

Louis Midgley

A Personal Introduction

As an honor to John Sorenson, I wish to describe and comment on the way in which some of the Latter-day Saints in New Zealand have approached the Book of Mormon. Sorenson justly deserves recognition for his work on the Book of Mormon. For many years he prepared learned responses to the critics of the Book of Mormon and also to those anxious to engage in woolly-headed speculation about its contents.[1] But his interest in the peoples of the South Pacific is less well-known. It turns out that he shares my interest in the Māori.[2]

On one occasion I discovered that Sorenson had prepared a detailed commentary and criticism on a 1965 study by Erik Schwimmer entitled "Mormonism in a Maori Village: A Study in Social Change."[3] In 1950 this so-called village consisted of four small Latter-day Saint branches clustered along a seven-mile

Louis Midgley is emeritus professor of political science at Brigham Young University.

stretch of coast just south of the entrance to the Bay of Islands. My mission for the Church of Jesus Christ of Latter-day Saints began that same year with visits to the Māori who in 1965 were members of the Whangaruru Ward and included in Schwimmer's study of what he considered a Mormon religious revival in that area. On another occasion John and I discussed Elder John H. Groberg's remarkable account of his missionary experiences in the early 1950s in Tonga.[4] Sorenson indicated that this book rang true; his own experiences among the Rarotongans in the Cook Islands, though they took place five hundred miles to the east and were several years earlier, were strikingly similar.

Differing Ways of Reading the Book of Mormon

"The Book of Mormon," according to Richard Bushman, "portrays another world in many ways alien to our own." This, he maintains, "is the hardest point for modern readers to deal with," and so "it has been difficult for Mormon and non-Mormon alike to grasp the real intellectual problem of the Book of Mormon."[5] Why? "The preconceptions of the modern age [have] led Mormons as well as critics to see things in the Book of Mormon that are not there."[6]

Bushman also argues that readers must realize that the Book of Mormon is "more than a patchwork of theological assertions, or a miscellany of statements about the Indians, like, for example, Ethan Smith's *View of the Hebrews*. We may miss the point if we treat the Book of Mormon as if it were that kind of hodgepodge."[7] And Enlightenment and post-Enlightenment assumptions about the world shield us from subtle matters found in the Book of Mormon. Unfortunately, readers tend to "employ a proof text method in [their] analyses, taking passages out of context to prove a point," while critics "seek to associate a few words or an episode with [Joseph] Smith or his time, the Masons here, republican ideology there, then a touch of Arminianism or of evangelical conversion preaching."[8]

There are dangers inherent in such readings. For example, those who approach the Book of Mormon assuming that it is an assortment of theological opinions or that it can be explained by currently fashionable secular explanations "lose sight of the larger world which the book evokes. The genius of the Book of Mormon, like that of many works of art, is that it brings an entire society and culture into existence, with a religion, an economy, a technology, a government, a geography, a sociology, all combined into a complete world."[9] We should strive to grasp "this larger world and relate individual passages to greater structures if we are to find their broadest meaning."[10] We need to focus our attention on the world from which the Book of Mormon speaks.

But how can we come to know this world? Bushman holds that the Book of Mormon has "a peculiar power to draw readers into its world."[11] Not all Latter-day Saints read the Book of Mormon the same way. What they see in the book depends to some extent on their particular cultural horizon. According to their immediate circumstances and the kinds of questions that concern them most—factors influenced at least partly by cultural differences—they necessarily appropriate its teachings and history in different ways. I will describe how the Māori in the early 1950s tended to read the Book of Mormon as an account of their past, or the past of a people much like themselves in various interesting ways.

The Māori Encounter the Restored Gospel

The first Latter-day Saint missionaries to New Zealand arrived in 1854. Their work in and near Wellington and

Christchurch was among those the Māori called Pākehā,[12] the white strangers who settled in Aotearoa[13] beginning in the early 1800s. Latter-day Saint missionaries took the restored gospel to the Māori in the 1880s. Initially, the missionaries were wholly unfamiliar with Māori customs, traditions, and language, and they had to rely on native translators.

Success with the Māori started north of Wellington with visits to Māori *pā*.[14] These small communities consisted of *whānau* (extended families) and perhaps one or more *hapū* (subtribes), often clustered around a *marae*.[15] When the missionaries arrived at a pā, they were often greeted by the Māori in the traditional fashion.[16] After they had explained the reason for their visit, they would be invited to preach and pray. When the missionaries made friends with the *rangatira* (heads of whānau) or the *ariki* (chiefs) of the hapū in control of a marae, they soon discovered that their new friends had kinfolk in other places who might assist in the favorable reception of their message. They crossed the Rimutaka Mountains east of Wellington to the Wairarapa area and then moved up the east coast to the Mahia Peninsula and Gisborne. There they encountered an *iwi* (a word meaning "bone" that identifies a tribe or alliance of hapū) known as the Ngati Kahungunu.[17]

In many instances the message and mode of prayer of the early Latter-day Saint missionaries seemed to those they encountered to be fulfillments of prophecies by Māori *tohunga* (skilled, learned persons, sometimes also charismatic figures). For example, unbeknown to the missionaries, the chiefs and leading tohunga of the Ngati Kahungunu had held a *hui* (meeting or conference)[18] in March 1881 at the dedication of a new meetinghouse at Te Ore Ore, near Masterton.[19] One of the questions considered at this hui was which of the Christian denominations was best for the tribe. They were dissatisfied with the Anglican and other sectarian versions of Christianity. After days of fasting and prayer, Paora Potangaroa, an aged ariki with great *mana* (prestige, authority, spiritual power), announced that none of the Christian denominations were right for the Māori.[20] He dictated what he called *Te Kawenata* (covenant), which soon thereafter some of the Māori converts saw fulfilled through their reception of the restored gospel.[21]

But other Māori tohunga had also issued what were considered prophecies that to the early Māori Latter-day Saints described the coming of their new faith and announced the signs by which it could be identified. From the Latter-day Saint perspective of the Māori, this new faith would be brought to their people by young men from the east who would travel in pairs, raise their right hands (or in one case their arms) over their heads when they prayed,[22] and so forth. The Latter-day Saint missionaries and their message seemed to the early Māori Latter-day Saints to fulfill prophecies of four tohunga since as early as 1830. Within a few decades thousands of Māori had joined the Church of Jesus Christ of Latter-day Saints, and numerous small branches had been established around the North Island. It seems that the Māori, especially those on the east coast of the North Island, had been prepared to receive the restored gospel.[23]

Some of the Māori accepted the restored gospel at least partly because they felt that Latter-day Saint beliefs were similar to teachings they already partly understood but could not find in the Christian denominations with which they were familiar. While Māori religion generally involved seeing the divine in oceans, trees, rivers, mountains, and so forth, some tohunga had preserved old teachings concerning a god known as *Io Matua* (Io, the father of all). The Io cult also included teachings about the origin of souls and their fate after death.[24] Pieter H. de Bres got it right when he argued in 1971 that "the Mormons have incorporated in their theology the Maori religious concept *Io,* believed by many to be the supreme God of the ancient Maori. The Io myth, which has become part of the belief of the Mormon Maori, proves to him that the ancient Maori had a conception of God similar to that of the Israelites. This does not only suggest that the ancestry of the Maori is rooted in the Bible, but it also gives lustre to the Maori past."[25] But some writers claim that the detailed teachings of the Io cult had been fashioned in the 1850s under Christian influences on traditional Māori lore.[26] One writer argues that "it will never be known for certain how old the Io tradition was. A number of modern scholars have doubted that the idea of a supreme God in Polynesia antedated Christianity."[27]

However, Io was also known in the Cook Islands and elsewhere in the eastern Pacific.[28] At least the name *Io* and some or even much of what went into the Io cult in Aotearoa/New Zealand seems to predate possible Christian influences on Māori traditions. For both the Māori and the Rarotongans to have independently fashioned both the name and a strikingly similar ideology would be crediting them with extraordinary imaginative powers. Be that as it may, striking parallels to the Māori Io cult can be found among the aboriginal peoples elsewhere in the eastern Pacific.

The best account of the Māori Saints is found in R. Lanier Britsch's history of Latter-day Saints in the Pacific.[29] Unfortunately, though this account is both detailed and competently done, it contains virtually nothing about how the Māori read the Book of Mormon. Peter Lineham, an astute non-Mormon historian, has written a sensitive treatment of what he believes were the transactions that took place between differing cultural horizons beginning in the 1880s as the Māori became Latter-day Saints.[30] But he also has little to say about the way the Māori read the scriptures, including the Book of Mormon.

There are reasons for the neglect of this topic. Most of what can now be recovered by historians about the Māori Saints is found in mission records and missionary diaries. For the most part, these sources are silent on many aspects of how the Māori experienced and understood the restored gospel. The Māori have oral traditions but have left virtually no records. Of course, a story can be built on memories and oral traditions, as well as on textual materials, but professional historians are apprehensive about grounding accounts in anything other than texts or text analogues.[31]

Getting Behind the Surface of Events

Lineham strove to discover "what was involved on both sides of the cultural exchange" as the Māori became Latter-day Saints. He viewed the process of Māori conversion to Mormon teachings as a cultural transaction wholly understandable in secular terms. Given his agenda, he had little to say about the way the Māori read the Book of Mormon. I wish to describe what I observed about the way the Māori tended to read the Book of Mormon. From 1950 through 1952 I heard the old stories, listened to the preaching, and conversed with the Māori Saints. I was a kind of naive participant-observer. My own enthrallment with the Book of Mormon, coupled with my fondness for making it the key to the restoration of the gospel, led to conversations about it with my Māori friends.

From virtually the beginning of their encounter with Anglican, Methodist, and Roman Catholic missionaries, the Māori entertained the notion that they were linked in some unknown way to ancient Israel, perhaps to the lost tribes or other descendants of migrating biblical peoples. This is, of course, rather well-known. Lineham argued that the Latter-day Saint missionaries "associated the Mormon message with the popular Maori desire to 'locate' themselves in the Bible."[32] And the Book of Mormon became the special link. Lineham thus noted that "when missionaries wanted to get support for translating the Book of Mormon, they emphasized that 'it was a history of God's dealings with their forefathers.'"[33]

It is, however, a mistake to assume that Latter-day Saint missionaries taught the Māori that the peoples described in the Book of Mormon were somehow part of their past. It seems just as likely that the Māori themselves made the connection between the Book of Mormon and their past, for the missionaries initially approached the Māori with virtually no understanding of their culture or lore. It is more likely that the Māori Saints, finding in the book of Alma the brief account of seafaring adventurers who eventually disappeared somewhere in the Pacific, drew the conclusion that Hagoth's people had somehow touched their own people, thereby linking them in some way to the Nephites and hence to Israel.[34]

It is also a mistake—all too common—to assume that the Māori Saints see themselves as Lamanites. Instead, the Māori Saints think of themselves as somehow at least partly of Nephite descent.[35] The Māori also do not see themselves as involved in the "Lamanite curse of a dark skin."[36] They may, it is true, sometimes liken themselves to the Lamanites, saying that in certain acts of forgetfulness or rebellion they are *like* the Lamanites; but the Māori Saints trace part of their roots to the Nephite faction, and not to the Lamanite faction, of Lehi's colony.

Lineham also mentions that the "passionate and fanciful exegesis of the Bible by Maori Saints (for example, rejecting Mihinare [Anglican] baptism because making the sign of the cross over a person was to consign the person to the evil power of the cross) reflected the way in which Maori interpreted stories of their own past."[37] Lineham is certainly correct in holding that the Māori tended to interpret the scriptures through the categories available to them in their own culture and traditions.

Lineham claims that the Book of Mormon accounts "of Israel in America fascinated many Maori," but he also believes "it is difficult to judge the extent to which it became part of Maori literature."[38] Difficult but not impossible, as I will attempt to show.

Kinship and Tribes

Traditional Māori society centers on kinship relations among extended families, subtribes, and tribes, all symbolized by ancestors common to each grouping. Elaborate genealogies keep these things sorted out. Many Māori can still trace their ancestral tribal identities back to, for example, a number of legendary canoes—the so-called Great Fleet—that brought them to New Zealand from places like Rarotonga in the Cook Islands or from Raiatea in the Society Islands in the 1300s and that seem to have moved them around Aotearoa/New Zealand. Archaeological evidence indicates that a people very much like the Māori may have inhabited Aotearoa/New Zealand perhaps as early as A.D. 800.[39] Be that as it may, the lives of the Māori were once entirely organized around what we tend to label myths, legends, and genealogies that provided them with an identity and a structured way of life. With the arrival of the Pākehā, at least some but not all of this knowledge was lost or transformed.

The Europeans found in the Māori a people who had to make do in a rather cold, densely forested, mountainous land and who lived without land mammals other than the rats and dogs they had brought with them from the eastern Pacific. The Māori lived on fern roots, fish, and other seafood, and they cultivated *kūmara* (a sweet potato). It is little wonder that the Māori were attracted by the material culture of the Pākehā. They soon acquired a taste for such things as firearms, land mammals, woolen blankets, metal tools, and leather. They could see that European clothing and woolen blankets were better than bird feathers and flax clothing. The Pākehā also made foods and drink available that were previously unknown to the Māori, who quickly became fond of pork and enslaved by beer. The encounter with the Pākehā immediately began the more or less rapid transformation of elements of Māori material culture.

The Pākehā also brought to the Māori the Bible and sectarian conflicts over its meaning. Soon after their initial contact with the Māori, Christian missionaries and others began recording Māori lore and established a remarkable written version of the previously unwritten Māori language.[40] With British rigor and persistence, they set out to teach the Māori to read their own language.[41] One reason for this effort was to make the Bible and the wonders of a Christian (and English) civilization available to the primitive, pagan Māori. Bronwyn Elsmore describes the process by which Māori became familiar with the Bible: "Bearing in mind the Maori's extraordinary enthusiasm for learning to read, and the extreme rapidity with which the skills of literacy spread, then even should the numbers of scriptures made available to the Maori be few to begin with, it is most likely that knowledge of the content of each volume spread quickly and widely."[42] So it was not long before many and eventually most Māori were literate and even eventually bilingual, and also at least nominally Christian.

One writer claims that "by the 1880s New Zealand had one of the highest rates of literacy in the world—a rate which was pushed up by the phenomenal levels of literacy among Maori youth. There was a pervading sense in Maori society of the new displacing the old."[43] As a result, "the impact of literacy, also introduced by the missionaries, quickly undermined the precepts of the Maori oral tradition."[44] The culture flowing from and regulated by oral traditions began to erode.

Soon after various Māori chiefs signed the Treaty of Waitangi[45] on 6 February 1840, at least some of the Māori found themselves increasingly at odds with the Pākehā. One reason was that the Pākehā saw themselves as bearers of a superior Christian civilization and loathed Māori learning and the culture it sustained and regulated. But even more important, it seemed to the Māori that Pākehā greed violated the very Christian principles they had been taught by Anglican and other missionaries. This greed was manifested in the theft of Māori lands, which presumably were protected by the Treaty of Waitangi. An old Māori saying runs something as follows: "The early Christian missionaries brought the Gospel of Jesus Christ to us, and taught us to go down on our knees and close our eyes in prayer to our Heavenly Father, but when we opened our eyes the land was gone."[46]

The Māori were aware of Pākehā hypocrisy. The Māori had sincerely embraced one or another of the competing sectarian brands of Christianity. Gradually they became somewhat dissatisfied with what they had adopted. But they did not cease reading their Bibles, nor did they give up their Christian convictions altogether: "Despite some outward appearances, and contemporary generalisations, many Maori did not abandon their faith when the stylized European Christianity they had welcomed began to take second place among the European settlers to more earthly interests. While some [Maori] stuck with their denominations, others forged new sects, which were a concoction of seventeenth-century English heretical sects, Judaism, and traditional Maori religion."[47]

The Māori who first heard the message of the restored gospel had at least partly entered the literate culture of the Pākehā; they treasured and were familiar with the Bible, which they consulted for an understanding of the circumstances in which they found themselves since the arrival of the Pākehā. For many years they were in the habit of drawing from the Bible—especially from the stories they found in the Old Testament—various parallels to their own life experiences, including their struggles with each other and with the Pākehā.

It was at this point, when some of the Māori were unhappy with the versions of Christianity given to them by early sectarian missionaries, that Latter-day Saint missionaries first approached them. The Māori who embraced the restored gospel began to be transformed by their new faith into what is essentially a doctrine-based community, rather than the more traditional tribal-based community. The restored gospel became the central organizing element in their Mormon Māori identity.[48] Lineham offered a nice inventory of reasons why the Latter-day Saint missionaries seem to have both succeeded and failed with the Māori.[49] On the positive side, the missionaries depended on their Māori hosts, learned their language and bits and pieces of their culture, and loved the Māori. In the Latter-day Saint missionaries, the Māori found—sometimes for the first time— Pākehā with whom they could enjoy a satisfactory, loving relationship.

A Difference in Readings

The largest branch of the Church of Jesus Christ of Latter-day Saints in Aotearoa/New Zealand in 1950 was in Auckland. It consisted of more than one hundred Latter-day Saint families spread over a large area. Since only a few families owned automobiles, this branch was possible because the Saints made use of trolleys and buses as transportation to social gatherings and meetings. Elsewhere in Aotearoa/New Zealand, circumstances were different. Outside of Auckland and a few other provincial towns, the church consisted of numerous small branches, many of which were located in traditional Māori pā.

My first experiences in Aotearoa/New Zealand were in the Northland, the area north of Auckland where there were two mission districts and dozens of small branches and home Sunday schools.[50] Initially, my missionary companions were Māori just out of high school. We had scant hope that the Pākehā would be interested in what they saw as a Māori church; nevertheless, we stopped at many of their farms. Sometimes they were kindly, but generally they were not interested in our message. Even when they were interested, they allowed us to visit only irregularly. Sometimes they were mildly curious about both Mormon and Māori things. Because they knew the Māori only at a distance and had almost never been in a Māori home, they were astonished to find that I depended on the Māori for food and shelter. Some of the Pākehā were sufficiently curious that they would eventually allow lessons, but only after a long period in which we had become friends and gained their confidence. For the Pākehā to become Latter-day Saints meant entering a world in which Māori culture dominated and in which Utah cultural mannerisms were secondary. For example, our branch and district conferences were conducted more or less in the tradition of Māori hui—in fact, they were called hui. The Saints and others assembled for these hui from long distances to enjoy the singing, preaching, considerable feasting, and other cultural events that were thoroughly Māori.

As missionaries we set out to visit the Māori, most of whom were scattered over the countryside in or near traditional pā. We were welcomed into every Māori home. Their mana was evident in their hospitality. They insisted that we have *karakia*,[51] a word that once meant a chant much like a prayer or incantation to the gods but that had come to identify praying, preaching, and singing. Our participation in these activities, our expressions of love, and our blessing on their homes and families was the *koha* (reciprocal payment) we offered them for their wonderful hospitality. During these karakia I would often explain the restoration, telling about Joseph Smith and the Book of Mormon. Even the Māori who were not Latter-day Saints had already heard this message and often said that although they believed what I told them, they liked beer or were enslaved by some other vice. Yet they still believed that the gospel had been restored through Joseph Smith. After karakia we consumed a large meal and continued in conversation as the old stories were repeated. Māori hospitality made it difficult to visit more than a few homes in a day. The habits of an oral culture lingered. Though at the time there were things that bothered me—the slow pace, rain, long distances, bad roads, cold, fleas, strange food—those were days never to be forgotten.

I had gone to Aotearoa/New Zealand anxious to argue that the gospel had been restored through Joseph Smith and that the Book of Mormon was the word of God. But the Māori explained that their problems were not with this message but with sin. I was stunned by their candor. Those whom Latter-day Saints would now call "less active" would explain in painful detail that they were weak and easily tempted by beer or another vice and thus had been in and out of the church. Others would try to explain why they had never joined, indicating that they had once been offended by someone or something. They seemed to give and receive insults easily, and they remembered each one. When I insisted that because they believed the Book of Mormon to be true they were obligated to follow its teachings, they would usually agree. But they pointed out that they found themselves in situations very much like those of the people described in the Book of Mormon. In fact, they saw the book as a description of their own situation, and they saw themselves as at least partly the descendants of Lehi's colony.

I soon discovered that the Māori read the Book of Mormon differently than I did. For example, I was anxious to find proof texts and was busy harmonizing its teachings with what I understood to be the received teachings among the Saints in Utah, whereas the Māori saw the tragic story of families in conflict and subtribes and tribes quarreling with each other and bent on revenge for personal insults and factional quarrels. They looked at the larger patterns of events and less at what might be construed from specific verses. They saw stories of ambitious rivals to traditional authority trying to carve out a space for themselves. They noticed how ambition led to quarrels within families and between extended families and tribes. They saw the atonement as an exchange of gifts between our Heavenly Father and his children somewhat in the way their own relationships were marked by reciprocity in acts of hospitality manifesting love. They found that the Book of Mormon described patterns of events similar to those in their traditional lore and also in their present situation. In that sense the book was their history or at least their kind of history—a mirror of both the noble and base in their own past and present, on an individual as well as community level.

For the Māori in the early 1950s, the Book of Mormon was not, as it was for me, a source of information about puzzling doctrinal matters. Instead, the Māori were fascinated by the narrative portions of the Book of Mormon. I merely glanced at the narratives to locate the more overt teachings, whereas they saw messages and moral instruction embedded in stories. I focused on individual verses and saw them as authoritative teachings on matters I had learned from other books that the Māori Saints were mostly unaware of. They tended to focus more on context, on the accounts of the evils inflicted on communities by pride and ambition, by struggles for power and the abuse of power, by quarrels and wars. They saw signs of kinship and the order it provides as well as the rivalry it engenders. In the Book of Mormon they found signs and consequences of divine blessings and also the curse brought on by the breakdown of family ties. The rise of secret combinations was seen as a result of law-less gangs led by ambitious leaders who had created surrogate families no longer controlled by traditional norms.

The Māori were also astonished by certain Book of Mormon events that I took for granted. For example, they were stunned by the audacity of Nephi in challenging his older brothers by claiming to be the rightful interpreter of his father's founding revelations. To the extent that their traditional norms were still in place, the Māori were deferent to age and birth order. Precisely because it defied traditional understandings, they saw importance in the story of Nephi. They could also understand the opposition of Laman and his faction to Nephi's claims. They noticed and understood the persistence of insults and quarrels that fuel the factional disputes recorded in the Nephite record, and they were reminded of similar tales of in-sults and resentments that constituted part of their own past. They also noticed that some of the successes of Nephite preach-ers seemed to depend on their dealing with their own distant brethren and hence on subtle matters of kinship.

The Māori also found nothing surprising in how rapidly individuals and communities of Lehi's descendants forgot their duties. This was exactly what they considered the reality of their own lives and the history of their people. They not only be-lieved that they were somehow related to Hagoth and hence to Nephi's tribe, but they also saw themselves as replicating the tragic tale told in the Book of Mormon of the woes that come upon a disobedient covenant people. To me, on the other hand, the ease with which the Nephite faithful fell away and, when chastened by preachers or adverse circumstances, returned to the fold was the least believable feature of the book.

It was not uncommon for missionaries to urge the Māori Saints to begin to cull from the scriptures the kinds of proof texts they employed in teaching the restored gospel to the

Pākehā. However, the Māori tended to ignore such admonitions, fastening instead on the historical narratives and the messages they carried. They seemed to think that much of importance to them was to be found in seeing the moral implications embedded in stories. As I look back on my experience living among the Māori, it seems that they were still operating as a culture in which stories and aphorisms provided, illustrated, and enlivened moral messages.

I had learned to mine the Book of Mormon for discreet bits of information about divine and human things, and I had little appreciation for the way in which stories and their plots can carry a message. I was not sensitive to aphoristic, highly symbolic, and formalized messages. Instead, I wanted the Māori Saints to read the Book of Mormon for the kinds of things that I found interesting in it. But the Māori loved the Book of Mormon for different reasons. They had their own way of reading it. First and foremost, they read the Book of Mormon as a tale of a people very much like themselves. The Māori were a tribal people with genealogies and accompanying accounts of noted ancestors, and they were keenly aware of the traditional hostilities between the different tribes, subtribes, and extended families. Much of the Māori lore was directly or indirectly related to tales of family and tribal conflicts. The Māori were known for the ease with which they gave and received insults, and the passion with which they kept alive over many generations real or assumed offenses of others. They saw a dire warning against this sort of thing when they read the Book of Mormon.

In the 1950s virtually all the Māori used English. Some were marvelous preachers in both Māori and English. I later discovered that this was the result of their own highly developed oratorical tradition, which was focused on the rituals of the marae and was the vehicle for transferring the culture to the next generation. But most of the Māori were no longer conducting their business in their homes in Māori, and the schools taught English exclusively. The Māori were therefore essentially bilingual, but their hold on their native language was slipping. They studied and knew the scriptures in English, though some treasured Māori translations. Looking back, I can now see that the Māori I encountered in the 1950s read the Book of Mormon with a different set of assumptions because of their unique cultural horizon.

Although the Māori Saints still seem to trace their identity to their whānau and hapū, they have added stories of how their ancestors became Latter-day Saints. In addition, they have the Book of Mormon, which they see as filled with materials that, similar to their traditional lore, helps give their lives meaning and moral direction. A significant part of their identity is found in their belief that part of what they are is set forth in the Nephite record. There is more to the Māori attachment to the Book of Mormon than a fascination with Hagoth: the Book of Mormon supplies them with a way of retaining certain of the noble portions of their traditional culture as they become a belief-centered people.

An Oral Culture Encounters the Literate World

In 1814, when Samuel Marsden, the first of many Christian missionaries to Aotearoa/New Zealand, arrived there, he found an indigenous people without a written language. Before the coming of the Pākehā, the culture of the written word was unavailable to the Māori. Those first Christian missionaries found that the Māori identity was grounded in stories about their past and embedded in elaborate genealogies providing what the Māori thought worth remembering about their past. This lore, which included elaborate myths tracing Māori origins back to Io and other divine beings, pointed them toward a future dependent on their actions here and now and preserved accounts of their notable individuals and the events out of which they drew moral instruction and the norms regulating their communities.

In order to have a past and thus an identity, the Māori had to commit to memory the knowledge that seemed to them to be normative. With the incursion of the Pākehā, however, all that began to change. Those who are products of a literate culture and whose life experiences are grounded in, and stored and communicated through, written artifacts may have difficulty appreciating the situation of a people who are grounded in oral tradition. It seems that when an oral culture comes in contact with a written culture, as happened in the late eighteenth century in Aotearoa/New Zealand, oral traditions are inevitably eroded, corrupted, and eventually perhaps even forgotten. Among the Māori, the introduction of writing reduced the need for the earlier elaborate, detailed oral transmission of traditional lore, a task that was assigned to gifted tohunga.[52] Inevitably, much of the old knowledge, including the cultural traditions and institutions grounded on that knowledge, would not be passed on, as it had been, to the next generation.

The Debasement of Mores

One particularly vexing challenge to understanding the past and the culture of a people whose identity is grounded in an essentially oral culture is that, as one writer has put it, an oral culture "leaves very little trace on the historical landscape."[53] Once the living link to the past is broken, it is difficult if not impossible to reconstitute it in its original form. The Pākehā who first encountered the Māori produced a written version of their language and taught them to read it and English as well. The Māori quickly became literate, but what Alexis de Tocqueville described as the "habits of the heart" remained largely embedded in the old oral culture.

When we attempt to understand or reconstitute the learning of an oral culture, even the little that may happen to have been written down suffers from the inaccuracies and the unavoidable misunderstandings of those who do both the telling and the writing. In addition, those who record oral traditions do so under the influence of their own agenda and the horizon of meaning they necessarily bring to their efforts. For these reasons, it is difficult to discover the intellectual world of the Māori before the Pākehā arrived. Nostalgia for such a thing— the longing for a noble past—expresses a desire for a solid guide for the present and a hope for the future, or at least a window to a different world.

To what degree those who recorded Māori lore were influenced by the notion that they were confronted with something primitive and pagan remains an open question. Because the Māori had lost much of their contact with the past that was previously kept alive in their oral culture by genealogies, carvings, rituals, traditions, and stories, those of Māori descent who now feel a nostalgia for a mostly lost past must struggle to recover that past through the medium of writing, that is, through what just happened to get recorded by the Pākehā—those who for the most part were from an alien culture and may not have understood much of what they were told. As one writer explains, "The outcome of this almost anarchic approach was that much of what was written, and what later formed the basis for further research, had been either significantly altered by the transcribers, or had been collected from poor sources."[54]

Other difficulties made the recording of Māori lore problematic. Much of the material that was recorded appeared as a jumble to the Pākehā. It seemed to them to be mythological or legendary even though on the surface it tended to "resemble eye-witness accounts of incidents." In these accounts, which did not take the form expected by the Pākehā, "there is a distinct focus on the main events, and generally less attention is paid to detail such as dates. Also, the emphasis is on what actually happened, and on the moral of the incident. There is little interpretation, and even less historiography. The center of interest is around the moral judgements of events, and the qualities of the people involved."[55]

Those whose life experience is essentially bound up with the written word, who live in a world in which writing rules, may have difficulty appreciating the time-consuming, somewhat cumbersome, and fragile way in which oral cultures transmit knowledge and a sense of identity. Those who live in a world where writing dominates may also have a low opinion of what could be remembered and transmitted in an oral culture, because they see writing as the primary way to acquire, store, and communicate information, and they sense the weakness of their own inattentive and untrained memories.

A recent brutal, vulgar, and powerful novel by Alan Duff, who has become perhaps the foremost Māori literary figure, depicts what has happened to his people as they have moved into an urban setting without having taken advantage of an education in which books—the written word—provide both the norm and the power to ennoble.[56] Duff depicts the social despoliation of Māori who have lost touch with their own past, or what remains of that past since the coming of the Pākehā: they have none of the traditional "cultural learning, no social precedents, rules, no regulated teaching."[57] Without the advantages of a literate culture, Duff contends, any semblance of traditional Māori ways simply cannot provide the means to move them from the bottom of the social heap.[58]

Duff argues that "as far back as Plato those opposed to the written word were loud and shrill in their arguments against it.

It is the reactionary standard of the oral cultures that they have an overpowering hatred of the written word."[59] Duff opposes the currently fashionable notion that there is a learning grounded in the traditional oral culture that can by itself fit the Māori for the world in which they find themselves. Thus he pictures in *Once Were Warriors* homes without books, and children and adults who simply do not read. One also notices that the women, as well as the men, in Duff's novels are constantly having their "smokes," even while children are going without food or other vital attention.

In these scenes Duff spells out some of the dreadful effects on the Māori of what he calls "the turning of the collective back on the written word." He points out that Māori women have "the highest lung cancer rate in the world. This is in stark contrast to our European fellow New Zealanders, who have been part of this vast written debate in every publication you could imagine, whose cigarette smoking consumption has gone the complete opposite direction: down."[60] He describes this as "but one graphic example of ignoring the written word." And so, according to Duff, "we Māori let it slip by our very noses as we languished in basically unread ignorance. And even now, there are a majority of us who refuse—point blank refuse—to recognize this failing on our part."[61]

Without their close attention to the written word and to education, Duff believes the Māori will continue to languish. And, ironically, without literacy those he pictures in his novels cannot even acquire the traditional lore of the Māori, for that lore is now available only in books written by Pākehā and in books by Māori scholars that build on those early Pākehā-written accounts, since the living link with the traditional past has long since been severed.

And so the salvation of the Māori, according to Duff, cannot be found in the social control exercised by extended families, or by the rituals and protocol of the marae, or even through a kind of nostalgic renaissance of some of the norms that once governed the Māori. Nor can a mere Māori cultural revival or Pākehā sentimentality about Māori things do much good. As Māori culture is presumably revived, it is also being transformed and re-created, but not exactly, according to Duff, in ways that fit the Māori to live well in a literate world where knowledge found in books rules.

Can the urban Māori now find in a nostalgia for the old traditions the discipline necessary to restrain them from enslavement to cigarettes, beer, violence, and sloth? Duff is confident that neither nostalgia nor a continued tribalism will improve the situation of the Māori. And he is right.

But Duff knows only too well the degradation of the urban Māori who have lost both their language and the moral discipline of the traditional culture and have turned away from the written word. For him the only hope seems to be in something much more than a mere continuation of, or even a revival of, the traditional culture, if such a thing were really possible. He pleads for attention to education—for the fruit of the written word. Unfortunately, he seems to know nothing of the Māori Latter-day Saints who have found ways of linking the more noble family and tribal elements of their traditional culture with a book that has offered them a form of Christianity filled with a prophetic message that they see—or at least once saw—as directed at their own condition. It is a mistake to neglect the role of the Book of Mormon in the lives of the Māori Saints, for it serves to stabilize and unify a people whose traditional culture is undergoing radical and not entirely desirable changes. It is a book that firmly grounds a moral and intellectual discipline, both communal and individual, and that strives to ground a community dedicated to achieving proper parenting, a community that insists on literacy and commends education, the very elements that Duff thinks the Māori currently lack.

And where Duff portrays deracinated youths—mongrels— leagued together in gangs that substitute for the extended families of traditional Māori culture, the Māori Saints fight a battle against these dreadful evils. The central message of Duff's terrible tales of degradation is that without their traditional past, the Māori have become slaves, for "without the past they were nothing."[62] But all the resources that flow from a genuine commitment to the Book of Mormon and the account of its recovery are meant to provide a meaningful past, and also a future in both this world and beyond the grave that nurtures a genuine hope.

Notes

1. See John L. Sorenson, *An Ancient American Setting for the Book of Mormon* (Salt Lake City: Deseret Book and FARMS, 1985).

2. The word *māori* when used as an adjective simply means "normal, usual, ordinary." As an adjective it is found in several cognate forms throughout the South Pacific. Hence the expression *tangata māori* (man, or human being as distinguished from supernatural beings) is *kanaka maoli* in Hawaiian. In Hawaiian the *l* sound displaces the Māori *r* sound. Hence *aroha* (love) becomes *aloha* in Hawaiian. As a proper noun, *Māori* first came into use on the Banks Peninsula near Christchurch, New Zealand, in 1836 to distinguish the indigenous people from the *Pākehā* (foreigners or strangers). See Herbert W. Williams, *A Dictionary of the Maori Language,* 7th ed., s.v. "maori."

3. Master's thesis, University of British Columbia, 1965. See Schwimmer's article "The Cognitive Aspect of Culture Change," *Journal of the Polynesian Society* 74 (June 1965): 149–81.

4. See John H. Groberg, *In the Eye of the Storm* (Salt Lake City: Bookcraft, 1993).

5. Richard L. Bushman, *Joseph Smith and the Beginnings of Mormonism* (Urbana: University of Illinois Press, 1984), 133.

6. Ibid.

7. Richard L. Bushman, "The Book of Mormon in Early Mormon History," in *New Views of Mormon History: Essays in Honor of Leonard J. Arrington*, ed. Davis Bitton and Maureen Ursenbach Beecher (Salt Lake City: University of Utah Press, 1987), 5.

8. Ibid.

9. Ibid.

10. Ibid.

11. Ibid., 14.

12. One writer claims that the immigrants to New Zealand from the United Kingdom were called *Pākehā* by the Māori because they "appeared to look like fairies or fair-skinned supernatural beings." He insists that the name *Pākehā* "is not used for all foreigners, only those who have white skin." And the name "is not a term of denigration in Māori usage, but rather one of respect in associating the new settlers with supernatural beings or godlike people (at least in terms of their appearance)" (Cleve Barlow, *Tikanga Whakaaro: Key Concepts in Maori Culture* [Auckland, New Zealand: Oxford University Press, 1991], 87).

13. *Aotearoa* is the Māori name for New Zealand, and it is now common to see the compound name *Aotearoa/New Zealand*. It means something like "land of the long white cloud."

14. Once a fortified place or stockade or its inhabitants, and hence a village.

15. This enclosed space, courtyard, or common (often but not necessarily a lawn) in front of a meetinghouse is constructed in such a way as to symbolize the traditional ancestor of the *tangata whenua* (people of that place) and is often decorated with carvings. For a useful account of the details concerning contemporary Māori marae and also something of their history, see Hiwi and Pat Tauroa, *Te Marae: A Guide to Customs and Protocol* (Birkenhead, Auckland, New Zealand: Reed Books, 1986). Currently the word *marae* identifies not merely the enclosed common area, but all of the buildings

associated with the community, including the symbolic representation of the tribal ancestor in the form of an elaborately carved sacred house, eating facilities, and so forth. Marae are a symbol of tribal identity. Once they were found only in rural areas, but urban marae have recently been established to serve the needs of those who now live in cities. See Barlow, *Tikanga Whakaaro*, 71–4.

16. For an indication of what that would have constituted, see the appropriate entry in Barlow, *Tikanga Whakaaro*; and Tauroa, *Te Marae*, 25–99.

17. Māori identity, until the Pākehā arrived, began with extended families *(whānau)* and mounted up through subtribes *(hapū)* to tribes *(iwi)*. Each level had male leaders: *kaumātua* (elders), *rangatira* (bosses or minor chiefs), and *ariki* (chiefs). At most levels the *mana* (the privileges, spiritual power, authority of chiefs) was mostly hereditary, though it was also an expression and extension of the group. Though the Māori now appear on the surface to have been assimilated into the larger Pākehā culture, remnants of these kinship structures still function in locating Māori identity. For some purposes, especially when facing the Pākehā, the Māori may see themselves as sharing a single identity. For other purposes, however, and perhaps for most purposes, they still tend to see themselves as divided into extended families, subtribes, and tribes.

18. For a rich account of various kinds of hui, see Anne Salmond, *Hui: A Study of Maori Ceremonial Gatherings* (Wellington, New Zealand: A. H. and A. W. Reed, 1975).

19. At one time, only properly endowed tohunga were permitted to enter the carved house that represented the founding ancestor of a hapū. See Barlow, *Tikanga Whakaaro*, 73.

20. This is a Latter-day Saint understanding of what went on at this hui. For details, see Matthew Cowley, "Maori Chief Predicts Coming of L.D.S. Missionaries," *Improvement Era* 53 (Sept. 1950): 697–8.

21. See Matthew Cowley, "Maori Chief Predicts," in *Matthew Cowley Speaks* (Salt Lake City: Deseret Book, 1954), 200–5, for a

translation of Potangaroa's prophecy, a description of its interpretation by the Māori Saints, and an account of how he came to possess a photograph of the original but lost text of *Te Kawenata*.

22. In 1830 Arama Toiroa, from Mahia, gathered his family and gave them his final testament, which included, among other things, the sign that the one who would eventually introduce to his descendants the true form of worship would "stand and raise both hands to heaven" when he prayed. In 1884 Elder William Thomas Stewart and others visited Korongata (Bridge Pa), where they held Sabbath services. When Elder Stewart closed those services, "he raised both hands and invoked God's blessings upon the people." Te Teira Marutu, a grandson of Toiroa, recognized this as the sign of the coming of the true faith to the Māori. Soon those living in Korongata and many in Mahia, familiar with Toiroa's prophetic testament, were baptized. See the translation of the account by Toiroa's famous Latter-day Saint descendant, Hirini Whaanga, entitled "A Maori Prophet," *Juvenile Instructor* 37 (1 Mar. 1902): 152–3.

23. For details see Ian Rewi Barker, "The Connection: The Mormon Church and the Maori People" (master's thesis, Victoria University, Wellington, New Zealand, 1967); and Brian W. Hunt, *Zion in New Zealand: A History of the Church of Jesus Christ of Latter-day Saints in New Zealand, 1854–1977* (Templeview, New Zealand: Church College of New Zealand, 1977), which is the published version of his 1971 master's thesis at Brigham Young University. However, the most accessible account has been provided by R. Lanier Britsch in "Maori Tohunga and the Growth of the Church," in his *Unto the Islands of the Sea: A History of the Latter-day Saints in the Pacific* (Salt Lake City: Deseret Book, 1986), 272–8.

24. The Io cult was celebrated and passed along through *wānanga* (special schools) of tohunga. A *whare wānanga* is the house in which the school meets. Hence a university is now called a whare wānanga (see Barlow, *Tikanga Whakaaro*, 156–9). The central teachings of the traditional whare wānanga concerned what the Māori involved in the Io cult called "baskets of wisdom," which included

elaborate cosmogenic lore such as knowledge of the ten heavens and other matters concerning the gods, the descent of man into this world, and the return of the soul to the divine realms governed by Io.

25. Pieter H. de Bres, *Religion in Atene: Religious Associations and the Urban Maori* (Wellington, New Zealand: Polynesian Society, 1971), 18. In an effort to explain how Latter-day Saints "get the Maori," de Bres adds that "the Mormon view of death as only a temporary separation of the deceased from the living ('we will meet again') is also important to the Maori. The study of genealogies *(whakapapa)* received a new meaning because it offered an opportunity to incorporate the ancestors [of the Maori] into the Church through baptism for the dead" (ibid.).

26. Hence the following from an anthropological study of a Māori village: "The ancient religion of the Maori is imperfectly understood since many of the early records were 'contaminated' by Christian conceptions either on the part of the authors or on the part of their informants. Much has been made by some of the esoteric cult of Io, reputed to have been a . . . being worshiped by a special secret priestly cult. There is practically no direct evidence upon which the existence, scope, or distribution of such belief and worship can be assessed" (James E. Ritchie, *The Making of a Maori: A Case Study of a Changing Community* [Wellington, New Zealand: A. H. and A. W. Reed, 1963], 20). "Much has been made of the so-called cult of Io. This is said to have been a special aristocratic worship of a supreme being whose very existence was kept hidden from the knowledge of common folk" (ibid., 120).

Eric Schwimmer has argued that a group of Māori "folk scholars, drawn from widely separated parts of the North Island, held two protracted meetings around the year 1860 in order to establish a common version of Maori cosmology, metaphysics, and very ancient history." Out of these meetings, Schwimmer argues, came "an elaborate doctrine that the ancient Maoris had a supreme God called Io. . . . It was maintained that though the Io traditions were very ancient they were also very secret and known only to the most esoteric class of tohungas. Thus it was explained why no surviving record of Io antedates the two meetings" (Eric Schwimmer, *The World of the Maori* [Wellington, New Zealand: A. H. and A. W. Reed, 1966], 114). Allan Hanson, a clever anthropologist, has argued that all "culture" and "tradition" are merely "inventions designed to serve contemporary purposes." He therefore brushes aside all Māori accounts of intentional migration to New Zealand and also claims that the antiquity of the Io cult is questionable. See his article "The Making of the Maori: Culture Invention and Its Logic," *American Anthropologist* 91 (Dec. 1989): 890–6.

27. Schwimmer, *World of the Maori*, 114. But another writer claims that "it is quite possible that in some of the historically late Maori cosmogonic texts, the composers were moved to create an account that maximized similarities with Christian ideas—not by borrowing from Christianity so much as by accentuating those indigenous ideas that most approximated Christian ones. I suspect that the *Whare Wananga* account was influenced in some way by the encounter with Christianity" (Gregory A. Schrempp, *Magical Arrows: The Maori, the Greeks, and the Folklore of the Universe* [Madison: University of Wisconsin Press, 1992], 107). But Schrempp is not inclined to say exactly how.

28. J. Frank Stimson (*Tuamotuan Religion* [Honolulu, Hi.: Bishop Museum, 1933], 69–80, 88–9) attempts to trace the Māori Io cult back to earlier high esoteric cosmology involving *iho, kio,* and *kiho,* found widely in the eastern Pacific. See also the many entries under *Io* in the impressive Rarotongan Māori dictionary. Perhaps because the Io cult among the Māori of New Zealand was found among the hapū on the east coast and was essentially secret, there is no entry on *Io* in Williams's *Dictionary of the Maori Language* (see n. 2). This dictionary, a wonderful source of information about the Māori language, was originally crafted by William Williams, an Anglican bishop, and published in Paihia in the Northland of New Zealand in 1844.

29. See Britsch, *Unto the Islands of the Sea,* 253–345. Incidentally, as an undergraduate at Brigham Young University, Britsch was a student of John L. Sorenson.

30. Peter Lineham, "The Mormon Message in the Context of Maori Culture," *Journal of Mormon History* 17 (1991): 62–93.

31. Even an anthropological study like that of Schwimmer contains little on how the Māori Saints in Whangaruru read the scriptures.

32. Lineham, "Mormon Message," 81.

33. Ibid.

34. One writer has argued that the notion of what he calls "the Semitic Maori lived on in the preaching of Mormon missionaries who began to proselytize among the Maoris in the late nineteenth century. According to the Book of Mormon, the Polynesians were descended from American Indian Semites who first landed in Hawaii in 58 B.C." This is an example of the confusion manifested by otherwise competent scholars concerning exactly what the Māori Saints believed about their links with the Lehi colony. See M. P. K. Sorrenson, *Maori Origins and Migrations: The Genesis of Some Pakeha Myths and Legends* (Auckland, New Zealand: Auckland University Press, 1979), 16–7, and the source he cites for his opinion.

35. See ibid. Also see Schwimmer, "Mormonism in a Maori Village," 149 (see n. 3). In 1991 I and a group of BYU students and other faculty heard a tribal elder *(kaumātua)* at the Takapuwahia marae in Porirua proclaim that Elder Spencer W. Kimball, next to Joseph Smith, was the greatest prophet of this dispensation. But, he added, Elder Kimball had made one serious mistake—he had wrongly assumed that the Māori were Lamanites.

36. Lineham, "Mormon Message," 83.

37. Ibid., 88.

38. Ibid.

39. For a detailed discussion from a number of different perspectives, see Douglas G. Sutton, ed., *The Origins of the First New Zealanders* (Auckland, New Zealand: Auckland University Press, 1994); or the discussion by Alan H. Grey in his *Aotearoa and New Zealand: A Historical Geography* (Christchurch, New Zealand: Canterbury University Press, 1994), 83–8.

40. The first efforts to construct a written version of the Māori

language began as early as 1820 with the preparation of a short lexicon and grammar by the Church Missionary Society. Samuel Lee, a professor of Arabic at Cambridge, eventually set out a satisfactory orthography. See Williams, *Dictionary of the Maori Language,* xxiii.

41. The Māori were thus made literate, first in Māori and then in English. They gradually became bilingual and then began to use only English.

42. Bronwyn Elsmore, *Mana from Heaven: A Century of Maori Prophets in New Zealand* (Tauranga, New Zealand: Moana Press, 1989), 24.

43. Paul Moon, *Maori Social and Economic History to the End of the Nineteenth Century* (Henderson, Auckland, New Zealand: Birdwood Publishing, 1993), 73.

44. Ibid., 77.

45. This treaty effectively made the British Crown the legal sovereign over New Zealand.

46. This version of the saying is in Lineham, "Mormon Message," 77.

47. Moon, *Maori Social and Economic History,* 79–80.

48. Eric Schwimmer seems to feel that the Māori used Mormonism to justify certain portions of their old traditions and lore as they found ways to change other elements of their culture. Schwimmer's study also tends to make Latter-day Saints out to be cultural imperialists bent on transforming Māori culture, or what he calls the old Māori ways. In reality, much of the traditional ways that Schwimmer thought were being replaced by an American religion amounted to such things as quarrels within and between families and especially the consumption of beer.

49. See Lineham, 72–93.

50. There are now two Latter-day Saint stakes in this same area.

51. See Barlow, *Tikanga Whakaaro,* 36–7.

52. See Barlow, *Tikanga Whakaaro,* xv, for an account of his own selection as "the keeper of the whakapapa or genealogy for the families in our district."

53. Moon, *Maori Social and Economic History,* 42.

54. Ibid.

55. Ibid.

56. Alan Duff, *Once Were Warriors* (New York: Vintage Books, 1990). The shocking, stunning, and depressing motion picture based on this novel does not do justice to the subtle messages offered by Duff.

57. Ibid., 127.

58. See Alan Duff, *Maori: The Crisis and the Challenge* (Auckland, New Zealand: HarperCollins, 1993).

59. Ibid., 7.

60. Ibid.

61. Ibid.

62. *Once Were Warriors,* 172. See the sequel to his novel entitled *What Becomes of the Broken Hearted?* (Glenfield, Auckland, New Zealand: Vintage, 1996).

CHAPTER 9

PATTERN AND PURPOSE OF THE ISAIAH COMMENTARIES IN THE BOOK OF MORMON

Garold N. Davis

The words of Isaiah . . . are written, ye have them before you, therefore search them (3 Nephi 20:11).

Ye ought to search these things. Yea, a commandment I give unto you that ye search these things diligently; for great are the words of Isaiah (3 Nephi 23:1).

As part of his marvelous vision recorded in 1 Nephi 11–14, Nephi saw that the gentiles in the last days would have a book (the Bible) containing the "covenants of the Lord" and "many of the prophecies of the holy prophets," which would include Isaiah (see 1 Nephi 13:20–5). Given that these "nations and kingdoms of the Gentiles" (1 Nephi 13:3) would have the writings of the biblical prophets, the question naturally arises, why would Mormon include in the Book of Mormon record twenty-one nearly complete chapters of Isaiah as well as quotations from them and other Isaiah chapters? Why this duplication of scripture?[1]

Garold N. Davis is professor of German and comparative literature at Brigham Young University.

One could argue that because eighteen of these twenty-one chapters were on the small plates of Nephi, which Mormon seems to have found among the Nephite records *after* he had completed his abridgment (see Words of Mormon 1:3) and which he apparently added to his abridgment without editing, this duplication was an oversight on the part of Mormon. But to those who believe in the divine stewardship of the production, transmission, and translation of Nephite records, the inclusion of this large body of information from the prophet Isaiah must surely be attributed to more than human oversight. Indeed, in this view the Book of Mormon's repeated affirmations of the great worth of Isaiah's words suggest a divine purpose behind their preservation in two different yet complementary collections of scripture. For example, Nephi indicates that the writings of Isaiah are for the benefit of the people in our day, or at least for the benefit of his own descendants: "In the days that the prophecies of Isaiah shall be fulfilled men shall know of a surety, at the times when they shall come to pass. . . . For I know that they shall be of great worth unto [mine own people] in the last days; for in that day shall they understand them; wherefore, for their good have I written them" (2 Nephi 25:7–8).

I suggest two possible reasons for the duplication of Isaiah's writings. First, the Isaiah text translated by Joseph Smith in the Book of Mormon contains numerous differences from the biblical translations of the same text available in his day and in ours. The doctrine of the LDS Church is that the Isaiah text in the Book of Mormon is an inspired translation of a transcript taken originally from the brass plates of Laban. Consequently, it predates our current Isaiah manuscripts by several centuries. After Lehi departed from Jerusalem with the writings of Isaiah firmly inscribed on the brass plates, changes were apparently introduced into the Isaiah manuscripts from which our current Bibles have been translated.[2] The Isaiah material in the Book of Mormon corrects textual errors perpetuated in the biblical versions.

A second reason for the duplication is that the Book of Mormon Isaiah text comes complete with a number of specific commentaries, an advantage that the biblical text of Isaiah does not have.

The Isaiah passages in the Book of Mormon occur within a very interesting lexical or contextual pattern. Careful readers of the book are aware that one of its major themes is the history and destiny of the Lord's covenant relationship with the house of Israel—a theme that includes the Abrahamic covenant, the covenant of the infinite atonement, the scattering of Israel, and the reestablishment of the house of Israel in the last days by a mighty gentile nation.

The contextual pattern is this: the Isaiah passages appear extensively on the small plates of Nephi and then not again (with the exception of Isaiah 53, quoted by Abinadi) until after the account of the Savior's appearance in 3 Nephi. Also, the term *house of Israel* and references to the Abrahamic covenant and to the gentile nation that will restore the house of Israel in the last days occur only where Isaiah is being cited. To illustrate, the term *house of Israel* occurs 107 times in the Book of Mormon (plus occasional references to the synonymous wording *house of Jacob*), but the term is not used randomly throughout the text. Like the Isaiah passages, this term appears with great frequency on the small plates and is not mentioned again (nor, with one exception, is Isaiah) until the tenth chapter of 3 Nephi—that is, no mention in Mosiah, Alma, Helaman, or the first part of 3 Nephi.[3] But when the Savior appears to the Book of Mormon people in 3 Nephi, the theme is reintroduced, one is tempted to say, with a vengeance.

In 3 Nephi 10:2 the text tells us "there was silence in all the

land for the space of many hours." This silence is broken by the
voice of the Savior, who immediately tells the people they are of
the house of Israel. He goes on to remind them of this four
more times in that chapter alone. In all, the Savior uses the term
house of Israel thirty-eight times during his visit with the people
as described in 3 Nephi—twenty-four times in chapters 16, 20,
and 21, the chapters that serve as commentary on and an introduction to Isaiah 52 and 54, which are quoted by the Savior.

This contextual pattern linking the Isaiah passages with the
term *house of Israel* has additional components. The term *covenant* appears in the same Book of Mormon sections in which
the Isaiah passages and the term *house of Israel* occur. In the
Book of Mormon the term *covenant* most frequently refers to
God's covenant promises, given through Abraham to the house
of Israel, of an "infinite atonement" (see 2 Nephi 9). The Book
of Mormon further teaches that the law of Moses and "all the
prophets who have prophesied ever since the world began"
(Mosiah 13:33) have pointed to the fulfillment of this covenant
promise (see Mosiah 13, 15) and, more specifically, that God
has not forgotten "scattered" Israel but will remember and restore them "in the last days." Frequently there is a reference
directly to the restoration of the "seed" of Lehi (see 1 Nephi
15:14–20; 22, especially verses 8–11). With the exception of
those few places where the word *covenant* is used in another
meaning (such as the covenant made by the Gadianton robbers
or the covenant made by the people of Alma at the time of their
baptism), the word appears prominently in the small plates and
then disappears until 3 Nephi, when the Savior reintroduces
the concept to the people in connection with his reintroduc-
tion of the theme of the house of Israel and his citation of the
prophet Isaiah.

Similarly, the term *gentile(s)* appears in the small plates of Nephi and then disappears from the text until the Savior's appearance in 3 Nephi. Understanding Isaiah in the Book of Mormon thus presumes an understanding of the terms *house of Israel, covenant,* and *gentile,* which predominate in the Isaiah commentaries in the Book of Mormon and do not occur elsewhere in the book.[4]

The scope of this paper does not allow a detailed explication of the Isaiah chapters in the Book of Mormon. Rather, my approach is to suggest how the commentaries unite in purpose to clarify and reinforce Isaiah's teachings. These commentaries are remarkably consistent in their interpretation and application of Isaiah's words. Lehi, Nephi, Jacob, and the Savior himself well understood the meaning, relevance, power, and authoritative nature of Isaiah's words, which often can be seen as stimulating the prophetic gift of those who so ably quoted and expounded them.

Lehi's Commentary on Isaiah

Perhaps because of the loss of the 116 manuscript pages of the Book of Mormon we have Lehi's commentary on Isaiah only through the words of Nephi. His words are sufficient, however, to indicate that Lehi taught his sons what specifically to look for in the prophet Isaiah's writings that would be of particular value to his people and to later readers of the Book of Mormon. Nephi tells us that in order to explain "my proceedings, and my reign and ministry" (1 Nephi 10:1), he must comment on the teachings of his father. He then gives a summary of Lehi's teachings that is a rather precise outline for all the commentaries on Isaiah that follow in the Book of Mormon. First Nephi 10 indicates that

1. Jerusalem will be destroyed and the Jews will be carried away (verse 3);

2. the Jews will return and "possess again the land of their inheritance" (verse 3);

3. the Messiah will come and "take away the sins of the world," but he will be rejected and slain and will then "rise from the dead" (verses 4–11);

4. the house of Israel will then be scattered "upon all the face of the earth" (verses 12–13);

5. the gentiles will receive "the fulness of the Gospel," and then the house of Israel will be gathered together and "come to the knowledge of the true Messiah, their Lord and their Redeemer" (verse 14).

Nephi returns from having been "carried away in the spirit" (1 Nephi 15:1) to find his brothers engaged in a dispute because they cannot understand Lehi's words concerning the scattering of Israel and the subsequent gathering through the fulness of the gentiles (see verses 7, 13). Nephi's explanation of these concepts follows the same pattern as that noted above in 1 Nephi 10:3–14: the house of Israel will be scattered (see verses 12, 17, 20), the Messiah "shall be manifested in body unto the children of men" (verse 13), "then shall the fulness of the gospel of the Messiah come unto the Gentiles" (verse 13), from the gentiles the gospel will be taken again to "the remnant of our seed" (verse 13), and "at that day shall the remnant of our seed know that they are of the house of Israel, and that they are the covenant people of the Lord" (verse 14). Nephi then reveals that he used the prophet Isaiah as his scriptural support for these teachings: "I did rehearse unto them the words of Isaiah, who spake concerning the restoration of the Jews, or of the house of Israel; and after they were restored they should no more be confounded, neither should they be scattered again" (verse 20). Apparently, Nephi's recourse to Isaiah's words satisfied his brothers, who "were pacified and did humble themselves before the Lord" (verse 20).

Nephi's Commentary on Isaiah 48–9 (1 Nephi 20–1)

Nephi's commentary on Isaiah 48 and 49 begins in 1 Nephi 19, where Nephi again mentions his father, Lehi, and states that Lehi's record and prophecies are contained on the other (large) plates. He then begins his own commentary, which asserts that "the God of Israel," who would come in six hundred years, would be rejected and crucified, and the signs of his death would be given to "all the house of Israel" (see 1 Nephi 19:7–8, 9–12). As a consequence, "those who are at Jerusalem . . . shall wander in the flesh and perish, and become a hiss and a byword" (verses 13–14). But the Lord, who "will remember the covenants which he made to their fathers," will also remember "all the people who are of the house of Israel" and will gather them again (see verses 15–16).

Nephi tells us that these things were written to persuade his people to "remember the Lord their Redeemer" (verse 18). Several texts from the brass plates helped him in this task, he states, but so that he "might more fully persuade them to believe in the Lord their Redeemer," he turned particularly to the prophet Isaiah (see verse 23). With this context and commentary as preparation for what will follow, Nephi then copies from the brass plates those sections from the writings of Isaiah that now constitute 1 Nephi 20–1 (Isaiah 48–9).

The introduction to Isaiah 48 serves, in a way, as an introduction to the purpose of all prophecy. God reveals future events through his prophets so that when those events transpire, people will not attribute them to natural (or even to supernatural but likewise ungodly) causes, but will recognize his supervening hand in human affairs. As stated by Isaiah, "Before it came to pass I showed them thee . . . for fear lest thou shouldst say—Mine idol hath done them, and my graven image, and my molten image hath commanded them" (1 Nephi 20:5).

In addition to inviting Nephi's illuminating commentary, the Book of Mormon text of Isaiah 48 fulfills the other purpose mentioned earlier by correcting two major errors that appeared in later biblical manuscripts and that were carried over into the King James Version of Isaiah. In 1 Nephi 20:1 (Isaiah 48:1) the information that the "house of Jacob" had come "out of the waters of baptism" is restored to the text, and in verse 2 the statement that the people of the holy city "stay themselves upon the God of Israel" is corrected to the exact opposite—they "*do not* stay themselves on the God of Israel."[5] This correction is important because it is consistent with the message that follows—that if the people had not broken the covenant, the house of Israel would not have been scattered (see 1 Nephi 20:18–19).

First Nephi 21 (Isaiah 49) presents the scattering of Israel as a result of breaking the covenant and specifically addresses "all ye that are broken off and are driven out because of the wickedness of the pastors of my people" (verse 1). If Israel is scattered, then is the Lord's work for the house of Israel all in vain? (see verse 4). No, because the Lord will gather them again through the gentiles, and all the nations of the earth will be blessed by his ministry, "that thou mayest be my salvation unto the ends of the earth" (see verses 5–6). The Lord will remember his covenant to those scattered, even to the "isles of the sea" (see verses 8–9, 15–16).

An interesting dialogue follows (verses 18–23) in which the Lord tells Israel that although she has lost her first children, she will have many more brought to her by the gentiles: "Behold, I will lift up mine hand to the Gentiles, and set up my standard to the people; and they shall bring thy sons in their arms, and thy daughters shall be carried upon their shoulders. And kings shall be thy nursing fathers, and their queens thy nursing mothers" (verses 22–3).

We have Laman and Lemuel to thank for Nephi's further commentary on Isaiah 48 and 49. "What meaneth these things which ye have read?" they ask (1 Nephi 22:1). Nephi explains that the house of Israel "will be scattered upon all the face of the earth, and also among all nations" (verse 3); that God will then "raise up a mighty nation among the Gentiles" who will continue the scattering of Israel (verse 7); and that God will then "proceed to do a marvelous work among the Gentiles" that will greatly benefit scattered Israel and "is likened unto their being nourished by the Gentiles and being carried in their arms and upon their shoulders" (verse 8).[6]

In the day when God brings "his covenants and his gospel unto those who are of the house of Israel . . . they shall be gathered together to the lands of their inheritance; and they shall be brought out of obscurity and out of darkness; and they shall know that the Lord is their Savior and their Redeemer, the Mighty One of Israel" (verses 11–12).

Nephi's commentary on Isaiah 48 and 49 in 1 Nephi 19 and 22 is entirely consistent with Lehi's commentary that Nephi recorded in 1 Nephi 10 and 15.

Jacob's Commentary on Isaiah 50–1 (2 Nephi 7–8)

Jacob quotes the next section of Isaiah and makes it clear that he is following the pattern set by his brother Nephi: "I will read you the words of Isaiah. And they are the words which my brother has desired that I should speak unto you . . . because ye

are of the house of Israel" (2 Nephi 6:4–5). Before quoting
Isaiah 50 and 51 (2 Nephi 7–8), Jacob begins his commentary
by quoting from Isaiah 49:22: "I will lift up mine hand to the
Gentiles . . ." (2 Nephi 6:6). The remainder of his preface to
Isaiah 50 and 51 is consistent with Lehi's and Nephi's commen-
taries on Isaiah discussed earlier. Jacob tells us in 2 Nephi 6 that

1. "those who were at Jerusalem" have been scattered (verse 8);

2. they will return (verse 9);

3. Christ will be born among them, but they will reject and
   crucify him (verse 9);

4. those at Jerusalem will be scattered again, "driven to and
   fro" (verses 10–11);

5. but the Lord will remember the covenant and will "set himself again the second time to recover them" (from Isaiah 11)
   through the gentiles (verses 12–14).

After this prefatory outline, Jacob then quotes Isaiah 50 and 51.

Isaiah 50 begins with a series of questions that, as understood
by Jacob, are concerned with the scattering of the house of Israel.
Speaking messianically, Isaiah uses the metaphor of divorce to
draw attention to this scattering: "Have I put thee away, or have
I cast thee off forever?" the Lord asks rhetorically. Isaiah then
answers his own question with the Lord's accusation: "For your
iniquities have ye sold yourselves, and for your transgressions is
your mother put away" (verse 1). Isaiah then asks Israel if this
separation could have been prevented had they only had faith in
the Lord's power: "O house of Israel, is my hand shortened at all
that it cannot redeem, or have I no power to deliver?" (verse 2).

The imagery of scattering and eventual gathering continues
through Isaiah 50 and 51, and at the outset of 2 Nephi 9 Jacob
clearly tells why he has quoted these two chapters and what

their major message is: "I have read these things [Isaiah 50–1] that ye might know concerning the *covenants* of the Lord that he has covenanted with all the *house of Israel*" (verse 1). One aspect of this covenant, as Jacob goes on to explain, is that the time will come when Israel "shall be restored to the true church and fold of God; when they shall be gathered home to the lands of their inheritance, and shall be established in all their lands of promise" (verse 2).

At this point in 2 Nephi 9, Jacob suddenly shifts the emphasis from this temporal gathering to a universal and spiritual gathering and suggests a second and even more important aspect of the covenant mentioned in verse 1: "I speak unto you these things that ye may rejoice, and lift up your heads *forever,* because of the blessings which the Lord God shall bestow upon your children" (verse 3). Jacob then proceeds to give a powerful sermon on universal death, the resurrection, and the atonement: "Our flesh must waste away and die" (verse 4), but Christ will die for all men and bring about a general resurrection (verses 5–6). Were it not for an "infinite atonement," the "first judgment [i.e., when mortals were, through Adam, cast out from the presence of God] . . . must needs have remained to an endless duration" (verses 6–7). Not only would we have died through a physical separation from God, but our spirits, without this "infinite atonement," would "have become . . . devils, angels to a devil, to be shut out from the presence of our God, and to remain with the father of lies, in misery, like unto himself" (verse 9).

Jacob refers to this double separation as a double "monster, death and hell, which I call the death of the body, and also the death of the spirit" (verse 10). But "because of the way of deliverance of our God, the Holy One of Israel, this death, . . . which is the temporal, shall deliver up its dead; which death is the grave. And this death . . . , which is the spiritual death, shall deliver up its dead; which spiritual death is hell" (verses 11–12). Now we understand why Jacob stated at the outset of the commentary that all mankind should "rejoice, and lift up [their] heads forever" (verse 3). Jacob's commentary expands on these points through verse 20, and with this commentary in mind we can now go back to Isaiah 50 and 51 (2 Nephi 7–8) and consider Isaiah's meaning in light of Jacob's commentary.

It seems clear that in Jacob's interpretation of Isaiah 50 and 51 the salvation spoken of may include, but goes much deeper than, the physical gathering of scattered Israel. Isaiah turns to the role of the Savior in gathering all mortal humanity from the ultimate scattering, death: "Is my hand shortened at all that it cannot redeem, or have I no power to deliver?" (2 Nephi 7:2). The verbs *redeem* and *deliver* seem to take on a more universal character when Isaiah then makes specific reference to the suffering of Christ: "I gave my back to the smiter, and my cheeks to them that plucked off the hair. I hid not my face from shame and spitting" (verse 6).

Second Nephi 7 (Isaiah 50) ends with the rather enigmatic comment that those who try to walk by the light of their own fire "shall lie down in sorrow" (verse 11). If I understand and apply Jacob's commentary in 2 Nephi 9 correctly, this metaphor has reference to the universal death that will come upon all mortals, and this theme then continues throughout Isaiah 51. As a word of caution, I should point out that when Jacob talks about the double monster, death and hell—that is, death of the body and death of the spirit—in 2 Nephi 9 as commentary on Isaiah 50 and 51, he is not suggesting that all mortals are doomed to suffer these two deaths. Rather, he is describing the result if a vital condition were not in place, a rhetorical style common to Book of Mormon writers. For example, beginning in 2 Nephi 9:7, Jacob details the sad state of all mortality "*save it should be* an infinite atonement." This rhetoric is similar to Nephi's phrasing "save Christ should come . . ." (2 Nephi 11:6), Alma's "except it were for these conditions . . ." (Alma 42:13), or Abinadi's "And now if Christ had not come . . ." (Mosiah 16:6). Following are a few quotations from Isaiah 51 (2 Nephi 8) with my own interpretive comments, both of which I believe correspond to Jacob's commentary in 2 Nephi 9: "Look unto the rock from whence ye are hewn, and to the hole of the pit from whence ye are digged" (2 Nephi 8:1). Look to Christ, the Holy One of Israel, for your salvation from the grave. "Look unto Abraham, your father, and unto Sarah, she that bare you" (verse 2). Remember the covenant that through Abraham's seed will come the Messiah, through whom all the nations of the earth will be blessed.[7] "The Lord shall comfort Zion. . . . Joy and gladness shall be found therein" (verse 3) because of the atonement that will overcome death.

The reader who proceeds through 2 Nephi 8 (Isaiah 51) with Jacob's commentary from chapter 9 firmly in mind will see the possibility that Isaiah 51 is a powerful commentary on the saving power of the "infinite atonement" (2 Nephi 9:7). For example, having in mind Jacob's discussion of physical and spiritual death and his characterization of death and hell as an "awful monster" (verse 10), the interesting parallelism in 2 Nephi 8:9 takes on a new dimension: "Art thou not he that hath cut Rahab [i.e., death] and wounded the dragon [i.e., hell]?" Then the verbs *ransomed* and *redeemed* in verses 10 and 11 take on a broader meaning, and of course "sorrow and mourning shall flee away" (verse 11), because of the infinite atonement that overcomes death and hell.

The remainder of 2 Nephi 8 continues to sustain the theme of the atonement that so clearly informs Jacob's commentary. "Among all the sons [Jerusalem] hath brought forth" (verse 18) there is no salvation (see verse 17), as there is no salvation in the law of Moses. The only sons left are "desolation and destruction" (verse 19)—that is, death and hell—and these two sons "lie at the head of all the streets" (verse 20), as death and hell lie at the end of every life, "save it should be an infinite atonement" (2 Nephi 9:7). Who, then, will comfort us, and why should we rejoice. The ultimate comfort—salvation—is of the Lord: "The Lord and thy God pleadeth the cause of his people; behold, I [the Lord and thy God] have taken out of thine hand the cup of trembling, the dregs of the cup of my fury; thou shalt no more drink it again" (verse 22). Christ has overcome death by drinking the bitter cup himself.

Certainly Jacob's commentary on Isaiah 50 and 51 allows a deeper, more personalized reading of these chapters than would otherwise likely be considered.

In 2 Nephi 10, Jacob's commentary on Isaiah continues, and his discussion of what he has just quoted from Isaiah also serves as an introductory commentary on the next group of Isaiah writings, 2 Nephi 12–24 (Isaiah 2–14).

Once again Jacob identifies the major themes that always accompany his citing of Isaiah. From 2 Nephi 10 we read that

1. Christ will come and the Jews will reject and crucify him (verse 3);

2. the Jews will be "scattered among all nations" (verse 6);

3. according to the covenant, the house of Israel will be "restored in the flesh, upon the earth, unto the lands of their inheritance" (verse 7);

4. the gentiles "shall be great in the eyes of [God]" in bringing about this gathering (verse 8).

Jacob's sermon shows further consistency with the teachings of his brother Nephi and his father, Lehi, because Jacob again quotes from Isaiah 49: "Yea, the kings of the Gentiles shall be nursing fathers unto them, and their queens shall become nursing mothers [Isaiah 49:23]; wherefore, the promises of the Lord are great unto the Gentiles" (2 Nephi 10:9; compare 1 Nephi 10:12, 14; 15:13–15; 22:8). Jacob then takes this promise to the gentiles one step further with a commentary on Isaiah 49:23: "I [God] will soften the hearts of the Gentiles, that they shall be like unto a father to them; *wherefore, the Gentiles shall be blessed and numbered among the house of Israel"* (2 Nephi 10:18).

With these background commentaries on Isaiah by Lehi, Nephi, and Jacob, we can better anticipate and understand the long section of Isaiah comprising 2 Nephi 12–24 (Isaiah 2–14).

Nephi's Commentary on Isaiah 2–14 (2 Nephi 12–24)

In introducing the next section of quotations from Isaiah, Nephi continues Jacob's emphasis on "the coming of Christ" (2 Nephi 11:4; compare 2 Nephi 9:21; 10:3), "the covenants of the Lord which he hath made to our fathers," (2 Nephi 11:5; compare 2 Nephi 6:12; 9:1, 53) and "the great and eternal plan of deliverance from death" (2 Nephi 11:5; compare 2 Nephi 9:10–13). Nephi is going to do this by quoting "more of the words of Isaiah, . . . for [Isaiah] verily saw my Redeemer, even as I have seen him. And my brother, Jacob, also has seen him" (2 Nephi 11:2–3). Finally, Nephi tells us that he will "write some of the words of Isaiah, that whoso of my people shall see these words may lift up their hearts and rejoice for all men" (verse 8). This final statement is an echo of Jacob, "rejoice, and lift up your heads forever" (2 Nephi 9:3), which was in turn a comment on Isaiah 51:11, "joy and holiness shall be upon their heads; and they shall obtain gladness and joy" (2 Nephi 8:11).

Nephi's major commentary on these thirteen chapters of Isaiah, however, comes by way of summary and conclusion in 2 Nephi 25, the chapter immediately following the long Isaiah section.

Because Isaiah's metaphoric and poetic language is difficult to understand, Nephi presents his own version of Isaiah's prophecy "according to [Nephi's] plainness" (see 2 Nephi 25:1–7). An important part of Nephi's commentary is to identify the time of fulfillment for Isaiah's prophecies: "In the days that the prophecies of Isaiah shall be fulfilled men shall know of a surety, at the times when they shall come to pass. . . . I know that they shall be of great worth unto [mine own people] *in the last days;* for in that day shall they understand them" (verses 7–8). Nephi then gives "in plainness" his own prophecy, which is also a commentary on the thirteen chapters of Isaiah he has just quoted. The pattern in 2 Nephi 25 is by now all too familiar:

1. the Jews have "been destroyed from generation to generation" (verse 9);

2. those who have been taken to Babylon "shall return again, and possess the land of Jerusalem; wherefore, they shall be restored again to the land of their inheritance" (verses 10–11);

3. Christ will come, they will reject and crucify him, he will be resurrected (verses 12–13);

4. Israel will be scattered again "by other nations" (verses 15–16);

5. the Lord "will set his hand again the second time" (quoting Isaiah 11:11) to gather and restore Israel, an event that Nephi (quoting Isaiah 29:14) refers to as "a marvelous work and a wonder" (verse 17).

Using Nephi's introductory commentary on Isaiah in 2 Nephi 11 and his summarizing commentary in 2 Nephi 25 as a guide, we can make our way more confidently through the thirteen chapters of Isaiah quoted in 2 Nephi 12–24 by watching for and identifying the themes discussed in the many commentaries on Isaiah: the Jews will be scattered and "scourged" (2 Nephi 25:16); the Messiah will come among them but will be rejected; yet in the "last days" the Lord will remember his covenant with the house of Israel and will, through the gentiles, "set his hand again the second time to recover the remnant of his people" (2 Nephi 21:11). It is interesting to note that Nephi's indication that the prophecies mentioned in Isaiah 11 will be fulfilled "in the last days" is confirmed by the visit of Moroni to Joseph Smith: "He [Moroni] quoted the eleventh chapter of Isaiah, saying that it was about to be fulfilled" (Joseph Smith—History, 1:40).

Nephi's Commentary on Isaiah 29 (2 Nephi 26–7)

Beginning in 2 Nephi 26 and continuing in 2 Nephi 27, Nephi's commentary on Isaiah 29 is different from the earlier commentaries because he provides not only an introductory and a summarizing commentary but also a type of intertextual commentary.

The first eleven verses of 2 Nephi 26 prophesy the eventual destruction of the Nephite nation, a branch of the house of Israel. Beginning with verse 14, however, Nephi turns his attention to the "last days," and his introductory remarks in verses 13 and 14 lead directly into the quotation of Isaiah 29. This type of commentary constitutes perhaps the most specific interpretation of Isaiah in the entire Book of Mormon, and I submit that no one without Nephi's commentary would be able to grasp the nuances of these writings of Isaiah.

Nephi begins: "But behold, I prophesy unto you concerning the last days; concerning the days when the Lord God shall bring these things forth unto the children of men. After my seed and the seed of my brethren shall have dwindled in unbelief, and shall have been smitten by the Gentiles . . ." (verses 14–15). And then, with only the word *yea* as a connector, Nephi begins quoting from Isaiah 29:3–4. In so doing he changes Isaiah's first-person narrative into a third-person narrative and expands the scriptural text. "Yea, after the Lord God shall have camped against them [i.e., against "my seed and the seed of my brethren"] round about, and shall have laid siege against them with a mount, and raised forts against them; and after they shall have been brought down low in the dust, even that they are not, yet the words of the righteous shall be written, and the prayers of the faithful shall be heard, and all those who have dwindled in unbelief [i.e., "my seed"] shall not be forgotten" (2 Nephi 26:15). Nephi continues this methodical explication of Isaiah 29 throughout 2 Nephi 26 and 27 by quoting sections of Isaiah, commenting, and then quoting further. For example, 2 Nephi 26:18, which paraphrases and quotes directly from Isaiah 29:5, is surrounded by Nephi's commentary.

It is perfectly understandable why Nephi should wish to give us such a careful comment on Isaiah 29. First, according to Nephi's understanding, Isaiah is prophesying in part about Nephi's own people—his "seed," a branch of the house of Israel that has been scattered and that "in the last days" will be brought back as part of the rebuilding of the house of Israel. Second, Isaiah is prophesying about Nephi's own book, the record of his people that later would become the Book of Mormon. We can only imagine the excitement and gratitude Nephi must have felt when through "the spirit of prophecy" (2 Nephi

25:4) he realized the prophecies in Isaiah 29 applied specifically to his people and his sacred record.

In 2 Nephi 27, Nephi speaks of the "sealed" record of "those who have slumbered in the dust" (verse 9) and of the learned person who is unable to read a sealed book (see verse 15–18). At the beginning of the chapter, Nephi is careful to indicate the time when this prophecy will be fulfilled and that its fulfillment is not restricted to his seed only: "But, behold, in the last days, or in the days of the Gentiles—yea, behold all the nations of the Gentiles and also the Jews, both those who shall come upon this land and those who shall be upon other lands, yea, *even upon all the lands of the earth*, behold, they will be drunken with iniquity [an interpretation of Isaiah 29:9, "drunken, but not with wine"] and all manner of abominations" (2 Nephi 27:1). Nephi then immediately resumes quoting Isaiah (see 2 Nephi 27:2; compare Isaiah 29:6), beginning at the point where he left off in chapter 26 (verse 18).

Nephi continues quoting Isaiah through 2 Nephi 27:7 and then inserts a long commentary of his own concerning the familiar story of the incident with Professor Charles Anthon (see Joseph Smith—History, 1:63–5). Following this careful combination of quotation and commentary, Nephi continues his own summarizing commentary in 2 Nephi 28, and once again he repeats the time when these prophecies of Isaiah will be fulfilled: "For it shall come to pass *in that day*" (2 Nephi 28:3).

Beginning with verse 30 of chapter 28, Nephi's revelation shifts from third person to first person; that is, it becomes a revelation directly from the Lord. For example: "I shall proceed to do a marvelous work among them [Isaiah 29:14], that I may remember my covenants which I have made unto the children of men, that I may set my hand again the second time to recover my people [changed from third person in Isaiah 11:11], which are of the house of Israel" (2 Nephi 29:1). Note that the

Lord's quoting of Isaiah's words anticipates his expressed approbation of Isaiah's writings to the Nephite survivors at Bountiful half a millennium later (see 3 Nephi 23:1).

It is also significant that the Book of Mormon makes a very important correction to the Isaiah text. As it stands in the Bible, Isaiah 29:10 reads: "For the Lord hath poured out upon you the spirit of deep sleep, and hath closed your eyes: the prophets and your rulers, the seers hath he covered." Here the Lord is represented as having closed the people's eyes. The Book of Mormon corrects this by making clear that "ye [the people] have closed your eyes, and ye have rejected the prophets." Consequently, the Lord has removed ("covered") their seers. Why? "Because of [Israel's] iniquity" (2 Nephi 27:5).

In summary, the words of Nephi (and the Lord) from 2 Nephi 26 through 29 constitute what must be the most careful and specific commentary on Isaiah in the entire Book of Mormon.

Abinadi's Commentary on Isaiah 52–3 (Mosiah 12, 14–15)

Abinadi's commentary on Isaiah is stimulated by one of the priests of King Noah's court who asks, "What meaneth the words which are written, and which have been taught by our fathers?" (Mosiah 12:20). The priest then quotes the well-known passage from Isaiah 52:7–10, which begins: "How beautiful upon the mountains are the feet of him that bringeth good tidings; that publisheth peace . . ." (see Mosiah 12:21–4). This quotation, concluding with the words "the Lord hath made bare his holy arm . . . ," initiates Abinadi's sermon on the Ten Commandments (see Mosiah 12:25–13:26).

As a preparatory commentary on Isaiah 53, Abinadi teaches that although it is necessary to keep these commandments, "salvation doth not come by the law alone," but by the "atonement, which God himself shall make for the sins and iniquities of his people" (Mosiah 13:28). He further explains that the "performances and ordinances" of the law of Moses were "types of things to come" (see verses 30–1). "For behold, did not Moses prophesy unto [the children of Israel] concerning the coming of the Messiah, and that God should redeem his people? Yea, and even all the prophets who have prophesied ever since the world began—have they not spoken more or less concerning these things?" (verse 33). With this introduction, Abinadi then quotes Isaiah 53, which Abinadi understands as referring to the Messiah: "Surely he has borne our griefs, and carried our sorrows . . ." (Mosiah 14:4; Isaiah 53:4).

In Mosiah 15 Abinadi provides a thorough commentary on Isaiah 53, emphasizing that those who accept Christ's sacrifice for sin will become the seed of Christ (see Mosiah 15:10–12). He then returns to the question asked earlier in Mosiah 12:20–4, setting up his response to it with a question of his own: Those who listen to the words of the prophets "are they whose sins he has borne; these are they for whom he has died, to redeem them from their transgressions, are they not his seed? Yea. . . . And these are they who have published peace, who have brought good tidings. . . . And O how beautiful upon the mountains were their feet" (Mosiah 15:12–15).

Abinadi's quoting of Isaiah leads into a commentary on the resurrection of mankind and the justice of God (see Mosiah 15:21–7). Like Nephi, Abinadi identifies a time for the events he will describe: "And now I say unto you that the time shall come that the salvation of the Lord shall be declared to every nation, kindred, tongue, and people" (verse 28). This establishes a helpful context for understanding the remaining Isaiah verses (Isaiah 52:8–10) that gave rise to the original question posed by the priest of King Noah in Mosiah 12:20–4. The last Isaiah verse Abinadi quotes, Isaiah 52:10 ("The Lord hath made bare his holy arm . . ."), is linked to, and thoroughly consistent with, Nephi's interpretation of the same verse in 1 Nephi 22 (see 1 Nephi 22:10–11 and surrounding commentary).

Abinadi concludes his sermon and Isaiah commentary with a return to the purpose of the law of Moses: "Therefore, if ye teach the law of Moses, also teach that it is a shadow of those things which are to come—Teach them that redemption cometh through Christ the Lord, who is the very Eternal Father" (Mosiah 16:14–15).

The Savior's Commentary on Isaiah 52 and 54 (3 Nephi 16, 20, 22)

The last full chapters of Isaiah quoted in the Book of Mormon, Isaiah 52 and 54, are quoted by the Savior himself in 3 Nephi 16, 20, and 22 and are preceded by a lengthy and detailed commentary beginning in 3 Nephi 16. Here the Savior tells of visiting his other sheep and then turns his attention to the destiny of the house of Israel, which according to the familiar pattern will be scattered and then gathered again in the last days by the gentiles: "O house of Israel, in the latter day shall the truth come unto the Gentiles, that the fulness of these things shall be made known unto them. . . . And then will I remember my covenant which I have made unto my people, O house of Israel, and I will bring my gospel unto them. . . . I will remember my covenant unto you, O house of Israel, and ye shall come unto the knowledge of the fulness of my gospel. But if the Gentiles will repent and return unto me, saith the Father, behold they shall be numbered among my people, O house of Israel" (3 Nephi 16:7, 11–13).

The Savior then concludes this section of his introductory commentary on Isaiah by returning to those same verses quoted in part by Nephi and in full by Abinadi, beginning with "Thy watchmen shall lift up the voice . . ." and concluding with "The Lord hath made bare his holy arm . . ." (see Isaiah 52:8–10; 3 Nephi 16:18–20).

The Savior's commentary on Isaiah continues in chapter 20 when he returns to the theme of the house of Israel: "Behold now I finish the commandment which the Father hath commanded me concerning this people, who are a remnant of the house of Israel. Ye remember that I spake unto you, and said that when the words of Isaiah should be fulfilled . . . then is the fulfilling of the covenant which the Father hath made unto his people, O house of Israel" (3 Nephi 20:10–12). The Savior has been sent "to bless you in turning away every one of you from his iniquities" (verse 26). The house of Israel will be scattered by the gentiles (see verses 27–8), but the Lord will remember the covenant and gather them again (see verse 29). The Savior then turns again to Isaiah 52:8–10, verses that, having been quoted by Nephi, the priest of Noah, Abinadi, and the Savior, have by this time become rather familiar to the readers of the Book of Mormon.

In this instance, however, the Savior gives an interesting commentary on the verse by quoting it differently. In Isaiah 52:9 the text reads, "Break forth into joy, sing together, ye waste places of Jerusalem: for the Lord hath comforted his people, he hath redeemed Jerusalem." As quoted by the Savior in the Book of Mormon, the text reads: "Then will the Father *gather them together again,* and give unto them Jerusalem for the land of their inheritance. Then shall they break forth into joy—Sing together, ye waste places of Jerusalem; *for the Father hath comforted his people,* he hath redeemed Jerusalem" (3 Nephi 20:33–4).

There is also a significant change in the verse that follows: "The Lord hath made bare his holy arm in the eyes of all the nations; and all the ends of the earth shall see the salvation of our God" (Isaiah 52:10). "The Father hath made bare his holy arm in the eyes of all the nations; and all the ends of the earth shall see the salvation of the Father; and *the Father and I are one*" (3 Nephi 20:35). The Savior then quotes the remainder of Isaiah 52 with some further variation, but he does not repeat verses 8 through 10.

Continuing this theme, 3 Nephi 21 begins with a specific statement that again identifies the time when these prophecies of Isaiah are to be fulfilled: "And verily I say unto you, I give unto you a sign, that ye may know the time when these things shall be about to take place—that I shall gather in, from their long dispersion, my people, O house of Israel, and shall establish again among them my Zion" (verse 1). The time prophesied by Isaiah for the gathering of Israel is identified here by the Savior as the last days, "when these works and the works which shall be wrought among you hereafter shall come forth from the Gentiles, unto your seed. . . . And when these things come to pass that thy seed shall begin to know these things—it shall be a sign unto them, that they may know that the work of the Father hath already commenced unto the fulfilling of the covenant which he hath made unto the people who are of the house of Israel" (see verses 5, 7).

At this point the Savior again quotes Isaiah and once again identifies the time of the fulfillment of Isaiah's prophecy: "*And when that day shall come,* it shall come to pass that kings shall shut their mouths" (3 Nephi 21:8, quoting Isaiah 52:15). "*For in that day,* for my sake shall the Father work a work, which shall be a great and a marvelous work among them" (3 Nephi 21:9, quoting Isaiah 29:14). "But if [the gentiles] will repent . . . I will establish my church among them, and they shall come in unto the covenant and be numbered among this the remnant of Jacob" (3 Nephi 21:22).

Third Nephi 21 continues to identify the time of fulfillment—"and then" (verses 24, 25, 26), "the work shall commence" (verse 27), "and then shall the work commence" (verse 28)—and concludes with an adaptation of Isaiah 52:12: "And they shall go out *from all nations;* and they shall not go out in haste, nor go by flight, for I will go before them, saith the Father, and I will be their rearward" (3 Nephi 21:29).

With this introduction, the Savior then quotes Isaiah 54 in its entirety. Verse 3 is perhaps the significant verse in the context of the Savior's commentary on the role of the gentiles in restoring the house of Israel: "For thou shalt break forth on the right hand and on the left, *and thy seed shall inherit the Gentiles* and make the desolate cities to be inhabited."

As mentioned earlier, the scope of this paper has not allowed an in-depth study of the Isaiah passages themselves.[8] The excitement of discovery is the rightful pleasure of each individual reader. This brief overview should, however, help the reader to understand that the key to understanding Isaiah in the Book of Mormon is in the commentaries.

In view of the significance of Isaiah in the Book of Mormon, it is perhaps fitting that Moroni should quote from Isaiah as part of his final exhortation and farewell: "And again I would exhort you that ye would come unto Christ, and lay hold upon every good gift, and touch not the evil gift, nor the unclean thing [from Isaiah 52:11]. And awake, and arise from the dust, O Jerusalem; yea, and put on thy beautiful garments, O daughter of Zion [from Isaiah 52:1]; and strengthen thy stakes and enlarge thy borders forever [from Isaiah 54:2], that thou mayest no more be confounded, that the covenants of the Eternal Father which he hath made unto thee, O house of Israel, may be fulfilled" (Moroni 10:30–1).

In summary, it should be emphasized that the Isaiah passages in the Book of Mormon are not unnecessary duplications of the biblical Isaiah. Rather, they are an inspired, integral part of that sacred text. Although the Book of Mormon Isaiah makes significant corrections to the biblical Isaiah, the greater value lies, first, in the contextual setting in which the doctrines of the covenant of Christ's atoning sacrifice, the prophesied scattering of Israel, and the restoration of the house of Israel in the last days through the instrumentality of the gentiles receive their full and proper emphasis; and, second, in the rich and detailed interpretations given us through the commentaries of Lehi, Nephi, Jacob, Abinadi, and the Savior.

Notes

1. Quoted in the Book of Mormon is Isaiah 2–14, 29 (except for verses 1–2), and 48–54 (except for verses 4–5 of chapter 52). A helpful listing of nearly all the quotations is found in Legrande Davies, "Texts in the Book of Mormon," *Encyclopedia of Mormonism*, 2:700. The most thorough listing of all Isaiah quotations found in the standard works as well as in the writings of selected General Authorities is found in Monte S. Nyman, *Great Are the Words of Isaiah* (Salt Lake City: Bookcraft, 1980), appendix B.

2. For a verse-by-verse comparison of the Book of Mormon Isaiah texts with five modern translations, see H. Clay Gorton, *The Legacy of the Brass Plates of Laban: A Comparison of Biblical and Book of Mormon Isaiah Texts* (Bountiful, Utah: Horizon, 1994). This study highlights textual differences and discusses the insertion of changes into the Isaiah texts "with malice aforethought" after Lehi's departure from Jerusalem with the brass plates.

3. Abinadi quotes Isaiah 53 in answer to a question concerning a passage found in Isaiah 52 (see Mosiah 12:20–4; 14). In so doing he relates the atonement of Christ to the law of Moses, but he does not use the term *house of Israel* in this context.

4. Often two and even three of these terms are found in the same verse: "For behold, I say unto you that as many of the *Gentiles* as will repent are the *covenant* people of the Lord" (2 Nephi 30:2). "The book that thou beholdest is a record of the Jews, which contains the

covenants of the Lord, which he hath made unto the *house of Israel;* . . . wherefore, they are of great worth unto the *Gentiles*" (1 Nephi 13:23). "Nevertheless, after they shall be nursed by the *Gentiles*, and the Lord has lifted up his hand upon the *Gentiles* . . . , behold these things of which are spoken are temporal; for thus are the *covenants* of the Lord with our fathers; and it meaneth us in the days to come, and also all our brethren who are of the house of Israel" (1 Nephi 22:6).

5. See Gorton, *Legacy of the Brass Plates,* for thorough commentary on these corrections.

6. In 1 Nephi 22:8–10, Nephi links Isaiah 29:14 ("a marvelous work . . ."), Isaiah 49:22–3 ("thy daughters shall be carried upon their shoulders . . ."), and Isaiah 52:10 ("the Lord hath made bare his holy arm . . ."), thus bringing together and explaining three of the most frequently quoted Isaiah verses in the Book of Mormon. This makes 1 Nephi 22 one of the most important Isaiah commentaries in the Book of Mormon.

7. Compare Galatians 3, in which the apostle Paul refers to the Abrahamic covenant in similar terms. During his visit to the Nephites, Jesus Christ indicated the precise nature of the blessing that would be extended to all nations: "In thy [Abraham's] seed shall all the kindreds of the earth be blessed—unto the *pouring out of the Holy Ghost* through me [Christ] upon the Gentiles, which blessing upon the Gentiles shall make them *mighty above all,* unto the scattering of my people. . . . Nevertheless, when they shall have *received the fulness of my gospel,* then if they shall harden their hearts against me I will return their iniquities upon their own heads, saith the Father" (3 Nephi 20:27–8).

8. Specific Isaiah selections in the Book of Mormon are discussed in detail in Donald W. Parry and John W. Welch, eds., *Isaiah in the Book of Mormon* (Provo, Utah: FARMS, 1998).

THE ANCIENT WORLD

CHAPTER 10

RESIST-DYEING AS A POSSIBLE ANCIENT TRANSOCEANIC TRANSFER

Stephen C. Jett

Introduction

The controversial question of whether significant cultural contact occurred between the peoples of the Eastern and Western Hemispheres before the time of Columbus is one of paramount cultural-historical and theoretical importance. Its potential resolution rests on many kinds of evidence.[1] Among these are cultural similarities of various sorts. A principal aim of research on this issue is determining which shared traits may have been the result of cultural exchange. From an evidentiary standpoint, the most convincing cultural commonalities involve either highly arbitrary traits (such as most lexemes) or highly complex phenomena whose independent development in distant geographical areas seems very improbable. Of the latter type is the technology of cloth manufacture, which includes fiber extraction, carding, spinning, and weaving, often in

Stephen C. Jett, professor of geography and of textiles and clothing at the University of California, Davis, is founding editor of Pre-Columbiana: A Journal of Long-Distance Contacts.

elaborate ways. When advanced coloring methods are added to all the other sophisticated aspects of textile production, the result is an exceedingly complicated system of phenomena. As one scholar noted, "Textiles are one of the strangest inventions ever produced by man."[2]

Unfortunately, very little research has been undertaken comparing Old and New World textile arts in the context of the transoceanic-diffusion question. In 1985 science historians Joseph Needham and Lu Gwei-Djen observed, "We have not found any comparative summary of textile technology in the Old and New Worlds, and without this it would be fruitless to offer any observations."[3] In view of this gap, I have attempted to address in a preliminary way the topic of textile manufacture as evidence for cultural diffusion between the hemispheres.

This complex topic offers many avenues for research, among them the technical attributes of spinning and ordinary weaving, including spindle and loom forms (e.g., the backstrap and vertical looms) and textile structures (the arrangements of the threads—e.g., in slit-tapestry weaves and cut pile); design motifs such as the stepped fret and the eight-pointed star; and textile coloring and the methods of obtaining designs through dyeing. The latter is a potentially fruitful area of investigation for cultural comparisons and is the basis for this study. In an earlier article examining four classes of dyestuffs, I compared their production and use in the two hemispheres. In their developed forms, each of these dyes—madder and its allies, indigo, insect dyes, and shellfish dyes—involved highly elaborate, even unlikely, procedures.[4] For instance, textiles specialists John Gillow and Nicholas Barnard have concluded that "red dyeing with a mordant is complex. It is a wonder that the many chemical interactions required should have been developed at all."[5] Although in my study I found no actual proof of transoceanic diffusion, or transfer, the co-occurrence in the ancient Old and

New Worlds of all four categories of dyestuffs—in highly developed form, in the case of three of them—indicated to me the improbability of independent invention. These three categories of highly developed dyestuffs are attested for the first millennium B.C. or earlier on both sides of the Pacific, while shellfish dyes are not known to have appeared in the Americas until later pre-Columbian times and did not involve elaborate techniques there.

To create pattern on cloth, a weaver has several options: weaving the design into the fabric using structures and techniques involving manipulations or additions of warps and wefts, with or without contrasting colored threads; embroidery; sewn-on appliqué; and, probably the most ancient method, painting the cloth with the fingers, a brush, or a stamp. All these approaches were known anciently in both the Old and New Worlds, with structural approaches becoming dominant in southwestern Asia and in the Andean region.

A variant of painting is applying mordant (a chemical required for certain dyes to "take") to those portions of the cloth that are intended to receive a mordant-dye color. Undoubtedly also deriving from painting is resist-dyeing. A resist is a substance or material that, when applied to a fiber such as cotton or wool, makes the reserved portion of the fiber impermeable to the dyestuff. Resist decoration, as opposed to structural decoration, came to be particularly characteristic of southern and southeastern Asia. Two broad categories of resist are used: impermeable-fiber wrapping and applied liquid or paste (stencils or stamps are sometimes employed with the latter). In the first method, the wrapping is removed after the yarn or cloth is dyed, revealing the design in undyed, negative form. In applying liquid or paste, the resist is washed, dissolved, or melted out of the yarn or cloth after it has been dyed, and a negative image (formed by the now-exposed blank areas) is unveiled. The three basic types of resist-dyeing carry Indonesian-derived names: ikat, tie-dye (the usual method is called plangi), and batik. I will examine each of these in the context of interhemispheric comparisons.

The two principal ancient world centers of textile manufacturing technology appear to have been southwestern Asia (Persia, Transcaucasia, southwestern Turkestan) and the central Andean area of what are now Bolivia and Peru. In the latter region, "textile construction was the primary technology of the Pre-Columbian world."[6] In the Eastern Hemisphere, the use of dyes and dyeing skills was concentrated somewhat to the east of that of pattern weaving, in the northwestern Indian subcontinent. Because textiles are perishable, direct archaeological evidence is in most cases scarce or absent. The major exception to this is the desert coast of South America, where preservation is remarkable—in fact, unique—although there have also been a certain number of finds from Old World drylands such as Egypt and inner Asia. Outside of the central Andean coastal region and a few other arid zones, we are obliged to depend almost entirely on evidence of historical and even contemporary textiles. This is less than fully satisfactory, but we must work with what we have.

Tie-Dye

Tie-dyeing involves using string, thread, or ribbon to bind woven fabric in any of several ways in order to prevent the dye from reaching the tied- or stitched-off portions of the cloth when the bundle is dipped (the terms *tie-dye* and *tying and dyeing* are sometimes used to include ikat).[7] The term *plangi* (from the Indonesian *pelangi*, "multicolored") is increasingly used in reference to all non-ikat tie-resist methods, although plangi is technically a subclass of tie-dyeing that involves tying off knobs of woven cloth. After dyeing, the binding is removed to reveal the negative, reserved zones. Experts can control the color patterns to a remarkable degree, making intricate designs and color combinations. Closely related to true plangi is fold-resist dyeing, in which the fabric is rolled or folded and tied or sewn in different places. Another related technique is stitch-dyeing (tritik), in which a sewn thread gathers the cloth, thereby excluding the dye from certain portions. Two other forms of resist-dyeing are reserving by knotting and plaiting the cloth itself.

Tie-dyeing in its evolved forms is quite complex. Because cultures in both hemispheres stressed the design motif of the spot or bar in a rectangle—a motif not entirely easy to achieve— the art of tie-dyeing would seem to be a good candidate for ancient interhemispheric transfer.

Old World Tie-Dye

Widespread in the Old World, tie-dyeing is found in southwestern, central, southern, southeastern, and eastern Asia; in southeastern Europe; in Hungary and Sweden; and in northern, western, and central Africa.[8] Plangi—called *bandhana* or *bandhei*, meaning "bound"—is particularly well developed in the Indian subcontinent, especially in Rajasthan (where tradition places its origin) and among Gujarati Muslims and Sindi Hindus. It also occurs in Punjab, Madhya Pradesh, Maharashtra, Hyderabad, Bengal, and Tamilnadu. The patterns produced are termed *chunari*, *chundadi*, or *shumgri*. Roll-resist dyeing *(lahariya)* is also found in Rajasthan.[9] In Southeast Asia, plangi occurs in Yunnan, in Thailand among the Mon and some Lao, in northeastern Malaya, in Cambodia (particularly among the Austronesian-speaking Cham), and sporadically in the islands from Sumatra to Lombok, along the western and southern coast of Borneo, on Sulawesi (among the Toradja people), and on Mindanao. The dot- and bar-in-square motifs are known in Indonesia and also in tie-dyed cloth produced in China and Japan.[10]

Because of a paucity of preserved specimens, it is impossible to date the origin of tie-dyeing, but it is presumably quite ancient. A number of archaeological plangi specimens found in dry Chinese Turkestan date from the fourth through the eighth centuries. Appearing in the written record about A.D. 700, tie-dyed *(jiao-xie)* silk cloth with a dotted-lozenge pattern is known archaeologically in China as early as A.D. 418, and tie-dyeing of the tritik type is recorded at A.D. 683 during the Tang period as well as later, in Gansu Province a bit to the east. Specimens before A.D. 749—some or all of Chinese origin—are known from Nara, Japan, where the various kinds of tie-dye are lumped under the term *shibori* (from *shiboru,* "to wring"). The ancient Japanese word *yuhata* ("knotting fabric") implies a pre-sixth-century use of tie-dye, and an A.D. 238 document suggests an even earlier presence in Japan. The more recent term, *kechi,* derives from the Chinese term for resist, *xie,* and the technique may have been imported from China. The Japanese emperor gave gifts of *kechi* in A.D. 720. The Nara specimens (and more recent ones) include variations on the dot-in-square design *(yokobiki,* "square ring dot").[11]

Ajanta Caves frescoes (A.D. 400–700) in Hyderabad State, India, depict simple roll-resist fabrics from about A.D. 500 to 700, and tie-dye *(pulaka bandha)* is mentioned in an Indian text from the early seventh century.[12] An archaeological plangi specimen from the eleventh or twelfth century in Mali, West Africa, displays a merged-double-dot-in-square design, a design still found in that country among the Soninke, Manding, and Dyula.[13] Interestingly, although the stiffer bast fiber and, in some areas, wild cotton were always available in Southeast Asia, cotton cultivation seems not to have been introduced there from India until the mid–first millennium A.D. Wanda Warming and Michael Gaworski suggest that tie-dyeing was first introduced into Indonesia by Indian and Moslem traders in the fourteenth and fifteenth centuries.[14] The earliest attestation of tie-dye in Indonesia is from the sixteenth century. In that archipelago "true plangi is not as firmly rooted in tradition as the other resist patterning techniques"; it was practiced mainly in ports by non-natives.[15]

Because of the complexity of designs of early Chinese plangi textiles and the breadth of resist techniques in China, Jack Lenor Larsen, following Alfred Bühler, suggested that "China or Central Asia may have been the cradle of plangi and other resist types as well."[16]

New World Tie-Dye

Tie-dyeing—mainly true plangi but including roll resist and tritik—was also an important and widely distributed dyeing method in the New World and is archaeologically the most frequently represented of the resist methods.[17] Concerning the specific occurrences of New World plangi, Mary Elizabeth King has observed: "In the Americas, plangi techniques are said to have occurred here and there in the Southwestern United States and Mexico. Centers of the craft are widely scattered on the west coast of South America and in parts of Argentina, [Paraguay, and Chile. Other ethnographic occurrences are in Mexico and Guatemala]. . . . The great majority of these American processes, whether pre-Columbian or post-Conquest, are extremely elementary . . . [involving] reserved circles or squares."[18]

In South America, tie-dye is said to have begun during the Formative period (1700–500 B.C.).[19] The earliest-known New World evidence of tie-dye is from the Chavín culture of Peru, the first "high culture" (beginning circa 1400 B.C.) of South America, which adopted the technique during an era in which textile technology blossomed.[20] These textiles, which include the bar-in-oblong motif,[21] may be the oldest tie-dyed ones known anywhere. However, according to King, "These earliest examples may instead be resist-painted to resemble tie-dye rather than actual tie-dye . . . [which] lead[s] me to suspect that craftsmen familiar with one resist method (batik) were copying [imported] fabrics decorated by an unfamiliar method in the only way they knew."[22] Later, clear evidence of tie-dyeing that employed up to five colors appears at Cañete on the central coast and at Paracas on the southern coast about 450–175 B.C. and again about A.D. 100.[23] A resist-painted Vicús pottery figurine of about the time of Christ depicts a plangi shirt.[24] Tie-dye is also recorded from the Lima area and in the southern coastal region from the middle horizon of the Nazca-Huari transition period (circa A.D. 500–800) and later, in the form of dotted rectangles appearing especially on patchwork tunics but also on effigy pots of the period.[25] Similar plangi fabrics are known from the Late Intermediate period (A.D. 1000–1476) of the central coast as well, and at Nazca on the southern coast.[26] But as Jane Feltham observed, "Forms of tie-dyeing go back to the Early Horizon, but neither ikat nor the *plangi* method was well developed in Peru" in terms of design and color complexity, although both were "carried to a certain degree of perfection."[27]

The easily achieved dot-in-circle tie-dye design is known from postclassic times in Mexico's Tehuacán region in the state of Puebla.[28] The process is also recorded ethnographically from Guatemala and Mexico (e.g., among the Otomí of Hidalgo and Querétaro).[29] Early Spanish colonial codices depict indigo-colored tie-dyed clothing featuring the spot-in-lozenge design. Worn by the Aztec emperor and by others of high status, such cloth was apparently called *xiutlapili* ("turquoise[-colored] tied item") and was a tribute article from eleven of the thirty-eight Aztec-controlled provinces. Its use was evidently a legacy from the pre-Aztec Toltec culture and likely predates the Toltec as well (see the section on batik).[30] The Aztecs also practiced roll resist *(tzitilli)*.

Dot-in-circle and dot-in-square tie-dyed cloth has been reported archaeologically from central and northern Arizona, New Mexico, and southern Utah, where the Anasazi were influenced by practices from Mexico and possibly from South America. An apparent red-colored example of tie-dyeing from the late prehistoric Mississippian Caddoan culture of the southeastern United States has also been reported.[31]

Tie-dyeing has been suggested as a possible transoceanic transfer,[32] but because of the relative technical and design simplicity of American tie-dyed textiles, Larsen, following Bühler, stated that "the view that they were borrowed from Asia is ill-founded." Larson also believed that plangi patterns are technique driven and thus are not of use in historical reconstruction.[33] However, the overall context of American tie-dye suggests that introduction from overseas is an excellent possibility. Textile specialist M. D. C. Crawford asserted, "Among the many fabrics from Peru which suggest so forcibly the textiles from Asia, none is so difficult to explain as a form of resist dye known as tie dyeing." Crawford saw all the occurrences in the Old World as certainly being historically related and as coming from Punjab, with only Peru providing a possible question mark.[34] Archaeologist Paul Tolstoy also considered tie-dye to be one of the "more convincing" evidences for possible overseas origin in the Americas.[35] In 1928 anthropologist Roland B. Dixon, referring to the extremely high development of weaving in Peru, wrote, "If anywhere, then, we might expect the invention of tie-dyeing . . . to have occurred here." On the other hand, he added that "if the simple tie-dying found in Peru is to be attributed to diffusion, it must certainly have been brought from Indonesia," because it is absent in Polynesia. However, Dixon also thought that if tie-dying had been introduced into Peru, ikatting and batikking also would have been introduced there. It turned out later that those techniques *were* present in Peru.[36]

If Peruvian tie-dyeing is of Asian origin, the puzzling association of it with a kind of patchwork may be illuminated by old Javanese practice: "[Non-tie-dye p]atchwork garments have a long-standing ceremonial importance" and were thought to afford protection from malevolent influences and misfortune for priests, rulers, and (by extension) rulers' subjects.[37]

Ikat

The Indonesian term *ikat* ("bundle," from *mengikat*, "to bind") refers to a highly laborious method of resist-dyeing that involves coloring the yarn prior to weaving rather than afterward, as in the case of tie-dyeing. Like tie-dyeing, ikat usually involves impermeable ties. "Before dyeing, skeins of yarn are reserved by knotting, partial wrapping, pressing by means of plates and other methods."[38] In the most common approach, the threads running in one direction (warp or weft, usually the former) that will ultimately be part of the woven web are stretched on tying frames with a disposition like that which they will have in the cloth after it is finally woven. Then individual stretched threads or small bunches of adjacent threads are tightly wrapped with an impenetrable fiber in those areas where it is intended that the cloth be free of the color in order to produce the pattern. When the wrapping has been accomplished, the yarn is dismounted, steeped in the dye, and then allowed to dry. The wrappings are then removed, revealing the absence of color underneath. The process is often repeated, with successive reductions or additions of wrapping and with different dyes, to produce sometimes highly complex patterns in several tints. After all the dyeing has been completed, the threads are stretched out on the loom and the weaving is accomplished. Although the pattern may be definitively created on the threads as they are stretched out for wrapping, sometimes the threads are adjusted before weaving to create or perfect the pattern.[39] According to Nora Fisher, "To separate the made-up weft into logical groups, to bind and dye it, and then to set up a system whereby the weft will be reeled back into the fabric in a logical order to form the desired pattern is a technically advanced and complicated procedure"[40]—a practice one might suppose unlikely to have developed independently in multiple areas and therefore an excellent subject for illuminating the transoceanic-contacts question.

What is termed single ikatting may be done on the warp threads alone or the weft threads alone. In combined ikat, both warp and weft are ikatted, with little or no overlap between the reserved areas in the two directions. Double ikatting also involves binding the threads in both directions, producing integrated patterns by the interaction of the warp and the weft resist areas—a very difficult and "highly labor-intensive process" indeed, yielding what is known in India as *patolu*.[41] Warp ikat, the most common, is the only kind of ikat known from South America. The technical complexity and laboriousness of even simple warp ikat is sufficient in my mind to suggest a single invention and elaboration, with all subsequent occurrences being historically derived from the place of first innovation.[42]

Old World Ikat

Textiles specialist Chelna Desai wrote: "While numerous legends and oral traditions indicate the existence of the single ikat technique in India in prehistoric times, the 6th century frescoes of the Ajanta Caves [in Hyderabad] provide the first visual records of it. Many of the world's ancient cultures practiced the single ikat craft, but the more complex double ikat exists only in India, where it is known as 'patolu' (plural 'patola'), in Bali, where it is called 'geringsing,' and in Japan, where it is named 'kasuri.'"[43] Centers of single-ikat *(khanjari)* production exist in India's Coromandel Coast states, Orissa (where the term *bandha* is used), Andhra Pradesh (since the turn of the twentieth century), and Gujarat in the northwest. In Gujarat the famous double-ikat silk *patola* have long been produced and are believed to date back to the fifth century A.D., with the name appearing in literature by the tenth century. Some double ikat is also produced in Maharashtra, Madhya Pradesh, Orissa, and Andhra Pradesh.[44] *Patola* are depicted in sixteenth- and seventeenth-century frescoes in temples in South India, and records indicate that the cloth was exported to Indonesia in the thirteenth century and to China and Japan in the 1500s, though it was "probably much earlier."[45] The designs and, in Bali and Japan, technique were widely copied.[46]

Single ikat in both southeastern and southwestern Asia is often attributed to diffusion from India.[47] Another possible source for at least Indonesian warp ikat is the Dongson culture centered in northern Vietnam during the first millennium B.C. Reflected in textiles, Dongson design motifs and objects diffused widely in the East Indies, especially in the Sunda Islands, and elsewhere.[48] Warming and Gaworski note that "sometime between the eighth and second centuries B.C., the Neolithic people who then lived in Indonesia came into contact with a bronze culture that developed in what is now northern Vietnam. This Dong-Son culture, as it is known, introduced metalwork and advanced agricultural methods to many islands in Indonesia, and it is generally believed that the backstrap loom and warp ikat appeared during this period, although a direct connection . . . has not been proven."[49]

The backstrap loom and the ikat technique are known today

in North Vietnam, southern and southwestern China, Cambodia, Thailand, and Burma,[50] as well as in Madagascar,[51] which was settled from Indonesia about the time of Christ. Thelma R. Newman unequivocally asserted that "we do know that it [ikatting] emanated from the Dongson and Late Chou [Zhou] cultures."[52] In Indonesia, warp ikatting occurs in Sumatra, Sumba, Timor, Flores, Savu, Roti, the Solor and Alor Islands, Bali (where the technique is called *endek*), Borneo (in Kalimantan among the Dyak people and in the Malaysian state of Sarawak), Sulawesi (among the Toradja people), and the Moluccas; in the Philippines on Mindanao, Luzon, and (archaeologically) Banton;[53] and elsewhere.

Weft ikatting is known from Japan, among the Tais of Thailand (where the technique is called *mat mii/mud mee*) and Laos, and in Cambodia (among the Khmer people), northeastern Malaya (the technique is called *kain cindai/kain limar*), Mindanao, Sumatra, Java, Bali, Lombok, and Sulawesi (among the Buginese).[54] Warming and Gaworski state that weft ikat, as well as double ikat, was introduced into Indonesia during the fourteenth and fifteenth centuries by Indian and Moslem traders.[55] In Japan, although imported warp ikats of unknown provenance have survived from the seventh and eighth centuries, and although ikatting of braided sashes was introduced during Heian times (A.D. 794–1185), warp, weft, and double ikat *kasuri* ("blurred," "hazy") was not introduced into the southern Ryukyu Islands (where it is called *kashiri*) until the fourteenth century, possibly by the same traders mentioned above. It spread to the main Japanese islands around 1700.[56]

In most areas, perishability of cloth has made it difficult or impossible to ascertain the age of ikatting. However, desert conditions at the medieval cemetery of Fostat, near Cairo, Egypt, have preserved inscribed ikats imported from Yemen (which had maritime trade relations with India) that date to the

eighth through twelfth centuries,[57] and the Cleveland Museum
of Art has a specimen from Sanaa, Yemen, dating to the tenth
century. Written sources indicate the presence of ikat in the
Yemen "perhaps as early as the seventh century."[58] Ikats from
Egypt and Nara, Japan, date to the sixth and eighth centuries,
and those from the Middle East date to the eighth century.[59]
Ikat is not directly documented in central Asia until the fifteenth century, but sources indirectly suggest a presence at least
as early as the seventh century.[60]

Widespread in the Old World,[61] single ikatting (in several
regions called by its Persian name, *abr*, "cloud") is important
not only in southern Asia, mainland southeastern Asia, and Indonesia but also in central Asia, Japan, Turkey, the formerly
Ottoman-occupied Balkans, Syria and Persia (both once controlled the Yemen), Arab North Africa (once part of the Otto-
man Empire), and in Nigeria, Burkina Faso, Ghana, and Ivory
Coast,[62] the African areas possibly influenced by Indonesians.[63]
The earliest-documented ikat is from China, although Bühler
believed this to reflect adoption from an older tribal tradition
in neighboring areas.[64] As mentioned, ikat is produced in Japan,
and in the West it spread into Mallorca, northern Italy, France,
the Alpine countries, and Scandinavia. Larsen wrote, "It seems
possible that ikat, like the other resist techniques, spread from
these tribal cultures [of south and southwestern China]" to
China proper and India, and from these putatively newer centers to other regions.[65]

New World Ikat

Its presence unrecognized by archaeologists before 1930,[66]
warp ikat appears to have been widespread in the pre-Columbian
New World, although archaeological evidence is lacking outside the central Andean area, where ikat is known in Quechua

as *watado.*[67] It is conceivable that the word *watado* is related to the lexeme *patolu,* because they both involve the following phonetic pattern: bilabial consonant, vowel, *t,* vowel, labio-palatal stop, and vowel (note that the Gujarati word for resist is *wa,* discussed later).

Unwoven "proto-ikat" fringe is recorded from Paracas (circa 600–400 B.C.) in combination with plangi,[68] but this may or may not be a precursor to woven true ikat. Speaking of true ikat, J. Alden Mason wrote, "Relatively few examples are known, and all are limited to the late Tiahuanaco horizon of the Chimú area [of the north coast of Peru, circa A.D. 900–1000]; however, the process is well known today in the Andean highlands and in Guatemala."[69] In 1977 Ann Pollard Rowe wrote that fifteen examples of pre-contact cotton ikat were known, largely from the Chimú area, with apparent exports to Pachacamac on the central coast as well, followed by alpaca ikats in Inca times.[70] King cited eighteen pre-Spanish ikat examples from the late intermediate and late horizons (circa A.D. 1000–1532), observing that the "designs are usually simple, and they are not expertly executed," but include both geometric and figurative motifs.[71] Currently, pre-Columbian ikatting is documented not only in Peru but also from Los Ríos Province, Ecuador, and from the Arica culture (A.D. 1000–1476) in northernmost Chile.[72] "Reconstructions of the [Peruvian] ikat patterns indicate a high stage of technical development," according to resist-dyeing specialist Jack Larsen.[73] But in the opinion of archaeological-textile expert Ann Pollard Rowe, "In South America, the ikat technique is not used with great finesse or elaboration, especially in comparison with ikats from other areas."[74]

Ethnographic studies indicate that at the turn of the nineteenth century the warp ikat method was in use among Indians in Bolivia (Potosí area), Peru (Cuzco, Piura, and Cajamarca areas),

Ecuador (Riobamba area), northern Colombia (Department of Bolívar), the Pampas of Argentina, the Arica area of northern Chile and the Araucanian area of south-central Chile, and Guatemala (where the technique is called *jaspe* or *jaspeado*—"jasper," "streaked"[75]—and whence large quantities are exported today), as well as in the Mexican states of Oaxaca (among the Mixtec people), Mexico, and Morelia.[76] Verla Birrell speculated that the technique may have spread to Central America from a Peruvian hearth,[77] while King felt that both northward and southward diffusions took place from northern coastal South America, perhaps in Classic times.[78] Ikat *rebozo* making in Mexico may reflect influences from Southeast Asian slaves imported in post-Columbian times, although the codices depict what seems to be maguey-fiber ikatted cloth (*netlapilli ixtlapalia*, which in Nahuatl means to be tied on the surface to dye something for someone).[79] Weft ikat is common among contemporary Mayas in Guatemala and occasional in Mexico, El Salvador, and possibly Honduras. It was introduced to New Mexico around 1800. Double ikat appears to be unique in Guatemala, as far as the Western Hemisphere is concerned.[80]

Ethnologist Erland Nordenskiöld wrote that, in connection with the textile complex, "it is especially the ikat and batik methods that have engaged the attention of those who have compared Indian culture with that of the Old World. Why especially ikat and batik should be considered such remarkable inventions I do not quite understand."[81] Daniel Shaffer, apparently following Larsen, wrote that the "ikat technique is so ubiquitous that it is unlikely to have spread only through cultural contact and diffusion, but was probably self-generated."[82] However, neither author specifies why wide distribution should imply independent development rather than diffusion. On the other hand, in 1916 M. D. C. Crawford, apparently speaking particularly about ikat (which was then yet to be recognized as having been present in pre-Columbian Peru), opined that "there are certain features of originality about this technique which make it difficult to see how it could have developed gradually. The whole process is required to produce design, and the several operations apparently owe their invention to a single mind."[83] Pierre Paris felt that ikat in the two hemispheres should be looked at in the context of transpacific contacts, and Gunnar Thompson believed that ikat was introduced to Peru from the Old World.[84] Textiles expert Peggy Gilfoy's observation concerning West African ikats is also applicable to South American ones: "Because there is so little ikat in Africa, and it is such a difficult technique, there seems justification for suspecting Indonesian influence rather than assuming the technique developed independently."[85] Alfred Bühler, the foremost expert on ikat and its history in the Old World, seemed to think that a unitary origin of the process was possible and advanced the opinion that east Asian ikat was probably the root of American ikat.[86] In an earlier article he was more explicit: "It is, therefore, to be assumed that the craft [in Peru] was very much under the influence of that of south-east Asia [specifically Indonesia]."[87] Following Bühler's lead, Larsen wrote, "Even the pre-Columbian American ikats may have very remote connections with east or southeast Asia."[88] Anthropologist Julian Steward considered ikat a plausible candidate for introduction from Asia,[89] and archaeologist G. H. S. Bushnell stated, "It [ikatting] was extremely rare in ancient Peru. . . . The rare occurrence of such a highly specialized technique suggests introduction from outside Peru, and it is tempting to look to Indonesia, but until something is known of its age there, speculation will be profitless."[90] Textiles specialist Mary Elizabeth King, in fact, contended that ikatting was introduced to America from the East Indies or elsewhere in Southeast Asia.[91]

Batik

The batik (from the Indonesian word *titik*, "dot," "drop") method involves applying a resist to the surface of woven cloth before applying the color. The resist is either a paste of some sort (e.g., starch, gum, mud, resin) or, most common today, melted wax, both of which may be applied by finger, brush, or pen painting; by block or roller stamping; or by using a stencil. The cloth is then dyed and subsequently washed or boiled to remove the resist. The reserved design is normally negative. Batikking may have evolved from the earlier practice of painting dark-colored wax on a fabric to create a design directly.[92] Also sometimes used, at least in Asia, is negative resist, in which selected threads are of a dye-resistant fiber.[93]

Old World Batik

Batik is known in Eurasia from Yugoslavia through the northern Middle East to Turkestan, in Yemen (which long traded with India via the Sabaean Lane), in parts of West Africa (which may have been influenced in recent centuries from Indonesia via the Dutch), among some Chinese peasants and in non-Han Miao- and Yao-speaking southern and southwestern China (and adjacent parts of Laos and Thailand) and Fujian, in Japan (where the technique is known as *rô-kechi*), in southern and southeastern Asia (including India, Burma/Myanmar, and Cambodia [among the Cham people]), and in parts of Indonesia (including southern Sumatra, Java, Madura, Bali, and Sulawesi [among the Toradja people]).[94] Although batik is best known today in the form of status-related wax-resist products from Java, its roots there appear to lie in India, where batik has a long history in Gujarat State and continues to be produced there, as it is in Bombay, Andhra Pradesh, Bengal, and, importantly, on the Coromandel Coast. In Gujarat, at least, use of both painted wax and block-printed wax (*wa*, "resist"; *ajrakh*, "resist-printed fabric") is old, as is block printing with mordants followed by dyeing (producing mordant-resist *sarasa*).[95] Rice-paste resist (Indonesian *kain simbat*) may precede wax historically and still survives in western Java (where modern batik seems to have been introduced along with Islam), central Sulawesi, and West Africa. Tofu-paste resist survives in China.[96]

The oldest-known resist-dyed cloths come from Greek-affiliated tombs in the Crimea, Ukraine, dating to the fourth century B.C.[97] Resist-dyeing involving a paste resist and entailing painting, printing, and stenciling on silk is recorded archaeologically from the Tang Dynasty (A.D. 618–907) in Gansu Province, China, as well.[98] The sophistication of this work implies a considerable history of batik in China. In India the Ajanta Caves paintings of the sixth and seventh centuries A.D. suggest the presence of batik, although it is not recorded historically until the 1500s.[99] Inner Asia provides specimens from about A.D. 520 to 700 and later. Eighth-century batiks of possible Chinese origin have been found in Japan, where wax printing became common. Stencil-resist indigo dyeing using a paste resist (*katazome* method) is traditional in southeastern Honshu. The technique was introduced there from China, and the oldest Japanese specimen dates to the sixteenth century.[100] (The use of stencils themselves as resists are omitted from the present discussion.) Early examples of batik, with classical and Christian iconography, also come from Fostat, Egypt. They date from the second through the tenth century A.D., and it seems likely that the method derived from India.[101] Indian batik specimens from the twelfth century and later, probably from Gujarat, have also been found at Fostat—even specimens dating to the first century, according to Stuart Robinson. A sixth-century piece, possibly imported, was found in Arles, France.[102]

Following Bühler, Larsen hypothesized that batik originated among the non-Han peoples, such as the Tibeto-Burman-
speaking Miao in what today is southern and southwestern
China. The technique was adopted and improved by the con-
quering Chinese, and it then diffused via the Chinese silk trade
to Japan, central Asia, the Caucasus, the Middle East, and India,
with West African batiks deriving from Indian ones.[103] However,
a diffusion from central Asia to China has also been suggested.
Birrell felt that wax batik probably spread to Indonesia from
southern India, presumably during the period of Indianization
in Southeast Asia peaking during the middle of the first millennium A.D.[104] Repeat designs appearing on temple walls from
around A.D. 800 and on statues from 1291 could represent batik, although it is not definitely recorded in Indonesia until the
seventeenth century.[105]

New World Batik

It is not widely known that forms of batik existed in ancient
nuclear America, and the process does not appear to have survived among American Indians into historic times. In fact, in
1976 Larsen wrote, "There are no known traces of indigenous
batik resists in the Americas," although he also stated more
equivocally in the same book that "it is not certain whether batik
methods are or were once known in America. Pre-Columbian
cotton fabrics found in Peru may be batiks but could also have
been painted. Certain kinds of ceramics decorated with 'negative patterns' may also point to a kind of batik technique. Post-
Conquest calabashes from El Salvador and Guatemala were
also resist-patterned with wax."[106] Peruvian batik was reported
as early as 1942[107] but was little noted. In reporting in 1963 a
presumably batikked fabric from Pachacamac, Peru, Ina VanStan
broke "a long-standing taboo against mentioning the likelihood
of a batik or batiklike technique in pre-Spanish America."[108]

Although details are scarce, painted-on resist-dyeing (as well as ordinary painting and printing) *is* found from pre-contact South America and appears to have commenced in the Formative period (1700–500 B.C.) and extended to the late Post-Classic period (A.D. 1000–1532). As far as is known, the resists were clay and resin.[109] Batik is earliest recognized in northern Peru's Chavín culture, which began about 1400 B.C.[110] It is also reported in later periods at such places as Pachacamac (after A.D. 1000), Maranga, and the Post-Classic Chancay culture of Peru's central coast.[111] One possibly resist-patterned painted cloth from around A.D. 1200 in Colombia has been described,[112] but because of environmental conditions hostile to the preservation of fabrics, there are no specimens of cloth, potentially batikked, from most of the pre-contact northern Andean region. However, various flat and roller clay stamps and seals, probably used to print cloth with colors or resist, have been found there; and resist-painted pottery was widespread in pre-Conquest Colombia, Ecuador, and Peru as early as the first millennium B.C., and in Costa Rica, Guatemala, and southern Mexico.[113]

King mentioned an evident batik for the Post-Classic Maya of Chiapas, Mexico, as well: "If so, this is the only known [archaeological] example of a resist-painted textile from Mesoamerica."[114] Nevertheless, experiments based on Spanish colonial depictions of the Aztec emperor's garments indicated that the patterns on such cloths were a combination of tie-dyeing and batikking. Colonial codices indicate that thousands of such cloths were taken to the Aztec capital, Tenochtitlán. As far as we know, New World batik was not highly evolved; it involved only simple resist painting (although, as mentioned, ceramic stamps could easily have been used as well).

Although he did not consider it particularly significant, Nordenskiöld noted the sharing of batik between Peru and Asia, displaying as evidence a cloth fragment that he labeled "batik" and that carried the typical bar-in-oblong motif often seen in tie-dying but also, apparently, in Mexican batiks.[115] While it is true that the principle of batikking could easily have been discovered by accident (e.g., by spilling some wax onto a cloth prior to dyeing), the fact is that the process remained absent in many areas and in developed form is sufficiently sophisticated that its reinvention as an evolved art seems less likely than its being imitated, especially in light of the interhemispheric sharing of the other two principal resist-dyeing techniques. Anthropologist Gunnar Thompson felt that batik was, in fact, introduced to South America.[116]

Conclusions

Conventional opinion is that Old and New World civilizations did not have important pre-Columbian interaction. For instance, in a discussion of ancient central Andean textiles, Mario Vargas Llosa wrote, "The ancient Peruvians with no contact with the occident or the great oriental civilizations of their time, created an original and complex culture"[117]—a culture that nevertheless supposedly independently duplicated many aspects of the civilizations of the Mediterranean/southwest Asian ecumene.[118] However, minority opinion favors the idea that significant, even fundamental, ancient transoceanic inputs took place, a hypothesis based on a great variety of evidence, little of which can be included here.[119]

This study stresses nonstructural techniques for the production of designs on cloth. Besides patterned weaves and simple and stamp painting, what Miguel Covarrubias, in reference to Peru, called "typically Oriental techniques"[120]—resist-dyeing by tie-dyeing, ikatting, and batikking—are all shown to have been shared between the two hemispheres, suggesting possible transoceanic transfer, most likely from southern Asia. Although some scholars have viewed these shared traits as comparable but coincidental,[121] several others have expressed a diffusionist opinion, if only tentatively,[122] or have at least acknowledged the plausibility of contact as an explanation.[123] Alfred Bühler, the world's expert on resist-dyeing and its history, opined that warp ikat was an Asian introduction to Peru and added, "This is in accordance with a fact which has been repeatedly verified with regard to the Pacific coast of the New World. Civilizatory influences of many kinds have reached the Americas across the ocean from southwest Asia. Such influence must go a long way back."[124]

Although large, stone-faced platform mounds reminiscent of the pyramids of Egypt and ziggurats of Mesopotamia appear in Peru before 3000 B.C.,[125] and although cotton raising and textiles can be documented in Peru as early as the first half of the third millennium B.C. and relbun dyeing with mordant is known from that same period as well,[126] resist-dyeing appears to date only from the Chavín period, which began around 1400 B.C. "The [Chavín] Early Horizon was a time of far-reaching technological changes in many media, including textiles [e.g., tapestry weave and discontinuous supplemental warps]. . . . Painted, tie-dyed, and batik cloth appeared. These innovations revolutionized Andean textile production."[127] The second millennium B.C.—a time of great population growth in Peru and growth of complex irrigation agriculture and urban centers there[128]—has sometimes been suggested as reflecting, among other things, stimulus from outside locations, including Asia.[129] Although "there is widespread consensus among archaeologists that Andean civilization developed *in situ* without any significant input from other autochthonous civilizations,"[130] the northwestern Indian subcontinent—with its irrigated cotton raising, the antiquity of its textiles and dyestuffs, and its adobe architecture—is increasingly being looked at by a

few scholars as one conceivable source area of cultural contributions over an extended period.[131]

The Indus Valley region shows the earliest Eastern Hemisphere evidence of cotton cloth and mordant dyeing.[132] "Above
all, . . . the hallmark of Indian textile genius was its mastery of
dyes and the use of mordants to form different colour combinations,"[133] to which may be added methods of obtaining patterns with dyes.

Certainly, vigorous Indian Ocean trade ranging from Africa, the Mediterranean, Indonesia, and China and involving
Indians, Malays, Arabs, and others was well developed by the
first century A.D.[134] "Gujarat . . . has been one of the foremost
textile producing areas of India for many centuries," along with
the Coromandel and Bay of Bengal coasts. "The Indian traders
obviously had the maritime skills to travel over vast areas of
oceans and the diplomatic or coercive talent to be widely accepted as trading partners."[135] "Gujarat, with its long coastline
and many harbours, dominated the seaborne cotton trade."[136]
As of A.D. 1512, "the textile trade was dominated by Gujarati
merchants."[137] These merchants from India's Gulf of Cambay
(Khambhat) region were very familiar with the Indian Ocean
shipping routes. In B.C. times, "on the west coast by far the
most important port was Bharukaccha (Broach), near the
mouth of the Narmada river [on the gulf]."[138] As I have argued
elsewhere, this maritime cloth-trading tradition may go back to
at least Harappan times in the third millennium B.C., and the
dyestuffs evidence points to this region as a center of origin.[139]
The Old World geographical distributions of resist-dyeing
techniques also seem consistent with the idea of their origins in
and diffusions from the northwestern Indian subcontinent, although this is, at present, impossible to directly demonstrate.
Mainland Southeast Asia, including southern China, is another
possible area of their inception.

There are many other textile-related matters worth investigating in this connection. For example, pioneering student of Peruvian textiles Junius Bird wrote the following of the Peruvian coast: "With the [archaeological] spindles are various small cups or bowl-like supports in which the lower ends of the spindles rested while they rotated. . . . Similar equipment has been used by cotton spinners in other parts of the world, such as Dakar, East Pakistan [Bangladesh]."[140] Roland B. Dixon noted that all Old World occurrences of gauze weaving are traceable to India and that Peru provides the only other ancient occurrence.[141]

The present chronological evidence, which begins earlier in South America than in Asia, allows for the possibility that plangi and batik (but not ikat) were invented in the New World and diffused to the Old World. However, the much higher degree of elaboration of resist-dyeing (as an alternative to the use of textile *structures*) in Asia argues—although not definitively—against true priority in the Western Hemisphere, where accidents of preservation are likely the explanation for the apparent priority.

Robert Heine-Geldern and others have suggested that the Chavín culture exhibits some influence from China's Zhou dynasty of the first millennium B.C.[142] Resist-dyeing could be among such imported traits, a theory specifically forwarded by Pierre Honoré, Wolfgang Marschall, and Paul Tolstoy.[143] In the New World, double ikat (and, largely, weft ikat) appears to have been confined to Guatemala, where it is known ethnographically among the Maya. In the Eastern Hemisphere, double ikat (and, possibly, weft ikat) is generally agreed to have had a single origin, in northwestern southern Asia, whence it was introduced to Japan and Bali. Crawford asserted that "we can safely say that the Moors carried the [ikat] craft into Spain, and the Spaniards in turn carried it to Mexico along with the silkworm.

Today the weavers of Guatemala apply this craft of ancient India to silk and cotton fibers."[144] Bühler also felt that weft ikat was a modern introduction to Guatemala.[145] However, in Guatemala the craft is practiced by American Indians, not by those of Hispanic culture. That fact, coupled with extensive evidence of pre-Columbian Hindu-Buddhist influence on the Maya, from Cambodia and possibly Java and southern India during the first millennium A.D.,[146] makes an earlier, Asian origin of Guatemalan weft ikat and double ikat plausible, although warp ikat could have come even earlier and from another source.

Migrations to northwestern South America from Indonesia, beginning in perhaps the fourth millennium B.C., have been suggested,[147] and the latest of these (perhaps in the middle of the first millennium B.C.) could conceivably have introduced resist-dyeing—if that technique was already present in Indonesia. In fact, King noted that the backstrap loom, certain resist-dyeing techniques, and the Indonesian *slendang* (Mexican *rebozo*) co-occur in Southeast Asia and ancient America. She observed: "I would postulate a Southeast Asian origin for the American backstrap loom. . . . One possibility is that ikat, plangi, and the loom were introduced together to [northern] coastal South America in Chavín times (after 1000 B.C.), but that either the complicated ikat technique did not really take hold until much later or . . . the dearth of early textiles from the North Coast has simply skewed our sample."[148] However, tie-dye and weft and double ikat seem to have been comparatively late introductions into Indonesia, and it is rather doubtful that even batik was present there early enough to account for Chavín use.

Other significant possibilities include proposed inputs to South America from Neolithic southeastern China (probably Tibeto-Burman Miao and Yao speaking at the time), which strikes me as a better possibility than Indonesia for the source of the American backstrap loom and perhaps tie-dye and batik.

Still, evidence for sufficient antiquity of these things in southern China (or anywhere else in the Old World) is not yet forthcoming. The highly influential Dongson culture (circa eighth to first centuries B.C.) of Tonkin and Yunnan, which may have inner Asian and even Pontic ties and which has been suggested to have introduced much metallurgical technology to northeastern South America,[149] would be too late to account for the first appearances of any of the resist methods in America other than ikat. It does, however, look like a potential source for warp ikat in northwestern South America, a region that might have served as a center for diffusion southward and perhaps northward as well. Michelle Pirazzoli-T'Serstevens wrote the following of the Kingdom of Dian, probably a Tibeto-Burman-speaking "cultural confederation" at the end of the first century B.C. and consisting of "Yue, Dông-son, and Shizhai shan": "At their apogee, at the end of the Bronze Age, these cultures found themselves subject to the pressure of the Chinese Iron Age civilization. Once caught in this grip, part of their populations may have emigrated, prolonging former contacts in Southeast Asia and as far as the Pacific, and increasing the dispersion of certain features particular to this confederation."[150]

The present survey is only a preliminary examination of the question of the possible origins and dispersals of resist-dyeing; much more research and synthesis are needed to fill in some of the many gaps and produce a more complete picture. Although some scholars view plangi, ikat, and batik as definite Old World introductions to the New World,[151] the study of resist-dyeing is not in itself sufficient to make a highly persuasive case for transoceanic transfer. In fact, Larsen, following Bühler, opined that resist "is so obvious and natural that patterning with resists, at least in their simple forms, is found in every major geographical area except the Arctic. Because such resists are so universal . . . we may assume that to a large extent discovery

of the resist principle was local and spontaneous."[152] But while
we may agree that the basic principle of resist might easily have
been discovered repeatedly and that the New World forms of at
least plangi and batik are relatively little elaborated, when these
methods are seen in the context of many other traits held in
common, transoceanic cultural transfer seems more than likely.
Larsen did acknowledge that "the more sophisticated developments of the techniques, on the other hand, seem to have occurred in a few major centers, then slowly spread with the
migration[s] of peoples, or at least of artisans." He also recognized the possibility that at least New World ikat derived from
Asia.[153] Although he was uncertain whether these centers of
resist-dyeing were all genetically related, Bühler acknowledged
that "the possibility of a joint origin should not be ruled out."
In fact, he felt that Peruvian ikat derived from Indonesia,[154] an
opinion foreshadowed or echoed to a greater or lesser degree by
other authors as well (e.g., Crawford, King, Steward, Paris,
Martínez, Covarrubias, Bushnell, Thompson). Again, given the
plethora of evidence for transoceanic contacts,[155] I believe that
the presence of these resist techniques in the Americas seems
most simply explained by contact and diffusion from the Old
World.

Notes

1. For a discussion of these evidences, see my "Before Columbus: The Question of Early Transoceanic Interinfluences," *BYU
Studies* 33/2 (1993): 245–71; and my "Diffusion versus Independent Development: The Bases of Controversy," in *Man across the Sea:
Problems of Pre-Columbian Contacts*, ed. Carroll L. Riley et al. (Austin: University of Texas Press, 1971), 5–53.

2. Daniel F. Rubín de la Borbolla, introduction to *Textiles of*

Oaxaca, by Gerald Williams (Hanover and Manchester, N.H.: Hopkins Center, Dartmouth College; Currier Gallery of Art, 1964), 3.

3. Joseph Needham and Lu Gwei-Djen, *Trans-Pacific Echoes and Resonances: Listening Once Again* (Singapore and Philadelphia: World Scientific Publishing, 1985), 52.

4. See my "Dyestuffs and Possible Early Contacts between Southwestern Asia and Nuclear America," *New England Antiquities Research Association Journal* 28/1–2 (1993): 31–8.

5. John Gillow and Nicholas Barnard, *Traditional Indian Textiles* (London: Thames and Hudson, 1991), 32; see Tamara E. Wasserman and Jonathan S. Hill, *Bolivian Indian Textiles: Traditional Designs and Costumes* (New York: Dover Publications, 1981), 7.

6. Elizabeth P. Benson, William J. Conklin, and Masakatsu Yamamoto, *Museums of the Andes* (New York: Newsweek; Tokyo: Kodansha, 1981), 132.

7. For definitions of resist-dyeing techniques, see Annemarie Seiler-Baldinger, *Textiles: A Classification of Techniques* (Washington: Smithsonian Institution Press, 1994), 143–8; see also Alfred Bühler, *Ikat, Batik, Plangi: Reservemusterungen auf Garn und Stoff aus Vorderasien, Zentralasien, Sudosteuropa und Nordafrika,* 3 vols. (Basel: Pharos Verlag, 1972); Verla Birrell, *The Textile Arts* (New York: Harper & Brothers, 1959), 405–9; Stuart Robinson, *A History of Dyed Textiles* (Cambridge, Mass.: M.I.T. Press, 1969); and Wanda Warming and Michael Gaworski, *The World of Indonesian Textiles* (Tokyo: Kodansha International, 1981), 122–6.

8. See, for example, Bühler, *Ikat, Batik, Plagi;* Christopher Spring, *African Textiles* (New York: Crescent Books, 1989), plates 7, 30; Jack Lenor Larsen et al., *The Dyer's Art: Ikat, Batik, Plangi* (New York: Van Nostrand Reinhold, 1976); Robinson, *History of Dyed Textiles,* 83; Renée Boser-Sarivaxévanis, *Les tissues de l'Afrique Occidentale,* Basler Beiträge zur Ethnologie, vol. 13 (Basel: Pharos, 1972); and Thelma R. Newman, *Contemporary African Arts and Crafts: On-Site Working with Art Forms and Processes* (New York: Crown, 1974), 69–72.

9. See Alfred Bühler, "Indian Resist-Dyed Fabrics," in *Handwoven Fabrics of India*, ed. Jasleen Dhamija and Jyotindra Jain (Ahmedabad: Mapin, 1989), 87–93; Alfred Bühler, Eberhard Fischer, and Marie-Louise Nabholz, *Indian Tie-Dyed Fabrics* (Ahmedabad, India: Calico Museum of Textiles, 1980), 102–42; Gillow and Barnard, *Traditional Indian Textiles;* Rustam J. Mehta, *The Handicrafts and Industrial Arts of India* (Bombay: D. B. Taraporevala, 1960), 126–8; Rustam J. Mehta, *Masterpieces of Indian Textiles: Hand Spun—Hand Woven—Traditional* (Bombay: D. B. Taraporevala, 1970), 38; T. M. Abraham, *Handicrafts in India* (New Delhi: Graphics Columbia, 1964), 142–3; Ethel-Jane W. Bunting, *Sindhi Tombs and Textiles: The Persistence of Pattern* (Albuquerque: Maxwell Museum of Anthropology and University of New Mexico Press, 1980), 62; Caroline Stone, "The Dye That Binds," *Aramco World* 47/5 (1996): 41; and Veronica Murphy and Rosemary Crill, *Tie-Dyed Textiles of India* (London: Victoria and Albert Museum, 1991).

10. See Larsen et al., *Dyer's Art*, 28–31; Sylvia Fraser-Lu, *Handwoven Textiles of South-East Asia* (Singapore: Oxford University Press, 1988), 118, 133; and Bronwen Solyom and Garrett Solyom, "Notes and Observations on Indonesian Textiles," in *Threads of Tradition: Textiles of Indonesia and Sarawak*, ed. Joseph Fischer (Berkeley: Fidelity Savings and Loan Association, 1979), 17.

11. See Bühler, *Ikat, Batik, Plangi*, 133–4; Larsen et al., *Dyer's Art*, 34; Murphy and Crill, *Tie-Dyed Textiles of India*, 9; Thelma Newman, *Contemporary Southeast Asian Arts and Crafts* (New York: Crown Publishers, 1977), 37; Shih Hsio-Yen, "Textile Finds in the People's Republic of China," in *Studies in Textile History: In Memory of Harold B. Burnham*, ed. Veronika Gervers (Toronto: Royal Ontario Museum, 1977), 317, 320, 321, 323; and Yoshiko Wada, Mary Kellog Rice, and Jane Barton, *Shibori: The Inventive Art of Resist Dyeing: Tradition, Techniques, Innovation* (Tokyo and New York: Kodansha International, 1983), 11–13, 58–64.

12. See Mehta, *Handicrafts and Industrial Arts of India*, 95; Mehta, *Masterpieces of Indian Textiles*, 38; Stone and Perlman, "The

Dye That Binds," 39, 41; Robinson, *History of Dyed Textiles*, 17, 79–81; Bühler, "Indian Resist-Dyed Fabrics," 93; and Murphy and Crill, *Tie-Dyed Textiles of India*, 9–11.

13. See Rita Bolland, *Tellem Textiles: Archaeological Finds from Burial Caves in Mali's Bandiagara Cliff*, trans. Patricia Wardle (Amsterdam: Tropenmusuem, 1991), 57, 67, 164.

14. See Joseph Fischer, "The Value of Tradition: An Essay on Indonesian Textiles," in *Threads of Tradition*, ed. Fischer, 9; Andrew M. Watson, "The Rise and Spread of Old World Cotton," in *Studies in Textile History*, ed. Gervers, 357; and Warming and Gaworski, *World of Indonesian Textiles*, 122.

15. See Larsen et al., *Dyer's Art*, 27, 34; see also Bühler, *Ikat, Batik, Plangi*, 131, 133; and Gillow and Barnard, *Traditional Indian Textiles*, 9.

16. Larsen et al., *Dyer's Art*, 34.

17. See M. D. C. Crawford, "Peruvian Fabrics," *Anthropological Papers of the American Museum of Natural History* 12/4 (1916): 153–4, 156, figs. 28–9.

18. Mary Elizabeth King, "Possible Indonesian or Southeast Asian Influences in New World Textile Industries," in *Indonesian Textiles*, ed. Mattiebelle Gittinger (Washington: Textile Museum, 1980), 367; see Larsen et al., *Dyer's Art*, 32, 47; and Robinson, *History of Dyed Textiles*, 82, 85.

19. See Yukihiro Tsunoyama, ed., *Textiles of the Andes: Catalogue of Amano Collection* (South San Francisco: Heian/Dohosha, 1979), 7–8.

20. See Fernando de Szyszlo, "The Excellence of Pre-Columbian Textile Art," in *The Textile Art of Peru*, ed. James W. Reid (Lima: Industria Textil Piura, 1991), 26.

21. See Karen Olsen Bruhns, *Ancient South America* (Cambridge: Cambridge University Press, 1994), 134.

22. King, "Possible Indonesian or Southeast Asian Influences," 367. For a discussion of later false tie-dyeing from the central coast, see Wolfgang Haberland, "Geweben mit unechtem Plangi von der Zentral-Peruanischen Küste," *Baessler-Archiv* 12 (1964): 271–9.

23. See Anne Paul, *Paracas Ritual Attire: Symbols of Authority in Ancient Peru* (Norman: University of Oklahoma Press, 1990), 151; and Larsen et al., *Dyer's Art*, 34, 50.

24. See Bruhns, *Ancient South America*, 163.

25. See Rebecca Stone-Miller, *To Weave for the Sun: Ancient Andean Textiles in the Museum of Fine Arts, Boston* (New York: Thames and Hudson, 1992), 21, 36–7, 99–101, 246, 252, 261; *Textile Art of Peru*, ed. Reid, 212–19; Benson, Conklin, and Yamamoto, *Museums of the Andes*, 95; Mary Elizabeth King, *Ancient Peruvian Textiles from the Collection of the Textile Museum, Washington, D.C.* (New York: Museum of Primitive Art, 1965), 28–9; Larsen et al., *Dyer's Art*, 47–9; Heinrich Ubbelohde-Doering, *The Art of Ancient Peru* (New York: Frederick A. Praeger, 1952), 29, 83, 131; Andre Emmerich, *Art of Ancient Peru* (New York: Andre Emmerich, 1969), 32; Lila M. O'Neale and A. L. Kroeber, *Textile Periods in Ancient Peru* (Berkeley and Los Angeles: University of California Press, 1930), pl. 27a, "Basic Table"; and Ann Pollard Rowe, "Textiles from the Nasca Valley at the Time of the Fall of the Huari Empire," in *The Junius B. Bird Conference on Andean Textiles, April 7th and 8th, 1984,* ed. Ann Pollard Rowe (Washington: Textile Museum, 1986), 161, 182 (hereafter cited as *Junius B. Bird Conference, 1984*).

26. See Stone-Miller, *To Weave for the Sun*, 230; and Larsen et al., *Dyer's Art*, 47. See also Ina VanStan, *The Fabrics of Peru* (Leigh-on-Sea, England: F. Lewis, Publishers, 1966), 15–16, figs. 49–51; Ina VanStan, *Textiles from Beneath the Temple of Pachacamac, Peru: A Part of the Uhle Collection of the University Museum, University of Pennsylvania* (Philadelphia: University Museum, 1967), 71–2, 84, 114, 124, 157, 158; G. H. S. Bushnell, *Peru* (New York: Frederick A. Praeger, 1957), 101; O'Neale and Kroeber, *Textile Periods in Ancient Peru*, pl. 27a, "Basic Table"; and Tsunoyama, *Textiles of the Andes*, 7–8, 12.

27. Jane Feltham, *Peruvian Textiles* (Aylesbury, England: Shire Publications, 1989), 89.

28. See Crawford, "Peruvian Fabrics," 154 (see n. 17).

29. See Alba Guadalupe Mastáche de Escobar, "Dos fragmentos de tejido decorados con la técnica de plangi," *Anales, Instituto Nacional de Antropología e Historia* 4 (1972): 251–62; and Mary Elizabeth King, "The Prehistoric Textile Industry of Mesoamerica," in *The Junius B. Bird Pre-Columbian Textile Conference, May 19th and 20th, 1973,* ed. Ann Pollard Rowe, Elizabeth P. Benson, and Anne-Louise Schaffer (Washington, D.C.: Textile Museum, 1979), 272.

30. See Lila O'Neale, *Textiles of Highland Guatemala* (Washington, D.C.: Carnegie Institute, 1945), 30; Robinson, *History of Dyed Textiles,* 85; Laura E. Start, *The McDougall Collection of Indian Textiles from Guatemala and Mexico* (Oxford: Oxford University Press, 1948), 102, pl. 16; Mastáche, "Dos fragmentos de tejido," 255–9; Virginia Davis, "Resist Dyeing in Mexico: Comments on Its History, Significance, and Prevalence," in *Textile Traditions of Mesoamerica and the Andes: An Anthology,* ed. Margot Blum Schevill, Janet Catherine Berlo, and Edward B. Dwyer (New York: Garland Publishing, 1991), 321–2; Patricia Reiff Anawalt, "The Emperor's Cloak: Aztec Pomp, Toltec Circumstance," *American Antiquity* 55/2 (1990): 219–307; Patricia Rieff Anawalt, "Riddle of the Emperor's Cloak," *Archaeology* 46/3 (1993): cover, 30–6, 70; and Patricia Reiff Anawalt, "Aztec Knotted and Netted Capes: Colonial Interpretations vs. Indigenous Primary Data," *Ancient Mesoamerica* 7 (1996): 187–206. For a dissenting view, see Carmen Aguilera, "Of Royal Mantles and Blue Turquoise: The Meaning of the Mexica Emperor's Mantle," *Latin American Antiquity* 8/1 (1997): 3–19.

31. See Emil W. Haury, *The Canyon Creek Ruin and the Cliff Dwellings of the Sierra Ancha* (Globe, Ariz.: Medallion, 1934), 99–100, pl. 61b; Robinson, *History of Dyed Textiles,* 82, 85; Clara Lee Tanner, *Prehistoric Southwestern Craft Arts* (Tucson: University of Arizona Press, 1976), 86; and Jenna Tedrick Kuttruff, "Mississippian Period Status Differentiation through Textile Analysis: A Caddoan Example," *American Antiquity* 58/1 (1993): 132–3, 140.

32. See, for example, Pierre Paris, "L'Amérique précolombienne et l'Asie Méridionale," *Bulletin de la Société des Études Indochinoises*

17/2 (1942–43); and Paul Tolstoy, "Transoceanic Diffusion and Nuclear Mesoamerica," in *Prehistoric America,* ed. Shirley Gorenstein (New York: St. Martin's Press, 1974), 131.

33. See Larsen et al., *Dyer's Art,* 34–5; and Alfred Bühler, "Plangi—Tie and Dye Work," *CIBA Review* 104 (1954): 3726–48, 3752.

34. See Crawford, "Peruvian Fabrics," 153.

35. See Tolstoy, "Transoceanic Diffusion and Nuclear Meso-america," 131.

36. See Roland B. Dixon, *The Building of Cultures* (New York: Charles Scribner's Sons, 1928), 199–202.

37. K. R. T. Hodjonogoro, "The Place of Batik in the History and Philosophy of Javanese Textiles: A Personal View," in *Indonesian Textiles,* ed. Gittinger, 227.

38. Seiler-Baldinger, *Textiles,* 148 (see n. 7).

39. See Alfred Bühler, "The Ikat Technique," *CIBA Review* 44 (1942): 1586–96; his "Dyes and Dyeing Methods for Ikat Threads," *CIBA Review* 44 (1942): 1597–1603; and his *Ikat, Batik, Plangi.* See also Larsen et al., *Dyer's Art,* 131; Birrell, *Textile Arts,* 409–10 (see n. 7); and Warming and Gaworski, *World of Indonesian Textiles,* 56–76 (see n. 7). The theoretical possibility of treating the threads with a liquid or paste resist rather than by wrapping has not, to my knowledge, been recorded.

40. Nora Fisher, "Weft Ikat Blankets," in *Spanish Textile Tradition of New Mexico and Colorado: Museum of International Folk Art,* ed. Sarah Nestor (Santa Fe: Museum of New Mexico Press, 1979), 133.

41. John Grey, "*Sarasa* and *Patola:* Indian Textiles in Indonesia," *Orientations* 20/1 (1989): 55.

42. For discussions of geographical origins and spreads of resist-dyeing methods in the Eastern Hemisphere, see Bühler, *Ikat, Batik, Plangi,* 316–40; Larsen et al., *Dyer's Art;* and Robinson, *History of Dyed Textiles.*

43. Chelna Desai, *Ikat Textiles of India* (San Francisco: Chronicle Books, 1987).

44. See Bühler, "Indian Resist-Dyed Fabrics," 95 (see n. 9); Mary

Golden De Bone, "Patolu and Its Techniques," *Textile Museum Journal* 4/3 (1976): 49–62; Bühler, Fischer, and Nabholz, *Indian Tie-Dyed Fabrics*, 7–101 (see n. 9); Alfred Bühler and Eberhard Fischer, *The Patola of Gujarat: Double Ikat in India* (Basel: Krebs, 1979); Gillow and Barnard, *Traditional Indian Textiles* (see n. 5); Mehta, *Handicrafts and Industrial Arts of India*, 128–30 (see n. 9); Mehta, *Masterpieces of Indian Textiles*, 39 (see n. 9); Abraham, *Handicrafts in India*, 146–7 (see n. 9); Ilay Cooper, John Gillow, and Barry Dawson, *Arts and Crafts of India* (London: Thames and Hudson, 1996), 92; Larsen et al., *Dyer's Art*, 131, 159; and Brigitta Hauser-Schaublin, Marie-Louise Nabholz-Kartaschoff, and Urs Ramseyer, *Textiles in Bali* (Berkeley: Periplus Editions, 1991), 116–35.

45. Grey, "*Sarasa* and *Patola*," 55; see Desai, *Ikat Textiles of India*, 8–11.

46. See Alfred Bühler, "Patola Influences in Southeast Asia," *Journal of Indian Textile History* 4 (1959): 1–43; Grey, "*Sarasa* and *Patola*," 44; Truade Gavin, *The Woman's Warpath: Iban Ritual Fabrics from Borneo* (Los Angeles: UCLA Fowler Museum of Cultural History, 1996), 70–1; Ann Hecht, *The Art of the Loom: Weaving, Spinning and Dyeing across the World* (New York: Rizzoli International Publications, 1989), 6, 122–40; and Warming and Gaworski, *World of Indonesian Textiles*, 102–8.

47. See, for example, Larsen et al., *Dyer's Art*, 131.

48. See, for example, Jan Fontein, *The Sculpture of Indonesia* (Washington, D.C.: National Gallery of Art; New York: Harry N. Abrams, 1990), 24, 116–21; and Fischer, *Threads of Tradition*, 9 (see n. 10).

49. Warming and Gaworski, *World of Indonesian Textiles*, 53, 92.

50. See Alfred Bühler, "The Origin and Extent of the Ikat Technique," *CIBA Review* 44 (1942): 1604–11; Larsen et al., *Dyer's Art*, 131–2; Fraser-Lu, *Handwoven Textiles of South-East Asia* (see n. 10); and Robinson, *History of Dyed Textiles*, 81.

51. See Spring, *African Textiles*, pl. 37 (see n. 8).

52. Newman, *Contemporary Southeast Asian Arts and Crafts*, 54 (see n. 11).

53. See Wilhelm G. Solheim II, "Philippine Prehistory," in *The*

People and Art of the Philippines, ed. Gabriel Casal et al. (Los Angeles: Museum of Cultural History, University of California, Los Angeles, 1981), 78–9; Hauser-Schaublin, Nabholz-Kartaschoff, and Ramseyer, *Textiles in Bali*, 12–30, 94–114; and Roy W. Hamilton, ed., *Gift of the Cotton Maiden: Textiles of Flores and the Solor Islands* (Los Angeles: Fowler Museum of Cultural History, University of California, Los Angeles).

54. See Newman, *Contemporary Southeast Asian Arts and Crafts*, 54–5; Bühler, "Origin and Extent of the Ikat Technique"; Larsen et al., *Dyer's Art*, 22–3, 130–1; Fraser-Lu, *Handwoven Textiles of South-East Asia;* Robyn Maxwell, *Textiles of Southeast Asia: Tradition, Trade and Transportation* (Melbourne: Australian National Gallery and Oxford University Press Australia, 1990), 165, 169–70, 228; and Mattiebelle Gittinger and H. Leedom Lefferts Jr., *Textiles and the Tai Experience in Southeast Asia* (Washington, D.C.: Textile Museum, 1992), 35–7.

55. See Warming and Gaworski, *World of Indonesian Textiles*, 114; and Fischer, "Value of Tradition," 10 (see n. 14).

56. See Mary Dusenbury, "Kasuri: A Japanese Textile," *Textile Museum Journal* 17 (1978): 41–5, 47.

57. See Bühler, *Ikat, Batik, Plangi*, 23, 27; and Larsen et al., *Dyer's Art*, 134.

58. Larsen et al., *Dyer's Art*, 134; see also Crawford, "Peruvian Fabrics," 153 (see n. 17).

59. See Jackie Battenfield, *Ikat Technique* (New York: Van Nostrand Reinhold Company, 1978), 12. The Cleveland specimen's accession number is 50.353.

60. See Doris Rau, Andy Hale, and Kate Fitz Gibbon, *Ikats, Woven Silks from Central Asia: The Rau Collection* (Oxford: Basil Blackwell, 1988), 8; and Janet Harvey, *Traditional Textiles of Central Asia* (New York: Thames and Hudson, 1996).

61. See Bühler, "Origin and Extent of the Ikat Technique"; his *Ikat, Batik, Plangi;* and his "Introduction: A Brief History of Ikat," in *Ikat*, ed. Lydia van Gelder (New York: Watson-Guptill Publications, 1980), 8–15. See also Larsen et al., *Dyer's Art;* and van Gelder, *Ikat*.

62. See Rau, Hale, and Gibbon, *Ikats*; Max Klimburg, *Ikat: Textile-kunds von der Seidenstrasse* (Textile art from the Silk Road) (Vienna: Kirdök, 1993); Robinson, *History of Dyed Textiles*, 80; Hecht, *Art of the Loom*, 92, 102–5, 109–11; Gavin, *Woman's Warpath;* van Gelder, *Ikat*, 18–19; and Boser-Sarivaxévanis, *Les tissues de l'Afrique Occidentale* (see n. 8).

63. See Peggy S. Gilfoy, "Textiles in Africa and Indonesia: A Connection?" in *Indonesian Textiles*, ed. Gittinger, 360 (see n. 37).

64. See Bühler, "Introduction," 14–15.

65. See Larsen et al., *Dyer's Art*, 131–5.

66. See P. Aug. Driessen, "Een Inka- of zelfs pré-Inka-Ikat," *Nederlandsh Indië, Oud en Nieuw* 15/3 (1930–31): 66–7; and E. H. Snethlage, "Ein figurliches Ikat-Gewebe aus Peru," *Der Weltkreis, Zeitschrift für Völkerkunde, Kulturgeschichte und Volkskunde* 2/3–4 (1931): 49–51.

67. See Wasserman and Hill, *Bolivian Indian Textiles*, 7 (see n. 5).

68. See Larsen et al., *Dyer's Art*, 50.

69. J. Alden Mason, *The Ancient Civilizations of Peru* (Harmondsworth, Middlesex: Penguin Books, 1957), 256; see Bushnell, *Peru*, 96 (see n. 26).

70. See Ann Pollard Rowe, *Warp-Patterned Weaves of the Andes* (Washington, D.C.: Textile Museum, 1977), 18; and Dieter Eisleb, "Altperuanische Ikat-Gewebe aus den Sammlungen des Berliner Museums für Völkerkunde," *Baessler-Archiv* 12 (1964): 179–91.

71. See King, "Possible Indonesian or Southeast Asian Influences," 367–8 (see n. 18).

72. See Feltham, *Peruvian Textiles*, 28 (see n. 27); Joan S. Gardner, "Pre-Columbian Textiles, Los Ríos Province, Ecuador," *National Geographic Society Research Reports* 18 (1985): 327–42; and Stone-Miller, *To Weave for the Sun*, 219 (see n. 25).

73. Larsen et al., *Dyer's Art*, 133.

74. Rowe, *Warp-Patterned Weaves*, 18; see Ina VanStan, "A Peruvian Ikat from Pachacamac," *American Antiquity* 23/2, pt. 1 (1957): 150–9.

75. See O'Neale, *Textiles of Highland Guatemala*, 25–7 (see n.

30); Hecht, *Art of the Loom*, 160–1; Feltham, *Peruvian Textiles*, 28; Rowe, *Warp-Patterned Weaves*, 19–23; Laura Matin Miller, "The Ikat Shawl Traditions of Northern Peru and Southern Ecuador," in *Textile Traditions of Mesoamerica*, 337–58 (see n. 30); Gerardo Reichel-Dolmatoff, "On the Discovery of the Ikat-Technique in Colombia, S.A.," *American Anthropologist* 59/1 (1957): 133; and Margot Blum Scheville, *Maya Textiles of Guatemela: The Gustavus A. Eisen Collection, 1902* (Austin: University of Texas Press, 1993), 62–3.

76. See van Gelder, *Ikat*, 63–4; and Start, *McDougall Collection*, 49–52, 77, 83 (see n. 30).

77. See Birrell, *Textile Arts*, 409 (see n. 7).

78. See King, "Possible Indonesian or Southeast Asian Influences."

79. See Davis, "Resist Dyeing in Mexico," 312, 315 (see n. 30); King, "Possible Indonesian or Southeast Asian Influences," 368–9; and Anawalt, "Aztec Knotted and Netted Capes," 192–3 (see n. 30).

80. See Larsen et al., *Dyer's Art*, 135; Fisher, "Weft Ikat Blankets" (see n. 40); Ann Pollard Rowe, *A Century of Change in Guatemalan Textiles* (New York: Center for Inter-American Relations, 1981), 73, 100–1, 104; and King, "Possible Indonesian or Southeast Asian Influences," 368.

81. Erland Nordenskiöld, "Origin of the Indian Civilizations in South America," *Comparative Ethnographical Studies* 9 (1931): 45–6.

82. Daniel Shaffer, "History and Technique [of Ikat]," *Hali* 7/3 (1985): 44; see Larsen et al., *Dyer's Art*, 13, 15.

83. Crawford, "Peruvian Fabrics," 154 (see n. 17).

84. See Paris, "L'Amérique précolombienne" (see n. 32); and Gunnar Thompson, *American Discovery: The Real Story* (Seattle: Misty Isles Press, 1992), 65.

85. Gilfoy, "Textiles in Africa and Indonesia," 360.

86. See Bühler, "Introduction," 14 (see n. 61).

87. Bühler, "Origin and Extent of the Ikat Technique," 1607 (see n. 50).

88. Larsen et al., *Dyer's Art*, 135.

89. Julian H. Steward, "South American Cultures: An Interpretive Summary," in *Handbook of South American Indians*, ed. Julian H.

Steward (Washington, D.C.: U.S. Government Printing Office, 1949), 5:744.

90. Bushnell, *Peru*, 101 (see n. 26).

91. See the quotation that corresponds to n. 148.

92. Alfred Steinmann, "Batik Work: Its Origin and Spread," *CIBA Review* 58 (1947): 2102.

93. Bühler, *Ikat, Batik, Plangi;* Birrell, *Textile Arts,* 411–12; and Robinson, *History of Dyed Textiles* (see n. 7). Discharge (bleaching out a design from an already-dyed cloth) is unknown ethnographically.

94. See Bühler, *Ikat, Batik, Plangi;* 158, 161–2, 164–6, 179–81, 191–205, 297; Larsen et al., *Dyer's Art,* 77, 79, 82–3; Steinmann, "Batik Work"; Fraser-Lu, *Handwoven Textiles of South-East Asia* (see n. 10); Spring, *African Textiles,* plates 5, 6, 27 (see n. 8); Robinson, *History of Dyed Textiles,* 39–43; Newman, *Contemporary Southeast Asian Arts and Crafts,* 73–8 (see n. 11); and Gilfoy, "Textiles in Africa and Indonesia," 360–1.

95. Grey, "*Sarasa* and *Patola*," 50–3, 58–60 (see n. 41). For a discussion of early block printing and mordant resist and their distributions, see Bühler, *Ikat, Batik, Plangi,* 189, 272–93, 297–8; Gillow and Barnard, *Traditional Indian Textiles* (see n. 5); Mehta, *Handicrafts and Industrial Arts of India,* 123 (see n. 9); Mehta, *Masterpieces of Indian Textiles,* 34–6 (see n. 9); Abraham, *Handicrafts in India,* 143–4 (see n. 9); Robinson, *History of Dyed Textiles,* 17, 39–40, 43; and Dhamija and Jain, eds., *Handwoven Fabrics of India,* 159 (see n. 9).

96. See Steinmann, "Batik Work," 2103, 2108–9; Fraser-Lu, *Handwoven Textiles of South-East Asia,* 2; and Hodjonogoro, "Place of Batik," 224, 227–8 (see n. 37).

97. E. J. W. Barber, *Prehistoric Textiles: The Development of Cloth in the Neolithic and Bronze Ages* (Princeton: Princeton University Press, 1991), 206–7, 226, 379.

98. See Shih, "Textile Finds in the People's Republic of China," 320–2.

99. See Larsen et al., *Dyer's Art,* 15, 79, 84.

100. See Amaury Saint-Gilles, *Mingei: Japan's Enduring Folk Arts* (Rutland, Vt.: Charles E. Tuttle Company, 1989), 28–9; Bühler,

Ikat, Batik, Plangi; 137–8; Robinson, *History of Dyed Textiles,* 39, 43, 52; Wada, Rice, and Barton, *Shibori,* 11 (see n. 11); and Eisha Nakano, *Japanese Stencil Dyeing Paste-Resist Techniques* (New York and Tokyo: John Wetherhill, 1982), 4.

101. See Bühler, *Ikat, Batik, Plangi,* 161–2; and Robinson, *History of Dyed Textiles,* 14, 40, 53.

102. See Gillow and Barnard, *Traditional Indian Textiles,* 11–12; Cooper, Gillow, and Dawson, *Arts and Crafts of India,* 91 (see n. 44); and Robinson, *History of Dyed Textiles,* 40, 74.

103. See Larsen et al., *Dyer's Art,* 84–5.

104. See Birrell, *Textile Arts,* 412; and George Coedès, *The Indianized States of Southeast Asia,* trans. Susan Brown Cowing (Honolulu: East-West Center Press, 1968).

105. See Sylvia Fraser-Lu, *Indonesian Batik: Processes, Patterns and Places* (Singapore: Oxford University Press, 1986), 1–2.

106. Larsen et al., *Dyer's Art,* 47, 83; see Dixon, *Building of Cultures,* 201 (see n. 36).

107. See Julius Rath, "Ein altperuanisches Batikmuster," *Paideuma* 2/4–5 (1942): 239–42.

108. Ina VanStan, "A Problematic Example of Peruvian Resist-Dyeing," *American Antiquity* 29/2 (1963): 173.

109. See Tsunoyama, *Textiles of the Andes,* 7–8, 12 (see n. 19).

110. See Szyszlo, "Excellence of Pre-Columbian Textile Art," 26 (see n. 20); Dwight T. Wallace, "A Technical and Iconographic Analysis of Carhua Painted Textiles," in *Paracas Art and Architecture: Object and Context in South Coastal Peru,* ed. Anne Paul (Iowa City: University of Iowa Press, 1991), 64; and Richard L. Burger, *Chavín and the Origins of Andean Civilization* (London: Thames and Hudson, 1992), 201.

111. See Benson, Conklin, and Yamamoto, *Museums of the Andes,* 130–2 (see n. 6); Robinson, *History of Dyed Textiles,* 40; and VanStan, "Peruvian Resist-Dyeing."

112. See Marianne Cardale Schrimpff, "Painted Textiles from Caves in the Eastern Cordillera, Colombia," in *Junius B. Bird Conference, 1984,* 207, 215 (see n. 25).

113. See Armand Labbé, *Colombia before Columbus: The People, Culture, and Ceramic Art of Prehistoric Colombia* (New York: Rizzoli International Publications, 1986); Alain Jacob, *Cerámica de los Paises Andinos, Colombia Ecuador, Céramiques des Pays Andines* (Paris: ABC Décor, 1975), 8, 22; Rafael Larco Hoyle, *Peru* (Cleveland and New York: World Publishing Company, 1966), 233, 239, plates 13, 132; Luis G. Lumbreras, *The Peoples and Cultures of Ancient Peru* (Washington, D.C.: Smithsonian Institution Press, 1974), 87, 98–9, 111–15; Mason, *Ancient Civilizations of Peru*, 255–6 (see n. 69); Emmerich, *Art of Ancient Peru*, 12, 13 (see n. 25); Christopher B. Donnan, *Ceramics of Ancient Peru* (Los Angeles: Fowler Museum of Cultural History, University of California, Los Angeles, 1992), 13, 22, 38–9, 70–9, 124; Nordenskiöld, "Origin of the Indian Civilizations," 66 (see n. 81). Note that seemingly wax-resist-painted pottery was also made in Tang times in China (see Larsen et al., *Dyer's Art*, 24).

114. King, "Prehistoric Textile Industry of Mesoamerica," 274 (see n. 29); see Irmgard Weitlaner Johnson, "Hilado y tejido," in *Esplendor de Mexico Antiguo* 1 (1959): 439–78, 464, 468.

115. See Nordenskiöld, "Origin of the Indian Civilizations," 44–6.

116. See Thompson, *American Discovery*, 65 (see n. 84).

117. See Mario Vargas Llosa, "Loquacious Weavings," in *Textile Art of Peru*, ed. Reid, 11 (see n. 20).

118. See John Howland Rowe, "Diffusionism and Archaeology," *American Antiquity* 31/3 (1966): 334–7.

119. See my "Diffusion versus Independent Development" (see n. 1); my "Pre-Columbian Transoceanic Contacts," in *Ancient South Americans*, ed. Jesse D. Jennings (San Francisco: W. H. Freeman and Company, 1983), 337–93; and my "Hypotheses of Mediterranean/ Southwest [Asian] Influences on New World Cultures," *New England Antiquities Research Association Journal* 26/3–4 (1992): 82–5.

120. Miguel Covarrubias, *The Eagle, the Jaguar, and the Serpent: Indian Art of the Americas; North America: Alaska, Canada, the United States* (New York: Alfred A. Knopf, 1954), 99.

121. See, for example, Dixon, *Building of Cultures* (see n. 36); Nordenskiöld, "Origin of the Indian Civilizations," 45–6; and Herbert W.

Krieger, "Indian Cultures of Northeastern South America," *Smithsonian Institution, Annual Report 1934* (1935): 401–21.

122. See, for example, Pierre Honoré, *In Quest of the White God* (New York: G. P. Putnam's, 1964), 194, 198; and Wolfgang Marschall, *Transpazifische Kulturbeziehungen: Studien zu iher Geschichte* (Munich: Klaus Renner, 1972), 135–43.

123. See, for example, Crawford, "Peruvian Fabrics," 153 (see n. 17); Steward, "South American Cultures," 744 (see n. 89); and Pablo Martínez del Río, *Los orígenes americanos* (Mexico City: A. V. Chavez, 1943).

124. Bühler, "Origin and Extent of the Ikat Technique," 1607 (see n. 50).

125. See Burger, *Chavín*, 27–8; and Michael E. Moseley, *The Incas and Their Ancestors: The Archaeology of Peru* (London: Thames and Hudson, 1992), 110–12, 116–17.

126. See Terence Grieder, "Fiber Arts," in *La Galgada: A Preceramic Culture in Transition*, ed. Terence Grieder et al. (Austin: University of Texas Press, 1988), 181.

127. Moseley, *Incas and Their Ancestors*, 157–8; see Burger, *Chavín*, 201.

128. See Luis Guillermo Lumbreras, "Textiles in Ancient Peru," in *Textile Art of Peru*, ed. Reid, 19 (see n. 20).

129. See my "Pre-Columbian Transoceanic Contacts," 354–5.

130. Burger, *Chavín*, 222.

131. See, for example, my "Dyestuffs," 35–6. Joseph B. Mahan has gone so far as to say that "it is beyond doubt that for more than a thousand years sailors from the Indus were to be seen throughout most of the inhabited world," colonizing widely (see Joseph B. Mahan, *The Secret: America in World History before Columbus* [Columbus, Ga.: J. B. Mahan, 1983], 188–91).

132. See Bridget Allchin and Raymond Allchin, *The Rise of Civilization in India and Pakistan* (Cambridge: Cambridge University Press, 1982), 191.

133. Cooper, Gillow, and Dawson, *Arts and Crafts of India*, 89 (see n. 44).

134. See Peter Muller and Raghubir Singh, "Kerala, Jewel of India's Malabar Coast," *National Geographic* 173/5 (1988): 597, 609.

135. Ruth Barnes, *Indian Block-Printed Cotton Fragments in the Kelsey Museum, The University of Michigan* (Ann Arbor: University of Michigan, 1993), 9–10.

136. Cooper, Gillow, and Barnard, *Arts and Crafts of India,* 91.

137. See Grey, "*Sarasa* and *Patola*," 49, 51 (see n. 41).

138. See F. R. Allchin, *The Archaeology of Early Historic South Asia* (Cambridge: Cambridge University Press, 1995), 141.

139. See my "Dyestuffs," 31. On Harappan overseas trade, see S. R. Rao, *Lothal: A Harappan Port Town* (New Delhi: Archaeological Survey of India, 1985), 685–8; compare Thor Heyerdahl, *The Maldive Mystery* (London: George Allen & Unwin, 1986), 294–5.

140. Junius B. Bird, "Fibers and Spinning Procedures in the Andean Area," in *Junius B. Bird Conference, 1984,* 15.

141. See Dixon, *Building of Cultures,* 202.

142. See my "Pre-Columbian Transoceanic Contacts," 354–5.

143. See Honoré, *In Quest of the White God,* 194, 198; Marschall, *Tranzpasifische Kulturbeziehungen,* 135–43; and Tolstoy, "Transoceanic Diffusion," 131 (see n. 32).

144. Crawford, "Peruvian Fabrics," 154.

145. See Bühler, "Origin and Extent of the Ikat Technique," 1607.

146. See my "Pre-Columbian Transoceanic Contacts," 374–81.

147. See my "Malaysia and Tropical America: Some Racial, Cultural, and Ethnobotanical Comparisons," *Congreso Internacional de Americanistas, Actas y Memorias* 37/4 (1968): 133–77; my "The Development and Distribution of the Blowgun," *Annals of the Association of American Geographers* 60/4 (1970): 662–88; and my "Further Information on the Geography of the Blowgun and Its Implications for Early Transoceanic Contacts," *Annals of the Association of American Geographers* 81/1 (1991): 89–102.

148. King, "Possible Indonesian or Southeast Asian Influences" (see n. 18).

149. See my "Pre-Columbian Transoceanic Contacts," 360–2; and Tolstoy, "Transoceanic Diffusion," 133–5.

150. Michele Pirazzoli-T'Serstevens, "The Bronze Drums of Shizhai shan: Their Social and Ritual Significance," in *Early South East Asia: Essays in Archaeology, History and Historical Geography*, ed. R. B. Smith and W. Watson (New York: Oxford University Press, 1979), 126–7.

151. See, for example, Kunz Dittmer, *Etnología general: Formas y evolución de la cultura* (Mexico City: Fondo de Cultura Económica, 1960), 211, 221.

152. Larsen et al., *Dyer's Art*, 13, 15.

153. See ibid.

154. See Bühler, "Origin and Extent of the Ikat Technique," 1606; and his "Introduction," 14 (see n. 61).

155. See my "Pre-Columbian Transoceanic Contacts"; Eugene R. Fingerhut, *Explorers of Pre-Columbian America? The Diffusionist-Inventionist Controversy*, 2nd ed. (Claremont, Calif.: Regina Books, 1996); and John L. Sorenson and Martin H. Raish, *Pre-Columbian Contact with the Americas across the Oceans: An Annotated Bibliography*, 2nd ed., 2 vols. (Provo, Utah: Research Press, 1996).

CHAPTER 11

PRE-COLUMBIAN AMERICAN SUNFLOWER AND MAIZE IMAGES IN INDIAN TEMPLES: EVIDENCE OF CONTACT BETWEEN CIVILIZATIONS IN INDIA AND AMERICA

Carl L. Johannessen

Sculptured representations of sunflower heads and maize ears are found in ancient temples in India. These images relate to the Lord Siva and to Hindu sun worship and date from seven hundred to thirteen hundred years ago. The fact that these crops were domesticated only in America several thousand years earlier suggests that people were able to sail far enough to transport cultural items across the world's oceans, perhaps both the Atlantic and the Pacific.

The conventional belief system of many historians, anthropologists, and geographers holds that the high civilizations in the New World (such as the pre-Inca, Inca, Olmec, Maya, Toltec, and Aztec) developed without any significant contact with or transfer of cultural traits from the Old World.[1] However,

Carl L. Johannessen is emeritus professor of geography at the University of Oregon.

ample field evidence of pre-Columbian cultural diffusion between the Neotropics and the Old World suggests a definite
need to reconsider that belief. The diffusion hypothesis has
been presented in multiple forms by many scholars.[2] For example, Betty J. Meggers, in her most recently published proposal
for determining the presence or absence of cultural diffusion,
points out that the chromosomes of living plant tissue that have
been modified in the New World provide solid evidence for
significant contact when those crops show up in Asia.[3] Such
crops display the rational characteristics identified by Meggers
as indicating diffusion. In the case of maize and sunflowers, it
does not matter where they came from; rather, the important
point is that these wild plants certainly were greatly changed by
farmers in the Americas and taken to Asia in that changed state
at an early date. Data presented in this chapter support a hypothesis that transoceanic voyagers carried American domesticated plants to India before the time of Columbus.

This study draws on evidence from temple carvings in India
that depict the American crop plants maize (*Zea mays* L.) and
sunflowers (*Helianthus annuus* L.). I have directly observed these
crops and ancient sculptures of them, studied many photographs
and literature citations, and interviewed epigraphers and archaeologists to test the diffusion hypothesis. In addition, I have
carefully considered counterindications to diffusion. The fact
that the conclusions of hundreds of other authors[4] who have
written on the general topic of diffusion have been rejected one
by one by traditional professionals continues to stimulate the
search for incontrovertible biological evidence that would be
impossible to be "independently invented" on the other continent an ocean away. This study shows that the highly detailed
stone images of sunflower and maize in Indian temple carvings
form a synergistic matrix in time and place that indicates that

in this case diffusion across the oceans was highly probable in pre-Columbian times.

Evidence of Diffusion

The morphology of the crop plants represented in India's temple art is quite detailed. Indian temple complexes often are composed of buildings constructed of polymorphic stone blocks, and temples and walls in India, the eastern Mediterranean, the Maldives, Easter Island, and especially Peru display essentially the same external design of construction. Both New and Old World temples were used in the worship of the sun. The maize images and polymorphic-block temple form in India may have been related to Peru, but the sunflowers may have come from northwestern Mexico to the southeastern United States.

The genus of the sunflower is American and includes between sixty-eight and several hundred species (according to different authors). It has no wild representatives in any early Asian biota from which an Asian sunflower could have evolved.[5] No bird can fly across the Atlantic or Pacific Oceans carrying sunflower seeds in a viable condition in or on its body, and sunflower seeds cannot float even a short time in ocean water without being eaten or spoiled by the salt. The cultivated sunflower appears to have come from the central United States area, from where it spread widely. The question of how far it spread in pre-Columbian times may be more difficult to determine. For example, according to Oakes Ames, eighteenth-century Swedish botanist Carolus Linnaeus relegated sunflowers to Mexico and Peru,[6] and in 1976 Charles B. Heiser Jr. reported that many other scientists over the last couple of centuries believed that sunflowers were more widely spread in the Americas than he

claimed was actually the case.[7] Apparently, none of the authorities recognized that transoceanic dispersal had occurred. I will
return to this point later in this report. The sunflower was domesticated in eastern North America over fifteen hundred years
ago. Space does not allow a full development of the question,
but ultimately the possible sources of *Helianthus* should be examined closely.

Sunflowers and Solar Calendric Dating

Now that references to the sunflower in the early religious
texts of India[8] appear to be verified by the flower's use in temple
architecture, more concrete examples and study are needed to
determine the broader significance of the presence of sunflowers
(*surya kanti* in Sanskrit) in early Hindu sun worship. To date,
little has been written about carvings depicting sunflowers in
southern India; it is as if the art historians have not differenti-
ated the sunflower from the lotus (*padma* in Sanskrit), except
for Thor Heyerdahl's report of finding carvings of ancient sunflowers in the Maldive Islands southwest of India.[9] The
Heyerdahl sunflower, however, may be a stylized symbol of the
sun instead of a sunflower, because this sunflower consists of only
three straight parallel lines radiating horizontally from a central
circle (as far as I can find), as opposed to a series of petals radiating all the way around a circle, representing a sunflower head.

Because young sunflower heads turn early in the day to face
the sun, the sunflower was an appropriate symbol for sunrise or
sun worship because it integrated ritual elements important to
the priests of Lord Siva: the horizon, the sunflower itself, Nandi
(a statue of the bull, transport vehicle of Siva), and the Siva
Lingam (a statue of the reproductive essence of Siva), which
was placed deep inside the temple where its alignment provided
a propitious observation point for the equinoxes. In India I first

encountered maize and sunflower representations (the latter associated with dawn or sunset) in the Keshava Temple at Somnathpur, Karnataka. I found a further example inside the Keshava Temple at Halebid, Karnataka, where due east of the Siva Lingam a Nandi figure had a sunflower carved on each side of its head. Subsequently, I observed multiple sunflower carvings in temples with different relationships to the solar calendar.

The sunflower identified in the carving over Nandi's ear in the temple at Halebid has (1) seventeen ray (petal) flowers carved so that every second petal is overlapped, (2) a large diameter, (3) a very gently rounded seed head in the center of the flower, and (4) a narrow, raised ring just inside the ray flowers that clearly represents the stigmas, styles, and stamens of the first florets that will develop the first mature seeds at the outside of the seed head in real sunflowers. These florets develop within a day or two of the unfolding of the ray flowers.

At Halebid during the equinox, a significant universal date for priestly astronomers, the dawn sun shines over a low-relief, distant horizon, past the notch between the left horn of Nandi and the sun-seeking sunflower positioned below it and above the ear, and in through the temple until it finally illuminates the Siva Lingam at the center of the inner *sanctum-sanctorum.* The sculptured sunflower is 16 centimeters across, its ray flowers 3.5 to 3.75 centimeters long. A central disk is 7 centimeters across, and the ridge ring just inside the ray flowers is 1 centimeter in width. Some present-day sunflowers in India have approximately the same relationship of size and shape (see fig. 1).

It might be suggested that another flower is represented here, but the large, gently domed seed head shown is not characteristic of the small-centered lotus flower (*Nelumbo* sp.) or the water lily *(Nymphaea),* and the lotus blossoms have been sculpted in a shape quite different from the sunflower. Normally the lotus symbol in these temples has two and sometimes three rows of petals, and each outer row is longer than the inner row. Its seed head is also proportionately smaller than the sunflower and regularly has no raised ring on the seed head. In both species the petals tend to alternate, with full petals overlapping the tips of petals of the same length. Rarely are the characteristics of each species shared, such as a ring on the lotus flower; the majority of the distributions leave no doubt of the species involved. In any case, sunflowers were placed where solar light was ritually significant for the worshipers.

Fig. 1. *Upper left:* Sunflower above the left ear and below the horn of Nandi, the bull, forming a notch through which the dawn light illuminates the Siva Lingam inside the temple on the equinox (Halebid, Karnataka, India). *Lower right:* A blooming sunflower. Note the ray flowers and the ring of disc florets. All photographs courtesy Carl L. Johannessen.

In at least five locations in India the sunflower is associated with Siva's bull, Nandi. The Hindu priests at these sites are aware that Nandi is located where the dawn's rays will pass over the bull figure at two periods during the year and illuminate the Siva Lingam inside the *sanctum-sanctorum* of the temple for a few minutes at dawn on only a few of these days.

At the Amruthteshvara Temple in the town of Amruthapura, Karnataka, the dawn sun rays pass between Nandi's two horns to illuminate the Siva Lingam on the eighth of February each year. Here, however, the sunflowers on Nandi that are carved just under the horns and above the ears do not protrude from the sides of the head (see fig. 2), so there is no major ear/sunflower notch for dawn sunlight as on the Nandi figure at Halebid. At Amruthteshvara the Nandi figure is oriented so that dawn light shines between Nandi's horns. Thus it is obvious that the sunflower is purposefully placed on the sculpted image in relation to the solar phenomena being observed or commemorated. In the Amruthteshvara Temple the azimuthal bearing of the gap between the temple's central colonnade provides barrier controls for the entry of the dawn sunlight. This colonnade is oriented

Fig. 2. Sunflower images on the Nandi figure at the Amruthteshvara Temple in Amruthapura, Karnataka, are carved on the sides of the head, below the horn and above the ear, as the sunflower shown here. Due to the azimuthal orientation of the temple, on 5–12 February dawn sunlight passes over and between the horns to illuminate parts of the Siva Lingam in the interior of the temple.

twenty to twenty-three degrees south of due east. The orientation of this temple allows light to enter from 5 to 12 February. The solar significance of the central date of 8 February is that it is halfway between the winter solstice and the spring equinox.[10]

Just 240 kilometers east of Amruthteshvara, at Bangalore, Karnataka, the incredibly complex cave temple called Sri Gave Ganadeshvara demonstrates the concern in ancient Hindu culture for obtaining solar calendric dating. The underground granite cave is cut to form a temple and maze into which the sunset rays enter only by passing over the top of a set of buildings, across a roadway, through a three-meter-high arch perched atop a boundary wall of the temple (the arch is designed only for the passage of light, not people or animals; see fig. 3), across the entryway of an open compound, through a window, across an outer room, through another window, across the main meeting room in front of Nandi, over Nandi's horns, through a doorway that has a sunflower carved on the first doorsill, and finally through a small anteroom and across another sill with a lotus carved on it. The rays then illuminate the Siva Lingam inside the inner sanctum on the evening of a single day, 14 January (marking approximately one-fourth of the period between winter solstice and spring equinox), to start the *Makrama Sankramana* (or *Makra Sankrante*) week of ceremonies. Another distinct lotus image, with its multiple rings of petals, is carved on the doorsill of the entrance to the main worship room and serves as a comparison to the sunflower on the other sill. The lotuses on the sills have relatively long petals and a very small, flat, circular center without the outer raised ring. The sunflower on the inner sill, however, has much shorter petals and a large, smooth, slightly mounded circular center with the small, raised ring between the central disc and the ray flowers.

Fig. 3. Arch that allows sunset light on the equinoxes to shine across the front of the Sri Gave Ganadeshvara Temple. This arch also permits sunset light to enter the temple on 14 January and to shine across Nandi, the bull, across a doorway threshold with a bas-relief of a sunflower, and then across another threshold with a bas-relief of a lotus flower before illuminating the Siva statue. All this is carved in granite. Bangalore, Karnataka, India.

A bearing of approximately nineteen degrees south of due west allows the near-sunset sunlight on 14 January at about 4:30 to 5:00 to descend more than three meters below the entrance walkway and down into the cave temple. The cessation of sunlight inside the cave signals the end of the opening ceremony as well as the beginning and, a week later, the ending of *Makrama Sankramana,* perhaps the most important Hindu religious period of the year in this part of southern India.

These complex architectural alignments obviously betoken the high degree to which the sunflower has been integrated into the ritual configuration of the Siva cult. It would be absurd to suppose that this association of flower, calendric sun angle, and temple architecture could have been achieved in less time than many centuries.

In southern India small Nandis with a sunflower on each side of the head or on the forehead have been found oriented to the sun in front of Siva Lingams at the following locations: the Virupaksha Temple in Bhatkal, Karnataka; the museum of Halebid; Bhagavatti (near Karwar), Karnataka;[11] and in a few other places in Karnataka.

The aforementioned giant arch on the temple wall at Sri Gave Ganadeshvara has another relation to the sunflower. At dusk on the equinoxes, the cusp on the uppermost design of the arch allows light to shine along the front of the temple and onto a large sunflower image sculpted and painted on the west-facing courtyard wall overlooking the temple (see fig. 3). This flower, located due east of the center of the arch, has a large, smooth center (see fig. 4). The surrounding ring represents the flower's stigmas, styles, and stamens. In addition, a single set of petals outside the ring allows us to classify the flower as a sunflower facing sunset.

The very large "equinox" Nandi in the temple at Halebid is highly distinctive because it is the only one known to have several sunflowers under the tail. Each small flower is seven centimeters in diameter and is carved on each side of the stone support for the bull's tail (see fig. 5). According to the priests, on the equinox six of the seven sunflowers tend to be in the shadow of the tail above them, whereas for a couple of days before and after the equinox they are a bit illuminated by the sun on either the north or south side, depending on whether it is spring or autumn. A few days before the solstices, the dawn lights the sunflowers entirely on the north or south side of the tail, depending on whether it is the winter or summer solstice. Thus, on the basis of this phenomenon the Hindu priests of the Keshava Temple at Halebid could know, a few days in advance, how close the dawn sun was to the equinox or solstice date. This knowledge became critical in determining the actual day of the equinox in the event of cloudy weather that obscured dawn's light on the equinox.

Fig. 4. This sunflower on a courtyard wall in line with the front of the temple in figure 3 is illuminated by equinox sunlight. Sri Gave Ganadeshvara Temple, Bangalore, Karnataka, India.

In the Mallikarjuna Temple at Pattadakal, Karnataka State, a representation of a dried, mature sunflower seed head is carved on a column in extended bas-relief. An Indian parrot is perched on the edge of the seed head as if it has just eaten the missing sunflower seeds on the edge of the seed head and is about to eat more seeds (see fig. 6). The bottom of dried sunflower heads indent as they dry out, as shown in figure 6, although the design may be somewhat stylized for sculpturing purposes.

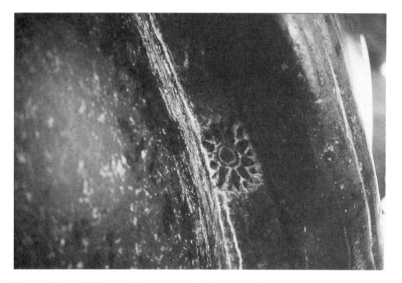

Fig. 5. One of the sunflowers under the tail of the Nandi figure in the Keshava Temple at Halebid (see fig. 1). These sunflowers are almost entirely in the shadow of the tail on the equinoxes but entirely illuminated on the north or south side of the tail at the respectively appropriate solstices, thereby providing a vernier for estimating some of the critical solar dates on the calendar.

In sun temples (those with special solar orientation) such as those found in Ellora and in the Ajanta cave complexes of temples in Maharashtra State, the sunflower design appears in about one in ten of the plaques in the sculptured ceilings. The square-shaped sunflower plaques are interspersed with plaques of lotus of similar shape. These images are in ceiling frescoes considered to have been made more than two thousand years ago. The flowers are somewhat inconsistent in design, but those that are sunflowerlike have the ring surrounding the seed head and only one set of petals. This clearly indicates that the sculptors' model for the sunflower was picked only a day after the sunflower opened. (I have carefully observed this ring phenomenon on sunflowers on my farm in Oregon.)

Fig. 6. In the eleventh-century Mallikarjuna Temple in Pattadakal, Karnataka, an Indian parrot perches on the edge of a dried and mature sunflower disc. A few seeds are missing from the edge of the flower, as if the bird had eaten them.

Fig. 7. Two sunflower images below the skirt and near the ankles of the Maize god in the Keshava Temple in Somnathpur, Karnataka, appear at the horizon level of the sculpture, as if representing the dawn and sunset. Perhaps these were the times for presenting offerings to the standing images of the gods and goddesses holding maize.

Dr. Madhav N. Katti, chief epigrapher at the Indian Archaeological Survey, helped in the discovery of sunflowers at the feet of the sculptured stone goddesses at Somnathpur. These several sunflower images at ground level may indicate the proper time of making offerings of corn (maize) at the many Hoysala dynasty (A.D. 1000–1268) temples that use the symbol. Figures 7 and 8 illustrate the appearance of these sunflower images.

Fig. 8. Detail of a sunflower at the feet of a stone goddess.

Literary evidence has been interpreted as supporting the identification of sunflowers in these temples. Dr. Katti's colleague, Dr. Shitala P. Tewari, showed my group his translations of the Sanskrit term *ashtapuspika*, which literally means "eight flowers" and can also refer to eight (or multiples of eight) parted flowers. He acknowledges that at least one of the translations for *ashtapuspika* in the religious literature is "sunflower," now commonly called *surya kanti* ("sun flower," that flower attracted to the sun).[12] Furthermore, the Tagare group's translation of the fifth-century *Bagavata Purana* interprets the Sanskrit word *arka* to mean "the sun plant" (sunflower) or "sun."[13]

None of the authors who have recently published on the cpDNA analysis of *Helianthus annuus* have recognized that the location of the plots of Chinese sunflower DNA lie on the graph beyond the bounds of what would normally be considered to be the same population source.[14] In the American distributions of sunflower DNA, the separation of the New World wild and domesticated sunflowers is shown to be so different from the Chinese (Russian and Turkish) sunflower DNA that this difference should have called into question the assumptions concerning the antiquity of races of sunflowers in Asia, but apparently this important point has been overlooked. If, as is indicated by the findings in this paper, sunflowers were in the Old World—especially in China and India—for more than one or two millennia, then we might expect some reasonable amount of genetic drift to have occurred. We do in fact find evidence of genetic drift in their DNA distributions: the seed cases of the sunflower fruits in China are significantly longer than those in most of the materials from early North American forms. This difference in the Chinese material can easily be hypothesized as being the result of the Chinese having selected for long seed cases, whereas the North American peoples may have been selecting for more seeds, more oil, more dye, different color, and so on. This evidence supports my postulation that significantly early cultural contact occurred between the New World and the Asian mainland, that this accounts for the presence of sunflowers in Asia in pre-Columbian times, and that once there the crop spread widely.

In summary, to be viable upon arrival in India, sunflower seeds had to have been carried across the sea in a dry place, perhaps stored on ships as long-term rations for voyaging. A complex set of iconographic data demonstrates that priests, planners, and artists engaged in constructing and utilizing the many sun temples in Karnataka State had live specimens of sunflowers available. These people incorporated the unique sun-seeking behavior of sunflowers purposefully into the Siva cult and its architecture no later than the tenth century and probably long before.

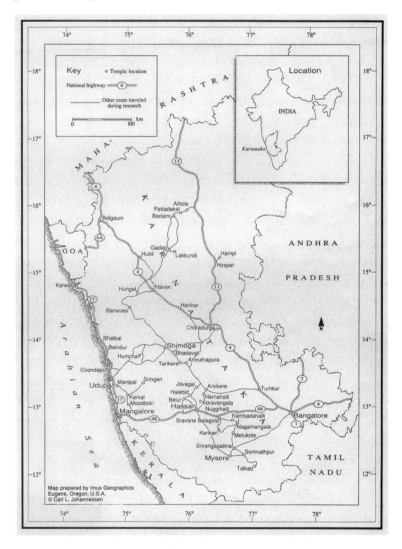

Fig. 9. Map of sites in Karnataka where the author conducted research on maize and sunflower sculpture commonly found in Indian temples.

Maize

The discoveries of ancient, excellently carved stone sculptures of American maize (*Zea mays* L., the same types grown in America one thousand years ago) in India in most, if not all, of sixty Hoysala dynasty temples are now well documented.[15] The evidence for pre-Columbian maize in Europe, Africa, and China has also been published.[16] However, despite the research demonstrating the presence of maize in sixth- to thirteenth-century temples at Amruthapura, Arsikere, Badami, Belur, Baindoor, Halebid, Harnahalli, Javagal, Nuggihalli, Somnathpur, Sravana Belagola, and sixty other temple sites in Karnataka (see fig. 9), many ethnobiologists have assumed that maize could not be a valid interpretation. Some who disagree have argued that the maize sculptures actually represent pomegranates (see fig. 10), upside-down cornucopia, or silk purses with cowry shells or pearls stitched on. However, the maize ears clearly do not have the placentas of the pomegranate, and the kernels do not have the proper shape and arrangement to be anything but maize.

The precise, intricate morphology of the sculpted ears normally shows the kernels arranged in pairs, with two kernels per cupule (see fig. 11). Just as in the natural world, this pairing is not always regular, and occasional shifts are found in the arrangement of the kernels. In the temple art the rows of kernels may be straight (see fig. 12), gently spiraling (see fig. 13), tightly spiraling or tessellated at the base (see fig. 14) or tip only, or tessellated throughout.

When the ears are shown in the husk, they are sometimes smooth, as if the silks had been pulled off, or they sometimes have the silks symbolized as an etched pair of curls on the husk (see fig. 15). Three times or more the curl of silk has subcurls on the larger curl, just the way one finds it in real maize ears when the ears still have their husks. Geographer Greg Howard suggests that this sculptural detail of silk on the ears is compelling

Fig. 10. Example from northern India of a pomegranate representation in the hand of Kartikeya at the Hindu University Museum, Varanasi, Uttar Pradesh. This pomegranate bears no resemblance to a maize ear, despite claims to the contrary by one observer who apparently interprets all maize images in Indian temples to be pomegranates.

evidence for the presence of maize plants in India, the live ears of which were used as models in sculpture. Occasionally the kernels are pointed and imbricated, though normally they are rounded as most flint and flour-starch kernels are. The width-

Fig. 11. This detailed maize-ear image of twelfth- or thirteenth-century
workmanship features paired kernels, interlocking rows, and smaller
kernels at the tip. Channakeshava Temple, Harnahalli, Karnataka.

to-thickness ratios for the kernels in the images (1:1.0 to 1:2.0,
with the mode, or most frequent ratio, being 1:1.3) are approximately the same as in archaeological maize one thousand
years ago from the Americas.[17] The size of the kernels in nature
depends on their location on the ear and whether they have

been pollinated. In the sculptures, smaller kernels usually appear near the ear's tip, and what would be unfertilized kernels are carved as smooth surfaces at the tip. Unfertilized kernels sometimes occur when the silks fail to protrude from the husk on one side of the ear. A thirteenth-century sculptor depicted

Fig. 12. Parallel rows of kernels in this sculpted maize ear show double kernels per cupule in ranks that become smaller at the tip. Someswara Temple, Harnahalli, Karnataka.

that reality by sculpting a maize ear with two rows of mature kernels, four rows immature kernels, and a third of the husk removed to show all this.[18] Nothing but an actual ear of this shape could have inspired this sculptor to capture such details!

Fig. 13. This maize image with spiral rows is held by the Maize goddess from the Kedareshvara Temple in Halebid and is an example of hundreds of maize images visible in friezes surrounding Hindu and other temples constructed during the Hoysala dynasty (A.D. 1000–1268) in Karnataka.

In Temple Cave III at Badami, Karnataka, we find another example of realistic modeling. In one of the oldest (sixth century A.D.) carved maize ears discovered so far, a bit of the stem protrudes from the base of the ear because the ear is held horizontally in Vishnu's hand rather than held with the base in the palm of the hand, covering the stem, as in all other sculptures (see fig. 16). Moreover, in the sculptures of seven hundred to nine hundred years ago, the maize ears often have warped, bent tips (see fig. 17), a detail supported by the fact that in nature even at present the antique varieties of maize ears grow and dry that way 5 to 10 percent of the time.[19]

Fig. 14. Maize ear with parallel rows at tip and tessellate arrangement of kernels on the right and front of the ear near the base, with parallel rows continuing to the bottom of the ear on the left side. Thirteenth century (A.D. 1286), Keshava Temple, Somnathpur, Karnataka.

In a 1990 study John Doebley was convinced that maize was not in Europe before the time of Columbus,[20] but he overlooked Carl O. Sauer's earlier study that proves that maize was in Italy (in Milan and Lombardy) and Spain (in Granada) before 1492.[21] Recent scholarship continues to provide evidence

Fig. 15. Maize ear in its husk with silk hanging in a curl from the tip. Note that the same *mudra* (hand position) is typically used with all maize images. Twelfth or thirteenth century, Javagal, Karnataka.

supporting the presence of maize in the Old World. Gunnar Thompson's 1997 study expands greatly on the evidence for the early presence of maize in the Mediterranean region. His illustration of a ceramic sculptural representation of maize in China is also a modestly good example of maize in the Old World, showing layers of husks attached to the base of the ear; but it is idiosyncratic and is not an absolutely identifiable reproduction.[22] In England's Rosslyn Chapel is a sculpted motif, made decades before Columbus, featuring what appears to be maize, though this motif lacks the intricate detail and perfection of the

Fig. 16. Maize ear with a stalk coming out of the bottom end (on left) and held in Vishnu's hand. Sixth century, Cave Temple III, Badami, Karnataka.

stone carvings found in Hoysala dynasty temples.[23] From what I have seen, the sculptures of India's Hoysala dynasty come closer than Aztec sculptures in the New World come to representing maize.

Fig. 17. Bent-tipped maize ears like this one, typical of certain ancient types and characteristic of some modern maizes, are frequently found in Hoysala temples of the eleventh through thirteenth centuries. Halebid, Karnataka.

The intricacy and completeness of maize-ear morphology represented in India's stone images leads inevitably to the conclusion that the sculptors had real models of maize ears on hand. Actual maize plants must have been growing in India.

It follows that maize must have been introduced into India from America, for virtually all botanists agree that it was native in America. Maize ears represented in the Hoysala temples often have characteristics similar to Peruvian maizes. Many of these Peruvian forms, which have relatively primitive characteristics typical of the ancient genetic maize variations pointed out by Zeven and Zhukovsky,[24] were taken from Peru to Central America and Mexico. Once there, they cross-pollinated with the original maizes of Mexico and Central America to create the races of maize we find there today. The frequency and distributions of the knobs that show on the stained chromosomes of maize in Peru and Central America can be explained by the acceptance of these translocations of South American forms of maize.[25]

The waxy-starch maize (*Zea certina* Collins) was a mutant in the Americas but was selected as a variety in Asia, similar to the way waxy wheat, barley, rice, foxtail millet, and sorghum had been selected for their consumption in Asia.[26]

Where is the gene pool of the early maize population that served the sculptors of India? Most likely it is in the fields of the Hill Tribes (the minority groups) of India. The search for the gene pool is in the future, as is the search for maize phytoliths under the one thousand-year-old buildings. In addition, the case for diffusion is strengthened when sculptures of American sunflowers and maize are found in India in buildings of the late Chalukyan culture (A.D. 1000–1200) that are homologous to distinctive buildings of cultures in the pre-Columbian Andes of South America of about the same age.

Polymorphic-Block and Massive-Stone Architecture

Early sun temples found in Karnataka State and in the eastern Mediterranean countries were built with massive polygonal stone blocks of approximately the same horizontal thickness throughout their length. The walls were built without mortar, but because of their stepped ends, the blocks interlock and tend to stay in place. Frequently in Karnataka's polymorphic-stone construction, walls surround or form the base of the temples, and the sun temples themselves are located in the same sacred complexes where we find the maize and sunflower sculptures of the Hoysala dynasty, which spanned the eleventh through the thirteenth centuries A.D. (see fig. 18). Some of these temples and some of their walls have essentially the same distinctive system of construction as that found in many pre-Inca and Inca temples, as well as in city walls, temples, and houses in the Andes from pre-Spanish times.[27] The most famous locations are near Cuzco, Peru, but this type of construction extends through many parts of the ancient realm of the Incas (see fig. 19).

Fig. 18. Polymorphic-block walls found at Sravanna Belagola, Karnataka, have protuberances or holes used for lifting.

Fig. 19. Polymorphic construction in Cuzco, Peru, resembles that in India with its use of "staples" but normally no mortar.

This construction involves the use of blocks of shaped stone. They do not necessarily have corners cut at ninety-degree angles, nor are their tops, bottoms, and end surfaces always parallel. The sides are parallel and similar in size, and the blocks are closely and intricately fitted together despite their lack of parallelism. No mortar was used on either continent with this type of construction. Frequently more than four surfaces touch because of the irregular shape of the blocks, which feature stair-step-like ends and many different angles. These large blocks commonly had either four protruding knobs or four small holes near the bottom of the sides that enabled them to be lifted (by ropes alone or by ropes with metal hooks) and maneuvered to fit with the blocks already on the rising wall. In both Peru and India the knobs at the bottom of the blocks, both inside and outside the building, were often left protruding. The masons doing the construction often did not retouch the surface of the walls after the stone units were supplied by the stone cutters and sculptors and put in place.

In Peru the masons who assembled the buildings sometimes ground the blocks together for a tighter fit, a detail I observed at the Temple of the Sun in Cuzco. The modestly sized blocks of a curved wall at the side of that temple apparently were swung by their knobs or hook holes into position for finish grinding using an A-frame. Each block was swung back and forth across the wall until the grinding motion created a convex surface on the bottom of the swinging block and a slightly concave surface on the top of the block already in the wall. Blocks were fitted together as they were stacked. So far I have not found this arcuate grinding used on the Indian subcontinent. In India the horizontal surfaces of the blocks appear to be flat, wherever I have been able to observe them. Modern stone masons in India always use iron chisels and hammers, and when shown photos of the South American work, they claim it would have been impossible to have cut granite in Peru on a large scale without iron chisels. Scientists need to think about that.

The construction system in both the New and the Old World incorporated bas-relief decorations on the sides of the walls, especially near the doorways of the polymorphic-block buildings. These ornaments included fish, snakes, turtles, or tenoned heads of other animals. The canons of construction allowed decorative carvings on door jambs and round, lathe-turned columns inside the temples, especially in India, but they are also reported near the coast in Peru.

In this type of polymorphic construction in Egypt, Greece, Anatolia, Spain, India, and the Andes, often the corner blocks and sometimes the wall blocks of the buildings are held together with metal bars. These bars, shaped like inverted staples or like *I*s and butterfly (abutting) triangles, lock into holes of the respective shapes and notches in the tops of the stone blocks. In India and in zones of high earthquake stress (in Peru, for example), iron, silver, bronze, and perhaps wood were used to make the fasteners that hold the mortarless blocks in place. Aspects of this general polymorphic construction are also found in slightly modified forms on Easter Island, in the Maldives, in the Indian Ocean, and in various other Old World cultural hearths.[28]

Peruvian features not found in the Old World are the beveled outer surfaces of the edge of the blocks on some Incan walls; the beveled, round corners; and the much larger blocks with curvilinear sides that were fitted smoothly together. It is possible that some of these specialized features were developed late in Inca times—too late to have been known to transoceanic travelers of an earlier day—or perhaps they have not been recognized in the Mediterranean area.

Conclusions

Aspects of ancient architecture in India and in the New World that exhibit a significant degree of correlation include (1) the polymorphic mode of construction at sites consecrated to sun worship and whose buildings have a solar orientation at dawn or dusk on specific dates, (2) animate decorations, (3) the metal clamping mechanisms that help hold those buildings together, and (4) especially the carvings of plants of American origin that were integrated into the local religious life and building decoration. This evidence compels us to see transoceanic contact and cultural diffusion, not independent invention, as the explanation.

The ability of Old and New World people to sail across the world's oceans is another major topic that has been amply demonstrated by several authors, although space does not permit its full documentation here.[29] According to these authors, the somewhat restricted fashions of rafts and ships in the New World are all represented in watercraft of the Old World, which are more diverse in size, shape, gear, and use. The literature cited demonstrates beyond question that transoceanic travel by rafts and ships was entirely feasible in periods of time that could account for the transmission of maize and the sunflower, which were surely used as models by the sculptors of the Karnataka State area.

The results of my personal investigation of sunflowers, maize, and building construction, in addition to my review of the bibliographic citations of many hundreds of other reports on diffusion (or its lack) assembled by John L. Sorenson and Martin H. Raish,[30] indicate contact between Asia and the Americas prior to European intrusion in A.D. 1492. The crop models of American sunflowers and maize ears for the sculpted stone images in India surely came from the Americas, most likely either Mexico, Central America, or the Andes, and perhaps Amazonia, where they were present many centuries ago. The polymorphic blocks used in several structures in India that exhibit these plants are similar to Peruvian stone structures and indicate significant contact between Asia and the Americas before A.D. 1000. It is time to recognize that many cultural traits and biological organisms diffused across the ocean earlier than the Iberian discoveries and transfers in the late fifteenth and sixteenth centuries.

Notes

I thank the National Science Foundation for helping me and Anne Z. Parker initiate this study on maize in the Himalayas. The following institutions and people are deeply appreciated for assisting in the funding of the seven other maize research trips for this report on artifacts in southern India: The Foundation for Ancient Research and Mormon Studies at Brigham Young University, the University of Oregon Research Services and the University of Oregon Foundation, Caterpillar Tractor Company, Brookhurst Mill, Alpine Map Company, Jerry's Home Improvement Center, Furrow Building Materials Company, Northrup Seed Company, and the Charles A. Lily Company. I thank the following people for their financial support of the research trips and activities: Professor George Carter of Texas A&M University, Robert and Sharon Wilson, Gordon Swoffer, and Rob Lewis. Invaluable help in the field was provided by Dr. Anne Z. Parker, Doris S. Johannessen, Barbara Northrup, Grace Schneiders, S. G. Samak, and Bruce and Laura Johannessen. Thanks also to the Archaeological Survey of India, particularly Drs. Mahadev N. Katti, C. Margabandhu, J. C. Joshi, K. V. Ramesh, K. P. Poonacha, and Shitala P. Tewari; university professors T. Dayananda Patel, P. D. Mahadev, Joginder Singh, Hugh Iltis, John L. Sorenson; students Greg Howard, K. Venkatesh, L. Ravi, Ananda Kumar, and Casey Dale; and a host of other helpful people. I am very grateful to David Imus of Imus Geographics for creating the map in figure 9.

1. See Gordon D. Gibson, "The Probability of Numerous Independent Inventions," *American Anthropologist* 50 (1948): 362–4; David M. Pendergast, "Further Data on Pacific Coast Fired Clay Figurines," *American Antiquity* 23 (1957): 178–80; John H. Rowe, "Diffusionism and Archaeology," *American Antiquity* 31 (1966): 334–7; Barbara Pickersgill, "Cultivated Plants as Evidence for Cultural Contacts," *American Antiquity* 37 (1972): 97–104; Zena Pearlstone, "Sujang: A Stirrup Spout Vessel from Nigeria," *American Antiquity* 38/4 (1973): 482–6; Juan Comas, *Origen de las culturas precolombinas* (Mexico: Universidad Autónoma de México, Instituto de Investigaciones Antropológicas, 1975), 175; Frank J. Frost, "Voyages of the Imagination," *Archaeology* 46/2 (1993): 44–51; O. Silva

384   *Carl L. Johannessen*

Galdames, *Prehistoria de América,* 3rd ed. (Santiago, Chile: Editorial
Universitaria, 1977); George Kubler, *The Art and Architecture of An-
cient America: The Mexican, Maya and Andean Peoples,* 3rd ed. (Baltimore: Penguin, 1984); Paul C. Mangelsdorf and Douglas L. Oliver,
"Whence Came Maize to Asia?" *Harvard University Botanical Mu-
seum Leaflets* 14/10 (1951): 263–91; Alan J. Osborn, "Limitations of
the Diffusionist Approach: Evolutionary Ecology and Shell-Tempered
Ceramics," in *The Transfer and Transformation of Ideas and Material
Culture,* ed. Peter J. Hugill and D. Bruce Dickson (College Station:
Texas A&M University Press, 1988), 23–44; John Doebley, "Molecu-
lar Evidence and the Evolution of Maize," in *New Perspectives on the
Origin and Evolution of New World Domesticated Plants,* ed. Peter K.
Bretting, (Lawrence, Kans.: Allen Press, 1990), 6–27 (supplement to
Economic Botany 44/3 [1990]); and Jeffrey Quilter et al., "Subsis-
tence Economy of El Paraíso, an Early Peruvian Site," *Science* 251
(January 1991): 277–83.
    2. See George F. Carter, "Pre-Columbian Chickens in America,"
in *Man across the Sea: Problems of Pre-Columbian Contacts,* ed.
Carroll L. Riley et al. (Austin: University of Texas Press, 1971), 178–
218; George F. Carter, "Domesticates as Artifacts," in *The Human
Mirror: Material and Spatial Images of Man,* ed. Miles Richardson
(Baton Rouge: Louisiana State Press, 1974), 201–30; Eugene R.
Fingerhut, *Explorers of Pre-Columbian America? The Diffusionist-
Inventionist Controversy* (Claremont, Calif.: Regina Books, 1994);
James A. Ford, *A Comparison of Formative Cultures in the Americas:
Diffusion or the Psychotic Unity of Man* (Washington, D.C.: Smith-
sonian Institution, 1969), 1–211, especially 188–94; Stephen C.
Jett, "Diffusion versus Independent Development: The Bases of
Controversy," in *Man across the Sea,* ed. Riley et al., 5–53; Carl L.
Johannessen, "Folk Medicine Uses of Melanotic Asiatic Chickens as
Evidence of Early Diffusion to the New World," *Social Science and
Medicine* 15 (1981): 427–34; Carl L. Johannessen, "Melanotic
Chicken Use and Chinese Traits in Guatemala," *Revista de Historia
de América* 93 (1982): 73–89; Carl L. Johannessen and Anne Z.
Parker, "Maize Ears Sculpted in Twelfth and Thirteenth Century

A.D. India as Indicators of Pre-Columbian Diffusion," *Economic Botany* 43 (1989): 164–80; John L. Sorenson and Martin H. Raish, *Pre-Columbian Contact with the Americas across the Oceans: An Annotated Bibliography,* 2 vols. (Provo, Utah: Research Press, 1990); C. R. Stonor and Edgar Anderson, "Maize among the Hill Peoples of Assam," *Annals of the Missouri Botanical Garden* 36 (1949): 355–404; Gunnar Thompson, *American Discovery: Our Multicultural Heritage* (Seattle: Argonauts Misty Isle Press, 1994); Gunnar Thompson, "Seeds of Paradise: Maize Diffusion before Columbus," *Ancient American* 19/20 (1997): 64–71.

3. See Betty J. Meggers, "The Transpacific Origin of Mesoamerican Civilization: A Preliminary Review of the Evidence and Its Theoretical Implications," *New England Antiquitities Research Association Journal* 31/1 (1997): 6–25.

4. For an exhaustive listing of the published works of these diffusionist authors, see Sorenson and Raish, *Pre-Columbian Contact.*

5. See Oakes Ames, *Economic Annuals and Human Cultures* (Cambridge, Mass.: Botanical Museum of Harvard University, 1939), 90; Edgar Anderson, *Plants, Man, and Life* (Berkeley: University of California Press, 1952), 164–74; Charles B. Heiser Jr., "The Origin and Development of the Cultivated Sunflower," *American Biology Teacher* 17 (1955): 161–7; Charles B. Heiser Jr., *The Sunflower* (Norman: University of Oklahoma, 1976), 32, 34, 35, 45, 110; Richard A. Yarnell, "Native Plant Husbandry North of Mexico," in *Origins of Agriculture,* ed. Charles A. Reed (The Hague: Mouton, 1977), 861–4; and A. C. Zeven and P. M. Zhukovsky, *Dictionary of Cultivated Plants and Their Centres of Diversity: Excluding Ornamentals, Forest Trees, and Lower Plants* (Wageningen, the Netherlands: Centre for Agricultural Publishing and Documentation, 1975), 130, 173–4.

6. See Ames, *Economic Annuals,* 90.

7. See Heiser, *Sunflower,* 50, 53–4.

8. See Shitala P. Tewari, *Contributions of Sanskrit Inscriptions to Lexicography* (Delhi, India: Agam Kala Prakashan, 1987); and Carl L. Johannessen and Anne Z. Parker, "American Crop Plants in Asia

prior to European Contact," *Yearbook 1988: Proceedings of the Conference of Latin American Geographers* 14 (1988): 14–19, especially p. 17.

9. See Thor Heyerdahl, *Early Man and the Ocean: A Search for the Beginnings of Navigation and Seaborne Civilizations* (Garden City, N. Y.: Doubleday, 1979), 67, 68, 84, 94, 108–9; and his *The Maldive Mystery* (Bethesda, Md.: Adler and Adler, 1986), 88 passim, 248–9.

10. This point was brought to my attention by Professor Fred Hirsch, a geographer in Oregon.

11. Here the Nandi figure is located outside without a roof, and the Siva Lingam stands in the ground.

12. See Tewari, *Sanskrit Inscriptions.*

13. See Johannessen and Parker, "American Crop Plants in Asia," 17.

14. See D. M. Airas and Loren H. Rieseberg, "Genetic Relationships among Domesticated and Wild Sunflower (*Helianthus annuus,* Asteraceae)," *Economic Botany* 49/3 (1995): 243–5; Loren H. Rieseberg and Gerald J. Seiler, "Molecular Evidence and the Origin and Development of the Domesticated Sunflower (*Helianthus annuus,* Asteraceae)," in *New Perspectives,* ed. Bretting, 83; and Peter K. Bretting, "New Perspectives on the Origin and Evolution of New World Domesticated Plants: Introduction," in *New Perspectives,* ed. Bretting, 3.

15. See my chapter "Maize Diffused to India before Columbus Came to America," in my *Across before Columbus* (*NEARA* [New England Antiquities Research Association], forthcoming); and Johannessen and Parker, "Maize Ears Sculpted in Twelfth and Thirteenth Century A.D. India," 165–74 (see n. 2). As illustrated in these two sources, Hoysala dynasty sculpture in India is, in accuracy of detail, equal to or better than the pottery in the early Americas. See Alan C. Lapiner, *Suns, Gods, and Saints* (New York: Andre Emmerich, 1969), fig. 36; and Julia Jones, *Art of Empire: The Inca of Peru* (New York: Museum of Art, 1964), figs. 58, 59. The majority of Indian sculptures show maize more accurately than the first European illustration of maize by Leonhart Fuchs in *De Historia Stirpium Com-*

mentarii Insignes (1542). Fuchs's illustration appears in Herbert G. Baker, *Plants and Civilization,* 2nd ed. (Belmont, Calif.: Wadsworth, 1970), 74.

16. See Carl O. Sauer, "Maize into Europe," *Akten des 34. Internationalen Amerikanisten Kongresses* (Vienna, 1960); reprinted in his *Seeds, Spades, Hearths, and Herds: The Domestication of Animals and Foodstuffs,* 2nd ed. (Cambridge, Mass.: M.I.T. Press, 1972), 147–67; M. D. W. Jeffreys, "Pre-Columbian Maize in the Philippines," *South African Journal of Science* 61 (1965): 5–10; M. D. W. Jeffreys, "Pre-Columbian Maize in Asia," in *Man across the Sea,* ed. Riley et al., 376–400; Tomasz Marszewski, "The Problem of the Introduction of 'Primitive' Maize into South-East Asia, Part II," *Folia Orientalia* 19 (1978): 127–63; and Edgar Anderson, *Plants, Man, and Life,* 139, 186 (see n. 5).

17. See Paul C. Mangelsdorf and C. E. Smith, "New Archaeological Evidence on Evolution in Maize," *Harvard University Botanical Museum Leaflets* 13 (1949): 213–47; and Johannessen and Parker, "Maize Ears Sculpted in Twelfth and Thirteenth Century A.D. India."

18. See Johannessen and Parker, "Maize Ears Sculpted in Twelfth and Thirteenth Century A.D. India," 172, fig. 12.

19. This tendency of some ears to develop bent tips can be viewed in the corn collection in the herbarium at the University of Wisconsin-Madison or in any other extensive collection that has not been selected against such morphology.

20. See John Doebley, "Molecular Evidence and the Evolution of Maize," 7 (see n. 1).

21. See Sauer, "Maize into Europe"; reprinted in his *Agricultural Origins and Dispersals: The Domestication of Animals and Foodstuffs* (Cambridge, Mass.: M.I.T. Press, 1969), 147–67, especially 156–7.

22. See Gunnar Thompson, "Seeds of Paradise," 64–6 (see n. 2).

23. See Andrew Sinclair, *The Sword and the Grail: Of the Grail and the Templars and a True Discovery of America* (New York, N.Y.: Crown, 1992), plate 23, bottom left, of the unpaginated illustration section.

24. See Zeven and Zhukovsky, *Dictionary of Cultivated Plants,* 150, 166–7 (see n. 4).

25. These knobs are described in Paul C. Mangelsdorf, *Corn: Its Origin, Evolution, and Improvement* (Cambridge: Harvard University Press, 1974), 28, 118–20.

26. See Zeven and Zhukovsky, *Dictionary of Cultivated Plants,* 33.

27. For detailed descriptions of this kind of construction in the New World, see George Bankes, *Peru before Pizarro* (Oxford: Phaidon, 1977), 127, 135, 185–95; Louis Baudin, *Daily Life in Peru under the Last Inca,* trans. Winifred Bradford (Oxford: Phaidon, 1977), 81, 96–7, 177; Hiram Bingham, "In the Wonderland of Peru," *National Geographic* 24/4 (April 1913): 416–18, 462–71, 488, 502–9, 529–30, 551; John Hemming, *Machu Picchu* (New York: Newsweek, 1981), 172, especially 23–32, 44–5, 60–1; Gérard Nicolini, *The Ancient Spaniards* (Farnsborough, Eng.: Saxon House, 1974), 92–3; J. Alden Mason, *The Ancient Civilizations of Peru* (Harmondsworth, Middlesex, England: Penguin, 1968), 144–8, 163–4; Thor Heyerdahl, *American Indians in the Pacific: The Theory behind the Kon-Tiki Expedition* (London: George Allen and Unwin, 1952); Arthur Posnansky, *Tiahuanacu: The Cradle of American Man,* trans. James F. Shearer (New York: J. J. Augustin, 1945); Jean-Pierre Protzen, *Inca Architecture and Construction at Ollantaytambo* (New York: Oxford University Press, 1993), 82–7, 222–37, 251–9; Ronald Wright, *Cut Stones and Crossroads: A Journey in the Two Worlds of Peru* (New York: Viking Press, 1984); and Luis E. Valcárcel and Pierre Verger (photographer), *Indians of Peru* (New York: Pocahontas Press, 1950), photos 1–6.

28. See Jean-Pierre Adam, *Roman Building: Materials and Techniques* (Bloomington: Indiana University Press, 1994), 48–58; Somers Clarke and Reginald Englebach, *Ancient Egyptian Masonry* (London: Oxford University Press, 1930), 96–116 (but these authors say Egyptians used thin mortar between blocks); Graziano Gasparini and Luise Margolies, *Inca Architecture,* trans. Patricia J. Lyon (Bloomington: Indiana University Press, 1980), 284–9, 324–32, figs. 316–24; Giuseppe Lugli, *La tecnica edilizia Romana, con partico-*

lare riguardo a Roma e Lazio, 2 vols. (Rome: G. Bardi, 1957), especially 2:i–xxii; Thor Heyerdahl, *Sea Routes to Polynesia* (Chicago: Rand McNally, 1968), 7–232, especially 160, 165–6, 190, 193, 195; Heyerdahl, *American Indians in the Pacific;* Heyerdahl, *Early Man and the Ocean* (see n. 8); Sindigi Rajasekhara, *Early Chalukya Art at Aihole* (New Delhi: Vikas, 1985); and Richard A. Tomlinson, *Greek Architecture,* ed. J. H. Betts (Bristol, Eng.: Bristol Classical Press, 1989), 22.

    29. See, for example, Edwin Doran Jr., "The Sailing Raft as a Great Tradition," in *Man across the Sea,* ed. Riley et al., 115–38; Clinton R. Edwards, *Aboriginal Watercraft on the Pacific Coast of South America* (Berkeley: University of California Press, 1965); Heyerdahl, *Kon-Tiki: Across the Pacific by Raft,* trans. F. H. Lyon (Chicago: Rand McNally, 1950), 408, fig. xvii; Thor Heyerdahl, "Voyage of Ra II," *National Geographic* 139/1 (1971): 44–71; Heyerdahl, *Early Man and the Ocean,* 20–5, 37, 204–15; Ling Shun-Shêng, "Formosan Sea-Going Raft and Its Origin in Ancient China," *Bulletin of the Institute of Ethnology* 1 (1956): 25–54; Betty J. Meggers, "Yes If by Land, No If by Sea: The Double Standard in Interpreting Cultural Similarities," *American Anthropologist* 78 (1976): 637–9; and James G. Nelson, "The Geography of the Balsa," *American Neptune* 21 (1961): 157–95.

    30. See Sorenson and Raish, *Pre-Columbian Contact* (see n. 2).

CHAPTER 12

DOUBLED, SEALED, WITNESSED DOCUMENTS: FROM THE ANCIENT WORLD TO THE BOOK OF MORMON

John W. Welch

A distinctive legal practice employed in Israel around 600 B.C. was the use of doubled, sealed, and witnessed documents to record the terms of various important legal transactions. These documents had two parts: one was left open for ready access, while the other was sealed up for later consultation by the parties or for the conclusive use of a judge in court. Is there any connection between the format of the Book of Mormon plates and this ancient legal practice, which spread widely throughout the eastern Mediterranean and into the Roman Empire?

My purpose is not to argue that the Book of Mormon plates were constructed in exactly the same fashion and in all respects as were these doubled, sealed documents from the Old World. Rather, it is to show that the basic concept of preserving important

John W. Welch, editor of BYU Studies *and Robert K. Thomas professor of law at Brigham Young University, is the founder of the Foundation for Ancient Research and Mormon Studies and is a member of its board of trustees.*

ancient documents by preparing them in two parts and then sealing one of the two was common throughout much of the ancient world, and thus to argue that this practice seems to have been known to Nephi and may well have influenced his prophetic expectations and statements about the final form of the Nephite records.

I have been intrigued by these ancient legal documents for several years. The hospitality of the Papyrological Institute at the University of Leiden shown to me in connection with the 1995 conference of the Society for the Study of Ancient Law made it possible to locate many otherwise obscure sources and complete the research for this paper. I hope, by this work, to express my collegial admiration and personal thanks to John L. Sorenson, whose keen ability to sense and explain the human and social ramifications of archaeological data has enriched my understanding of sacred texts, especially the Book of Mormon.

A Preexilic Biblical Legal Form

An intriguing Old Testament passage, Jeremiah 32:6–15, relates an event that occurred about 590 B.C. Pursuant to his right of redemption within the family and with prophetic fore-knowledge of the transaction, Jeremiah bought from his cousin a field located at Anathoth in the lands of Benjamin. His willingness to make this long-term investment was supportive of God's enduring promise that "houses and fields and vineyards shall be possessed again in this land" (Jeremiah 32:15), notwithstanding the prophecy that Jerusalem would soon fall to the invading Babylonians (see Jeremiah 32:3).

In order to memorialize his purchase as impressively and as permanently as possible, Jeremiah as purchaser drafted and executed not just a single document but a two-part deed. One part

of its text "was sealed according to the law *[mitzvah]* and custom *[huqqim]*," and the other part of the document "was open"
(Jeremiah 32:11; compare 32:14). Jeremiah signed this double
document and sealed it, as did several other people who witnessed the transaction and subscribed the text (see Jeremiah
32:10, 12). Moreover, in order to preserve this evidence of his
purchase, Jeremiah took his doubled, sealed document and, in
the presence of his witnesses, securely deposited it with both of
its parts in a clay jar, "that they may continue many days"
(Jeremiah 32:14). A slightly different version of this pericope is
found in the Septuagint (LXX) in Jeremiah 39:6–15.

Jeremiah's detailed account reflects many interesting legal
technicalities that were evidently customary in his day.[1] As John
Bright says of Jeremiah's text, "Technical legal terminology is
no doubt involved," even though the precise nature of the Hebrew text and some of its phrases cannot be ascertained.[2]

While Jeremiah 32:14 clearly points to some form of
double documentation, it is not clear whether the two parts of
that documentation were written on one piece of papyrus or
two. Jeremiah 32:14 has been confusing to some commentators
in this regard because it uses both the plural and the singular:
"Take these evidences *[sepharim]*, this evidence *[sepher]* of the
purchase, both which is sealed *[hatom]*, and this evidence
which is open *[galoi]*."

Likewise, while it would appear, both from what is known
about normal Israelite practices and also from the use of the
word *sepher*, that Jeremiah wrote his contract of conveyance on
parchment, papyrus, or leather, and not on a clay sherd,[3] it is
less clear what he means by *sepher* or *sepharim*. He calls the
document a *sepher*, which may mean a scroll, a letter, or any
other writing (see also LXX Jeremiah 39:10, *eis biblion*). Indeed, when Isaiah speaks of "a book that is sealed" (Isaiah

29:11), his word for book is also *sepher,* the same word that appears in both of Jeremiah's expressions, "book of the purchase" and "evidence of the purchase" (Jeremiah 32:12, 14).

While his document obviously deals with a transfer of title to the land, Jeremiah does not say anything about the content of the two parts of this document or how the texts of these two parts related to each other. Were their contents identical? Was one a copy or summary of the other? Or did they contain entirely different materials?

Jeremiah clearly relates that he "sealed" part of the documentation (Jeremiah 32:10; LXX Jeremiah 39:10, *esphragisamen*). Presumably he did this by rolling the document up and tying it with strings or strips of leather and then impressing his signet ring or other seal into a clay or wax fastener to keep the roll closed. The use of seal impressions by biblical personages is well attested during Jeremiah's day.[4] He also records that the witnesses "subscribed" the document (LXX Jeremiah 39:10, *diemarturamen marturas,* and 39:12, "wrote in the book of the purchase"), but it is unclear in what fashion they did so, or if in addition to signing they also affixed their seals to the conveyance.

Furthermore, intriguing linguistic ambiguities exist in the words *ḥatom* (sealed) and *galoi* (open). As Ben Zion Wacholder observes: "Literally this word *[ḥatom]* refers to a document upon which a seal has been affixed. Yet there are additional nuances to the term as well, such as 'closed' in the sense of 'unavailable' or 'complete.' . . . The 'sealing' may refer to the contents of the document, to the document itself, or to its mode of storage."[5]

The open part of the documentation is said to be *galoi,* which similarly has a broad range of meaning. It may refer to the openness or availability of the document itself or to its contents being "revealed." The root *gala* means "to uncover, remove," and hence is used in such expressions as "to open [uncover] one's eyes or ears" (e.g., LXX Numbers 24:4; 1 Samuel 9:15), "to show, or to reveal" (as in Amos 3:7, the Lord "revealeth his secret"), and "to open in widespread communication or proclamation" (compare *published* in Esther 3:14; 8:13). In another sense it means to "go forth into the world," and hence to remove or to go into exile. Each of these meanings may find relevance to the open segments of important legal or religious documents.

Moreover, the King James Version says that the closed part of the documentation was sealed "according to the law and custom" (Jeremiah 32:11), but nothing more is known from preexilic times in Israel about the origins or nature of any such legal requirements or customs in Jerusalem. Other translations indicate that the closed part was sealed simply "according to the correct legal procedure,"[6] but this diminishes the force and effect of the words *mitzvah* and *ḥuqqim,* which convey a sense that this procedure was not only correct but also long-standing and mandatory. Bright prefers to translate these words narrowly, by rendering them as containing "the contract and the conditions,"[7] and others have followed suit with "the title and conditions"[8] and "the terms and conditions."[9] But such translations have two drawbacks: they imply that only the sealed part of the document contained the essential "terms" or "title" and "conditions"—which flies in the face of the archaeological evidence, a discussion of which follows—and they give little clue as to what the "title" or "terms" in the contract might be. Interestingly, the Septuagint omits this particular phrase altogether, perhaps because its meaning was unclear to the Greek translators.[10] Although in such particulars we cannot be sure of the precise technical meaning of Jeremiah 32:6–15, it appears that Jeremiah was following some legal pattern well-known to his family, his witnesses, and his contemporary audience.

Archaeological and Textual Evidences
of Double Documents

Several archaeological discoveries made in the twentieth century shed considerable light on this interesting form of ancient legal documentation.[11] As discussed most recently by Elisabeth Koffmahn, these discoveries tend to clarify to a considerable extent both the terminology found in Jeremiah 32 and the history of the use of doubled, sealed documents, which expanded into the Hellenistic world and throughout the Roman Empire.[12] Several ancient documents give a fairly precise picture of what these double documents looked like; how they were executed, witnessed, and sealed; and what they contained.

The Two Parts

These documents, when written on parchment or papyrus, were written on a single sheet, the text standing in two parts, one at the top and the other at the bottom of the sheet. Archaeological evidence thus argues quite persuasively that Jeremiah 32 describes the use of a single document with two parts, not two separate scrolls or sheets. Several instances of such two-part documents have been found. Because each single document contains two parts, the singular and plural forms of the word *sepher* in Jeremiah 32:14 can both "refer to one and the same double document."[13]

Typically, "the same text was written twice on one and the same papyrus, leaving an empty space about 2–3 cm wide between the two texts."[14] For example, "the legal documents found at Dura are without exception double: that is to say, the text of the agreement or transaction was copied twice on the same sheet of parchment or papyrus" (see fig. 1).[15] Accordingly, Jeremiah 32 is not describing two separate documents, one for

Fig. 1. A typical double document on parchment found at Dura-Europos, in modern-day Syria. This Jewish bill of divorcement was written in Greek in A.D. 204. Note the care with which the lower part was written compared to the cursive speed of the writing in the upper part. Reproduced from Perkins, ed., *Excavations at Dura-Europos* (Yale University Press), plate XIV. © 1959 by Yale University. All rights reserved.

daily use and the other that is sealed and preserved as Friedrich
Bilabel has suggested,[16] but one scroll with two parts that are
both preserved. Not only does the archaeological evidence support this view, but, as Koffmahn points out, so does the fact
that Jeremiah placed both parts of his documentation into the
clay vessel, an action that would contradict the idea that the
two parts were intended to remain physically separate to serve
two distinct purposes: one open, or public, and the other closed,
or private.

In preparing these documents, the ancient legal scribes and
notaries had various options available to them. In the earlier
texts the sealed and the open parts are often identical. In one
collection of documents from the third century B.C., each has a
"fully developed inner and outer text,"[17] and the Hibeh Papyri
(ca. 300 B.C.) present their full texts twice.[18] Two bronze tablets
of the Roman emperor Trajan, with a Roman date equivalent to
A.D. October 103 (see fig. 2), present the full text in neat lettering on the open side of the first bronze plate and then repeat
exactly the same text in more hurried lettering on the inside
faces of the two plates.[19]

In a world without copy machines or county recorders' offices, the use of double documentation in this fashion made
very good sense in preventing fraud or alteration of documents.[20] This was apparently the overriding purpose behind all
double documents that contained a nearly verbatim repetition
of the *scriptura interior* (inner portion) in the *scripta exterior*
(outer portion): "The purpose of this institution lay not only in
the daily inspection of the open text, which allowed each party
to orient himself concerning the content of the contract, but
also deterred, particularly through the sealing of the closed portion (the *scriptura interior*), any tampering and guarded against
unauthorized emendations."[21]

Bronze Plate 1 (Exterior)   Bronze Plate 2 (Exterior)

Bronze Plate 1 (Interior)   Bronze Plate 2 (Interior)

Fig. 2. The bronze tablets from the time of the Roman emperor Trajan, in Latin, A.D. 103. In order to create these Roman tablets, the scribe impressed the letters into a wax blank with a heated metal stylus. On the front (exterior) of plate 1, he wrote close together in capital letters, with more serifs than he used when he repeated the same text in a rustic style on the two interior faces. He formed an ornamental frame by sliding a scraper along the edges of the two exterior faces to give them a formal appearance. The names of the witnesses appear on the back (exterior) of plate 2. Photographs courtesy the Roman-German Central Museum, Mainz, Germany.

But the second part of many double documents was not a verbatim repetition of the first part, and "the form of the double document, especially with respect to the order and position of the two texts, changed over the course of the centuries."[22] In several cases one of the two texts would be an abridgment of the other. In the papyri from Murabba'at,[23] for example, some of the double documents have a "greatly abridged *[stark verkümmerter]* scriptum interior,"[24] with the *scriptura exterior* counting as the original. At Dura-Europos[25] the "upper version was written in a smaller hand than the lower [open] and deviates from it intentionally or otherwise, being reduced to a brief notation in the later period."[26] A demotic marriage contract (363 B.C.) did not repeat the text twice in full, but featured excerpts from the main text that were written on the open part of the document so that the basic contents of the scroll could be known without having to unroll the whole papyrus.[27]

Abridgments typically reduced the main text by a factor of three or four (see fig. 1). Ten lines in one text were reduced to three; twenty lines in another text were shortened to five.[28] In these cases the abridged text served as a working summary or general identification of the main contents of the transaction, so the shortened text would only prevent falsification of the main document in a limited number of cases. In any event, "both texts are always formatted in the same way and written in the same hand,"[29] although the handwriting of the second text is often less deliberate.

Whenever one creates two copies or versions of a legal document, the question is likely to arise as to which of the two is the controlling document; that is, which is the more important of the two? In the earliest cases it appears that the *scriptura interior* (the sealed portion) was viewed as the "original,"[30] for it bore the signatures of the witnesses (ca. fourth century B.C.), although both texts were written at the same time and both

were probably considered "virtually primary."[31] Later, the
scriptura exterior bore the signatures of witnesses and thus was
probably viewed as the "primary document."[32] This development is attested as early as the third century B.C. in many Hellenistic documents in which the exterior text was the main text
and the interior text was the "sealed abridgment" *(versiegelte Innen-
schrift verkümmerte).*[33]

Sealing and the Seals

Sealing (closing the document) was essential, and the manner of sealing papyrus or parchment documents was relatively
standard. Typically, these documents have a horizontal slit from
the edge of the papyrus to the middle, between the two texts (as
seen in fig. 1). The top half was rolled to the middle and then
folded across the slit. Three holes were punched from the slit to
the other side, thin papyrus bands were threaded through these
holes and wrapped around the rolled-up and folded-over upper
portion of the document, and on these bands the seals (wax or
clay impressions) of the participants were affixed (see fig. 3).[34]
In other cases the documents were just rolled down from the
top without a slit and fold, and the top half was then sealed.[35]
At Dura the upper part of the papyrus was rolled and "then tied
with a single string in five knots across the sheet," with a tassel
on each end of the string so it could not be pulled through the
holes without tearing the papyrus (see fig. 4).[36] The use of three
seals was common, but sometimes four or two are also found.[37]
The documents at Dura bear the seals both of "the witnesses
and principals."[38]

The manner of sealing metal documents was somewhat different. The principles involved in the practice of doubled,
sealed documents needed to be modified slightly depending on
the writing materials used. The two bronze metal plates from

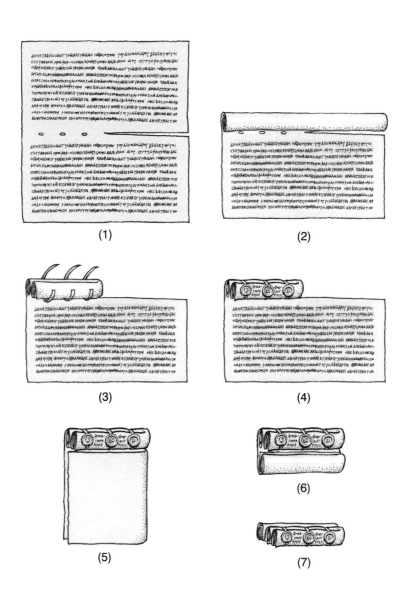

(1)

(2)

(3)

(4)

(5)

(6)

(7)

Fig. 3. The drawings above show seven stages in folding and sealing a typical double document used by Hellenistic scribes in Egypt. The intent was to make a small, durable packet that could be stored easily. Reproduced by Michael P. Lyon from Rubensohn, *Elephantine-Papyri, 6, 7.*

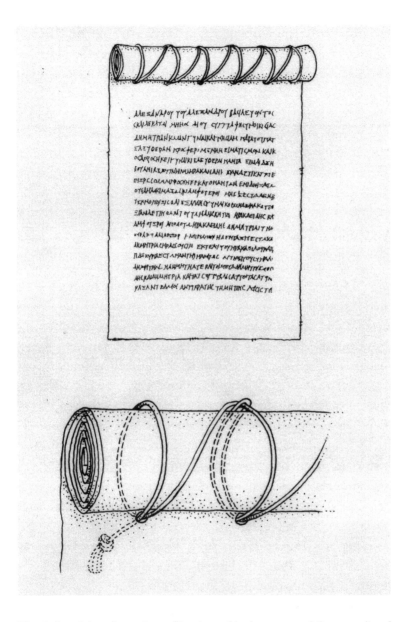

Fig. 4. An elaborate system of knots and lacing ensured the security of the sealed portion of documents from Dura-Europos. Drawings by Michael P. Lyon.

the time of Trajan, found in Mainz, Germany (see fig. 2), have four holes, two on the corners and two in the middle: "The seal was fashioned in the following manner: A cord made out of bronze wire threads was laced through the middle holes of both plates and the two ends were tied together on the back side of the second plate. Over these knots a film of wax was poured, on which the witnesses impressed their seals. A half-cylindrical bronze seal was soldered over the wax for protection [see fig. 5]."[39]

The Witnesses

Witnesses were necessary, although their number could vary. In one Assyrian agreement on a clay tablet from 651 B.C. that documented the sale of a property, twelve witnesses are listed.[40] Ten documents, each subscribed by six witnesses, come from the third century B.C.[41] In Egypt it was common to use five or, most often, six witnesses.[42] The Hibeh documents bear "the signatures of the witnesses, whose names are also given on the verso and who seem to have been seven in number."[43] The Babylonian Talmud stipulated that "at least three witnesses were required by law."[44] Accordingly, in most Jewish texts three witnesses were common, and normally not more than seven seem to have been used,[45] although in principle one witness was required to sign on each fold and "if there are more than three folds more witnesses must be added, one for each fold."[46] The number of witnesses in the Bar-Kokhba documents is "usually five or seven."[47] In Dura-Europos "the standard number of witnesses is three; five occur in the two camp texts."[48] The decree of Trajan on two bronze plates contains the names of seven witnesses listed on the back open side of the second plate (see fig. 2). All of these sealing and witnessing procedures, of course,

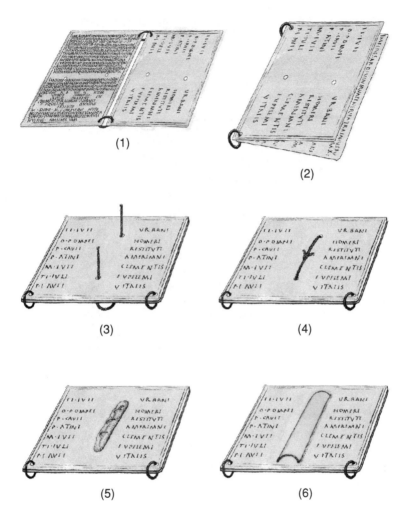

(1)

(2)

(3)

(4)

(5)

(6)

Fig. 5. The Roman citizenship "diploma" shown earlier in figure 2 was sealed in the manner represented here. Found in the area of Mainz, Germany, the document is an extract of Trajan's declaration on a bronze tablet stored in a temple in Rome. Citizenship was granted by the emperor in A.D. 103 to soldiers of the Roman army who came from Germanic tribes. The bequest itself stated that they received this great gift "for themselves and their posterity" along with the right to marry within their own tribes under the protections of Roman law. Drawings by Michael P. Lyon.

may bring to mind the book with seven seals envisioned by John in Revelation 5:1–4 (see fig. 6).

Fig. 6. This reconstruction of a wax-covered wooden diptych from Pompeii records the sale of a dyeworks. The upper papyrus document was sealed in its compartment with five seals. Photograph courtesy the Roman-German Central Museum, Mainz, Germany.

The functions of witnesses could vary. In some cases (demotic and Mishnaic) all of the witnesses attested to the entire document, whereas in other Jewish cases one witness affirmed each line of text (after each line on the recto a witness signed on the verso). Some witnesses testified to the execution of the document or formation of the contract; others certified the correctness of the content of the document. Thus, for example, "the Dura witnesses attested the act or declaration which constituted the document. . . . [In documents executed outside of Dura] it is evident that the action indicated by the verb took place 'before,' 'in the presence of' the specific persons named as witnesses at the end."[49] In documents drawn up within Dura itself, this element is lacking, "perhaps because it could be assumed that the act which they documented was performed in an official place."[50]

The Signatures

The signatures of the witnesses are typically found on the back of the document, on the sealed part in early times, and on the open part in later times.[51] The witnesses typically signed on the back of the document in ascending order from the bottom, with the first line of signatures directly opposite the last line of the text on the front side, the second line of signatures opposite the penultimate line of text on the other side, and so forth.[52] In one of the documents from Dura-Europos, the witnesses signed "on the verso opposite knots in the string tying shut the upper text."[53] In all cases except one, the signatures of the witnesses are found on the verso.[54] Similarly, on the twenty-three double deeds found among the Bar-Kokhba letters, "the witnesses signed their names on the back (the *verso*), each next to one knot," with the names running from the knot toward the bottom of the document (see fig. 7).[55]

The Babylonian Talmud, written in the centuries directly after the time of Christ, describes two similar kinds of double documents. The difference is slight, principally with respect to the manner in which the signatures are to be affixed. In the first type, the entire scroll containing both parts of the document is rolled up into a single roll and sealed, with the signatures of the witnesses either on the front of the document in the space between the two blocks of text or on the back of the document. In the second type, only the closed text is rolled up and sealed; the signatures run on the right side of the open text, beginning at the last line and continuing to the first line of text, as proof that nothing was missing (see fig. 8).[56]

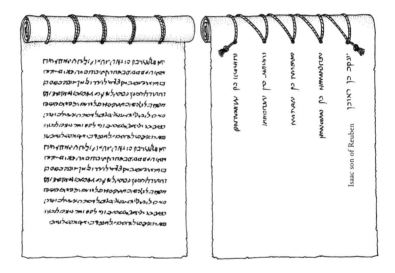

Fig. 7. This drawing shows how witnesses affixed their signatures to specific places on the Bar-Kokhba documents from the second century A.D. Redrawn by Michael P. Lyon from Yadin, *Bar-Kokhba*, 229, 231.

According to the Talmud, "an open document [has] its witnesses on the inside; and a bound [document has] its witnesses on the outside." If this procedure is not followed correctly, the document is invalidated, as in a bill of divorcement, according to the majority opinion. For unsealed documents, two witnesses will suffice; but a sealed document requires three. In the

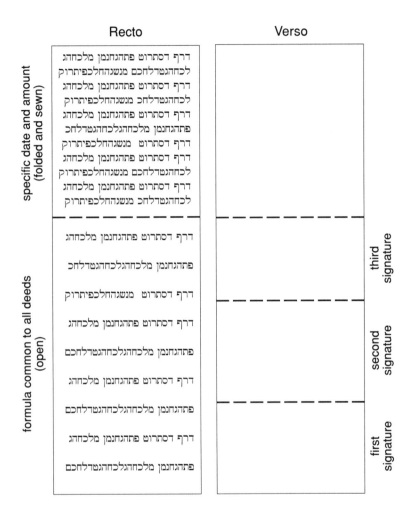

Fig. 8. This stylized schematic follows the talmudic instructions for witnessing and sealing a document. The rabbis evidently knew of the widespread custom of sealed documents but did not comment on the doubled text. The commentaries stipulated that the sealed portion was to contain the date and amount, while the open portion was to contain the standard formula used in all deeds. Although they did not come to a consensus on the direction and number of signatures, the rabbis realized that the practice of sealing documents precluded unauthorized additions to, or deletions from, the bottom of the document. Redrawn and adapted by Mary Mahan from Fischer, "Die Urkunden im Talmud," 86.

case of a discrepancy between the top portion of the document and the bottom, "everything follows the bottom," since the sealed, or upper, portion is only there "so that if one letter from the bottom should be erased, it will be derived from the top."[57] The signing of a sealed or bound document under the Rabbinic practice required the paper to be folded over each line, sewn, and signed: "each fold requires the signature of a witness, with a different witness on each fold." All such documents were required to conclude with the words *firm and established.*[58]

The Legal Contents

The contents of these doubled, sealed documents covered a wide spectrum of legal subjects. Bilabel lists thirty-seven Ptolemaic double documents (mostly receipts, *Quittungen*) and sixteen certain and five other probable documents that involve royal decrees *(Königseide)*.[59] Portions of contracts are found in the Dead Sea Scrolls, but they are often so fragmentary that it is not possible to determine what kinds of documents they are;[60] one is a double deed regarding the sale of land.[61] The double documents from Dura-Europos, written in Greek from the first through the third centuries A.D., feature a wide variety of transactions. They include a bequest *(Schenkungsvertrag)* with a complete inner and outer text, a division of property *(Teilungsvertrag)*, loan documents *(Darlehnsvertrag)*, purchases, a sale of a vineyard (five witnesses, with an abridged interior text of three lines), a deposit *(Verwahrungsvertrag)*, marriage contracts, divorce documents (one with complete inner and outer text), and a receipt.[62] The double documents from Murabbaʿat and from the region around Naḥal Ḥever[63] involve legal matters including acknowledgment of indebtedness, marriage, divorce, and purchases.[64]

The Sealing Up, or Preserving

Security in preservation was provided by placing the double documents in vessels to secure and protect them. Jeremiah's instructions are explicit on this: "Put them in an earthenware jar, so that they might last a long time" (see fig. 9).[65] During the time of the Neo-Babylonian Empire, "private archives of tablets were stored in clay jars in the homes."[66] Security in maintaining the integrity of the deed was provided by the use of seals, common in Babylonian administrative texts, but only after the Old Babylonian period with respect to legal texts.[67]

Fig. 9. This jar and lid come from the first century A.D. at Qumran. One of the reasons for the survival of the Dead Sea Scrolls was their storage in large pottery jars created by the community's potters. This practice is reminiscent of Jeremiah 32:14. Photograph by David Hawkinson, courtesy the Church of Jesus Christ of Latter-day Saints and Brigham Young University, Museum of Art.

Opening the Document

When and by whom could these seals be opened? It appears that only a judge or some other duly authorized official could break the seals and open the document. In Babylonia, if a dispute ever arose concerning the correct wording of the contract, a judge could remove the outer envelope and reveal the original tablet.[68] This rule seems to reflect the prevailing practice in the world of the Bible: "Only a judge could open the sealed copy to settle disputes."[69] "In case of doubt, and only then, the *interior* could be opened in the appropriate office."[70] Accordingly, John the Revelator "wept much, because no man was found worthy to open and read the book" that he beheld, until "the Lion of the tribe of Juda . . . prevailed to open the book, and to loose the seven seals thereof" (Revelation 5:4, 5; compare Isaiah 29:11).

Origins and Applications

What can be said about the origins of this practice? Emphasizing its Israelite origin, Koffmahn argues that the archaeological record indicates that the double document originated as a Hebrew practice or custom. She concludes, "Everything appears to point to a Semitic origin."[71] In Egypt "double documents first appear among the Hellenistic papyri from Elephantine (fourth century B.C.)," which shows that this legal form of documentation did not originate earlier in Egypt.[72] Elsewhere throughout the Hellenistic world, she argues, double documents "surface wherever any contact with the Semitic culture can be also demonstrated."[73] While Koffmahn acknowledges that in the centuries after Christ the Jewish legal practice was modified under Hellenistic and Roman influences, especially with respect to "private documents, such as prenuptial agreements, divorce documents, debt instruments, and other such matters, for which the Old Testament does not prescribe the use of this particular form,"[74] she stands by her conclusion that "certainly in the first instance we are to call this the original Semitic law, as has been handed down to us through Jeremiah 32:10ff."[75]

Other scholars, such as Hans Julius Wolff, do not see this practice as originating among the Israelites.[76] They look to parallels in the earlier Mesopotamian practice of preserving legal documents in case tablets with the interior text repeated on the envelope (see fig. 10). Examples of case tablets are found as early as 2900 B.C.,[77] but they do not surface in all eras or centuries of Mesopotamian history: they appear as Sumerian deeds from the third dynasty of Ur and also come under the heading of the so-called Cappadocian clay tablets of about 2000 B.C.[78] Examples have been found that date to the middle of the second millennium,[79] but they drop out during the time of the Amorites. Case tablets surface again in the old and new Assyrian empires but were not used in the Neo-Babylonian period, when other practices such as giving each party a copy of the document were used to protect the transaction.[80] Case tablets are found again in Persian-Kurdistan.[81] In these documents both the inner tablet and the outer case repeated the basic text verbatim, and both bore the impressions of the cylinder seals or other seals of the witnesses.[82] In regard to Mesopotamian clay tablets at one location, "from some fragmentary examples, these tablets were all doubled, the one encased in the other, and by comparing the text on the inside and outside one could readily see that the seal and the inscription *(Inschrift)* were the same."[83]

The traditional material used since prehistoric times to make tablets such as these was the clay found prevalently in the alluvial riverbeds.[84] Tablets were formed from the clay and either sun dried, as prescribed, or fired. The sun-dried tablets became a gray color; those that were fired were red or black. Thanks to the protection of desert gravel and sand, many ancient tablets are still clearly legible today.[85]

Fig. 10. *Top:* This Mesopotamian case tablet dating to about 1900–2050 B.C. shows the use of an exterior text written on the outside of a clay envelope to preserve the integrity of the interior message. *Below:* The signature, seen in this model within the rectangle, was an impression made by rolling a cylinder seal across the bottom of the tablet. Reprinted, by permission, from Chiera, *They Wrote on Clay* (University of Chicago Press, 1938), 70, 73. Photograph courtesy University of Chicago, Oriental Institute.

Writing on clay was not easy; scribes were hired to prepare these legal documents. Starting with a somewhat flattened lump of clay, the scribe would use a stylus made of wood or a reed[86] to impress the characters, rather than scratching them in.[87] The parties to the contract would have their personal seals ready to be rolled in the clay to form a signature. Because it would have been easy to add or subtract from the contract before it dried out, a second lump of clay was formed into a case tablet by flattening it, "reducing it to the thickness of a pie crust."[88] The signed document would then be folded into this second piece of clay and the outer tablet formed around it. The scribe would then inscribe the same words of the transaction on the outer tablet, and the parties would affix their seals to it in the same way. Surprisingly, the clay of the inner tablet did not adhere to the outer tablet; both copies were preserved. During the drying process both tablets shrank, again providing security because any attempt to replace the outer envelope with new clay would result in damage to the inner tablet from the moisture.[89]

Although these Mesopotamian practices seem to be somewhat related to the papyrus procedures of the eastern Mediterranean, John Bright prefers to discount any connection.[90] Hammershaimb and most others, however, do not: "The procedure [on papyrus or parchment] corresponds in principle to the Babylonian case-tablets, where the outer one serves to give information about the content and the inner one is only taken out if a dispute about the content arises."[91] Wolff assumes that "the Babylonian tradition of the case-tablet must have been adapted and extended for use in connection with new writing materials."[92] Rubensohn agrees.[93] Fischer sees the practice as "perhaps a general custom throughout antiquity."[94] If the western papyrus procedures developed out of the eastern cuneiform cultures, then the Israelite conventions made no particularly

unique contribution to legal practices in these regards. But if
the papyrus procedures are independent of the practices connected with clay tablets, then Jeremiah 32 is the earliest known
instance of such a doubled, sealed document, and the Israelite
influence in the history of this convention becomes more
prominent. Although Koffmahn's position is not highly regarded among scholars today, her evidence still shows that the
use of doubled, sealed documents was significant and prominent among the Israelites and Jews for many centuries, even if
an Israelite origin of the basic underlying concept per se cannot
be proved.

Applying this legal custom widely, the Romans undoubtedly borrowed the idea of double documents from the general
legal practice in the Hellenistic world and incorporated it into
their own practice and law (see fig. 11).[95] Many Roman double
documents have been found involving military instructions,[96]
military retirements and benefits,[97] slave purchases, horse purchases, requests for information *(Bittgesuch),* and marriage contracts.[98] Indeed, Roman law in the first century A.D. expressly
required this form of documentation in order to prevent falsification;[99] Paulus explained that double documentation was necessary to preserve the integrity of the transaction: "ut exteriori
scripturae fidem interior servet."[100]

Moreover, these Roman documents, consistent with the
broad cultural practice of the ancient Mediterranean and
Mesopotamian worlds, were subscribed by witnesses and
sealed. The practical value and enduring importance of the use
of seals in antiquity is further illustrated by the frequent presence of stamp and cylinder seals in Mesoamerica, as several
items listed in John L. Sorenson's monumental bibliography
amply document.[101] Such seals and their arguable connection
with the ancient Near East offer some evidence that the practice

Fig. 11. Front and back sides of a bronze tablet from the time of Vespasian, with a date equivalent to A.D. 77. This document grants citizenship to a group of German military veterans (and their wives) who had served in the Roman Empire. Photographs courtesy the Roman-German Central Museum, Mainz, Germany.

of sealing documents was known and used in pre-Columbian America.

In addition, the Old Testament demonstrates that physical records were not the only items that could be thought of as being sealed up: the Song of Moses refers to God's vengeance being "sealed up among my treasures" (Deuteronomy 32:34), and Job's "transgression is sealed up in a bag" (Job 14:17). Modern revelation brings us the promise that we can be "sealed up unto eternal life" through the "sure word of prophecy" (D&C 131:5; compare Mosiah 5:15), but the wicked, or those who reject the gospel, will have the testimony of the prophets sealed up from them. In other words, the legal practice of sealing important documents or judgments was impressive enough that it formed the basis of several scriptural images and idioms.

To sum up, while some of the particulars vary from culture to culture and from one writing medium to another, doubled, sealed, witnessed documents were common in the ancient world and were fundamental in preserving important written records. The standard elements included the presentation of the essential components of the document twice, the certification of witnesses, and the physical sealing (binding) together with the sealing up (concealing) of the document itself.

The "Sealed Torah" in the Dead Sea Scrolls and Pseudepigrapha

Much as the idea of a "sealed book" proved useful in the creative biblical language of Isaiah and Jeremiah, it also captured the theological fascination of Jewish sectarians, as seen in the Dead Sea Scrolls. Ben Zion Wacholder argues that Jeremiah 32 holds the key to understanding *Damascus Document* 5:1–6. This text from the Dead Sea community developed or used the idea that a sealed book of the law of Moses existed, and the

Essenes used this idea in rationalizing David's sins as inadvertent (except for the blood of Uriah), because "David had not read in the sealed Book of the Law which was inside the ark." This sealed version of the law of Moses was reportedly "hidden and was not revealed until the son of Zadok arose." Wacholder finds traces of Jeremiah 32 in this text in its use of the key words *sealed* and *revealed* (open). It is possible that Jeremiah 32 influenced the sectarians or that Jeremiah's language and the Dead Sea exegetes were both influenced by a widespread general tradition even more ancient than Jeremiah himself.

Similarly, several traditions springing largely out of Deuteronomy 31:26–30 are found among the Jewish legends and pseudepigraphic writings. In Deuteronomy 31:26, Moses was commanded, "Take this book of the law, and put it in the side of the ark of the covenant of the Lord your God, that it may be there for a witness against thee." Various understandings of this scripture arose. Did Moses write one copy of the law for open and public use and then deposit a duplicate copy of the law in some ark (perhaps the ark of the covenant) for use at the judgment bar of God? Or, as the author of the *Damascus Document* seems to claim, did Moses write two different versions of the law—one for present use and circulated in multiple copies among David and his people, and the other for eschatological use and inscribed in two copies, both of which "were in storage"?[102]

Whatever the case may be, the idea of there being a sealed Torah sealed up somewhere for God's future use in addition to the open, or revealed, Torah is clear enough. An account relates that, on the last day of his life, Moses "wrote thirteen scrolls of the Torah, twelve for the twelve tribes, and one he put into the Holy Ark, so that, if they wished to falsify the Torah, the one in the Ark might remain untouched." This thirteenth scroll was "fetched by Gabriel, who brought it to the highest heavenly court to show the piety of Moses. . . . It is this scroll of the Torah out of which the souls of the pious read."[103]

The idea of thirteen scrolls is upheld by Maimonides in the *Mishneh Torah*,[104] and even before Maimonides, the Zadokite sages "arrived at the conception of *two* Mosaic recensions."[105] Those sages further concluded from Deuteronomy 31:26 that the second Torah was put in a "sealed container," that is, a "box or chest in which scribes wrap their manuscripts for preservation and safekeeping."[106] This box or chest may have been thought of as the ark of the covenant, since 2 Maccabees 2:5–8 says that Jeremiah hid the ark in a secret place that he sealed, and this ark was the storage place of the law.[107]

In the *Testament of Moses* 1:16–18, Moses was told: "Take this writing so that later you will remember how to preserve the books which I shall entrust to you. You shall arrange them, anoint them with cedar, and deposit them in earthenware jars in the place which (God) has chosen from the beginning of the creation of the world, (a place) where his name may be called upon until the day of recompense when the Lord will surely have regard for his people."[108]

In *Jubilees* 1:5–29, Moses was given two stone tablets and was shown a vision of "what was in the beginning and what will occur in the future" (compare Moses 1; see no. 5 in table on p. 477). He was instructed to write a book containing everything the Lord would tell him on the mountain so that it might serve as a testimony in the future against the people. While the *Testament of Moses* and the book of *Jubilees* do not say that this eschatological and prophetic book of Moses would be sealed, the authors of those works presume that those writings of Moses would be preserved until the final day of judgment.

Jewish texts such as these show that the idea of doubled, sealed documents attracted attention far beyond the sphere of mundane secular transactions. The Israelite tendency to use daily practices to carry theological cargoes virtually assured that an institution as laden with solemn formality as the doubled, sealed, witnessed document would be carried into the literary imagery and religious discourse of the people in and around Jerusalem.

The "Sealed" or "Sealed Up" Documents in the Book of Mormon

The legal use of doubled, sealed, witnessed documents during Jeremiah's (and Lehi's) lifetime in Jerusalem, together with the secular use of such instruments throughout much of the ancient world and the religious utilization of this formalism in biblical and intertestamental literature, raise the distinct possibility that Lehi knew of this practice and that Nephi and his successors had this form of double documentation in mind when they contemplated the preservation of their own records, constructed and assembled their written texts, and ultimately sealed and deposited the Book of Mormon plates. The following factors relate the form of the double documents of the ancient world to that of the Book of Mormon.

Nephi knew that the Nephite record would eventually be a two-part book. As early as about 550 B.C., he described the time when "the words of a book," meaning the Book of Mormon, would come forth (2 Nephi 27:6). Although Nephi could sometimes speak of that doubled book as a single document, just as Jeremiah had spoken of his two-part deed of purchase as a single document *(sepher)*, Nephi, like Jeremiah, saw the final Nephite record as having two parts, one sealed and the other not: "The things which are sealed shall not be delivered in the day of the wickedness and abominations of the people" (verse 8), but the "words which are not sealed" shall be taken and delivered "to another" (verse 15) who shall be told to "touch not the things which are sealed, for I will bring them forth in mine own due time" (verse 21). Indeed, one portion of the Nephite record was sealed; the other part was open. Consistent with the ancient practices and requirements, witnesses were promised; in particular, at least three witnesses were stipulated. Others would be provided for, according to God's will: "as many witnesses as seemeth him good" (verse 14) to "testify to the truth of the book and the things therein" (verse 12). For security and preservation, the plates were buried; they were both sealed and sealed up. Similarly, Jeremiah both sealed his document and then sealed it up in an earthen jar, to preserve the document for later official use. These prima facie points of comparison call for a thorough inspection of descriptive material found in three parts of the Book of Mormon: 2 Nephi 27, Ether 3–4, and Ether 5.

2 Nephi 27: Nephi's Conception of the Nephite Record

The idea of a doubled, sealed, witnessed document is encountered in 2 Nephi 27. Although this chapter draws heavily on Isaiah 29, its terminology does not come entirely from that chapter of Isaiah, which talks only about a sealed book (see Isaiah 29:11–12). The text in 2 Nephi 27 goes on to deal with witnesses and "sealing up" and contemplates a two-part collection of records.

Nephi begins by prophesying that because of iniquity among the gentiles, the eyes of their rulers and seers will be "covered" (verse 5). Nevertheless, the Lord will bring forth to the gentiles "the words of a book"—not the book itself but only the words of that book—which shall be the words of Nephites who "have slumbered" (verse 6). Moreover, while the words of the book will be open, the book itself will be sealed: "And behold the book shall be sealed" (verse 7). In other words, it appears that the book will be in the form of a sealed document, part of which will be open and part closed.

There seems to be a distinction in Nephi's mind between being "sealed" and being "sealed up." The former, according to the Old World practice, would normally have to do with physically tying the document shut and affixing a wax or clay seal to the closure. The latter has to do with whether or not a portion will be revealed: "because of the things which are sealed up, the things which are sealed shall not be delivered in the day of the wickedness and abominations of the people" (verse 8). Because of the unrighteousness of the gentiles, "the book shall be kept from them [the gentiles]" (verse 8). In other words, the plates themselves will be kept from the people, but the book itself "shall be delivered [given] unto a man [Joseph Smith]" (verse 9). He shall "deliver [translate] these words," and "the words of the book . . . he shall deliver [dictate] . . . unto another [Oliver Cowdery]" (verse 9). Concerning the part of the book that is sealed, "he [Joseph Smith] shall not deliver [translate], neither shall he deliver the book [that is, show the plates themselves to the world]" (verse 10).

Moreover, Nephi indicates that the seals on the book were affixed by the power and authority of God: "For the book shall be sealed by the power of God" (verse 10). In this way the contents could become available in the day of the Lord, presumably for use on the day of judgment: "and the revelation which was sealed shall be kept in the book until the own due time of the Lord, that they may come forth" (verse 10). The plural *they* in this text may be taken to refer to the two parts of this record; in other words, "that they [the open and the sealed parts] may [both eventually] come forth" according to the Lord's timetable. For "the day cometh that the words of the book which were sealed shall be read upon the house tops; and they shall be read by the power of Christ" (verse 11). That is, just as these words were sealed by the power and authority of Christ, they shall be read by that same power and authority. Christ, as judge, maker, and sealer of the document, would have the authority to open and disclose the sealed text.

Nephi also mentions witnesses in connection with this document. In 2 Nephi 27:12 he reaffirms that, apart from Joseph Smith, "the man of whom I have spoken, . . . three witnesses shall behold it, by the power of God." As previously noted, the minimum number of witnesses required under Jewish law in order for a sealed document to be legally valid was three. According to Nephi, these three witnesses will have two functions: to "testify to the truth of the book and [of] the things therein" (verse 12; compare "The Testimony of Three Witnesses," in the forepart of the current edition of the Book of Mormon). Testifying to "the truth of the book" corresponds with the ancient function of verifying the validity of the formation of the contract and the formalities of the execution of the document; testifying to the truth of "the things in the book" corresponds with the legal role of affirming the accuracy of the words themselves.

Besides these three witnesses, "a few" others shall view "it" (presumably the external features of the book itself) so that they might "bear testimony of his [God's] word [singular]" (verse 13). In other words, they will attest to the fulfillment of God's promise (word) "that the words of the faithful [the slumbering Nephites] should speak as if it were from the dead" (verse 13). However, it was not anticipated that these other witnesses should testify of the words or contents of the book itself (which is consistent with "The Testimony of Eight Witnesses," in the front matter of the current printing of the Book of Mormon). Thus God will bring forth "the words of the book," as distinguished from the book itself, and in the mouths of "as many witnesses as seemeth him good will he establish his word" (verse 14). As in the ancient practice, the total number of witnesses mentioned by Nephi was not rigidly fixed, although he gives assurances that more than the required minimum of three would be provided. The testimonies of the Three and Eight Witnesses appeared at the back of the first edition of the Book of Mormon, just as the signatures of witnesses stood at the end of ancient documents, marking the conclusion of the document. Anything that came after the bottom witness's name was presumptively not a part of the original document but an unauthorized addition.

Nephi next places a curse on anyone who rejects the word of God (see verse 14). Once an ancient legal statement was established by witnesses, it carried a high degree of seriousness. Unwitnessed statements could be disregarded at one's own discretion, but witnessed documents were far more authoritative. Disregarding them was tantamount to rejecting the validity of the entire legal system and of the deity in whose name the witnesses swore; thus, rejecting sworn testimony would amount to a denial of the whole word of God, warranting the curse.

Moreover, in 2 Nephi 27:15–18 the ancient seer prophesies how the "words which are not sealed" (the open part of the book) would be delivered to another (Martin Harris) so that he could show them to the learned (Charles Anthon and others). Harris would explain that "it is sealed," and Anthon would respond that he cannot read it (see verses 17–18). But the Lord will "deliver again the book and the words thereof" to the unlearned (verse 19), and he shall read "the words which I [the Lord] shall give" (verse 20). In other words, he shall read only those words, namely, the open part of the document. Joseph would be commanded to "touch not the things which are sealed," for they will come forth in the Lord's due time (see verse 21).

The contents of this two-part, sealed document are described four times by Nephi throughout this passage. We are told that "it" (the book as a whole) will contain "a revelation from God, from the beginning of the world to the ending thereof" (verse 7); that "they" will "reveal all things from the foundation of the world unto the end thereof" (verse 10); that when the sealed words are read upon the housetops, "all things shall be revealed unto the children of men which ever have been among the children of men, and which ever will be even unto the end of the earth" (verse 11); and that the sealed words will be preserved until the Lord sees fit to "reveal all things unto the children of men" (verse 22). While the latter two statements indicate that the sealed words will be made known *at the time* when the Lord will reveal all things, it is not clear whether all those things will be revealed entirely, partially, or perhaps not at all by means of this particular sealed text or in some other manner at that time. Moreover, the first two statements seem to say that information about things from the foundation to the end of the world will be contained in the book as a whole, both in the sealed portion and also to some extent in the open portion. It is unclear whether the book as a whole, or the sealed portion alone, will consist of a single revelation about all these things, "a revelation from God," or whether that revelation will be found among or embedded in other sorts of records. Indeed, to a very significant degree, the open portion of the Book of Mormon already reveals great and precious knowledge from the fall and before the foundation of the earth (see 2 Nephi 2; Alma 12) to the atonement and end of the world (see 1 Nephi 14; 2 Nephi 9, 28–30; Alma 7, 13; 3 Nephi 21–5). Therefore, the general contents of the open and sealed parts of this two-part record need not be very different from each other.

Nephi anticipated that, after the open part of the text had been read and the witnesses obtained, Joseph would be required to "seal up the book again" (verse 22). This might simply refer to putting the book back into its container (that is, simply sealing, or closing, it up), or it may indicate that the open portion of the book was initially closed with outer seals (in addition to the inner seals that were on the sealed portion) and that those outer seals would be reaffixed. Either way, the book was to be sealed by Joseph Smith "again," and Nephi seems to have had something like the conventional legal practices of his day in mind.

Modern readers may wonder why Nephi would envision and thereby effectively prescribe the use of these practices, employed in the ancient world to memorialize and preserve secular legal contracts, when he spoke of the future configuration of the Nephite records, which were sacred, not secular. To the ancient mind, however, formalities such as these were the essence of validating and conserving documents and proclamations of utmost significance. More specifically, the Book of Mormon is indeed a binding document, a legal warning, a proclamation, a testament, covenant, and contract. Its provisions are about covenants of the Lord. It has much to do with rights of land possession, and it contains the terms and conditions that the owner of the land of promise requires those who occupy that land to obey. In other words, the religious and secular spheres were not widely separated in antiquity, and the Book of Mormon presents sacred materials often by using legalistic forms or concepts. These factors may well explain why Nephi would associate this legal form, typically used for legal contracts, with the final presentation of the Nephite records.

Moreover, the process of sealing up the Nephite records served several practical and religious purposes. To keep the record pure, Nephi and his posterity were instructed that the records should be "sealed up to come forth in their purity" (1 Nephi 14:26). As further protection against destruction, the Lord instructed his scribes to seal up the writings in a book so that "those who have dwindled in unbelief shall not have them, for they seek to destroy the things of God" (2 Nephi 26:17).

Prophetically, Nephi reported that the book would be dedicated to the Lord, "sealed up again unto the Lord" (2 Nephi 30:3).

Ether 3–4: Instructions to the Brother of Jared

Interestingly, the book of Ether, which also speaks of revelations being sealed, deals with two distinct times and sealings: first, the sealing up of a record written and sealed up by the brother of Jared; and second, the sealing up of an abridgment of that record by Moroni after he had included that material as part of the book of Ether at the end of the plates of Mormon. In describing this document and its abridgment, the brother of Jared and Moroni never use the word *seal* (or *sealed*) by itself, while the phrase *seal up* (or *sealed up*) is used eight times (see Ether 3:22, 23, 27, 28; 4:5 [3 times]; and 5:1). By contrast, 2 Nephi 27 uses the word *seal (sealed)* by itself nine times (see verses 7, 8, 10 [3 times], 11, 15, 17, 21), while the expression *seal up (sealed up)* is used only twice (see 2 Nephi 27:8 and 22; in verse 8 its meaning is unclear, but in verse 22 it means "to seal up" in the sense of "to hide up"). The dominance of *seal up* in Ether indicates that "sealing up" something meant something different, especially in the mind of the brother of Jared, from what "sealing" meant for Nephi. Culturally, one would expect to find a difference between these two texts. Nephi came from Jerusalem; the brother of Jared came many centuries earlier from Mesopotamia, a culture that even in its earliest days kept records on clay tablets; and Moroni lived in the fourth century A.D.

Perhaps the Jaredites knew of the practice of "sealing up" documents by use of cylinder seals and case tablets; but it is doubtful that, away from the river culture of Mesopotamia, the Jaredites would have had the clay and other resources necessary to record their words in this fashion. Although we do not know what medium the brother of Jared used to write on, his background and experience would still have inclined him to take special steps to protect and preserve written texts. Thus the brother of Jared was told to "treasure up" and "seal up" (Ether 3:21, 22) the things that he had seen, but nothing indicates that he prepared his record with one part open and the other part closed, as Jeremiah did in writing his deed and as Nephi contemplated would be done with the Nephite record.

The Jaredite document described by the brother of Jared in Ether 3:21–4:2 differs in many ways from the Nephite record discussed in 2 Nephi 27. Whereas Nephi spoke of the Nephite record as being "sealed," that is, closed with a seal, the Jaredite account seems to envision something quite different in speaking about the record of the brother of Jared as being "sealed up." For the Jaredite text, being "sealed" means that the holders of the document should "show it to no man" (Ether 3:21) and should write the words in a language in which "they cannot be read" (verse 22), since "the language which ye shall write I [the Lord] have confounded" (verse 24).

Moreover, the two records differ in content and in the time when they shall come forth. The brother of Jared's record reports his two-part revelation: first, he was shown Christ's premortal body (see Ether 3:13); and second, he saw "all the inhabitants of the earth which had been, and also all that would be; and he [the Lord] withheld them not from his sight, even unto the ends of the earth" (verse 25). Following his vision of the premortal Christ, the brother of Jared was told by Christ that the prophet's account of this great vision should not be made public "until the time cometh that I shall glorify my name in the flesh" (verse 21) or "until after that he should be lifted up upon the cross" (Ether 4:1). In fulfillment of this prophecy, "after Christ truly had showed himself unto his people [the Nephites], he commanded that they [the records] should be made manifest" (verse 2); this does not match the time when the sealed Nephite records would come forth. Regarding the second part of the revelation given to the brother of Jared, the Lord told him to "write these things and seal them up; and I will show them in mine own due time unto the children of men" (Ether 3:27). This may or may not correspond with the manifestation of all things to the children of men mentioned in 2 Nephi 27.

Together with the Jaredite record, two stones were also sealed up (see Ether 3:23). This is reiterated later: "The Lord commanded him that he should seal up the two stones which he had received, and show them not, until the Lord should show them unto the children of men" (verse 28). No stones are mentioned in 2 Nephi 27 in connection with the sealed Nephite book. Thus, on several grounds, it appears that the record that the brother of Jared "sealed up" in very ancient times is a different record from the sealed part of the Nephite book.

Ether 4–5: Moroni's Handling of the Jaredite Record

In Ether 4:3–5:4 Moroni speaks of "sealing up" the record of the brother of Jared. After all of the Nephites and Lamanites had "dwindled in unbelief," the Lord commanded Moroni to "hide them [the words of the brother of Jared] up again in the earth" (Ether 4:3). After writing or abridging "the very things which the brother of Jared saw" and including them on the plates of Mormon (verse 4), Moroni "sealed up" those records and the interpreters (verse 5). The Lord told Moroni that the full record of the brother of Jared would not go forth to the gentiles until they repented and became clean and had the same faith as the brother of Jared (see verses 6–7).

Moroni then pronounced a curse on anyone who might "contend against the word of the Lord" (verse 8). Nephi's curse, somewhat differently, was aimed at anyone who might "reject" the word. Moroni, like Nephi, however, set his warnings in connection with the judgment bar of God: "for ye shall know that it is I that speaketh, at the last day" (verse 10; see also 5:6). Moroni then invited the gentiles to come to Christ and learn "greater things, the knowledge which is hid up because of unbelief" (Ether 4:13), indicating yet another way—namely, by unbelief—in which the great revelations given to the brother of Jared were "sealed up."

Moroni affirmed that he had "told [the reader] the things which [he had] sealed up," and thus he prohibited the translator from touching the things that he, Moroni, had sealed up (see Ether 5:1). He promised the translator that he could "show the plates unto those who shall assist to bring forth this work" (verse 2), but Moroni's text does not indicate that those people would necessarily become formal witnesses. Three others, however, would be shown the plates "by the power of God" (verse 3), for "in the mouth of three witnesses shall these things be established" (verse 4). They will be joined at the last day by the testimony of three others, namely, the Father, the Son, and the Holy Ghost (see verse 4).

While certain similarities exist between the prophetic statements of Nephi and Moroni, Moroni made little use of the full legal model used by Nephi. Moroni did not speak in terms of the open and sealed nature of the document, the particular roles and functions of the witnesses, or of the significance of the document itself being sealed, not just sealed up. Apparently, Moroni simply sealed up the records without thought of, or recourse to, the ancient legal customs or practices.

I leave it to the reader to judge the extent to which the concept of doubled, sealed, witnessed documents employed anciently in various media is relevant to the composition, sealing, and witnessing of the Book of Mormon and to sort out the

Comparison of the Passages in the Book of Mormon That Mention Sealed or Sealed-Up Documents

	2 Nephi 27 *Nephi's Conception of the Nephite Record*	Ether 3–4 *Instructions to the Brother of Jared concerning His Record*	Ether 4–5 *Moroni's Comments on His Abridgment of the Writings of the Brother of Jared*
1. Will the document be in a sealed format?	Yes. The book itself shall be "sealed" (27:7, 8, 10, 11, 17, 21, 22).	No. The record will be "sealed up" (3:22, 23, 27; cf. 4:5; 5:1).	Not indicated. Great things are "hid up because of unbelief" (4:13).
2. Will the document be in two distinct parts?	Yes, words that are "not sealed" (27:15) and words that are "sealed" (27:8, 21).	Not in the same sense. The vision of the brother of Jared came in two parts, but only one record was made.	Yes. Moroni told the reader somewhat concerning the contents (thereby adding text to the unsealed part) but forbade the translator from touching that which he had sealed up (5:1).
3. Will the document be supported by witnesses?	Yes, three (27:12) and a few others (27:13).	Nothing is said about witnesses.	Yes, three (5:3), joined by the three members of the Godhead (5:4).
4. When will the document come forth?	The open part will come forth in "the own due time of the Lord" (27:10).	The first part of this record is to remain confidential "until the time cometh that	The record of the brother of Jared was manifested by Christ (4:2) but will not

		"I shall glorify my name in the flesh" (3:21); the second part will come forth in due time (3:27).	come forth among the gentiles until they repent and become clean and have faith as the brother of Jared (4:6–7).
5. What does the document contain?	The book as a whole contains "a revelation from God, from the beginning of the world to the ending thereof" (27:7).	The brother of Jared saw the premortal Christ (3:13) and "all the inhabitants of the earth which had been, and also all that would be" (3:25).	Things the brother of Jared saw (4:4), of which Moroni told part (5:1).
6. Is there a curse associated with rejecting the record?	Yes, a curse on anyone who "rejecteth the word of God" (27:14).	Not mentioned.	Yes, a curse on "he that will contend against the word of the Lord" (4:8).
7. Is the document to be sealed or sealed up again?	Yes, after the text has been read and witnesses obtained (27:22).	Not expected.	Moroni was commanded to hide the record of the brother of Jared again so that it would not be destroyed by the unfaithful (title page; 4:3).
8. Was anything else sealed up with this record?	No.	Two stones were also sealed up (3:23).	The interpreters were "sealed up" (4:5).

differences and similarities between Nephi's expectations, the
instructions given by the Lord to the brother of Jared, and the
actions taken by Moroni with respect to the records under his
jurisdiction. Beyond the texts in the Book of Mormon and the
comparative studies explored above, there is little further information to go on. We know that part of the plates of Mormon
were sealed, but ultimately the descriptions of the plates known
to us from history are too brief to provide much further assistance. Joseph Smith once briefly described the plates of Mormon as bound together as a single document, the plates having
uniform dimensions and comprising two parts, and that "a
part" of the plates "was sealed."[109]

In 1878 David Whitmer was asked, "Did the angel turn all
the leaves before you as you looked on it?" He answered: "No,
not all, only that part of the book which was not sealed, and
what there was sealed appeared as solid to my view as wood."
Responding to the question "How many of the plates were
sealed?" he said: "About the half of the book was sealed. . . .
There is yet to be given a translation about Jared's people's doings and of Nephi, and many other records and books, which
all has to be done, when the time comes."[110] In 1881, 1885,
and 1888, David Whitmer added the following comments:
"About one-third of which appeared to be loose, in plates, the
other solid, but with perceptible marks where the plates seemed
to be sealed."[111] "A large portion of the volume was securely
sealed, but on the loose pages were engraved hieroglyphics."[112]
"A large portion of the leaves were so securely bound together
that it was impossible to separate them, but upon those loose
leaves were engraved hieroglyphics."[113] "A large portion of the
volume was securely sealed, but on the loose pages were engraved hieroglyphics."[114] "A large portion of the leaves were so
securely bound together that it was impossible to separate
them, but upon the loose leaves were engraved hieroglyphics."[115]

Conclusions

From this study I conclude that Nephi was familiar with the Israelite legal practice of using double documents or deeds and that he instructed his posterity to construct the Nephite record in a fashion that would conform with that tradition. His discussion in 2 Nephi 27 not only expands on Isaiah 29 but also draws on Jeremiah 32 or the general tradition of doubled, witnessed documentation, one part of which was sealed and the other left open.

Nephi envisioned that the Nephite record would eventually consist of two parts—one being sealed, hidden, sacred, and protected and the other being open, public, revealed, and revealing. In this regard the record of the brother of Jared and the rest of the Book of Mormon differ; Nephi's conception of a sealed text differed from that reflected in Moroni's abridgment and description of material in the book of Ether. Although these two sealed or sealed-up records may come forth at the same future time, they are different.

According to the double-document practices of the ancient Mediterranean, the two parts of the doubled document were closely associated with each other: the sealed portion typically provided confirmation of the revealed portion. Moreover, because the revealed, or open, portion (the published Book of Mormon) is itself an abridgment of other records, one may surmise that the sealed portion of the plates of Mormon is a longer version of, and closely related to, the material that has been revealed to us. In conformance with the concepts of the double deed, then, the purpose of the sealed portion will be to confirm the truth of the revealed portion. Moroni himself said, "Ye shall see me at the bar of God; and the Lord God will say unto you: Did I not declare my words unto you?" (Moroni 10:27). Thus a primary purpose of the sealed portion of the Book of Mormon will be to stand as a witness that what has been declared unto us in the Book of Mormon is true.

The format of the double documents in antiquity was somewhat flexible, depending on materials available and the individual needs and circumstances. One cannot expect that the Book of Mormon plates physically conformed exactly to patterns used in other ancient legal and administrative practices. Double documents could be inscribed in various fashions on papyrus, parchment, metal tablets, or clay-case tablets. Although the particular details of implementation varied to suit the available writing media and sealing materials, the underlying concepts remained essentially the same.

The necessity for, and functions of, witnesses are attested through many ancient legal documents. Although the number of witnesses varied, it could not be less than three for a sealed document, according to Jewish law. Biblical law called for two or three witnesses in judicial settings. The witnesses were crucial for verifying the validity of the document, the sealed part standing as a witness for the revealed part in time of judgment, when the seal was broken by an authorized person. Since the witnessed document was received under oath, curses fell upon those who failed to give heed to these documents: "Cursed be he that confirmeth not all the words of this law to do them" (Deuteronomy 27:26). All this gives additional force to the comment found in Job, "For God speaketh once, yea twice, yet man perceiveth it not" (Job 33:14).

In ancient societies, where duplicating equipment and central record offices did not exist, the practice of stating important decisions or transactions twice provided an important degree of certitude concerning the accuracy of crucial official records. No wonder this practice was impressive and memorable to many ancient people: it provided a powerful image to the prophet Jeremiah, it grew to be prevalent in Hellenistic

Egypt, it was remembered by the Dead Sea sectarians, it was useful in the hands of apocryphal writers, it became mandatory in certain cases under Jewish law, and it persisted in Roman administration. For many of the same reasons, it also was paradigmatic for Nephi and the plates of Mormon.

Notes

I thank Alison Coutts for her careful and valuable assistance in completing this project, and Michael Lyon for his expertise in producing the illustrations.

1. See Leopold Wenger, "Über Stempel und Siegel," *Zeitschrift der Savigny-Stiftung* 42 (1921): 626, in which Wenger correlates Jeremiah's double deed to Assyrian double deeds while noting the difference in material.

2. John Bright, ed., *Jeremiah,* The Anchor Bible, vol. 21 (Garden City, N.Y.: Doubleday, 1965), 237 n. 11.

3. See Elisabeth Koffmahn, *Die Doppelurkunden aus der Wüste Juda* (Leiden: Brill, 1968), 19.

4. See Tsvi Schneider, "Six Biblical Signatures: Seals and Seal Impressions of Six Biblical Personages Recovered," *Biblical Archaeology Review* 17 (July/August 1991): 26–33; Yigael Shiloh, "A Group of Hebrew Bullae from the City of David," *Israel Exploration Journal* 36 (1986): 33.

5. Ben Zion Wacholder, "The 'Sealed' Torah versus the 'Revealed' Torah: An Exegesis of Damascus Covenant V, 1–6 and Jeremiah 32, 10–14," *Revue de Qumran* 12 (December 1986): 353.

6. Bright, *Jeremiah,* 237 n. 11.

7. Ibid., 236.

8. Jeremiah 32:11, New American Bible.

9. Jeremiah 32:11, Revised Standard Version; see Daniel C. Browning, "Contracts, Deeds and Their Containers," *Biblical Illustrator* (spring 1990): 64.

10. See Bright, *Jeremiah,* 237 n. 11.

11. See especially Leopold Fischer, "Die Urkunden in Jer 32 11–14

nach den Ausgrabungen und dem Talmud," *Zeitschrift der Altertums Wissenschaft* 30 (1910): 136–42; Leopold Wenger, "Über Stempel und Siegel," 611–38.

12. Koffmahn, in *Doppelurkunden*, tends to overstate the Hebraic origin of double documents; nevertheless, she provides the most extensive recent discussion of the topic available. Translation from her German is mine.

13. Ibid., 17, citing Friedrich Bilabel, "Zur Doppelausfertigung ägyptischer Urkunden," pt. 2, *Aegyptus* 6/2–3 (1925): 94, which refers to ten examples from a collection of Egyptian double documents dating from 300 B.C.

14. Koffmahn, *Doppelurkunden*, 11.

15. Ann Perkins, ed., *The Excavations at Dura-Europos*, final report 5, pt. 1 (New Haven: Yale University Press, 1959), 14.

16. See Koffmahn, *Doppelurkunden*, 18; see also Friedrich Bilabel, "Zur Doppelausfertigung ägyptischer Urkunden," pt. 1, *Aegyptus* 5/3 (1924): 98.

17. Koffmahn, *Doppelurkunden*, 23.

18. See Bernard P. Grenfell and Arthur S. Hunt, eds., *The Hibeh Papyri*, pt. 1 (London: Egypt Exploration Fund, 1906), 242, 266. Hibeh is on the east bank of the Nile between Benisuêf and Shêkh Fadl; the papryi form part of the John Rylands Library, demotic collection.

19. See Alfred v. Domaszewski, "Ein neues Militärdiplom," in *Die Altertümer unsere heidnischen Vorzeit* (Mainz: Römisch-Germanisches Zentralmuseum, 1911), 5:181.

20. See Fischer, "Die Urkunden in Jer 32 11–14," 139; Otto B. Rubensohn, *Elephantine-Papyri* (Berlin: Weidmann, 1907), 7.

21. Koffmahn, *Doppelurkunden*, 11.

22. Ibid., 15.

23. Wadi Murabbaʿat is located in the Judean desert. Excavation there revealed archaeological remains in four caves. These remains included full papyri, papyri fragments with traces of letters, several small ostraca, and two coins. See Emanuel Tov and Stephen J. Pfann,

eds., *Companion Volume to the Dead Sea Scrolls Microfiche Edition* (Leiden: Brill, 1995), 115.

24. Koffmahn, *Doppelurkunden*, 13.

25. In the 1930s archaeologists uncovered a Roman garrison town, Dura-Europos, once located at the edge of the Persian empire of the Sassanians, now found in the Syrian desert near Dayr az-Zawr.

26. Perkins, *Excavations at Dura-Europos*, 14.

27. See Koffmahn, *Doppelurkunden*, 14.

28. See ibid., 15.

29. Leopold Fischer, "Die Urkunden im Talmud," in *Jahrbuch der Jüdisch-Literarischen Gesellschaft* (Frankfurt: J. Kauffmann, 1912), 138.

30. Browning, "Contracts, Deeds," 64.

31. See Koffmahn, *Doppelurkunden*, 13–15.

32. See ibid., 13–14, as in the talmudic practice.

33. Ibid., 15.

34. See Rubensohn, *Elephantine-Papyri*, 6–8; Fischer, "Die Urkunden in Jer 32 11–14," 138; Friedrich Preisigke, *Griechische Papyrus* (Leipzig: Hinrichs, 1912), 1:221.

35. See Fischer, "Die Urkunden in Jer 32 11–14," 138.

36. See Perkins, *Excavations at Dura-Europos*, 14.

37. See Friedrich Preisigke, *Griechische Papyrus* (Leipzig: Hinrichs, 1920), 2:15.

38. Perkins, *Excavations at Dura-Europos*, 14.

39. Domaszewski, "Ein neues Militärdiplom," 181.

40. See E. Hammershaimb, "Some Observations on the Aramaic Elephantine Papyri," *Vetus Testamentum* 7 (January 1957): 24.

41. See Koffmahn, *Doppelurkunden*, 23.

42. See Hans J. Wolff, "Die hellenistische Zeugen-Hüterurkunde," in *Das Recht der griechischen Papyri Ägyptens* (Munich: Beck, 1978), 2:63. For a long list of published six-witness documents from Egypt, see Bilabel, "Doppelausfertigung," pt. 1, 156–7; see also Paul M. Meyer, *Juristische Papyri* (Chicago: Ares, 1976), 103.

43. Grenfell, *Hibeh Papryi*, 266.

44. Koffmahn, *Doppelurkunden*, 12.

45. See Fischer, "Die Urkunden in Jer 32 11–14," 139; Wolff, "Die hellenistische Zeugen-Hüterurkunde," 63 n. 39.

46. TB *Gittin* 81b.

47. Yigael Yadin, *Bar-Kokhba: The Rediscovery of the Legendary Hero of the Last Jewish Revolt against Imperial Rome* (New York: Random House, 1971), 230.

48. Perkins, *Excavations at Dura-Europos*, 15.

49. Ibid.

50. Ibid.

51. See Koffmahn, *Doppelurkunden*, 11.

52. See Fischer, "Die Urkunden in Jer 32 11–14," 138.

53. Koffmahn, *Doppelurkunden*, 26.

54. See ibid., 27.

55. Yadin, *Bar-Kokhba*, 229.

56. See Koffmahn, *Doppelurkunden*, 12, citing Mishnah Tosephta *Baba Bathra* 10:12 (TB and TY). See also Fischer, "Die Urkunden im Talmud," 51–88.

57. Koffmahn, *Doppelurkunden*, 12, citing Mishnah Tosephta *Baba Bathra* 10:12 (TB and TY).

58. Talmud *Baba Bathra* 160b. Compare *firm and steadfast* in 1 Nephi 2:10 and 3 Nephi 6:14.

59. See Koffmahn, *Doppelurkunden*, 23; see also Bilabel, "Doppelausfertigung," pt. 2, 105.

60. It has been said that five fragments of doubled manuscripts from Qumran Cave 4 may be dated to the second century before Christ (see Koffmahn, *Doppelurkunden*, 20). While they have not been published, these fragments (4Q344, 345, 346, 348, and 349) have been identified as including a debt acknowledgment, a sale of land, an act regarding ownership, and a seal of property, but they are highly fragmentary and difficult to read. It is not clear what kinds of documents they are.

61. See Jozef T. Milik, "Deux documents inédits du désert de Juda," *Biblica* 38 (1957): 255–60.

62. See Koffmahn, *Doppelurkunden*, 25–7.

63. Naḥal Ḥever is located in the Judean desert. Cave 5/6 contained the Babatha archive, the contents of which include many double documents (see Tov and Pfann, *Companion Volume to the Dead Sea Scrolls*, 117).

64. See Koffmahn, *Doppelurkunden*, 27.

65. Bright, *Jeremiah*, 236.

66. Browning, "Contracts, Deeds," 63; see A. Leo Oppenheim, *Ancient Mesopotamia: Portrait of a Dead Civilization*, rev. Erica Reiner (Chicago: University of Chicago Press, 1977), 241.

67. See Oppenheim, *Ancient Mesopotamia*, 282.

68. See ibid.

69. Browning, "Contracts, Deeds," 64, citing Nahman Avigad.

70. Yadin, *Bar-Kokhba*, 230; emphasis in original.

71. Koffmahn, *Doppelurkunden*, 22.

72. Ibid., 21–2.

73. Ibid., 28.

74. Ibid.

75. Ibid.

76. See Wolff, "Die hellenistische Zeugen-Hüterurkunde," 61.

77. See Wenger, "Über Stempel und Siegel," 626. The practice of enclosing tokens in clay envelopes has been dated to the early fourth millennium B.C. See Denise Schmandt-Besserat, "Strings of Tokens and Envelopes," in *From Counting to Cuneiform*, vol. 1 of *Before Writing* (Austin: University of Texas Press, 1992), 108.

78. See Marian San Nicolò, "Die Tontafel als Urkundenform des Privatrechtes," in *Beiträge zur Rechtsgeschichte im Bereiche der Keilschriftlichen Rechtsquellen* (Oslo: Aschehoug, 1931), 126.

79. See Oppenheim, *Ancient Mesopotamia*, 282.

80. See ibid.

81. See Wenger, "Über Stempel und Siegel," 626.

82. See ibid., 625; Browning, "Contracts, Deeds," 63.

83. Fischer, "Die Urkunden in Jer 32 11–14," 141, citing S. N. Strassmaier.

84. See San Nicolò, "Die Tontafel," 116.

85. See ibid., 116–17.

86. San Nicolò refers to the instrument as a *qân ṭuppi*.

87. See Edward Chiera, *They Wrote on Clay* (Chicago: University of Chicago Press, 1938), 69–70.

88. Ibid., 70.

89. See ibid., 71–2.

90. See Bright, *Jeremiah*, 238 n. 13.

91. Hammershaimb, "Aramaic Elephantine Papyri," 25.

92. Wolff, "Die hellenistische Zeugen-Hüterurkunde," 62.

93. See Rubensohn, *Elephantine-Papyri*, 8.

94. Fischer, "Die Urkunden in Jer 32 11–14," 141.

95. See Koffmahn, *Doppelurkunden*, 29.

96. See Wenger, "Über Stempel und Siegel," 631.

97. See Géza Alföldy, "Zur Beurteilung der Militärplome der Auxiliarsoldaten," *Historia* 17 (1968): 215–27; Theodor Mommsen and Herbert Nesselhauf, *Corpus Inscriptionum Latinarum volumen XVI, Diplomata militaria* (Berlin: de Gruyter, 1936, 1955); Instrumentum Domesticum, fascicule 1 (military diplomata, metal ingots, tesserae, dies, labels, and lead sealings), ed. S. S. Frere, Margaret Roxan, and R. S. O. Tomlin, vol. 2 of *The Roman Inscriptions of Britain*, by R. G. Collingwood and R. P. Wright (Oxford: Clarendon, 1990); and the following by Margaret Roxan: "Epigraphic Notes," *Epigraphische Studien* 9 (1972): 246–50; *Roman Military Diplomas, 1954–1977* (London: Institute of Archaeology, 1978); "The Distribution of Roman Military Diplomas," *Epigraphische Studien* 12 (1981): 265–86; *Roman Military Diplomas, 1985–1993* (London: Institute of Archaeology, 1994).

98. See Koffmahn, *Doppelurkunden*, 24–5.

99. See ibid., 15.

100. Cited in ibid., 15–16.

101. See John L. Sorenson and Martin H. Raish, eds., *Pre-Columbian Contact with the Americas across the Oceans: An Annotated Bibliography*, 2nd ed. rev. (Provo, Utah: Research Press, 1996), from which the following references and notations have been drawn: José Alcina Franch, "Distribución geográfica de las pintaderas en

América," *Archivo de prehistoira levantina* 3 (1952): 241–55, discussing the distribution of stamp seals in America; José Alcina Franch, "Diffusion of Pottery Stamps (summary)," *Proceedings of the 30th International Congress of Americanists* (Cambridge: n.p., 1952): 248, which deals with the seals or pottery stamps of Mexico and the hypothesis that they were introduced to America in Neolithic times, originally from the Near East by way of the Mediterranean; José Alcina Franch, "Hipótesis acerca de la difusión mundial de las 'pintaderas,'" *Trabajos y conferencias* 3 (1955): 217–23, arguing for a worldwide diffusion of stamp seals; José Alcina Franch, "Las 'Pintaderas' de Canarias y sus posibles relaciones," *Anuario de estudios atlánticos* 17 (1971): 103–49, regarding the possibility of an Atlantic diffusion of seals; Stephan F. de Borhegyi, "Notas sobre sellos de barro existentes en el Museo Nacional de Arqueología y Etnología de Guatemala," *Antropología e Historia de Guatemala* 2 (1950): 16–26, examining the dating of cylinder seals and stamps throughout most of the archaeological sequence of highland Guatemala, especially in the Early Preclassic period; George W. Brainerd, "A Cylindrical Stamp from Ecuador," *Masterkey* 27/1 (1953): 14–17, reporting a stamp that incorporates the Mesoamerican concept of the speech scroll in its design; George F. Carter and Sol Heinemann, "Pre-Columbian Sellos: Another Artifact Showing Possible Cultural Contact and Trans-Pacific Diffusion," *Anthropological Journal of Canada* 15/3 (1977): 2–6, analyzing the writing on Mexican cylinder and stamp seals; Gabriel deCicco and Donald Brockington, *Reconocimiento arqueológico en el suroeste de Oaxaca,* informes 6 (Instituto Nacional de Antropología e Historia, Dirección di Monumentos Pre-Hispánicos, 1956): 22–5, featuring a presentation of a stamp seal found in Oaxaca; David H. Kelley, "A Cylinder Seal from Tlatilco," *American Antiquity* 31 (1966): 744–6, discussing the inscription on a cylinder seal apparently from the Olmec occupation at Tlatilco; Carlos Navarrete, *Un reconocimiento de la Sierra Madre de Chiapas: Apuntes de un Diario de Campo,* cuadernos 13 (Universidad Nacional Autónoma de México, Centro de Estudios Mayas, 1978), examining nonpictorial characters on a stamp seal found in the Sierra

Madre. See also Carl Hugh Jones, "The 'Anthon Transcript' and Two Mesoamerican Cylinder Seals," *Newsletter of the Society for Early Historic Archaeology,* no. 122 (September 1970), 1–8.

102. Wacholder, "'Sealed' Torah," 360. Consider also 4Q203, a fragment that speaks of a "copy of the second tablet" that "has not been read up till now," as rendered in Florentino García Martínez, ed., *The Dead Sea Scrolls Translated: The Qumran Texts in English,* trans. Wilfred G. E. Watson (Leiden: E. J. Brill, 1994), 260.

103. Louis Ginzberg, *The Legends of the Jews,* trans. Henrietta Szold (Philadelphia: Jewish Publication Society of America, 1988), 3:439–40, citing Petirat Mosheh.

104. See Wacholder, "'Sealed' Torah," 354.

105. Ibid., 355; emphasis in original.

106. Ibid., 357 and n. 21.

107. See ibid., 362 and n. 34.

108. As translated by J. Priest, in James H. Charlesworth, ed., *The Old Testament Pseudepigrapha* (Garden City, N.Y.: Doubleday, 1983), 1:927.

109. *History of the Church,* 4:537; compare *The Papers of Joseph Smith,* ed. Dean C. Jessee (Salt Lake City: Deseret Book, 1989), 1:399–400.

110. As quoted in *David Whitmer Interviews: A Restoration Witness,* ed. Lyndon W. Cook (Orem, Utah: Grandin, 1991), 20–1.

111. Ibid., 75.

112. Ibid., 172.

113. Ibid., 221.

114. Ibid., 248.

115. Ibid., 254.

CHAPTER 13

FESTIVALS AS CONTEXT FOR EXCHANGE IN THE GREAT BASIN–COLUMBIA PLATEAU REGION OF WESTERN NORTH AMERICA

Joel C. Janetski

We soon found out that [the] Provo River region was the great place of gathering of all Ute tribes of central Utah valleys, too, on account of the wonderful supply of fish moving up the stream from the Lake to their spawning ground every spring. . . . While these Bands of Indians met each spring for fishing, they engaged in good sporting as well, horse-racing, trading, gambling, footracing, wrestling, etc. Some spent weeks here.[1]

The exchange of goods and ideas in western North American aboriginal societies occurred in diverse social and economic contexts, such as festivals, life-crisis events, opportunistic bartering, structured trade, and gambling. As indicated by the introductory quotation, festivals, the focus of this study, were

Joel C. Janetski is professor of anthropology and director of the Museum of Peoples and Cultures at Brigham Young University.

times of excitement, sociability, and renewal for the hunting and gathering peoples of the Great Basin and Columbia Plateau. W. Raymond Wood argues that the intense and regular interaction that occurred at festivals was an important catalyst for cultural change among the participants.[2] Likewise, Robert F. Spencer, in his study of trade fairs among the North Alaskan Eskimo, states, "Trade, in short, was the factor which brought tremendously widely separated people together and which promoted the spread of ideas and culture elements from one center to another."[3] H. Edwin Jackson also has emphasized the importance of trade fairs as a mechanism for social and economic interaction among hunter-gatherers across the globe during recent times and has argued for the existence of similar events rather deep in prehistory.[4] However, the incomplete ethnographic record and the difficulties inherent in identifying short-term social gatherings (however large) through archaeology tend to distort or underplay the importance of regular social interactions that occurred among ethnically distinct groups, even in demographically sparse areas such as the Great Basin–Columbia Plateau region of the western United States.

Wood has described a "trade net" that blanketed pre-European North America.[5] Critical to his model are major (primary) and secondary centers, which acted as points of regional aggregation. Primary centers are defined as villages occupied by sedentary populations, a circumstance made possible by the presence of a substantial resource base (such as crops or fish). Populations swelled at these centers during the trade fairs. Secondary centers were impermanent or floating concentrations of people who aggregated solely for the short-term trade activity. The mountain man rendezvous epitomizes secondary centers, while the Missouri River horticultural villages are typical of primary centers. The trade-oriented gatherings at both the primary and the secondary centers have often been referred to as trade fairs.

Following a probe of the ethnographic and historic literature for the southern Columbia Plateau and the Great Basin
area, I offer a refinement of Wood's characterization of the
trade net by suggesting a tertiary level of distributory mechanisms in the Great Basin. This level consists of the ubiquitous
"festivals" recorded for most Great Basin peoples. I propose that
these events, whose basis was more social than economic, were
effective links in exchange systems (with emphasis on the exchange of information and ideas rather than goods alone) of the
desert West. The empirical basis for this conclusion follows a
brief discussion of the social role of exchange.

Exchange in Small-Scale Societies

How, when, and why did exchange occur in aboriginal societies in western North America? George Dalton's comments
from more than three decades ago are worth repeating as preface to this issue: "Primitive economy is different from market
industrialism not in degree but in kind."[6] Joseph G. Jorgensen,
in his exhaustive review of western Indian society, notes the variety of contexts wherein goods were moved from one individual to another and comments that trade in the formal sense
may have been the least important of these.[7] This notion is
made clear in Marshall Sahlins's classic treatment of economics
in simple societies, wherein he states that redistribution of
commodities cannot be understood apart from social context.
Circumstance, kinship, and history all play a part in determining direction, quantity, and quality of the flow of goods. In
Sahlins's scheme of reciprocities, which reflects the array of circumstances and expectations that surround gift giving and
trade, reciprocity has three levels—generalized, balanced, and
negative—with kin distance decreasing and economic interests
and potential for tension increasing at each level.[8] For example,

gift giving among kin on such occasions as birth, puberty, marriage, and death carries little economic expectation and exemplifies generalized reciprocity, whereas balanced and negative reciprocity characterize exchange among distant relations and unrelated persons and carries greater economic impact.

Exchange relaxed tensions between unrelated groups. Sahlins, paraphrasing Marcel Mauss from *The Gift: Forms and Functions of Exchange in Archaic Societies*, states, "Menaced always by deterioration into war, primitive groups are nevertheless reconciled by festival and exchange."[9] Similarly, Lorna Marshall quotes an African bushman: "The worse thing is not giving presents. If people do not like each other but one gives a gift and the other must accept, this brings a peace between them. We give what we have. That is the way we live together."[10] Viewed in this light, exchange assumes diplomatic dimensions apart from economics: "The gift is the primitive way of achieving the peace that in civil society is secured by the State."[11]

Feasting solidified social relations, and giving food demonstrated generosity. Sahlins argues that food moved mostly in generalized rather than balanced exchange. He states as principle that "one does not exchange things for food, not directly that is, among friends and relatives. Traffic in food is traffic between foreign interests."[12] Spencer's account of restrictions on trade in food among the Alaskan Eskimo illustrates this notion: "Again, the feeling was present that to trade for food was reprehensible, but since each setting had its own specialties, this attitude was in some measure obviated. . . . The pattern with respect to food was less concerned with formal exchange. It was used to cement good relations between partners and when given as a gift, the notion of trading for food was avoided."[13]

It is no surprise that trade events typically included or concluded with feasts, a pattern that is exemplified by numerous cases. North Alaskan trade fairs concluded with the Messenger

Feast, and the Pomo of California participated in trade feasts during which foodstuffs, especially fish, were traded for shell or stone beads.[14] Feasts were associated with most gatherings in the Great Basin–Columbia Plateau region: the Sun Dance (Ute), datura ceremony (Southern Paiute, Chemehuevi), Bear Dance (Ute), and Girls' Dance (Washo) all concluded with feasting.[15] Social, political, and economic purposes blended in these occasions. In ecologically or economically contrasting regions, food naturally and appropriately became a common commodity in the marketplace. Mandan/Arikara-Plains and Plains-Pueblo peoples exemplified this kind of complementary, mutualistic relationship; in both cases garden produce of the farmers moved against the meat and hides brought by hunters.[16]

Several expectations concerning festivals can be surmised from the foregoing discussion. The social atmosphere of festivals should vary depending on who attended: close kin, distant relatives, or unrelated groups. Underlying tensions would be most expected in the context of intertribal trade, and gift exchange and feasting would reduce that tension and set the scene for serious trading. In all cases festivals should occur during times of food abundance. Trade in foodstuffs, however rationalized, would be more likely to occur between individuals from ecologically contrasting regions. And importantly, festival participants attended for social rather than commercial purposes.

Accounts of Festivals and Trade in the Ethnographic Great Basin and Columbia Plateau Region

Great Basin

The hydrographic Great Basin encompasses the region from the Sierra Nevada of eastern California on the west, Utah's Wasatch Mountains on the east, and the drainages of the Snake and Virgin Rivers on the north and south, respectively. The

cultural Great Basin, however, spilled beyond this physio-
graphic area well into the Columbia Plateau to the north to
include portions of eastern Oregon, western and southern
Idaho, the Colorado Plateau of eastern Utah and western Colorado, and the plains of Wyoming.[17] Linguistic and cultural
similarities combine to group the aboriginal peoples of this
area, which once encompassed the Northern Paiute, Western
and Northern Shoshone, Ute, and Southern Paiute peoples (see
figure 1).

Information on trade among Great Basin peoples is generally sparse or at best erratic. It is not clear whether this defi-
ciency is due to the interest (or lack of it) of ethnographers or to
real patterns. Festivals, on the other hand, are mentioned or
described for most groups (see table 1, located at the end of this
chapter). Richard E. Hughes and James A. Bennyhoff, in their
synthesis of exchange in the ethnographic Great Basin, conclude that organized festivals provided the context for much
traditional trade activity in this region.[18] Areas with particularly
rich information include Owens Valley, Humboldt Sink, and
Yainax Butte.

Western Great Basin

Owens Valley, on the extreme western edge of the Great
Basin, was home to the Northern Paiute. Julian H. Steward described their annual festival, or fandango: "The Paiute . . . assembled each fall for dancing, gambling, and festivities."[19] Typically,
fandangos were held after seed harvest or around rabbit-hunt
time, with the location varying annually. Steward does not discuss trade as an activity accompanying the fandango, although
the Owens Valley Paiute were certainly involved with trade.[20]
Most trade occurred with California peoples, particularly the
Western Mono and Miwok, and was accomplished in "hurried

Fig. 1. Locations of documented primary (●), secondary (○), and tertiary (•) locations for socioeconomic gatherings across the Great Basin and southern Columbia Plateau.

trips."[21] There is no mention of just how the trade occurred, but considerable quantities of goods—mostly perishables (foodstuffs such as pine nuts and berries, salt, rabbit-skin blankets, baskets) but some nonperishables (clamshell beads, obsidian)—were toted in burden baskets, mostly by women, across the Sierras. The Paiute traded little with other Great Basin peoples to the east. Steward stressed the importance of gambling during the fandango, although gambling occurred year-round.

East and north of Owens Valley, the Humboldt Sink is the terminus of the Humboldt River, which drains all of northern Nevada, and was another population center for Northern Paiute people.[22] Broad, grassy, and rich in wetland resources that flourished in the marshes and ephemeral lakes, the sink was attractive to hunting and gathering peoples who lived in the arid environment of the western Basin. Early travelers commented on the large numbers of people concentrated there. Jedediah Smith camped at the sink in 1827 and was threatened by twenty to thirty mounted Paiute who, because they had buffalo robes and Spanish blankets with them, were apparently involved in long-distance trading with both Plains Indians and the Spanish.[23] Two years later, in May 1929 at the Humboldt Sink, Peter Skene Ogden had a similar encounter with "upwards of two hundred" mounted Indians, probably from California, whom he described as not "well inclined toward us."[24] Ogden was struck by the large populations of Indians along the Humboldt River. As he traveled east of Winnemucca along the Humboldt in November 1928, he wrote, "It is almost indescribable how numerous the natives are in this quarter."[25] Zenas Leonard, who traveled down the Humboldt in September 1833 with the Joseph Walker party, also described large numbers of people at Humboldt Sink, although these people were not mounted: "Here [at the sink] the country is low and swampy, producing an abundance of very fine grass. . . . On taking a view of the surrounding waste with a spy-glass, we discovered smoke issuing from the high grass in every direction. This was sufficient to convince us that we were in the midst of a large body of Indians. [Eventually] the Indians issued from their hiding places in the grass, to the number, as near as I could guess, of 8 or 900."[26]

Eight or nine hundred people seems a very large concentration by Great Basin standards. It is possible, given the fall date and the abundant resources of the sink, that the people had gathered for fall festivities (see table 1); however, such a conclusion is conjecture. On the basis of the presence of mounted, apparently hostile Indians, Thomas N. Layton concludes that the Humboldt Sink was a trading center, albeit a secondary one, that also functioned as a stopover where raiders and traders from Walker River and California fed their horses as they moved across the Great Basin to Idaho for buffalo products.[27]

Yainax Butte in southern Oregon, an area in traditional Klamath territory, was apparently another location for annual trade fairs.[28] In 1873 Clarke described a fair in the area: "To this mountain's base came the Columbia River Indians to exchange fleet cayuse coursers for slaves, to barter the blankets and nicknacks furnished by the Fur Company traders for the furs gathered by Modocs and Klamaths, and the bows and arrows. . . . Yainax was a great slave mart in the long ago, for Klamaths and Modocs, being first cousins, . . . made war indiscriminately on weaker tribes and took captives to swell the importance of the Yainax fairs." In a 1905 account Clarke related the following: "The Yahooskin or Summer Lake Snakes did not hesitate to take part in these gatherings, for, though neutral as to their fellow Snakes, they liked to take a hand in the games, make good trades, and swap horses—when they could do so to advantage.

There was pleasure and honor, as well as plenty of business, here at Yainax on those gala days in October."[29]

Layton described the Humboldt Sink and Yainax Butte as intermediate nodes for trade. The former linked California with the Rockies via the Humboldt River, and the latter connected California with the major trade center at The Dalles on the Columbia River. Layton maintains that the pattern was in place before 1800, although the movement along these routes, especially long-distance movement, would have increased greatly with the introduction of the horse.[30]

To the west of the Northern Paiute lay Washo territory, which centered on Lake Tahoe and its outlet, the Truckee River. James F. Downs describes Washo trade with the neighboring Paiute as "lively."[31] Commodities of exchange included deer for antelope or occasionally bison hides, pigments, and tool stone. The Washo, whom Downs characterizes as middlemen between the "rich country of California and the relatively impoverished Basin," traveled to California to obtain shell and obsidian knives for exchange with groups to the east. James T. Davis names the Miwok, Maidu, and Mono as primary trading partners for salt, pine nuts, rabbit-skin and buffalo robes, baskets, and shell beads, among other things. He does not mention trade with Pyramid Lake or other Northern Paiute neighbors.[32]

The annual Washo festival, or *Gumsaba*, included games, fasting, feasting, gambling, and dancing. Warren d'Azevedo describes late spring and early summer first-fish rites held by the Washo at the mouth of Long Valley Creek near Honey Lake, and he makes note of gift exchanges that occurred during these and other festivals.[33] Attendees other than the Washo are not mentioned, although nearby Honey Lake was occupied by Northern Paiute and Maidu.[34] Interestingly, ethnographer Francis Riddell states that Honey Lake Paiute described gambling as a form of trade that served to move deer hides, baskets, dentalia, and rabbit-skin blankets between them and the Washo.[35] These comments suggest that gambling occurred at intertribal gatherings of Washo, Northern Paiute, and perhaps Maidu.

Central Great Basin

There is little information about trade activities among the Western Shoshone in the central Great Basin. In fact, Julian Steward, the premier ethnographer of Basin aboriginal peoples, maintains that Nevada Shoshone traded little or not at all.[36] Festivals, on the other hand, were typical; people from nearly every valley participated in them at least annually (see table 1). The following excerpts from Steward's monograph describe what occurred at these festivals:

Owens Valley. "Six-day festivals, involving dances, gambling, and rabbit drives, were held by each band in the fall after the pine-nut harvest. These were planned, organized, and managed by the band chief. Invitations were sent to neighboring villages. Large villages . . . attracted people from distant places. . . . Sometimes villages held festivals at different times in the fall so that people from elsewhere could attend after completing their own festival."[37]

Steptoe Valley. "Festivals, involving the round dance, back-and-forth dance, 'war dance' or *paminukep*, and considerable gambling, were held, usually after pine-nut harvest, at various localities, depending partly upon abundance of seeds. People after dancing at home, often went elsewhere to dance again; there was frequent reciprocation in this manner."[38]

Skull Valley/Deep Creek. "Festivals were held independently at Skull Valley, Deep Creek, and perhaps elsewhere under different directors. . . . Festivals were held by members of several neighboring villages, principally in the spring. They performed the round dance to make seeds grow. If, however, many people were assembled in some area of abundant seeds during the summer, and especially when gathering pine nuts in the fall, they might also hold dances. . . . When such dances were to be held the chief sent out messengers to invite people to attend. The main festivals lasted 5 days."[39]

Steward mentions festivals for each Great Basin valley he describes, and although these festivals varied somewhat, some common patterns are evident. Festivals were not located in the same place each year, nor did the same people attend each time, though the events usually included people from nearby valleys. Festivals were held when foods were relatively abundant, especially around the pine-nut harvest and fall rabbit drives. Activities included dances and gambling. Trade is seldom mentioned for regions south of the Snake River.

Eastern Great Basin

The Shoshone, Ute, and Southern Paiute peoples occupied the eastern Great Basin and the northern Colorado Plateau to the east. Traditional Ute territory covered much of eastern Utah and Colorado, with the groups in the former region often referred to as the Western Ute and those in the latter as the Eastern Ute. Reference was made in the introductory quote to the spring gathering in Utah Valley, which was in Western Ute territory. Various sources make clear this area's importance, a result of its rich fishery and population concentrations.[40] Utah Valley as a gathering place is further documented in an 1849 book by T. J. Farnham: "The great Yutas tribe . . . is divided into two families which are contradistinguished by the names of their respective head-quarters; the Taos Yutas, so called, because their principal camp is pitched in the Taos mountains, seventy miles north of Santa Fe; and the Timpanigos Yutas who hold their great camp near the Timpanigos lake."[41]

Farnham's reference to sizable camps at Taos and "Timpanigos lake" (Utah Lake) in the same breath could imply that both were locations for trade fairs. Taos is well-known as a major fair location that attracted Plains Indians as well as Pueblos.[42] The description of the spring gathering of "all Ute tribes of central Utah valleys" (see introductory quotation) at Utah Lake strongly suggests that Utah Valley served as the location for a large festival. Omer C. Stewart's comments regarding the Bear Dance imply that this renewal ceremony was very likely a part of the festival in Utah Valley. One of his informants reported that the Bear Dance started after the "*Pagonunts* (Utah Lake Indians) came to [the] Uintah Reservation."[43]

Another indication that Utah Valley was a trade center is the fact that it was a primary stop for the Dominguez-Escalante party. They traded in the valley for fresh supplies and pondered establishing a Spanish colony. Subsequently, Spanish traders visited the valley to barter for slaves and horses.[44] Utah Valley's rich fishery and permanent population density also suggest the area was a primary trade center.

Utes in the southern portion of the region traded with their linguistic cousins—the Southern Paiute, the Navajo, and the Pueblos.[45] Isabel T. Kelly identifies the Utes as important in Southern Paiute trade activities (see section below).

Southern Great Basin/Colorado Plateau

Kelly's research on the Southern Paiute is by far the most important source of information on trade in the southern Great Basin. She reports trade activity for all groups studied (Kaibab, Kaiparowits, San Juan, and Panguitch).[46] The Kaibab, for example, traded with other Southern Paiute bands as well as with the Ute and Navajo. Most intriguing are insights into trade between nonagricultural and agricultural groups. The Kaibab, who did not farm, traded with Paiutes at St. George, receiving "about 50 lbs of maize, beans" for a deer hide.[47] After 1800, trade was vigorous with the Ute, who brought horses, buffalo robes, metal knives, and guns to trade for buckskins and Navajo blankets. In this latter case the Southern Paiute acted as middlemen. Little trade crossed the imposing Grand Canyon and Colorado River. Kelly offers no insights into when such trade occurred or the circumstances surrounding the exchange. She collected no information on social gatherings such as the Washo *Gumsaba*, although she and Stewart both record dances and numerous gambling activities that would have taken place during such festivals. Dances most commonly occurred in the fall, in concert with communal rabbit hunts and pine-nut gathering and after crops were harvested.[48]

Steward's brief description of Southern Paiute bands in southern Nevada is important because it does mention fall festivals reminiscent of the central Great Basin pattern. These three- or four-day events included several villages in the Las Vegas or Moapa area and consisted of dances and annual mourning rites.[49] Robert C. Euler, in his exhaustive compendium of Southern Paiute ethnohistory, relates numerous accounts of Navajo in the vicinity of Kanab during the 1870s. He cites John D. Lee's journal, which remarks that Kanab was "full of NavaJoes in to trade" and that "13 NavaJoes started to visit the settlements North as far as Beaver [Utah]."[50] Euler also cites Lee's midsummer descriptions of Indians at Panguitch Lake (in south-central Utah) who had laid out "Strings of Trout to trade."[51] These Indians were likely from the Panguitch band of Southern Paiute. Like Kelly, however, Euler provides no accounts of gatherings other than those orchestrated by Anglos, though he offers many instances of individual bartering. Given the accounts of annual festivals among the Moapa Paiute, it seems reasonable to assume that festivals occurred among Paiute to the east as well.

Columbia Plateau

The Snake River–Columbia River system drains the vast region north of the Great Basin from Yellowstone to Canada and was a traffic corridor for aboriginal peoples in southern Idaho, Oregon, and Washington. Its role as a transportation route was and is critical to the lives of people in these areas. The Columbia River, which forks near Umatilla, Washington, drains eastern Washington, and the Snake drains the country to the east and south across southern Idaho. Aboriginal peoples in this area include the Northern Shoshone and Bannock of southern Idaho, the Northern Paiute of southeast Oregon, the Nez Percé of western Idaho and Oregon, the Cayuse and Umatilla of eastern Oregon, the Spokane of eastern Washington, the Kalispel of northern Idaho, and others. Two important trading centers flourished in protohistoric times on the Snake River: the first and the best known was Camas Prairie, located on the northern edge of the Snake River plain; the second was at the mouth of the Weiser River, close to the Idaho-Oregon border.

Camas Prairie lies northwest of Twin Falls, in southern Idaho. Camas roots were abundant in late spring and attracted people from throughout the Snake River country.[52] These gatherings were important social and economic events: "This was also a time of dances and festivities, for a large part of the Shoshone and Bannock population of Idaho, plus a sprinkling of the Nez Perce and Flathead resorted at the same time to these root grounds. These were probably the largest gatherings of people among all the Shoshone. There was no large single encampment, but families and camp groups were in such close contiguity that social interaction was intense."[53]

Trade was an important aspect of the Camas Prairie gathering. Bannock, Shoshone, Nez Percé, Flathead, Pend d'Oreilles, and people from the Northern Great Basin all participated. According to Sven Liljeblad, "The Bannock traded buffalo hides to the Nez Perce for horses. The downstream Shoshoni came loaded with salmon; groups who wintered in northern Utah brought seeds and pine nuts; the impoverished local Shoshoni had nothing to offer but seeds, roots, and dried crickets."[54]

In the years after the demise of bison on the Snake River plain, Camas Prairie was also the point of departure for the annual buffalo hunt over the Bannock Trail, which went across extreme northwestern Wyoming in the area of present-day Yellowstone National Park. Much could be said about the importance of Camas Prairie in the lives of the Shoshone and Bannock of southern Idaho. Suffice it to say that the intrusion of whites into this area was the impetus for the Bannock War of 1878.[55]

It is important to note that Liljeblad considered the tradition of gathering at Camas Prairie in the late spring for camas harvest, trade, and socializing as predating the European invasion, although the arrival of the horse greatly intensified these activities: "From time immemorial, the Nez Perce had traded with the Pacific coastal Indians along the lower Columbia River at The Dalles. They now came into the position of controlling a flourishing exchange of goods between east and west. In addition to the traditional dentalium and other sea shells, they now brought in this trade European articles which had passed through the hands of the Chinook who were the chief traders on the Northwest Coast."[56]

Steward places several villages along Camas Creek, which

flows through Camas Prairie, although he locates winter camps along the Snake River below Twin Falls.[57]

The mouth of the Weiser River, about 150 miles down the Snake from Camas Prairie, was another major trading center. Robert F. Murphy and Yolanda Murphy note that "the Nez Perce joined the Cayuse, the Umatilla, and the Shoshone at an annual trading market" there.[58] Again, Liljeblad asserts that trade activity on the Weiser dated to pre-Anglo times:

> From early prehistoric times there was communication up and down the Snake River. . . . Olivella shells have been found in sites far upstream. Also in more recent times, the Shoshoni in East Idaho, on their trading expeditions to the Weiser River, obtained obsidian which they rated higher than the inferior kind from Yellowstone and the Big Butte. This obsidian must have come from Glass Buttes in central Oregon. Direct contact between the upper Snake River area and the Weiser region without intermediary agents could not have taken place, however, before the Fort Hall Indians had horses. From then on, [the Weiser River area] became the most important center of intertribal horse trade west of the Rockies.[59]

Much farther down the Snake and the Columbia, at the upstream end of the Columbia River Gorge, is The Dalles, one of the best-documented aboriginal trade centers west of the Rocky Mountains (see figure 1). The local Wishram and Wasco exploited their enviable position as middlemen moving goods from the coast to the interior and vice versa. Washington Irving, in his invaluable *Astoria*, captures the essence of the hustle and bustle of this marketplace:

> We have given this process at some length, as furnished by the first explorers, because it marks a practiced ingenuity in preparing articles of traffic for a market, seldom seen among our aboriginals. For like reasons we would make

especial mention of the Village of Wish-ram at the head of the Long Narrows, as being a solitary instance of an aboriginal trading mart, or emporium. Here the salmon caught in the neighboring rapids were "ware housed" to await customers. Hither the tribes from the mouth of the Columbia repaired with the fish of the sea cast, the roots, berries and especially the Wappatoo, gathered in the lower parts of the river, together with goods and trinkets obtained from the ships which casually visited the coast. Hither also the tribes from the Rocky Mountains brought down horses, bear grass, Quamash and other commodities of the interior. The merchant fishermen at the Falls acted as middle men or factors: and passed the objects of traffic as it were cross handed, trading away part of the wares received from the mountain tribes, to those of the river and the plains, and vice versa: their packages of pounded salmon entered largely into the system of barter and being carried off in opposite directions, found their way to the savage hunting camps far in the interior, and to the casual white traders who touched upon the coast.[60]

The image communicated by Irving is vivid indeed, as is the economic emphasis of these sharp traders. This mecca of intertribal trade clearly functioned as a profit-making enterprise. The participation of "tribes from the Rocky Mountains" and "hunting camps far in the interior" most likely refers to the Nez Percé, but they could be mounted Bannock or Shoshone who were exploring well beyond their traditional grounds.

Green River Basin

An important point of trade on the northeastern periphery of the Great Basin culture area was apparently the Green River Basin of southwestern Wyoming. Raymond Wood, for example, identified this area as a major center of trade, a "Shoshone rendezvous," although it is difficult to identify specifics on the trade activities or the exact area where aboriginal trading occurred.[61] Liljeblad specifically mentions Black's Fork, and Murphy and Murphy identify the Green River Basin as an important resource area.[62] Demitri B. Shimkin describes "intertribal games" that were held in the summer months and attended by Shoshone and Bannock. These games took place "in the mountains," but there is no mention of which mountains.[63]

Apparently the source that first identified southwestern Wyoming as a trading center is a book by John C. Ewers, who stated that "no contemporary source definitely located this Shoshoni rendezvous. On my map I have placed it in its most probable location, in the river valleys of southwestern Wyoming west of the South Pass. This was the same region in which the Mountain Men later held their annual rendezvous."[64]

Although the location of this trading center is uncertain, its existence is important to various arguments on aboriginal trade. In describing his trade net, Wood, building on the arguments of Ewers, characterizes the southwestern Wyoming locale as a "trading center in the Great Basin."[65] Both Wood and Ewers suggest that the highly popularized mountain man rendezvous were held at locations that were established aboriginal trade centers, a conclusion that Dale L. Morgan and Eleanor T. Harris tend to view with caution.[66] Historic fur trade rendezvous certainly occurred in the general region (Hamm's Fork and Black's Fork of the Green River),[67] and this may have been related to a preexisting pattern, although historical accounts (such as those available for the previously described Weiser River, Camas Prairie, and Utah Valley gatherings) of this area as a place for intertribal gatherings are lacking. In addition, this area is not known for its seasonally abundant resources, and such resources appear to have been a requisite for aboriginal trade centers (e.g., The Dalles, Utah Valley, and Camas Prairie).

It is also of interest that no mountain man rendezvous are known to have been held in the places just mentioned, although they were without question important points of social aggregation and economic interaction for native peoples. It could be that the Shoshone gatherings described by Ewers and Wood was held elsewhere but nearby, perhaps Bear Lake, Utah Valley (both have great fisheries), or Cache Valley.[68]

Discussion

Wood's definition of primary and secondary trade centers allows some expansion of his western trade net[69] to include the area south of the Snake River. As noted, Thomas Layton considers Yainax Butte in southern Oregon to be an important node in trade between the Klamath, Modoc, and Great Basin peoples. However, Yainax Butte is poorly described in the literature. Leslie Spier makes only a couple of passing remarks about it, and there is no reference to it as a trade area. The Humboldt Sink, on the other hand, is well described in a number of places, and along with the bottomlands along the Humboldt River, it clearly supported large numbers of people in the past. On the eastern perimeter of the Great Basin, Utah Valley may have been a primary center because of its resident population and ready supply of fish and other resources. The available ethnographic data certainly argue for large gatherings in Utah Valley in the spring. Interestingly, these discussions not only extend Wood's western trade web to the south but also suggest that Steward accurately concluded that trade occurred mostly on the perimeters in the Great Basin (he was referring to the northern and western peripheries, of course). Adding Utah Valley to the trade net would include the eastern periphery as well.

The trading that occurred at the primary and secondary centers offers only a partial explanation of how goods moved from group to group. As intimated in the introductory section, I would argue that socially important festivals that occurred at least annually provided both a context and a mechanism for moving goods and ideas across all of the Great Basin. Although these festivals are not usually described as commercial or even as including trade, trade was imbedded in the always-present hand game or in other forms of gambling that occurred at social gatherings. The explicit recognition by Honey Lake Paiute that gambling was trading is evidence that this social form of entertainment also served commercial ends. This conclusion, and the fact that festivals were held in nearly every Great Basin valley, clarifies the role of these events in terms of cultural exchange. Figure 1 displays known festival locations in the Great Basin and surrounding areas based on Steward's work and the several other sources cited herein. The distribution represented in the chart is obviously incomplete. However, the ubiquity of these events, their typical inclusion of attendees from adjacent valleys, and the fact that festival locations moved on a regular basis suggest that information and goods could have moved across this region relatively rapidly to reach even the most remote populations within a couple of seasons.

Why is trade seldom mentioned in the Great Basin ethnographic literature? This is a difficult question because, to begin with, one cannot be completely sure whether the scarcity of information is due to (1) the biases of ethnographers, (2) the loss of trading traditions through cultural change, or (3) reality (i.e., actual infrequency of trade activity within the Great Basin). Wherever they went, Fremont and Ogden encountered people who were very willing to trade, suggesting that commerce was not a new concept. Trade is documented for all groups around the Great Basin, including the Southern Paiute, whose populations and resource abundance were also low. Steward's explanation for the near absence of trade within the

Great Basin (resources were too scarce to provide surpluses for
trade) may apply only to the Western Shoshone of the central
Basin, where the ecology and resources, compared with those
elsewhere in the Basin, were not unique or diverse enough to
stimulate the kind of exchange seen on the Basin perimeter and
elsewhere. Thus exchange in the central Basin occurred mostly
in the form of gift giving at important social events and as a
consequence of gaming during festivals.

Interestingly, the empirical data make clear that trading
food was very common. At The Dalles, for example, the primary item for barter was fish; at Camas Prairie roots, pine nuts,
salmon, and crickets traded hands. What do these examples say
about the earlier remarks that traffic in food was reprehensible?
Were such attitudes reflective of an ideal that simply was not
practiced? Was trade in foodstuffs actually as common as the
evidence suggests? It may be that the majority of the food
moved between tribal groups rather than among tribal members. Robert Spencer's comments make a good argument that
food from outside one's area was an acceptable trade item.[70]
Inland Nuunamiut, for example, traded caribou marrow or
pemmican and berries to coastal dwellers for *muktuk* (skin and
fat from baleen whales). This pattern is somewhat supported by
James Davis, who reported that foods from the interior of California moved against foodstuffs from the coast. It is clear, however, that in some cases items (acorns, for example) were traded
that must have been available in both areas.[71] Isabel Kelly's description of southern Paiute food trade, in which food moved
between hunter-gatherer groups and horticultural groups, although all were Paiute, also supports Spencer's model.

To return to the several expectations stated at the onset, it is
clear that social gatherings, though variable, can be broadly
characterized. Festivals varied in timing, scale, attendees, and
economic emphasis. Those that were held on major transporta-

tion routes or in regions of resource abundance and that were attended by numerous ethnic groups were characterized by greater commercial interests or balanced reciprocity. Thomas Layton's accounts of trade activity at the Humboldt Sink suggest the tension present during Indian-European exchange, and although few additional accounts were noted in the literature reviewed for this paper, Raymond Wood has described the "latent hostility" underlying trading activities on the Plains.[72] In the central Basin, where resource availability was variable, festivals were more about sociability, and exchange took the form of generalized reciprocity. The rarity of both formal trade and warfare in the Great Basin may, in fact, be related.[73] In all cases, however, as with the Plains groups described by Wood, festivals constituted social interaction and thus were instruments of change. Without exception, aboriginal festivals were held in places and at times when a major food item was in season, be it rabbits, pine nuts, fish, or camas roots.

Despite the often highly ethnocentric descriptions by early travelers of native peoples living in the lowest form of humanity,[74] people in the Great Basin and surrounding regions were not isolated. They maintained and participated in a structured system that facilitated information flow and, to a lesser extent, goods. This system interacted in down-the-line fashion, although probably not in a strictly linear sense. Ultimately, this tertiary system connected with Wood's trade net that stretched from coast to coast. Components of this system were primary as well as secondary trade nodes that have been well described in the historic and ethnographic literature. This paper argues for the importance of tertiary nodes—annual festivals that, characterized by a strong social flavor, also served to move thoughts, people, and sometimes things into all the valleys of the lightly populated regions of the Great Basin and southern Columbia Plateau.

Table 1. Characteristics of known festivals across the Great Basin and Columbia Plateau.[75]

Location/Group	Duration	Season	Gambling
Northern Paiute			
Owens Valley	5–7 days	fall	yes
Humboldt/ Carson Sinks	5–6 days	fall (pine-nut harvest)	yes
Pyramid Lake	5 days	May (Kuyui fish harvest)	no data
Stillwater	5 days for fall pine-nut dance	fall pine-nut dance; also dances in summer (to ensure fall pine-nut harvest), spring (start of harvest year), fall (rabbit dance)	yes
Deep Springs	6 days	fall	yes
Washo	up to two weeks	early fall, late spring	yes
Western Shoshone			
Lida	no data	no data	no data
Southern Death Valley, Panamint Valley, Koso	no data	fall	yes
Northern Death Valley	no data	fall	no data
Beatty	5 days	fall	no data

Interval	Attendees	Trade	Source
annual	adjacent valleys	not mentioned	Steward 1938
at least annual	no data	not mentioned	Stewart 1941
annual?	no data	no data	Lowie 1924:306
several times during year		not mentioned	Fowler 1992:185, 260
annual	adjacent valleys	not mentioned	Steward 1938
annual, early fall	all Washo; in the past probably more than one festival was held for different groups	not mentioned	Downs 1966; d'Azevedo 1986
irregular	adjacent valleys		Steward 1938:70
annual	adjacent valleys	not mentioned	Steward 1938:74
annual	adjacent valleys	not mentioned	Steward 1938:90
annual	adjacent valleys		Steward 1938:98

Location/Group	Duration	Season	Gambling
Reese River, Ione Valley, Smith Creek Valley	5 days	fall (festivals in spring and summer)	no data
Kawich Mountains	no data	fall (during pine-nut harvest)	no data
Little Smokey Valley	no data	fall (fewer festivals in spring and summer)	no data
Railroad Valley	no data	spring (when plants begin to grow), midsummer (when seeds ripen), fall	no data
Steptoe Valley	no data	fall (after pine-nut harvest)	yes
Spring, Snake, Antelope Valleys	no data	no data	no data
Cave, Skull Valley, Deep Creek Mountains	5 days	spring (main festival), summer and fall (after pine-nut harvest)	no data
Pine Creek, Diamond Valley	no data	fall (before pine-nut harvest)	no data
Ruby Valley	no data	spring or fall	no data
Humboldt River	5 days	fall (before pine-nut harvest)	no data
Battle Mountain	no data	probably fall (mentions pine nuts)	no data
Northern Shoshone			
Snake River	5 days (dances)	different seasons, summer at Camas Prairie	yes

Interval	Attendees	Trade	Source
annual	adjacent valleys		Steward 1938:106
annual	Kawich camps only	not mentioned	Steward 1938:112
annual	adjacent valleys		Steward 1938:115
three times	adjacent valleys	not mentioned	Steward 1938:120
annual	adjacent valleys	not mentioned	Steward 1938:122
no data	adjacent valleys	not mentioned	Steward 1938:130
up to 3 per year	adjacent valleys	not mentioned	Steward 1938:139
annual	no data	not mentioned	Steward 1938:143
up to 2 per year	Egan Canyon	not mentioned	Steward 1938:148
annual	Ruby Valley	not mentioned	Steward 1938:159
no data	adjacent valleys	not mentioned	Steward 1938:154
erratic	adjacent valleys in south-central Idaho		Steward 1938:168

Location/Group	Duration	Season	Gambling
Lemhi	no data	spring and fall, Camas Prairie	no data
Fort Hall Bannock and Shoshone	no data	late spring or early summer gathering at Camas Prairie	no data
Boise, Weiser Rivers			
Ute			
Utah Valley	no data	spring (fish runs)	yes
Southern Paiute			
Pahrump and Las Vegas	3–4 days	fall	no data
Panguitch	no festivals reported		
Kaibab	no festivals reported		

Interval	Attendees	Trade	Source
twice a year	adjacent valleys in south-central Idaho		Steward 1938:193
warm months	adjacent valleys in south-central Idaho	yes	Steward 1938; Liljeblad 1957
		yes	Liljeblad 1957; Murphy and Murphy 1960
annual	adjacent valleys	not mentioned	Bean 1945
annual	adjacent valleys	not mentioned	Steward 1938:184
			Kelly 1964
			Kelly 1964

Notes

1. *Autobiography of George Washington Bean: A Utah Pioneer of 1847*, comp. Flora Diana Bean Horne (Salt Lake City: Utah Printing, 1945), 51–2.

2. See W. Raymond Wood, "Plains Trade in Prehistoric and Protohistoric Intertribal Relations," in *Anthropology on the Great Plains*, ed. W. Raymond Wood and Margot Liberty (Lincoln: University of Nebraska, 1980), 98.

3. Robert F. Spencer, *The North Alaskan Eskimo* (New York: Dover, 1976), 199.

4. See H. Edwin Jackson, "The Trade Fair in Hunter-Gatherer Interactions: The Role of Intersocietal Trade in the Evolution of Poverty Point Culture," in *Between Bands and States*, ed. Susan A. Gregg (Carbondale: Center for Archaeological Investigations, Southern Illinois University, 1991).

5. See Wood, "Plains Trade," 99.

6. George Dalton, "Economic Theory and Primitive Society," *American Anthropologist* 63 (1961), 20.

7. See Joseph G. Jorgensen, *Western Indians: Comparative Environments, Languages, and Cultures of 172 Western American Indian Tribes* (San Francisco: W. H. Freeman, 1980), 138.

8. See Marshall Sahlins, *Stone Age Economics* (Chicago: Aldine-Atherton, 1972), 191–6.

9. Ibid., 182.

10. Lorna Marshall, "Sharing, Talking, and Giving: Relief of Social Tensions among !Kung Bushmen," *Africa* 31 (1961): 245.

11. Sahlins, *Stone Age Economics*, 169.

12. Ibid., 216.

13. Spencer, *North Alaskan Eskimo*, 204–5.

14. See Lowell J. Bean and Dorothea Theodoratus, "Western Pomo and Northeastern Pomo," in *California*, ed. Robert F. Heizer, vol. 8 of *Handbook of North American Indians*, ed. William C. Sturtevant (Washington, D. C.: Smithsonian Institution, 1978), 298.

15. See Joseph G. Jorgensen, "Ghost Dance, Bear Dance, and

Sun Dance," in *Great Basin*, ed. Warren L. d'Azevedo, vol. 11 of *Handbook of North American Indians*, ed. Sturtevant, 660–72.

16. For examples of Plains-Pueblo mutualism, see the various articles in Katherine A. Spielmann, ed., *Farmers, Hunters, and Colonists* (Tucson: University of Arizona, 1991).

17. See Warren L. d'Azevedo, introduction to *Great Basin*, ed. d'Azevedo.

18. See Richard E. Hughes and James A. Bennyhoff, "Early Trade," in *Great Basin*, ed. d'Azevedo.

19. Julian H. Steward, *Ethnography of the Owens Valley Paiute* (Berkeley: University of California Press, 1933), 320.

20. See James T. Davis, *Trade Routes and Economic Exchange among the Indians of California* (Ramona, Calif.: Ballena Press, 1974), 20–1.

21. Steward, *Owens Valley Paiute*, 257.

22. See Catherine S. Fowler, ed., *Willlard Z. Park's Ethnographic Notes on the Northern Paiute of Western Nevada, 1933–1940* (Salt Lake City: University of Utah Press, 1989).

23. See Thomas N. Layton, "Traders and Raiders: Aspects of Trans-Basin and California-Plateau Commerce, 1800–1830," *Journal of California and Great Basin Anthropology* 3/1 (1981): 127–37.

24. *Peter Skene Ogden's Snake Country Journals: 1827–28 and 1828–29*, ed. Glyndwr Williams (London: Hudson's Bay Records Society, 1971), 153.

25. Ibid., 108.

26. Zenas Leonard, *Adventures of a Mountain Man: Narrative of Zenas Leonard*, ed. Milo Milton Quaife (Lincoln: University of Nebraska Press, 1978), 112–14.

27. See Layton, "Traders and Raiders," 135.

28. See ibid., 128.

29. Cited in Layton, "Traders and Raiders," 129.

30. See ibid., 135.

31. James F. Downs, *The Two Worlds of the Washo* (New York: Holt, Rinehart and Winston, 1966), 36–7.

32. See Davis, "Trade Routes and Economic Exchange," 42.

33. See Warren L. d'Azevedo, "Washo," in *Great Basin*, ed. d'Azevedo, 470.

34. See Francis A. Riddell, *Honey Lake Paiute Ethnography* (Carson City: Nevada State Museum, 1978); and William S. Evans Jr., *Ethnographic Notes on the Honey Lake Maidu* (Carson City: Nevada State Museum, 1978).

35. See Riddell, *Honey Lake Paiute*, 89.

36. See Julian H. Steward, *Basin-Plateau Aboriginal Sociopolitical Groups* (1938; reprint, Salt Lake City: University of Utah Press, 1970), 44–5.

37. Ibid., 54.

38. Ibid., 122.

39. Ibid., 139.

40. See my *The Ute of Utah Lake* (Salt Lake City: University of Utah Press, 1991) for discussions.

41. T. J. Farnham, *Life, Adventures, and Travels in California* (New York: Nafis and Cornish, 1849), 371.

42. See, for example, Charles H. Lange, "Relations of the Southwest with the Plains and Great Basin," in *Southwest*, ed. Alfonso Ortiz, vol. 9 of *Handbook of North American Indians*, ed. Sturtevant (1979), 202.

43. Omer C. Stewart, *Ute–Southern Paiute*, Culture Element Distributions XVIII (Berkeley: University of California Press, 1942), 348.

44. See Joseph J. Hill, "Spanish and Mexican Exploration and Trade Northwest from New Mexico into the Great Basin," *Utah Historical Quarterly* 3/1 (1930): 3–23.

45. See Jorgensen, *Western Indians*, 142.

46. See Isabel T. Kelly, *Southern Paiute Ethnography* (Salt Lake City: University of Utah Press, 1964).

47. See ibid., 90.

48. See ibid., 103; and Stewart, *Ute–Southern Paiute*, 321.

49. See Steward, *Basin-Plateau*, 184.

50. Robert C. Euler, *Southern Paiute Ethnohistory* (Salt Lake City: University of Utah Press, 1966), 82–3.

51. Ibid., 83.

52. Various scholars report on the importance of Big Camas Prairie. For helpful insights, see Sven Liljeblad, "Indian Peoples in Idaho" (Pocatello: Idaho State University, 1957, manuscript on file), 47; Dawn S. Stratham, *Camas and the Northern Shoshoni* (Boise: Boise State University, 1982), 74; and Steward, *Basin-Plateau*, 191.

53. Robert F. Murphy and Yolando Murphy, *Shoshone-Bannock Subsistence and Society* (Berkeley: University of California, 1960), 319.

54. Liljeblad, *Indian Peoples*, 46–7.

55. For a full discussion, see Brigham D. Madsen, *The Northern Shoshoni* (Caldwell: Caxton, 1980).

56. Liljeblad, *Indian Peoples*, 46–7.

57. See the map in the front of Steward, *Basin-Plateau*.

58. Murphy and Murphy, *Shoshone-Bannock*, 286.

59. Liljeblad, *Indian Peoples*, 88–9.

60. Washington Irving, *Astoria* (Boston: Twayne Publishers, 1976), 69–70.

61. See Wood, "Plains Trade," 100.

62. See Liljeblad, *Indian Peoples*, 47; and Murphy and Murphy, *Shoshone-Bannock*.

63. Demitri B. Shimkin, "Eastern Shoshone," in *Great Basin*, ed. d'Azevedo, 323.

64. John C. Ewers, *Indian Life on the Upper Missouri* (Norman: University of Oklahoma, 1968), 17 n. 2.

65. See Wood, "Plains Trade," 102.

66. See Dale L. Morgan and Eleanor T. Harris, *The Rocky Mountain Journals of William Marshall Anderson* (Lincoln: University of Nebraska, 1967), 18.

67. See ibid., frontispiece maps.

68. Steward, *Basin-Plateau*, 218–19, mentions that Cache Valley was the site of the 1826 rendezvous and discusses the importance of Bear Lake to Cache Valley Shoshone. Ethnographers have paid little attention to Cache Valley since Steward, despite its probable importance to indigenous peoples.

69. See Wood, "Plains Trade," 101, fig. 1.

70. See Spencer, *North Alaskan Eskimo*, 204–5 (see n. 3).

71. There are various examples of this in Davis, *Trade Routes* (see n. 19).

72. See Wood, "Plains Trade," 104.

73. See Steward, *Basin-Plateau*, 238.

74. See Fremont, *The Exploring Expedition to the Rocky Mountains* (Washington, D.C.: Smithsonian Institution, 1988), 276.

75. Sources that are not found in the endnotes for this paper are S. Catherine Fowler, *In the Shadow of Fox Peak: An Ethnography of the Cattail-Eater Northern Paiute People of Stillwater Marsh* (Washington, D.C.: U.S. Government Printing Office, 1992); Robert H. Lowie, *Notes on Shoshonean Ethnography*, Anthropological Papers, vol. 20, no. 3 (New York: American Museum of Natural History, 1924); and Julian H. Steward, *Nevada Shoshoni*, Culture Element Distributions XII (Berkeley: University of California Press, 1941).

A Bibliography of the Published and Unpublished Works of John Leon Sorenson

Compiled by David J. Whittaker

Abbreviations

BYU   Brigham Young University. Provo, Utah.
BYUS   *Brigham Young University Studies.*
DRC   Defense Research Corporation. Santa Barbara, Calif.
Dialogue   *Dialogue: A Journal of Mormon Thought.*
FARMS   Foundation for Ancient Research and Mormon Studies. Provo, Utah.
GRC   General Research Corporation. Santa Barbara, Calif.
NWAF   New World Archaeological Foundation. Orinda, Calif., 1952–60; Provo, Utah, 1961–present.
SEHA   Society for Early Historic Archaeology. Provo, Utah.
UAS   University Archaeological Society. Provo, Utah.

1950

Maori Study. Apia, Samoa: Samoan Mission of the Church of Jesus Christ of Latter-day Saints, 1950. A Rarotongan grammar. Mimeographed.

1951

"The Challenge of the Maya Mystery." *Improvement Era* 54 (October 1951): 712, 738, 740.

"Dating Archaeological Finds by Radioactive Carbon Content." *Bulletin of the University Archaeological Society,* no. 2 (September 1951): 1–6.

1952

"Book of Mormon Geography in the Light of Ceramic Distributions." *U.A.S. Newsletter,* no. 8 (25 November 1952).

"Comparison of Fundamental Traits of the Book of Mormon and Ancient American Civilizations." *U.A.S. Newsletter,* no. 4 (20 January 1952). Abstract in *Progress in Archaeology: An Anthology,* edited by Ross T. Christensen, 108. Provo, Utah: BYU, 1963.

"The Elephant in Ancient America." *U.A.S. Newsletter,* no. 4 (20 January 1952).

"Evidences of Culture Contacts between Polynesia and the Americas in Precolumbian Times." Master's thesis, Brigham Young University, 1952.

"Further on Authentication and Elucidation of the Book of Mormon." *U.A.S. Newsletter,* no. 6 (10 May 1952). Abstract in *Progress in Archaeology: An Anthology,* edited by Ross T. Christensen, 147–9. Provo, Utah: BYU, 1963.

1953

"Asia–North American Linguistic Tie-Up." *U.A.S. Newsletter,* no. 14 (10 August 1953).

"Explorations in Southern Mexico: Report of Field Work, NWAF Expedition of 1953." *U.A.S. Newsletter,* no. 13 (25 June 1953). With Gareth W. Lowe.

"Report of Archaeological Reconnaissance—in West-Central

Chiapas, Mexico." Report on behalf of the NWAF presented to the Departmento de Monumentos Prehispánicos, Instituto Nacional de Antropología e Historia de Mexico. Typescript in author's possession.

"Teotihuacán Sequence Revised." *U.A.S. Newsletter*, no. 14 (10 August 1953).

1954

Review of *Book of Mormon Evidences in Ancient America*, by Dewey Farnsworth. *U.A.S. Newsletter*, no. 18 (25 February 1954). Abstract in *Progress in Archaeology: An Anthology*, edited by Ross T. Christensen, 103–6. Provo, Utah: BYU, 1963.

"Early Archaeological Sequences in Highland Guatemala." *U.A.S. Newsletter*, no. 17 (18 January 1954).

"Indications of Early Metal in Mesoamerica." *Bulletin of the University Archaeological Society*, no. 5 (October 1954): 1–15.

"New Evidence of Migration of Biblical Peoples to the New World." *U.A.S. Newsletter*, no. 21 (2 July 1954). Abstract titled "Incense-Burning and 'Seer' Stones in Ancient Mesoamerica: New Evidence of Migrations of Biblical Peoples to the New World" in *Progress in Archaeology: An Anthology*, edited by Ross T. Christensen, 118–19. Provo, Utah: BYU, 1963.

"Preclassic Metal?" *American Antiquity* 20 (July 1954): 64.

"True Arch." *U.A.S. Newsletter*, no. 17 (18 January 1954).

1955

A Chronological Ordering of the Mesoamerican Pre-Classic. Middle American Research Records, vol. 2, no. 3. New Orleans: Tulane University, 1955.

"Some Mesoamerican Traditions of Immigration by Sea." *El México Antiguo* 8 (1955): 425–39. Reprinted by FARMS, 1981.

The World of the Book of Mormon. Provo, Utah: BYU Extension

Service, 1955. Mimeographed. Leadership Week lecture series: (1) "The Physical World," 1–14; (2) "The Cultural World, Part 1," 15–28; (3) "The Cultural World, Part 2," 29–44; (4) "The World of Ideas," 45–60; (5) "The Transmission of Ideas," 61–75.

1956

"An Archaeological Reconnaissance of West-Central Chiapas, Mexico." *New World Archaeological Foundation Publication No. 1* (1956): 7–19.

"Pre-Hispanic Culture History of Central Chiapas." Paper presented at the annual meeting of the American Anthropological Association, Santa Monica, Calif., December 1956.

1957

"A Bibliography for *Yucatán Medicinal Plant Studies,* by William E. Gates." *Tlalocán* 3 (1957): 334–43.

"The Current Status of Knowledge of the Origins of Agriculture in the Americas." 1957. Typescript in author's possession.

"The Historical and Functional Roots of Mexico's Racial Attitudes." 1957. Typescript in author's possession.

"The Twig of the Cedar." *Improvement Era* 60 (May 1957): 330–1, 338, 341–2. Reprinted as "Bible Prophecies of the Mulekites" in *A Book of Mormon Treasury,* 229–37. Salt Lake City: Bookcraft, 1959. Also reprinted by FARMS, 1981.

1958

"Industrialization and Tradition in a Mormon Village." Paper presented at the annual meeting of the American Anthropological Association, Washington, D.C., 20 November 1958.

1959

Anthropology and the Latter-day Saints. Provo, Utah: BYU Adult Education and Extension Services, 1959. Mimeographed. Leadership Week lecture series: (1) "Mankind's Proper Study," 1–12; (2) "Society and Culture in the Gospel Plan," 13–24; (3) "Mirror for Mormons," 25–36; (4) "Every Nation, Kindred, Tongue and People," 37–49.

Review of *Little Smoky Ridge*, by Marion Pearsall, and *Millways of Kent*, by John Kenneth Morland. *American Anthropologist* 61 (December 1959): 1109–10.

"What Archeology Can and Cannot Do for the Book of Mormon." Circa 1959. Copy in Special Collections and Manuscripts, Harold B. Lee Library, BYU. Typescript.

1960

Review of *Being a Palauan*, by H. G. Barnett; *Bunyoro: An African Kingdom*, by John Beattie; *The Tiwi of North Australia*, by C. W. M. Hart and Arnold R. Pilling; *The Cheyennes: Indians of the Great Plains*, by E. Adamson Hoebel; and *Tepoztlán: Village in Mexico*, by Oscar Lewis. *Rural Sociology* 25 (1960): 451–4.

1961

"Culture Capsules." *Modern Language Journal* 45 (December 1961): 350–4. With H. Darrel Taylor. Reprinted in *The Teaching of German, Problems and Methods: Anthology*, edited by Eberhard Reichmann, 350–4 (Philadelphia: National Carl Schurz Association, 1970); *A Handbook on Latin America for Teachers: Methodology and Annotated Bibliography*, edited by H. Ned Seelye, 15–18 (Springfield: State of Illinois, Office of the Superintendent of Public Instruction, 1968); and *Teaching Cultural Concepts in Spanish Classes*, edited by H. Ned Seelye, 81–5 (Springfield: State of Illinois, Office of the Superintendent of Public Instruction, 1972).

"Industrialization and Social Change: A Controlled Comparison of Two Utah Communities." Ph.D. diss., University of California, Los Angeles, 1961.

"Patterns of Mormon Funeral Behavior." *Utah Academy of Sciences,*

Arts, and Letters: Proceedings 39 (1961–62): 202–3. Abstract based on an unpublished 1957 paper, "Mormon Funeral Behavior." Copy in Special Collections and Manuscripts, Harold B. Lee Library, BYU. Typescript.

1962

"Anthropological Approaches [to] the Book of Mormon." In *Book of Mormon Institute, December 5, 1959*, 25–36. Provo, Utah: BYU Extension Publications, 1962.

"The Development of a Model for the Society and Culture of Vietnam." U.S. Naval Ordnance Test Station, China Lake, Calif., 1962. Duplicated. With Paul V. Hyer.

"An Outline for the Analysis of Unconventional Warfare." U.S. Naval Ordnance Test Station, China Lake, Calif., 1962. Duplicated. With David K. Pack, Paul V. Hyer, Mark W. Cannon, Ray G. Hillam and R. Joseph Monsen.

"Plain and Precious Prophecy." *Instructor* (September 1962): 309, 319.

1963

"Anthropology Applied to Unconventional Warfare." Paper presented at the Northwest Anthropological Conference, Logan, Utah, April 1963.

"Civil Rights Problems to an Anthropologist." Paper presented at meetings of the Utah Academy of Sciences, Arts, and Letters, Logan, Utah, 9 November 1963.

"A Cultural Summary of Israelite Palestine at the End of the Middle Iron Age [seventh century B.C.]." Book of Mormon Working Paper, no. 1 (September 1963). Mimeographed.

"Directions in Book of Mormon Geography." Book of Mormon Working Paper, no. 3 (September 1963). Mimeographed.

"A Possible Absolute Chronology for the Jaredites." Book of Mormon Working Paper, no. 5 (December 1963). Mimeographed.

Revised as "The Years of the Jaredites" in 1972 and issued as a FARMS Preliminary Report in 1980.

"Some Observations on the Brass Plates." Book of Mormon Working Paper, no. 4 (September 1963). Mimeographed.

"Some Uses of Theory in Archaeology." Paper presented at the annual meetings of the Society for American Archaeology, Boulder, Colo., spring 1963.

"A Systemic Approach to the Analysis of a Society for the Purposes of Unconventional Warfare." U.S. Naval Ordnance Test Station, China Lake, Calif., January 1963. Duplicated. With David K. Pack.

"Where in the World? Some Views on Geography, Part 1." Book of Mormon Working Paper, no. 2 (September 1963). Mimeographed. Revised 1963, 1971; revised and expanded with appendix and map 1973, 1974.

1964

Applied Analysis of Unconventional Warfare. Technical Publication 3458. China Lake, Calif.: U.S. Naval Ordnance Test Station, April 1964. With David K. Pack.

"Communicating with the Latin American." As told to Dennis C. Regenauer. *Galaxy Magazine* (9 March 1964): 4 (published by the BYU *Daily Universe*).

Condensed Account, DRC Urban Insurgency Conference, 31 Aug.–4 Sept. 1964. Santa Barbara, Calif.: DRC, 1964.

"Is Anthropology 'the Study of Man'? Problems in the Study of Complex Societies." *BYUS* 5 (winter 1964): 115–24.

"Missionaries and the 'Spirit.'" In *Buying the Wind,* edited by Richard M. Dorson, 520–2. Chicago: University of Chicago Press, 1964.

"Nephite Social Structure." Book of Mormon Working Paper, no. 7 (February 1964). Duplicated. Lecture to UAS, Salt Lake Chapter, February 1964.

"The Relation of Rural and Urban Insurgency in Colombia and Venezuela." Internal Memorandum 219-Releasable. DRC, Santa Barbara, Calif., 1964.

"The Relation of a Scientific Picture of Man's Appearance and Cultural History on the Earth to a Scriptural Picture." Book of Mormon Working Paper, no. 6 (1964). Duplicated. Revised as "A Mormon Picture of Creation," 1979.

"Some Field Notes on the Power Structure of the American Anthropological Association." *The American Behavioral Scientist* 7 (February 1964): 8–9. Based on a paper presented at the sixty-second annual meeting of the American Anthropological Association, San Francisco, Calif., 23 November 1963.

Unconventional Warfare and the Venezuelan Society. Technical Publication 3583. China Lake, Calif.: U.S. Naval Ordnance Test Station, November 1964.

Unconventional Warfare and the Vietnamese Society. Technical Publication 3457. China Lake, Calif.: U.S. Naval Ordnance Test Station, July 1964. With David K. Pack.

"Urban Disorders Research—Tentative Program Formulation." Internal Memorandum-Releasable 175. DRC, Santa Barbara, Calif., 1964. With Richard Holbrook.

"Use of Automated Tools in Archaeology." *American Antiquity* 30 (October 1964): 205–6.

"Workbook for Participants: Urban Insurgency Conference, August 31–September 4, 1964." Internal Memorandum-Releasable 154. DRC, Santa Barbara, Calif., August 1964. With others.

1965

"Counterinsurgency Assistance for Latin America." Internal Memorandum-Releasable 291. DRC, Santa Barbara, Calif., September 1965. Secret. With T. F. Cave, C. T. Clark, and A. D. Stathacoupolos.

"Some Reports of Insurgent and Potential Insurgent Activity around the World." Internal Memorandum-Releasable 288. DRC, Santa Barbara, Calif., June 1965.

"Urban Insurgency Cases." Internal Memorandum-Releasable 176. DRC, Santa Barbara, Calif., February 1965.

"Urban Insurgency and Military Requirements." Internal Memorandum-Releasable 307. DRC, Santa Barbara, Calif., November 1965. Confidential. Summary in *Proceedings: 16th Military Operations Research Symposium, 26–29 October 1965.* Seattle, Wash.: Sandpoint Naval Air Station, 1996, 264–5. Secret.

1966

An Analysis of Urban Insurgency Tactics. Technical Manual 415. Santa Barbara, Calif.: DRC, August 1966. Confidential. With others.

Counterinsurgency Assistance for Guatemala. Technical Manual 341. Santa Barbara, Calif.: DRC, March 1966. Secret.

Counterinsurgency Assistance for Venezuela. Technical Manual 340. Santa Barbara, Calif.: DRC, March 1966. Secret. With T. F. Cave.

Relations between Urban and Rural Insurgents. Technical Manual 386. Santa Barbara, Calif.: DRC, May 1966. Confidential. Reprinted in *Proceedings: First Counterinsurgency Research and Development Symposium, 14–16 June 1966,* 1:237–45. Arlington, Va.: Infrared Physics Laboratory, Willow Run Laboratories, Institute of Science and Technology, University of Michigan, n.d. Secret.

"Some Voices from the Dust: A Review of Papers of the Fifteenth Annual Symposium on the Archaeology of the Scriptures." *Dialogue* (spring 1966): 144–9.

Urban Case Studies II and III (classified subtitle). Technical Manual 413. Santa Barbara, Calif.: DRC, August 1966. Secret.

"Urban Insurgency Studies, Final Report." Contract Report 124–1. DRC, Santa Barbara, Calif., August 1966. Secret.

"Venezuelan Society and the Prospects for Insurgency." Internal
Memorandum-Releasable 355. DRC, Santa Barbara, Calif.,
March 1966. With Dean E. Mann.

1967

"A Critique of Some Assumptions." Internal Memorandum 685.
GRC, Santa Barbara, Calif., August 1967. Top secret.

"Evaluation of Indian Community Action Programs at Arizona State
University, University of South Dakota, and University of
Utah." Contract Report 82-1. GRC, Santa Barbara, Calif., Oc-
tober 1967. With Larry Berg.

"Identification of Social Costs and Benefits in Urban Transportation
Planning." Internal Memorandum-Releasable 595. GRC, Santa
Barbara, Calif., May 1967. Reprinted in *Network Flow Analyses,*
2–38. Vol. 3 of *Systems Analysis of Urban Transportation.* Santa
Barbara, Calif.: GRC, 1967.

"Problems of Implementation of Urban Transportation Policy." Internal Memorandum-Releasable 499. GRC, Santa Barbara, Calif.,
February 1967. With Murray Frost.

"Some Significance of Mormon Missionary Activity in California in
the Twentieth Century: Where Have the Converts Gone?" Paper
presented at the annual meeting of the Mormon History Association, Stanford University, 28 August 1967. Copy in Special
Collections and Manuscripts, Harold B. Lee Library, BYU.

"Vietnam: Just a War, or a Just War?" *Dialogue* (winter 1967): 91–
100. Third article in a series titled "Roundtable: Vietnam."

1968

"Comparison of Costs and Benefits for Major Transportation Alternatives." Internal Memorandum-Releasable 770. GRC, Santa Barbara, Calif., January 1968. Reprinted in *Systems Analysis of Urban
Transportation,* 269–324. Santa Barbara, Calif.: GRC, 1968.

"Enemy Responses in Vietnam to New Weapons and Techniques." Internal Memorandum-Releasable 925. GRC, Santa Barbara, Calif., October 1968. Reprinted in *Third Counterinsurgency Research and Development Symposium (CIRADS III): Proceedings*, 2-77 to 2-92. Columbus, Ohio: Battelle Memorial Institute, 1968. Classified.

"Problems and Answers: A Review of Sidney B. Sperry, *Answers to Book of Mormon Questions.*" *Dialogue* (spring 1968): 118–20.

1969

"Ancient America and the Book of Mormon Revisited." *Dialogue* (summer 1969): 80–94.

"CLOARAD—High Intensity Phenomena Program." Final Technical Report. GRC, Santa Barbara, Calif., November 1969. With others.

"The Social Bases of Instability in Rural Southeast Asia." *Asian Survey* (Institute of International Studies, University of California, Berkeley) 9 (July 1969): 540–5. First presented as a paper at the Western Conference of the Association for Asian Studies, San Francisco, October 1968. Also issued as Internal Memorandum-Releasable 953. Santa Barbara, Calif.: GRC, November 1968.

1970

"Mobility of Academic Anthropologists." American Anthropological Association. *Newsletter* 11 (April 1970): 4–5.

"Observations on Nephite Chronology." Book of Mormon Working Paper, no. 8 (1970). Mimeographed.

1971

"A Collection of References to Trans-Oceanic Contacts with the Americas before the Recognized Discoveries." Part 1. *New England Antiquities Research Association Newsletter* 67 (1971): 78–80.

"The Significance of an Apparent Relationship between the Ancient Near East and Mesoamerica." In *Man Across the Sea: Problems of Pre-Columbian Contacts*, edited by Carroll L. Riley et al., 219–40. Austin: University of Texas Press, 1971. Reprinted by FARMS, 1981. Initially presented as a paper at the annual meetings of the Society for American Archaeology, Santa Fe, N. Mex., spring 1968.

1972

"Assessment of Social and Environmental Costs and Benefits." In "Evaluation of Economic and Social Benefits and Costs of Data from ERTS–A (Phase I)." Contract Report 1-321. Santa Barbara, Calif.: GRC, 1972, 236–64.

"A Collection of References to Trans-Oceanic Contacts with the Americas before the Recognized Discoveries." Part 2. *New England Antiquities Research Association Newsletter* 68 (1972): 38–40.

"Emergent Systems Analysis." In *First Annual Symposium on LDS Intercultural Communications and Language Concerns*, 159–64. Provo, Utah: BYU Language Research Center, 1972.

"On Being a Graduate: Thoughts and Opinions of the Latter-day Saint High School and College Graduate." *New Era* (July 1972): 38–40. With Jay M. Todd.

Review of *The Quest for America*, by Geoffery Ashe et al. In *BYUS* 12 (spring 1972): 329–31.

"The Years of the Jaredites." Revision of Book of Mormon Working Paper, no. 5, December 1963. Issued as a FARMS Preliminary Report in 1980.

1973

"The Language of the Mormons: A Sociocultural Perspective." In *Conference on the Language of the Mormons, 1970*, edited by Harold S. Madsen and John L. Sorenson, 1–6. Provo, Utah: BYU Language Research Center, 1973.

"Mormon World View and American Culture." *Dialogue* (1973): 17–29.

1974

"Evaluation." Paper presented at the Second Annual Symposium on LDS Intercultural Communications and Language Concerns, Provo, Utah, 7–10 October 1974. Sponsored by the BYU Language Research Center.

"Notes on the Margin." Review of *Religious Movements in Contemporary America,* edited by Irving I. Zaretsky and Mark P. Leone. *Dialogue* (winter 1974): 82–3.

"Social Structure and Cult among the Nephites." Paper presented at the annual SEHA symposium, Provo, Utah, October 1974.

"The West as a Network of Cultures." In *Essays on the American West, 1972–73,* edited by Thomas G. Alexander, 69–86. Charles Redd Monographs in Western History, no. 3. Provo, Utah: BYU Press, 1974.

"Word Frequencies in the Messages of the First Presidency, 19th vs. 20th Century." In *Conference on the Language of the Mormons, 1974.* Provo, Utah: BYU Language Research Center, 1974.

1975

"Brief History of the BYU-New World Archaeological Foundation." Typescript in author's possession.

"Channels of Innovation in Mormon Life." Typescript in author's possession. Published in *Mormon Culture: Four Decades of Essays on Mormon Society and Personality* (1997), 97–110.

"The Gates of God." *New Era* (March 1975): 18–25. Sorenson is the unattributed author of the text accompanying the photographs.

"The Land of Promise." *New Era* (January 1975): 20–9. Sorenson is the unattributed author of the text accompanying the photographs.

"The Role of BYU-NWAF in Middle American Archaeology." Address on the work of the NWAF, given at the opening of the BYU centennial exhibit *Uncovering Mesoamerican Civilization*, 28 October 1975. Typescript in author's possession.

"The Second Gathering: The New Migrants to Utah." In *Social Accommodation in Utah*, edited by Clark S. Knowlton, 65–70. Salt Lake City: American West Center, University of Utah, 1975.

1976

"The Book of Mormon as a Mesoamerican Codex." *Newsletter and Proceedings of the S.E.H.A.*, no. 139 (December 1976): 1–9. Reprinted by FARMS, 1981.

"Instant Expertise on Book of Mormon Archaeology." *BYUS* 16 (spring 1976): 429–32. Review of *The Americas before Columbus*, by Dewey and Edith Farnsworth; *The Book and the Map: New Insights into Book of Mormon Geography*, by Venice Priddis; *Trial of the Stick of Joseph*, by Jack West; and *These Early Americans: External Evidences of the Book of Mormon*, by Paul Cheesman.

"A Reconsideration of Early Metal in Mesoamerica." *Katunob* (Greeley, Colo.) 9 (March 1976): 1–8. Reprinted in *Metallurgy in Ancient Mexico*. Greeley, Colo.: University of Northern Colorado, Museum of Anthropology, 1982. Also reprinted by FARMS, 1982.

"The Third Century: An Anthropologist Looks at America's Future." *BYU Today* (August 1976): 14–15.

"Toward a Characterization of 'Mormon Personality.'" *Committee on Mormon Society and Culture Newsletter* (Provo, Utah), no. 2 (1976): 2–8. Revised and reprinted in *Mormon Culture* (1997), 171–81.

1977

Review of *America B.C.: Ancient Settlers in the New World*, by Barry Fell. *BYUS* 17 (spring 1977): 373–5.

"The 'Brass Plates' and Biblical Scholarship." *Dialogue* (autumn 1977): 31–9. Reprinted by FARMS, 1977 and 1981. Translated and reprinted as "Las 'Planchas de Bronce' y la erudición bíblica" in *El Libro de Mormón ante la Crítica,* edited by Josué Sánchez, 301–13. Salt Lake City: Publishers Press, 1992. Reprinted in *Nephite Culture and Society: Collected Papers* (1997), 25–39.

"Mesoamerican C-14 Dates Revised." *Katunob* 9 (February 1977): 56–71.

"A Mesoamerican Chronology: April 1977." *Katunob* 9 (February 1977): 41–55.

"Spotlight" (interview with John L. Sorenson). *Century 2* (BYU student journal, fall 1977): 48–54.

Review of "A Worldwide Evolutionary Classification of Cultures by Subsistence Systems," by Alan Lomax and Conrad M. Arensberg. *Current Anthropology* 18 (December 1977): 704–5.

"Writing Systems among the Book of Mormon Peoples." *New Era* (November 1977): 48–50. Reprinted as "Schriftsysteme der im Buch Mormon erwahnten Volker" in *Der Stern* (January 1978): 26–30. Also printed in other languages.

1978

"Comments." In *Mormonism: A Faith for All Cultures,* edited by F. Lamond Tullis, 28–32. Provo, Utah: BYU Press, 1978. Remarks on cultures as tabernacles.

1979

"Four Theories of Culture and Their Application to Communication." In *Bridges of Understanding Symposium, November 30–December 2, 1978,* edited by V. Lynn Tyler and Deborah L. Coon, 22.1–22.3. Provo, Utah: BYU Language and Intercultural Research Center, 1979.

"Linguistics and Cultural Activity." Paper presented at meetings of the Deseret Language and Linguistics Society, Provo, Utah, April 1979.

"Science and Mormonism as Traditions." In *Science and Religion: Toward a More Useful Dialogue,* edited by Wilford M. Hess, Raymond T. Matheny, and Donlu D. Thayer, 1:11–14. Geneva, Ill.: Paladin House, 1979. Reprinted in *Mormon Culture* (1997), 69–77.

1980

"'Being Wrong' in Mormon Thought." Paper presented at the Sunstone Theological Symposium, Salt Lake City, August 1980. Published in *Mormon Culture* (1997), 55–67.

"Consider Their Origin: Interpreting and Enriching American Family Histories through an Understanding of Cultural Differences." In *North American Family and Local History,* part 2. Vol. 4 of *World Conference on Records: Preserving Our Heritage, August 12–15, 1980.* Salt Lake City: The Church of Jesus Christ of Latter-day Saints, 1980. Reprinted in *Mormon Culture* (1997), 39–53.

"The Hierarchy of Mormon Cultures." Paper presented at the plenary session of the Mosaic of Mormon Culture Symposium, Charles Redd Center for Western Studies, BYU, fall 1980.

1981

"Ritual as Theology." *Sunstone* (May/June 1981): 10–14.

"Wheeled Figurines in the Ancient World." FARMS Preliminary Report, 1981.

1982

"A New Evaluation of the Smithsonian Institution's 'Statement regarding the Book of Mormon.'" FARMS Preliminary Report, 1982. Revised 1995.

"Toward Linguistic Archaeology." Paper presented at meetings of the Deseret Language and Linguistics Society, Provo, Utah, March 1982.

1983

Lands of the Book of Mormon. Video recording and a discussion with John L. Sorenson, Truman G. Madsen, Stephen D. Ricks, and Susan Roylance, 1983. Learning Resource Center, Harold B. Lee Library, BYU.

"Mormon Folk and Mormon Elite." *Horizons* (Sydney, Australia) 1 (spring 1983): 4–18. Originally a paper presented at the Mormon History Association annual meeting, Canandaigua, New York, May 1980, under the title "Conflict between Mormon Folk and Mormon Elite." Reprinted in *Mormon Culture* (1997), 17–27.

1984

"Digging into the Book of Mormon: Our Changing Understanding of Ancient America and Its Scripture." Parts 1 and 2. *Ensign* (September 1984): 26–37; (October 1984): 12–23. Reprinted in other languages in LDS Church magazines and by FARMS, 1984. Also reprinted as "Excavando en el Libro de Mormón" in *El Libro de Mormón ante la Crítica,* edited by Josué Sánchez, 74–115. Salt Lake City: Publishers Press, 1992.

"External Evidences of Scripture: A Panel." In *Scriptures for the Modern World,* edited by Paul R. Cheesman and C. Wilfred Griggs, 121–35. Provo, Utah: BYU Religious Studies Center, 1984. With Noel B. Reynolds, Arthur Wallace, and Paul R. Cheesman.

1985

An Ancient American Setting for the Book of Mormon. Salt Lake City and Provo, Utah: Deseret Book and FARMS, 1985. Softbound edition with enlarged index printed in 1996.

Changing Views of the Book of Mormon. Audiotape of lecture. Learning Resource Center, Harold B. Lee Library, BYU. Also taped and distributed by FARMS as a forum address presented at

Ricks College, Rexburg, Idaho, 4 March 1985, and titled "A Methodological Approach to the Book of Mormon."

"Human Issues in the Development of the American West and Other Less Developed Areas." In *Community Development in the American West: Past and Present Nineteenth and Twentieth Century Frontiers,* edited by Jessie L. Embry and Howard A. Christy, 1–22. Provo, Utah: Charles Redd Center for Western Studies, BYU, 1985. Excerpted in *BYU Today* (November 1981): 6.

"Study Maps of the Book of Mormon." FARMS, 1985. Packet of maps excerpted from *An Ancient American Setting for the Book of Mormon* (1985).

1986

"Book of Mormon." In *Encyclopedia USA: The Encyclopedia of the United States of America, Past and Present.* Vol. 7. Gulf Breeze, Florida: Academic International Press, 1986.

"Five Theories in Search of 'Mormon Personality.'" Honored alumni lecture presented to College of Family, Home, and Social Sciences, BYU, 23 October 1986. Published in *Mormon Culture* (1997), 183–95.

"Report on Education Research in St. George, January–April 1985." Report on a grant from BYU College of Education. Typescript in author's possession.

1987

"Excellence: Escaping a Superficial Life." Speech presented at a BYU graduation banquet, Provo, Utah, 13 August 1987. Typescript in author's possession.

1988

"Transoceanic Crossings." In *The Book of Mormon: First Nephi, the Doctrinal Foundation,* edited by Monte S. Nyman and Charles D.

Tate Jr., 251–70. Provo, Utah: BYU Religious Studies Center, 1988. This chapter from a volume containing papers from the Second Annual Book of Mormon Symposium is an analysis of 1 Nephi 17–18. Reprinted by FARMS, 1988. Reprinted, with postscript, in *Nephite Culture and Society* (1997), 41–63.

Transoceanic Culture Contacts between the Old and New Worlds in Pre-Columbian Times: A Comprehensive Annotated Bibliography. Provo, Utah: FARMS, 1988. Preliminary edition, March 1988. With Martin H. Raish.

1989

"Ancient Oceanic Crossing to America—the Evidence; Newly Discovered Complexities in the Book of Mormon." Video recording of lecture presented at FRAA (Foundation for Research in Ancient America) Book of Mormon Day, Independence, Mo., 1989. Learning Resource Center, Harold B. Lee Library, BYU.

Review of *Mapping the Action Found in the Book of Mormon*, by Harold K. Nielsen. *Review of Books on the Book of Mormon* 1 (1989): 119–20.

1990

"The Composition of Lehi's Family." In *By Study and Also by Faith: Essays in Honor of Hugh W. Nibley*, edited by John M. Lundquist and Stephen D. Ricks, 174–96. Vol. 2. Salt Lake City and Provo, Utah: Deseret Book and FARMS, 1990. Reprinted by FARMS, 1990. Reprinted, with postscript, in *Nephite Culture and Society* (1997), 1–23.

"Fortifications in the Book of Mormon Account Compared with Mesoamerican Fortifications." In *Warfare in the Book of Mormon*, edited by Stephen D. Ricks and William J. Hamblin, 425–44. Salt Lake City and Provo, Utah: Deseret Book and FARMS, 1990.

The Geography of Book of Mormon Events: A Source Book. Provo, Utah: FARMS, 1990. Revised edition, 1992.

"The Mormon Community: An Anthropologist's View." Keynote address prepared for the meeting of the Canadian Mormon Studies Association, Lethbridge, Alberta, Canada, 23 June 1990. Revised and published as "The Mormon People: A View from Anthropology" in *Mormon Culture* (1997), 1–16.

"The 'Mulekites.'" *BYUS* 30 (summer 1990): 6–22. Reprinted by FARMS, 1990.

Pre-Columbian Contact with the Americas across the Oceans: An Annotated Bibliography. 2 vols. Provo, Utah: Research Press, 1990. Second edition, revised, printed in 1996. Guide to 5,600 items. With Martin H. Raish.

"Seasonality of Warfare in the Book of Mormon and in Mesoamerica." In *Warfare in the Book of Mormon,* edited by Stephen D. Ricks and William J. Hamblin, 445–78. Salt Lake City and Provo, Utah: Deseret Book and FARMS, 1990. Reprinted, with postscript, in *Nephite Culture and Society* (1997), 155–93.

"The Significance of the Chronological Discrepancy between Alma 53:22 and Alma 56:9." FARMS Preliminary Report, 1990.

1991

"Commentary." In *American Epigraphy at the Crossroads,* edited by James P. Whittall Jr., 109–12. Rowley, Mass.: Early Sites Research Society, 1991.

Rediscovering the Book of Mormon. Salt Lake City and Provo, Utah: Deseret Book and FARMS, 1991. Edited by John L. Sorenson and Melvin J. Thorne.

"Seasons of War, Seasons of Peace in the Book of Mormon." In *Rediscovering the Book of Mormon,* edited by John L. Sorenson and Melvin J. Thorne, 249–55. Salt Lake City and Provo, Utah: Deseret Book and FARMS, 1991.

1992

Animals in the Book of Mormon: An Annotated Bibliography. Provo, Utah: FARMS, 1992.

The Book of Mormon in Ancient America. FARMS Lecture Series, 1992. Learning Resource Center, Harold B. Lee Library, BYU. Video recording.

"Book of Mormon Peoples." In *Encyclopedia of Mormonism,* edited by Daniel H. Ludlow, 1:191–5. New York: Macmillan, 1992. Reprinted in *Selections from the Encyclopedia of Mormonism: Scriptures,* edited by Daniel H. Ludlow, 168–77. Salt Lake City: Deseret Book, 1995.

Review of *Fantastic Archaeology: The Wild Side of North American Prehistory,* by Stephen Williams. *Review of Books on the Book of Mormon* 4 (1992): 254–7.

"I have heard that the sizes of the Nephite and Lamanite populations indicated in the Book of Mormon do not make sense. What do we know about their numbers?" I Have a Question. *Ensign* (September 1992): 27–8.

Metals and Metallurgy Relating to the Book of Mormon Text. Provo, Utah: FARMS, 1992.

"Origin of Man." In *Encyclopedia of Mormonism,* edited by Daniel H. Ludlow, 3:1053–4. New York: Macmillan, 1992. Reprinted in *Selections from the Encyclopedia of Mormonism: Jesus Christ and His Gospel: Doctrine,* edited by Daniel H. Ludlow, 374–6. Salt Lake City: Deseret Book, 1994.

"When Lehi's Party Arrived in the Land, Did They Find Others There?" *Journal of Book of Mormon Studies* 1 (fall 1992): 1–34. Reprinted in *Nephite Culture and Society* (1997), 65–103.

Research for chapters in John W. Welch, ed., *Reexploring the Book of Mormon* (Salt Lake City and Provo, Utah: Deseret Book and FARMS, 1992):

- "Two Figurines from the Belleza and Sanchez Collection." With Robert F. Smith.
- "Old World Languages in the New World." With Gordon C. Thomasson and Robert F. Smith.
- "Winds and Currents: A Look at Nephi's Ocean Crossing."
- "Parallelism, Merismus, and Difrasismo." With Angela Crowell and Allen J. Christensen.
- "Lost Arts." With Paul Y. Hoskisson.
- "Ancient Europeans in America?"
- "'Latest Discoveries.'"
- "Barley in Ancient America." With Robert F. Smith.
- "Possible 'Silk' and 'Linen' in the Book of Mormon."
- "'A Day and a Half's Journey for a Nephite.'"
- "Mesoamericans in Pre-Spanish South America."
- "Mesoamericans in Pre-Columbian North America."
- "Nephi's Garden and Chief Market."
- "Prophecy among the Maya."

1993

"Comments on Nephite Chronology." *Journal of Book of Mormon Studies* 2 (fall 1993): 207–11.

Review of *Health and Medicine among the Latter-day Saints: Science, Sense, and Scripture,* by Lester E. Bush Jr. *BYUS* 33 (1993): 624–9.

1994

"Viva Zapato! Hurray for the Shoe!" Review of "Does the Shoe Fit? A Critique of the Limited Tehuantepec Geography," by Deanne G. Matheny. In *New Approaches to the Book of Mormon,* edited by Brent Lee Metcalfe, 269–328. *Review of Books on the Book of Mormon* 6 (1994): 297–361.

"Zur Geographie des Buches Mormon." In *F.A.R.M.S.* German ed. Vol. 1. Bad Reichenhall, Germany: LDS Books Schubert und Roth OHG, 1994. Chapter 1 of *An Ancient American Setting for the Book of Mormon* (1985).

1996

"New Technology and Ancient Questions." Part 1. FARMS Update. *Insights* (December 1996): 2.

Pre-Columbian Contact with the Americas across the Oceans: An Annotated Bibliography. 2nd ed., rev. Provo, Utah: Research Press, 1996. With Martin H. Raish.

1997

"The Book of Mormon as a Mesoamerican Record." In *Book of Mormon Authorship Revisited: The Evidence for Ancient Origins,* edited by Noel B. Reynolds, 391–521. Provo, Utah: FARMS, 1997.

Mormon Culture: Four Decades of Essays on Mormon Society and Personality. Salt Lake City: New Sage Books, 1997. Includes:

- "The Mormon People: A View from Anthropology."
- "Mormon Folk and Mormon Elite."
- "Ritual as Theology."
- "Consider Their Origin: Interpreting and Enriching American Family Histories through an Understanding of Cultural Differences."
- "'Being Wrong' in Mormon Thought."
- "Science and Mormonism as Traditions."
- "Mormon World View and American Culture."
- "Channels of Innovation in Mormon Life."
- "The Second Gathering: New Migrants to Utah."
- "The West as a Network of Cultures."
- "The Language of the Mormons: A Sociocultural Perspective."
- "Industrialization and Tradition in a Mormon Village."
- "Mormon Funeral Behavior."
- "Toward a Characterization of Mormon Personality."
- "Five Theories in Search of Mormon Personality."

Nephite Culture and Society: Collected Papers. Salt Lake City: New Sage Books, 1997. Includes:

- "The Composition of Lehi's Family."

- "The Brass Plates and Biblical Scholarship."
- "Transoceanic Crossings."
- "When Lehi's Party Arrived in the Land, Did They Find Others There?"
- "The 'Mulekites.'"
- "The Settlements of Book of Mormon Peoples."
- "Seasonality of Warfare in the Book of Mormon and in Meso-america."
- "The Political Economy of the Nephites."

"New Technology and Ancient Questions." Part 2. FARMS Update. *Insights* (February 1997): 2.

1998

Images of Ancient America: Visualizing Book of Mormon Life. Provo, Utah: FARMS, 1998.

In Press

"The Complex Structure of Religious Groups among the Nephites, 200–1 B.C." To appear in a Festschrift for Richard L. Anderson. Provo, Utah: FARMS.

John L. Sorenson oral history. Interview by Davis Bitton. Tape recording. Salt Lake City, Utah, 1996. Harold B. Lee Library archives, BYU.

Mindful of Every People: Anthropological Perspectives on Mormons. Edited by John L. Sorenson and Mark P. Leone. To be published as a *BYUS* book.

INDEX

Abinadi, commentary on Isaiah in Book of Mormon 296–8
Abraham, Mormons as adopted heirs of God's covenant with 15, 16, 18
Abrahamic covenant, theme of, in Book of Mormon 279, 289, 298–301
Alma, on kingship 160–1
An Ancient American Setting for the Book of Mormon, seminal work by
     John L. Sorenson xxxvi, xliii
Animals in the Book of Mormon: An Annotated Bibliography, work by
     John L. Sorenson xlii
anthropology
  at Brigham Young University xxxii–xxxiii
  John L. Sorenson teaches, at Brigham Young University xxv
  John L. Sorenson's professional work in applied xxv–xxvi, xxviii–
     xxx, xxxiii
archaeology
  at Brigham Young University xxi, xxxii–xxxiii
  provides insufficient data for conclusive correlation between Book of
     Mormon and Mesoamerica xxxv
Asherah (mother of the gods). *See also* Yahweh: association with Asherah
  associated with trees 205–6, 233
  disappearance of, from Israelite history 199
  early Israelite veneration of 196–209, 218–19
  identification of 196
  opposition to 199–202

atonement, infinite 279, 280, 287–90
Avery, Amy, assists Navajo girl in desire to attend school 91, 92

Baker, Shirley W.
    assassination attempt on 125–6
    deported from Tonga 126
    influence of, on Tongan king 124, 125
baptism, covenant of 9–11, 12
batik (dyeing technique)
    defined 324
    in New World 326–8
    in Old World 324–6
Bible
    acceptance of, among Māori 254–6
    erasing of Asherah veneration 200
    wisdom literature of 209–18
bishop, role of, in Zion 8–15
Bonneville Research Corporation, General Research Corporation
        subsidiary formed by John L. Sorenson xxix
Book of Mormon
    Abinadi's commentary on Isaiah in 296–8
    ancient double documents related to, plates 391–2, 421, 435–6, 437
    as stabilizer for Māori culture 267–8
    contextual pattern of Isaiah passages in 279–81
    different ways of reading 246–7
    Hagoth account (Alma 63) in 59, 252, 262
    identifies events to be fulfilled in latter days 6–7
    Jacob's commentary on Isaiah in 285–91
    Jesus Christ's commentary on Isaiah in 279–80, 298–301
    Lehi's commentary on Isaiah in 281–3
    Māori interpretation of 245, 258–62
    Nephi's commentary on Isaiah in 283–5, 291–6
    Nephi's conception of sealing of 422–8
    published in French and German 65
    published in Hawaiian 67
    sealing up of Jaredite record 428–34
    tree of life imagery in 191–2, 214
    unlike *View of the Hebrews* 246
    wisdom literature themes in 210

Book of Mormon archaeology xix, xx
Book of Mormon geography xix, xxxiv–xxxv
  John L. Sorenson's views on xxxiv–xxxvi
  John L. Sorenson's views on, published in Ensign xxxv
Book of Mormon studies
  John L. Sorenson's budding interest in xix
  John L. Sorenson's contributions to xxxiv–xxxviii, xli–xliii
brass plates, source of Book of Mormon Isaiah text 278
Brigham Young University
  anthropology at xxxii–xxxiii
  archaeology at xix, xxi, xxv, xxxii–xxxiii
  John L. Sorenson enrolls at xviii
  John L. Sorenson hired as professor at xxx
  John L. Sorenson pursues master's degree at xix
  Museum of Peoples and Cultures at xxxi
Bright, John, on legal terminology of Jeremiah's deed 393, 395
Buchanan, Golden, role in origin of Indian student placement service
  91–3
Bureau of Indian Affairs 94–5
Bushman, Richard, on different ways of reading Book of Mormon 246–7
Butler, Alva J., early LDS missionary to Tonga 126

Calvin, John, on justness of God's will 34
Cannon, Abraham H., apostle eulogized by Wilford Woodruff and
  Joseph F. Smith 31
Cannon, George Q.
  activities after release from Pacific Mission 70–1
  considers fiction to be potentially corruptive 69
  continues Parley P. Pratt's publishing activities 64
  eulogizes martyred Mormon missionaries 44
  founds *Western Standard* newspaper 67–8
  Hawaiian mission 65
  notes opposition in California to missionary work 68, 69
chastity, law of 17
Chiapas, Mexico, John L. Sorenson initiates successful archaeological
  research in xxi
Christ. *See* Jesus Christ; Yahweh
Church of Christ. *See also* Church of Jesus Christ of Latter-day Saints
  as element of Mormon religious identity 5, 9–12

Church of Christ (*continued*)
  concept of, related to Mormon history 19–20
  latter-day, organized by Joseph Smith 6–7
  Parley P. Pratt declares apostasy from primitive 55
Church of Jesus Christ of Latter-day Saints, The
  membership in, defined by covenant of baptism 9–11
  organized by Joseph Smith 6
  progress of, in Tonga 141
  Tongan exclusion law causes problems for 130–2
Churchill, Winston, endorses law banning LDS missionaries from
    Tonga 130
Clayton, William, eulogized by Joseph F. Smith 30–1
Columbia Plateau (western U.S.), trade activity in 459–64
consecration, law observed in Zion 13–15
Coogan, Michael D., on Israelite and Canaanite religions 195
Coombs, M. Vernon
  efforts to repeal Tonga's discriminatory passport law 137–9
  presides over Tongan Mission 127
  reports discouraging state of missionary work in Tonga 131–2
  successfully pleads for continuation of Tongan Mission 140–1
covenant, term cited in Book of Mormon 280–1
Cowdery, Oliver, sustained as "second elder" of restored church 6
Cox, Kay, helps Navajo foster child succeed in school 98–100
Cross, Frank Moore, Jr., on Canaanite gods in early Israelite religion
    195–6
cultural diffusion. *See* diffusion, cultural

Defense Research Corporation, recruits John L. Sorenson for employ-
    ment xxvi
Dever, William H.
  on Asherah as paired with Yahweh in ancient Israel 204
  on disappearance of Asherah from Israelite history 199–200
  on Israelite figurines representing Asherah 197–8, 202, 205
diffusion, cultural. *See also* transoceanic contact
  arguments against, between Old and New Worlds 328, 333–4
  counterindications to 352
  evidence of, summarized 382
  maize as evidence of 368–77
  much evidence supports, between Old and New Worlds 328–34

opposition to hypothesis of 351
search for absolute proof of 352
sunflowers as evidence of 353–4, 354–67
textile dyeing, promising line of research in study of 308, 311, 315–16
diffusion hypothesis. *See* diffusion, cultural
documents, ancient double
archaeological and textual evidences of 396–418
debated origin of 412–16
Jeremiah's deed an example of 392–5
preservation of 393, 411
purposes of 410
related to Book of Mormon 391–2, 421
sealed Torah an example of 418–21
sealing of 393, 394, 395, 401–4
signatures on 407–10
talmudic description of 407–10
two parts of 396–401
witnesses of 404–7
Duff, Alan, on social despoliation of Māori 265–8
Durkheim, Emile
on society's fundamental concept of God 3
dyeing, textile
batik 324–8
fruitful line of research regarding transoceanic diffusion
308, 311, 315–16
ikat 316–23
resist-dyeing 309–10
tie-dye 310–16

Edmunds Act 122
El (father of the gods) 195–6
Elsmore, Bronwyn, on Māori acceptance of Bible 254
Endowment House 21, 34
Enoch and his "City of Holiness" 13
Ensign, John L. Sorenson's views on Book of Mormon geography
published in xxxv
"Evidences of Culture Contacts between Polynesia and the Americas in
Precolumbian Times," John L. Sorenson's master's thesis xx
exaltation, alluded to in Mormon funeral sermons 37, 43
exchange of goods. *See* trade

family
    as basic unit in mortality and eternity 16
    belief in continuation of, after death 35–6
    devotional activities encouraged in LDS Church 21
family history research 22
FARMS
    John L. Sorenson's enthusiastic involvement in xxxvi
Ferguson, Thomas Stuart, organizes New World Archaeological
        Foundation xx
festivals
    as catalyst for cultural change 446
    attended for social rather than commercial purposes 449
    map of, in Great Basin and Columbia Plateau 7 fig. 451
    table of characteristics of 468–73 table 1
figurines, Israelite and Canaanite 197–8, 202, 205
Free Church of Tonga, established 124–5
Freedman, David Noel
    on Asherah as paired with Yahweh in ancient Israel 204
    on fate of Asherah worshipers 201
    on veneration of Yahweh and Asherah in Israel 198
funeral sermons, Mormon
    defining features of 28–50
    standard scriptural passages used in 41–6

General Allotment Act of 1887 87
General Research Corporation xxxiv
    nature of John L. Sorenson's work at xxvii–xxix
Geography of Book of Mormon Events: A Source Book, work of John L.
        Sorenson xli
George, Dan (Swinomish Indian chief), remarks on impact of
        modernism on his people 85–6, 110
gift giving, role of, in primitive societies 448, 449
God, kingdom of (Zion). *See also* Zion
    as element of Mormon religious identity 5, 12–15
    concept of, related to Mormon history 20–1
gospel, law of the
    embraces code of conduct 11
    purifies adherents from unrighteousness 12
Grant, Heber J., eulogizes President John Taylor 29
Grant, Jedediah M., after-death experience of 34–5

Great Basin (western U.S.), early trade activity in 450–9
Grijalva River, viewed as part of "land of Zarahemla" xxxiv
Guerrero, Manuel P., criticizes Indian student placement service 107

Hagoth
    Book of Mormon account of xx, 59
    Māori conception of account of 252, 262
Hawaiian edition of Book of Mormon published 67
heaven, Mormon, social structure of, defined 5
Heiser, Charles B., Jr., on distribution of sunflowers 353–4
Heyerdahl, Thor, 1949 voyage of xx
house of Israel. *See* Israel, house of
Howard, Greg, on maize sculptures in India 368
Huntington, Dimmick B., eulogy at funeral of 30
Hutchison, John, successful Christian mission to Tonga 122
Hyde, John, Jr., anti-Mormon lectures of 69
Hyde, Orson, assists George Q. Cannon in establishing print shop 66

ikat (dyeing technique)
    defined 316–17
    in New World 320–3
    in Old World 317–20
India
    American crop plants in 352
Indian Child Welfare Act of 1978 107
Indian student placement program
    conversion of participants 94–95, 105–6
    criticism of 94–5, 107–8, 109–10
    early development of 88–92
    effects of, on participants 100–6
    enrollment 93, 94, 96, 107, 108
    impact on family relationships 106
    LDS Church leaders' support of 93
    purpose of 86–7
    success in meeting major objective 110
infant resurrection. *See* resurrection of infants
invention, independent
    as counterindication to diffusion 352
    improbability of, regarding dyestuffs in ancient Old and New Worlds
    309

Io cult, among the Māori 249–50
Irving, Washington, describes trade activity at The Dalles 461–2
Isaiah
   Abinadi's commentary on, in Book of Mormon 296–8
   contextual pattern of, passages in Book of Mormon 279–81
   Jacob's commentary on, in Book of Mormon 285–91
   Jesus Christ's commentary on, in Book of Mormon 279–80, 298–301
   Lehi's commentary on, in Book of Mormon 281–3
   Nephi's commentary on, in Book of Mormon 283–5, 291–6
   reasons for Book of Mormon duplication of writings of 277–9
Israel, house of
   as element of Mormon religious identity 5, 9–10, 15–18
   citations of the term, in Book of Mormon 279–81
   concept of, related to Mormon history 21–2
   references to scattering of, in Book of Mormon 279, 280, 282–3,
      284–8, 290, 292–3, 294–5, 299, 302
   spiritual ideals of, reflected in Mormon social behavior 5
Israelite and Canaanite figurines 197–8, 202, 205

Jacob
   commentary on Isaiah in Book of Mormon 285–91
   sermon of, in 2 Nephi 166
Jakeman, M. Wells, mentor of John L. Sorenson xviii, xxxiv
Jeremiah, two-part legal deed of 392–5
Jesus Christ
   as essential role model 12
   becoming disciples of, through baptism 11
   commentary on Isaiah in Book of Mormon 279–80, 298–301
   Joseph Smith and Sidney Rigdon receive vision of 8
   second coming of 6
   to reign as King of Zion 13
John, Helen, as catalyst for Indian student placement service 88, 91–2, 109

Kane, Thomas L., lobbies on behalf of LDS Church interests 71
Katti, Madhav N., discovery of sunflowers in India 364
Kelly, Isabel T., on trade activity in southern Great Basin 457–8
Kimball, Heber C., describes Jedediah M. Grant's after-death experience
   34–5

Kimball, Spencer W.
    as advocate for Native Americans 89, 90
    reproves church members for hypocrisy toward Native Americans 89
    role in establishing Indian student placement service 91, 93
King James Version of the Bible, errors in 284
kingdom of God (Zion)
    as element of Mormon religious identity 5, 12–15
    concept of, related to Mormon history 20–1
kingship, Nephite
    compared with ancient Israelite monarchy 151–2, 169–72
    Laman and Lemuel's claim to 152–3, 154–5, 157, 184–6
    Nephi's claim to 152–8, 178–85, 185–6
Kirtland Temple, inaugurates gathering of house of Israel 7

land of Nephi, John L. Sorenson's identification of, in highland
        Guatemala xxxiv
land of Zarahemla, John L. Sorenson's identification of, in southern
        Mexico xxxiv
Latter-day Saints
    persecution of, in Tonga 131
    prohibited from entering Tonga 121
    religious identity of 6–18
    settle in Yerba Buena 54
Latter-day Saints' Book Depot, efforts to establish 52, 53, 59
Latter-day Saints' Millennial Star, impact of, on Mormon publishing 53
law of the gospel
    embraces code of conduct 11
    purifies adherents from unrighteousness 12
law of Moses 280, 297–8
Lawry, Walter, failure to gain converts in Tonga 122
LDS Church. *See* Church of Jesus Christ of Latter-day Saints, The
LDS Social Services, oversees Indian student placement service 96
Lehi
    commentary on Isaiah in Book of Mormon 281–3
    passes ruling authority to Nephi 154
Lemaire, André, on Yahweh's absorption of El's role 202
Liljeblad, Sven, on Native American trade practices 460, 461
Lineham, Peter, on LDS influence on the Māori 250–3

Linnaeus, Carolus, on distribution of sunflowers 353
London Missionary Society (LMS), failure to gain converts in Tonga 122
lotus, mistaken for sunflowers in Indian temple art 354–6

maize
    as evidence of diffusion 368–77
    depicted in temples of India 352
    realistic modeling of, in temple art in India 377
Man across the Sea: Problems of Pre-Columbian Contacts, important work
    by John L. Sorenson published xxxiv
Māori
    effects of literacy on 254, 262–8
    interpretation of Book of Mormon 245, 258–62
    origin of 253
    reception of first encounter of LDS missionaries 247–50, 256
Marden, Belinda, writes pamphlet on plural marriage 63
marriage
    Indian student placement participants and 101, 103, 105
    sealing of, in LDS temples 16
marriage, plural 21
    Belinda Marden writes pamphlet on 63
    cause of intolerance toward Mormons 122, 133
    George Q. Cannon uses non-Mormon material to defend 69
    Parley P. Pratt defends 51, 58
    plagues Parley P. Pratt's missionary efforts in California 63–4
Marsden, Samuel, first Christian missionary to Māori 262
Mary
    Nephi's vision of 193–4
    veneration of, as mother of son of God 194, 207–9
Meggers, Betty J., on evidence for diffusion 352
Mesoamerica
    Brigham Young Univeristy library's outstanding collection of books on
        xxxiii
    John L. Sorenson believes Nephite lands lay in xxxiv
    John L. Sorenson specializes in archaeology of xxii, xxxiv
    John L. Sorenson's approach to correlating Book of Mormon with
        xxxv, xliii
Mexico
    John L. Sorenson's 1953 archaeological expedition to southern xx–xxii
    possible site of some Book of Mormon events xxxiv

millennium, Book of Mormon identifies events prior to 6–7

Mindful of Every People: Anthropological Perspectives on Mormons, work of
    John L. Sorenson xliii

missionary work 19, 20
    adverse effects of plural marriage on 122, 133
    impeded by Tongan legislation 130–2
    in spirit world 34
    opposition to, in California 68, 69
    Parley P. Pratt undertakes, in Chile 55–7
    Parley P. Pratt's publishing efforts as form of 51–2, 55, 56, 58–64

Mormon (Nephite prophet-historian), reasons for duplicating Isaiah's
    writings in Book of Mormon 277–9

Mormon Herald, Parley P. Pratt's plans to publish 52, 60

Mormonism. *See* Church of Jesus Christ of Latter-day Saints, The

Mormons. *See* Latter-day Saints

Moses, Nephi compared to 152, 159, 170–8

Moses, law of, sealed 418–20

Moulton, J. Egan, on reign of terror in Tonga 126

mourning, paradox of 39

Museum of Peoples and Cultures, expanded under John L. Sorenson's
    direction xxxi

National Science Foundation, John L. Sorenson a recipient of predoctoral
    fellowship offered by xxii

Native Americans
    experiences of, in Indian student placement program 91–2, 96–100
    Parley P. Pratt addresses, in tract 55

Nauvoo Temple, importance of sacred ordinances performed in 8

Nephi
    commentary on Isaiah in Book of Mormon 283–5, 291–296
    compared to Moses 152, 159, 170–8
    kingly authority of 152–8
    possible coronation story of 178–85, 185–6

Nephi's vision
    of virgin Mary 193–4, 207–8
    parallels to 209, 213–17

"new and everlasting covenant of marriage," related to organization of
    house of Israel among Latter-day Saints 8, 16

New World Archaeological Foundation xx, xxii, xxxiv

Nibley, Hugh W., scholarship of, inspired John L. Sorenson xviii

Ollenburger, Ben C., on Israelite political traditions 171
Olyan, Saul
    on origin of Asherah opposition 201
    on relationship of Yahweh and Asherah 202
    on removal of Asherah from Bible 200

paradise, Mormon concept of 34
Patai, Raphael
    on Asherah as paired with Yahweh 204
    on veneration of Israelite female deities and quasi deities 206
patriarchal blessings 16
patriarchs 16
plangi (dyeing technique)
    defined 310, 311
    origin of, linked to China or Central Asia 313
plural marriage
    Belinda Marden writes pamphlet on 63
    cause of intolerance toward Mormons 122, 133
    George Q. Cannon uses non-Mormon material to defend 69
    Parley P. Pratt defends 51, 58
    plagues Parley P. Pratt's missionary efforts in California 63–4
Pratt, Orson
    on resurrection of infants 38
    sermonizes at funeral of Caroline Smith 44
Pratt, Parley P.
    called as president of Pacific mission 54
    defends plural marriage 51, 58
    early writings 52–3
    efforts to establish LDS press and book supply agency 59–60
    mission to Chile 55–7
    second call to Pacific Mission 58
*Pre-Columbian Contact with the Americas across the Oceans: An Annotated
    Bibliography,* monumental work of John L. Sorenson xl
priesthood
    Aaronic 19
    explicated in section 84 of the Doctrine and Covenants 5
    Melchizedek 10, 12, 16, 19
    presiding offices in 12
procreation 17, 18

reciprocities, Marshall Sahlins's scheme of 447–8
repentance, possibility of, in spirit world 16
resist-dyeing
    defined 309
    three basic types of 310
resurrection
    frequent reference to, in Mormon funeral sermons 36
    John Taylor speaks on, and eternal life 43
resurrection of infants
    Franklin D. Richards's view of 39
    Orson Pratt's view of 38
    Wilford Woodruff recalls Joseph Smith's teaching on 39
Richards, Franklin D.
    eulogized 32
    letter of, to Parley P. Pratt explaining printing delay 61–2
    on resurrection of infants 39
    Parley P. Pratt requests LDS literature from, to distribute 55
Rigdon, Sidney, receives vision of Christ 8

sacrament, covenant of baptism renewed during 11, 12
Sahlins, Marshall, on economics in simple societies 447
Sālote, Queen (queen of Tonga), discharges head of Free Church of
    Tonga 134
Sauer, Carl O., on maize in pre-Columbian Italy and Spain 373
scripture
    modern, used in funeral sermons 46, 47
    standard passages used in funeral sermons 41–6
sealings, temple 16
Siva, Lord (ancient Hindu god) 351, 354
Smith, Caroline (Joseph Smith's sister-in-law), eulogized 44
Smith, Ethan, assessment of his *View of the Hebrews* 246
Smith, Joseph, Jr.
    as latter-day Enoch 13
    on importance of establishing Zion 7
    organizes Church of Christ 6–7
    receives section 84 of the Doctrine and Covenants 5
    receives vision of Christ 8
Smith, Joseph F.
    acknowledges in eulogy William Clayton's faults 30–1

Smith, Joseph F. (*continued*)
    on faithfulness of Abraham H. Cannon 31–2
    on growth in millennium of children who die 39
    on presence of deceased's spirit at funeral 40
    vision of spirit world canonized 35
Smith, Joseph, Sr.
    eulogized 41
    likened to biblical Abner in funeral sermon 41
Smith, Mark
    on Israelite religion 195
    on nurturing aspects of the asherah 206
Smith, Samuel H.
    death noted in *Times and Seasons* 33
    eulogized 32
Smith, Willard L., presides over Tongan Mission 127
Smoot, Brigham, early LDS missionary to Tonga 126
Smoot, Reed
    protests British ban of LDS missionaries in Tonga 127
    seeks to repeal discriminatory Tongan passport law 135
Society for Early Historic Archaeology xxxvi
Sorenson, John L.
    academic training xii–xiii, xiv, xviii–xxiv
    Book of Mormon studies xxxiv–xxxviii, xli–xliii
    mission to Polynesia xv–xviii
    personal life xxxviii–xxxix
    professional career xxv–xxxiv
    studied funeral behavior among religious groups 27–8
    upbringing x–xii
Sperry, Sidney B., scholarship of, inspired John L. Sorenson xviii
spirit world
    Joseph F. Smith's vision of, canonized 35
    possibility of repentance in 36
Steward, Julian H., on Native American festivals and trade
        450, 455, 458, 464
Stewart, Omer C., on Native American festivals 457, 458
sunflowers
    as evidence of diffusion 354–67
    depicted in temples of India 352
    distribution of cultivated 353–4

evidence of genetic drift in 366
origin of 353

Taking a Closer Look: Four Decades of Essays on Mormon Culture and Personality, work of John L. Sorenson xliii
Tāufaʻāhau, Chief. *See* Tupou I
Taylor, Grant Hardy, studies Native American students at Brigham Young University 100, 101
Taylor, J. Glen, on veneration of Yahweh and Asherah 198
Taylor, John
    eulogizes Dimmick B. Huntington 30
    eulogy at funeral of 29
    on emphasizing the positive 30
    on resurrection and eternal life 43
    publishes Book of Mormon and newspapers in French, German 65
temples
    similarities of, in New and Old Worlds 353, 378
    sun, of India 354–67, 378–81
Ten Commandments, Abinadi's sermon on 296
Tewari, Shitala P., on sanskrit translation of term *sunflower* 365
textile arts, dearth of research on, in context of diffusion 308
Thomas, John, successful Christian mission to Tonga 122
Thompson, Gunnar, on evidence of maize in Old World 374
Thompson, John S., on Jacob's sermon as part of festival season 166
Thompson, Robert B., eulogizes Joseph Smith Sr. 41
tie-dye
    as possible transoceanic transfer 315–16
    defined 310
    in New World 313–16
    in Old World 311–13
Tonga
    Christianization of 123
    Free Church of Tonga established 124–5
    passes law banning LDS missionaries 130
    progress of LDS Church in 141
    reign of terror in 126
trade
    as catalyst for spread of ideas and culture elements 446

trade (*continued*)
    in Columbia Plateau 459–64
    in Great Basin 450–9
transfer. *See* diffusion, cultural
transoceanic contact. *See also* diffusion, cultural
    John L. Sorenson's *Man Across the Sea* treats topic of xxxiv
    John L. Sorenson's *Pre-Columbian Contact with the Americas* a
        significant contribution to study of xl
Treaty of Waitangi 255
tree of life imagery 191–2, 212, 214, 217, 219, 234
tritik (dyeing technique) 311, 312
Tupou I (king of Tonga)
    converts to Christianity 123
    influence of Shirley W. Baker on 124, 125
Tvedtnes, John A., on Israelite Feast of Tabernacles 181–3

values in City of Zion 14, 20
View of the Hebrews, different from Book of Mormon 246
vision
    Joseph Smith's, of Jesus Christ 8
    Nephi's, of Mary 193–4

Watkin, Rev. Jabez Bunting
    becomes president of Free Church of Tonga 125
    discharged from post 134
Welch, John W.
    founds FARMS xxxvi
    on inclusion of Jacob's speech in 2 Nephi 166
Western Standard
    George Q. Cannon's plans to establish 67–8
    publication of 68, 70
Whitmer, David, on sealed portion of Book of Mormon 434
Wiggins, Steve A.
    on Asherah as wisdom 211
    on removing Asherah from Bible 200
Wood, W. Raymond
    on festivals as catalyst for cultural change 446
    "trade net" theory of 446, 463–4
    "trade net" theory of, expanded 464–7

Woodruff, Wilford
  on presence of deceased's spirit at funeral 39–40
  recalls Joseph Smith's teaching on resurrection of infants 39
  remarks at funeral of children 37–8
  remarks on service of Abraham H. Cannon 31
Word of Wisdom, Indian student placement participants more likely to heed 105
work, as exalted labor 14

Yahweh
  absorbs role of El (father of the gods) 196, 199, 202, 204
  association with Asherah (mother of the gods) 197, 198, 202–3, 227–8 n. 42
Young, Brigham
  calls Parley P. Pratt to preside over Pacific Mission 54
  delivers funeral sermon without specific scriptural text 41
  explains what it means to "die in the Lord" 45

Zion. *See also* kingdom of God
  as most important temporal object 7
  as socioeconomic and territorial order 13–15
  blessings and glories of 15
  law of consecration observed in 13–15
  role of bishop in 13–14, 15
  spiritual ideals of, reflected in Mormon social behavior 5
  values of 14, 20
Zion, City of
  model for restored church 13
  nature of life in 7
Zondajas, Edouardo, notes inadequacy in Indian student placement program 97–8

THE FOUNDATION FOR ANCIENT
RESEARCH AND MORMON STUDIES
(FARMS)

The Foundation for Ancient Research and Mormon Studies encourages and supports research and publication about the Book of Mormon, Another Testament of Jesus Christ, and other ancient scriptures.

FARMS is a nonprofit, tax-exempt educational foundation, affiliated with Brigham Young University. Its main research interests in the scriptures include ancient history, language, literature, culture, geography, politics, religion, and law. Although research on such subjects is of secondary importance when compared with the spiritual and eternal messages of the scriptures, solid scholarly research can supply certain kinds of useful information, even if only tentatively, concerning many significant and interesting questions about the ancient backgrounds, origins, composition, and meanings of scripture.

The work of the Foundation rests on the premise that the Book of Mormon and other scriptures were written by prophets of God. Belief in this premise—in the divinity of scripture—is a matter of faith. Religious truths require divine witness to establish the faith of the believer. While scholarly research cannot replace that witness, such studies may reinforce and encourage individual testimonies by fostering understanding and appreciation of the scriptures. It is hoped that this information will help people to "come unto Christ" (Jacob 1:7) and to understand and take more seriously these ancient witnesses of the atonement of Jesus Christ, the Son of God.

The Foundation works to make interim and final reports about its research available widely, promptly, and economically, both in scholarly and popular formats. FARMS publishes information about the Book of Mormon and other ancient scripture in the *Insights* newsletter; books and research papers; *FARMS Review of Books; Journal of Book of Mormon Studies;* reprints of published scholarly papers; and videos and audiotapes. FARMS also supports the preparation of the *Collected Works of Hugh Nibley.*

To facilitate the sharing of information, FARMS sponsors lectures, seminars, symposia, firesides, and radio and television broadcasts in which research findings are communicated to working scholars and to anyone interested in faithful, reliable information about the scriptures. Through Research Press, a publishing arm of the Foundation, FARMS publishes materials addressed primarily to working scholars.

For more information about the Foundation and its activities, contact the FARMS office at 1-800-327-6715 or (801) 373-5111.